Classic American Furniture

Christopher Schwarz
& the Editors of
Woodworking Magazine

POPULAR WOODWORKING BOOKS
CINCINNATI, OHIO
www.popularwoodworking.com

Metric Conversion Chart

TO CONVERT	TO	MULTIPLY BY
Inches	Centimeters	2.54
Centimeters	Inches	0.4
Feet	Centimeters	30.5
Centimeters	Feet	0.03
Yards	Meters	0.9
Meters	Yards	1.1

About the Authors

Christopher Schwarz is the publisher at Lost Art Press, the former editor of *Popular Woodworking Magazine* and *Woodworking Magazine*, and he teaches hand-tool woodworking at schools around the world.

He began woodworking at the age of eight when his family built their first home on their farm outside Hackett, Arkansas, using hand tools because they had no electricity. After studying journalism at Northwestern University and The Ohio State University, Chris became a newspaper reporter, while studying woodworking at night at the Univeristy of Kentucky. He joined the staff of *Popular Woodworking Magazine* in 1996 as managing editor, worked his way up to editor and helped establish *Woodworking Magazine* in 2004.

He's also hosted numerous DVDs on hand tools for both Popular Woodworking and Lie-Nielsen Toolworks.

After writing his first book, "Workbenches: From Design & Theory to Construction & Use" (Popular Woodworking Books), Chris and a partner established Lost Art Press LLC, a business that publishes books on traditional woodworking techniques, including "The Anarchist's Tool Chest," "The Joiner and Cabinet Maker" "The Essential Woodworker" and, most recently, "To Make as Perfectly as Possible: Roubo on Marquetry."

Chris remains an avid woodworker, building projects for his Lost Art Press books, *Popular Woodworking*, his family and occasionally for sale. When he's not woodworking or teaching others about the craft, he's cooking or editing.

He lives in Fort Mitchell, Ky., with his wife, Lucy, who is also a journalist, and his two children, Maddy and Katy.

Steve Shanesy was one of the founders of *Woodworking Magazine* and part of *Popular Woodworking's* staff for 19 years, serving as editor and publisher during that time. Steve is an avid woodturner and also likes to make contemporary furniture. In his retirement, he's spending as much time as possible in the shop with his son.

Megan Fitzpatrick is the editor of *Popular Woodworking* and was a contributor to *Woodworking Magazine*. She has been a mamber of the *Popular Woodworking* staff since 2005, when she joined as managing editor. Already an avid DIY carpenter, she quickly began learning everything she could about building fine furniture and now gravitates toward hand tools to build 19th and early 20th-century pieces. She is finishing her Ph.D. in English literature and teaches journalism, composition and literature part time, in addition to woodworking.

Robert W. Lang is executive editor of *Popular Woodworking* and was a contributor to *Woodworking Magazine*. A lifetime professional woodworker and noted author of books on Arts & Crafts-style furniture, he also is considered a foremost authority on Google SketchUp and a power user who Google consults regularly.

Glen Huey has been associated with *Popular Woodworking* for 13 years and now serves as managing editor. In addition to his work as an editor, author, video host and woodworking teacher, Glen is a long-time professional woodworker, who specializes in period reproductions.

David Thiel was a senior editor with Popular Woodworking Magazine for 12 years before moving to our book division. He new serves as editor for the woodworking books and is also responsible for our woodworking video products..

Contents

SLIDING LID BOX: PAGE 63

A SIMPLE SEA CHEST: PAGE 81

AMERICAN WALL CUPBOARD: PAGE 41

A BETTER BLANKET CHEST DESIGN: PAGE 66

A TALE OF TWO TABOURETS: PAGE 129

STICKLEY MAGAZINE STAND: PAGE 142

CIRCULAR CUTTING BOARD: PAGE 177

TOOL TOTE: PAGE 179

CABINETS

18th-century Dry Sink

This vanished furniture form is still useful. It can teach you a few lessons about wood movement and still find work in the modern home.

The concept of building a reproduction of a dry sink seems – on its surface – ridiculous. It's on par with building a set of Egyptian canopic chests and jars – the vessels that held the internal organs of mummified royalty.

Dry sinks were the kitchen cabinetry in early American homes until plumbing became commonplace. The dry sink would hold a bowl and pitchers of water so you could do the washing. The oversized rim around the dry sink's top (sometimes lined with metal) was called the splash, and it kept the water from running everywhere.

This form of cabinet evolved in the 19th century to include drawers, frame-and-panel doors and even sets of additional cabinets above the splash. In other words, it started looking like a modern kitchen cabinet.

So why build one today? There are a couple good reasons. From a woodworking perspective, building a dry sink is an interesting journey into the mind-set of the early woodworker. The form will cause you to question a lot of the woodworking dogma that permeates the magazines, books, schools and web sites that deal with the craft.

The best reason to build one, however, is that your family members will fight about who gets to own it (my wife and sister-in-law are at odds about the one in this article).

There is something inexplicably appealing about the form, especially to Americans. I like to think dry sinks are like leather jackets. Both are impractical in many ways, but that doesn't stop you from wanting one.

This particular dry sink is based on an original example circa 1780 that came from a Connecticut estate. It would make an excellent entertainment center, changing table or even a sideboard in a rustic dining room.

PHOTO BY AL PARRISH

Early dry sinks, such as this one, seem to be a lesson in what not to do when building a carcase. You can journey down the same path as the maker or alter the plan to use modern construction methods.

Curious Construction Details

In many ways, this cabinet is a simplified version of a modern face-frame cabinet. There is a primitive face frame on the front. The carcase is assembled with the bottom and two rails nailed into dados and rabbets in the side panels. The back of the dry sink is a traditional shiplapped back that is also nailed in place.

The splash, however, is a curious thing. The originals were built in a way that defied modern rules for accommodating wood movement. You will have to decide if you are willing to risk your project being wrenched apart by seasonal expansion and contraction, or if you will apply a modern (and more complex) solution to deal with the splash. We'll be discussing both approaches in this article.

Begin With the Panels

Unlike later examples of dry sinks that used frame-and-panel construction, this example uses wide solid-wood panels. The original was built with Eastern white pine, which is what I've used for this project.

This species of pine is easy to work with hand and power tools, but it blotches horribly if you color it with dyes or pigments. So if you choose a pine, you should also consider a paint for the finish – or an amber shellac if you just cannot bear to paint your work.

Begin your project by preparing all the wood and gluing up the panels you need for the sides, bottom and top of the dry sink.

Once the panels are complete, you should flatten them before you begin the joinery. I use a jointer plane. If you are more power-tool inclined, a hand-held belt sander will also do the trick. Set the panels aside and gather the parts for your face frame. The first struggle between antique and modern is nigh.

Face Frame or Forget It?

The original of this dry sink didn't have a proper face frame. The two stiles on either side of the door were independent of the splash rail above them. On the original piece, that rail was only nailed to the other splash pieces and to the top of the carcase.

You can build it this way and it will simplify construction – you'll just nail on the stiles and splash rail after you build the carcase. You can skip to the section about building the carcase if you choose the antique approach.

I, however, decided to build a face frame. Why? Because I wanted to be able to get the splash rail and stiles joined tightly and without gaps. The best way to do this is to build a face frame and tweak the mortise-and-tenon joints until the fit is flawless.

To build the face frame, first cut a ¼"-thick x 1¼"-long tenon on the end of each stile. I used a dado stack in a table saw, a procedure we have advocated since Issue 1.

The stiles are too wide to have just one tenon. After tenons gets 6" wide you should split them into two (sometimes three) tenons. This creates a balanced joint – a single enormous mortise will be too weak. I split each tenon into two 4"-wide tenons with ½"-wide shoulders at each end.

Cut your tenons' edge shoulders with a dovetail saw, then remove the waste with a bowsaw. Clean up your work with a chisel.

Then use your finished tenons to mark the locations of the mortises on your splash rail. Cut your mortises. I used a hollow-chisel mortiser. In this situation I would usually use a mortising chisel; however deep mortises in small pieces of pine are a recipe for a heartbreaking split.

Before assembling the face frame, it's ideal to

Here I'm preparing the wide panels for the sides of the dry sink. First I plane across the grain of the panel, then I plane diagonally and I finish up with strokes with the grain.

To make the tenon, I use a dado stack and my miter gauge. Set the dado stack to ¼" high and set the fence 1¼" from the left-most tooth of your dado stack. Nibble the end of the tenon, then shift the tenon until it touches the fence and complete the tenon cut.

Use a dovetail saw or tenon saw to cut the edge shoulders of your twin tenons on each stile of the face frame. Each tenon should end up 4" wide. Get as close to the shoulder as you dare and then stop sawing.

A bowsaw or a coping saw is the perfect tool for removing waste between tenons. The band saw can get unwieldy with bigger workpieces.

Using your mortises to mark out your tenons requires fewer math equations. The only downside is that you need to test your tenons in a sample mortise first.

A cabinetmaker's rasp makes quick work of the curve (especially in pine). Use the flat face of the rasp for the straight section of the foot. Use the curved face for the curved section of the foot.

cut the curved foot shape in each stile. The curve is a segment of a circle with a $3\frac{1}{4}$" radius. Lay out the curve, cut it close with a bowsaw (or a jigsaw) and then use a rasp to clean up your work.

Adjust your face frame's joints with a chisel or shoulder plane until everything fits to your satisfaction. Then assemble the face frame with glue and four bar clamps.

With the face frame complete, you can then determine the size of your carcase and make adjustments to your plan. Fetch your glued-up panels and head to the table saw to cut them to finished size.

An Old-school Carcase

Trim your sides, bottom and rails to their finished sizes. Now cut the joinery in the side panels that will hold the entire carcase together. Using a dado stack in your table saw, cut the following:

- A $\frac{3}{4}$"-wide x $\frac{1}{4}$"-deep through-dado. This dado should be $4\frac{1}{4}$" up from the bottom of the side panels. This dado holds the bottom piece.
- A $\frac{3}{4}$"-wide x $\frac{1}{4}$"-deep rabbet at the top of each side panel. This holds the two rails.
- A $\frac{1}{2}$" x $\frac{1}{2}$" rabbet on the back edge of each side panel. This rabbet houses the back pieces.

Then cut the foot shape on the side pieces. Note that the original dry sink didn't have the foot on the sides. If you want to be authentic, leave it off. We toyed with it both ways and decided the shape on the sides made the whole piece look a little more finished.

Now sic your smoothing plane on all your panels. Smooth plane the bottom until it fits into the dado (use cross-grain strokes on the underside of the bottom if you want to remove material quickly). Smooth plane the outside surfaces of the side panels (I leave the jointer plane marks

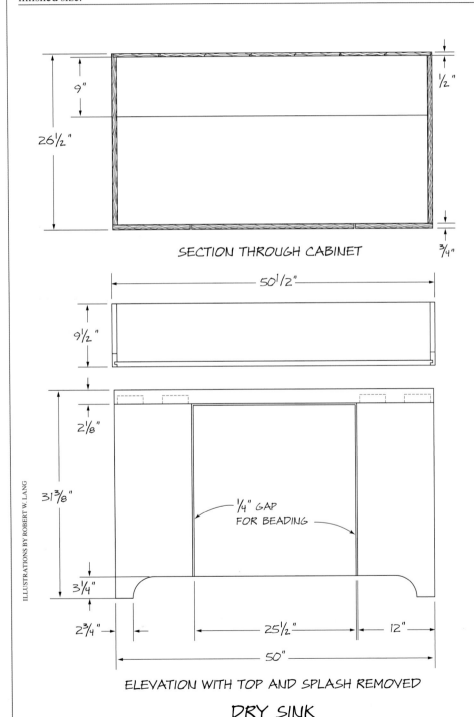

You can cut all the joinery in your side pieces using a dado stack in your table saw plus an accessory fence facing on your rip fence.

The footwork on the side panels is a modern addition, so I decided to use a modern tool as well. Cut things close with a jigsaw and clean up the shape with a rasp.

on the inside surfaces).

To assemble the carcase, run a bead of glue in the dados and knock the bottom into the dados. Put the rails in place in their rabbets and get out your hammer and nails.

I assembled the carcase using Tremont Nail's 6d "fine finish nails" and a 16-oz. hammer. The Tremont cut nails require a pilot hole (I used $3/32$"). Drive the nails almost flush with the surface, then set them about $1/16$" below the surface (see the Shortcuts in this issue for a tip on this).

Drive five nails into each end of the bottom and two nails into each end of your rails.

Once the glue has cured, use a plane (I use a jointer plane, but any plane will do) to true up the front edges of the carcase. Shift the carcase around until it is square – it will be quite flexible. Then glue the face frame to the carcase.

Once the glue has dried, you can smooth plane the outside of the entire carcase to remove tool marks, excess glue and layout lines.

Now you can add any interior shelving. The original had a single narrow shelf as shown in the plan. I added the shelf to the carcase using a period-appropriate method: cleats.

Nail the cleats to the sides 9" up from the bottom of the carcase. Because the grain of the cleat runs contrary to the side pieces, use glue only at the back of the cleat. The nails will bend as the side piece moves with the seasons.

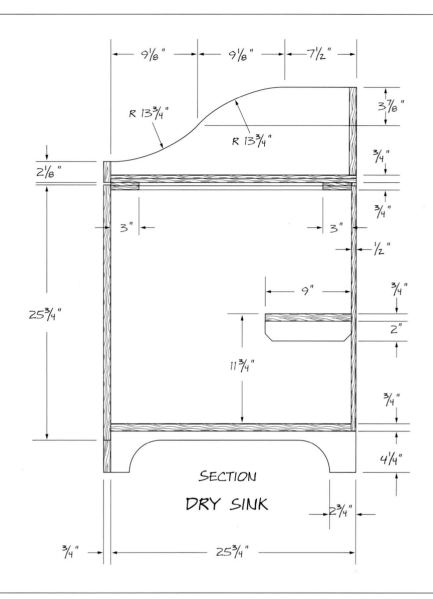

SECTION
DRY SINK

I use painter's tape to lay out the locations of cut nails when I need to repeat that layout. The tape makes transferring the layout easy and requires less cleanup of my layout lines after assembly.

Dry Sink

	NO.	PART	T	W	L	MATERIAL	NOTES
Face Frame							
❑	2	Stiles	$3/4$	12*	$30^1/2$	Pine	$1^1/4$"-long tenons on one end
❑	1	Splash rail	$3/4$	$2^1/8$	50	Pine	
Carcase							
❑	2	Sides	$3/4$	$25^3/4$	$29^1/4$	Pine	
❑	1	Bottom	$3/4$	$25^1/4$	49	Pine	Nailed in dados in sides
❑	2	Rails	$3/4$	3	49	Pine	Nailed in rabbets in sides
❑	2	Shelf cleats	$3/4$	2	9	Pine	Nailed to sides
❑	1	Shelf	$3/4$	9	$48^1/2$	Pine	Nailed to cleats
❑	1	Back pieces	$1/2$	$49^1/2$	27	Pine	Nailed to bottom, rail & shelf
❑	1	Door	$3/4$	$25^1/2$*	$25^3/4$*	Pine	Fit inside beading moulding
Splash							
❑	1	Top	$3/4$	$26^1/2$*	$49^3/4$	Pine	Rabbeted on ends
❑	2	Splash sides	$3/4$	$9^1/2$	$26^1/2$	Pine	Rabbeted on ends
❑	1	Splash back	$3/4$	$8^3/4$	50	Pine	Nailed to splash sides

* Make slightly larger for trimming later

I hate to show you this photo because it points out that I have a clamp problem. You don't need this many clamps to glue the face frame to the carcase, but because I had them at hand … .

I brace my carcase against a sawbench to smooth plane it. The sawbench is braced against my bench. This prevents me from ramming into the bench with my plane.

Then nail the shelf to the top edge of the cleats. The top of the shelf will be a little too flexible at this point, but don't fret. Once you nail it to the backboards it will be stiff.

The back of the carcase is comprised of $\frac{1}{2}$"-thick boards that are random widths. They are "shiplapped," which means they have interlocking $\frac{1}{4}$" x $\frac{1}{4}$" rabbets on their long edges.

Cut the rabbets using your dado stack on your table saw and then arrange them on the carcase so there is about a dime's space between them. Then nail them in place to the rail, shelf and bottom piece. I also nailed the boards on the ends to the side pieces.

Struggling With the Splash

On the original dry sink the cabinet's top was surrounded by the four splash pieces. These four pieces were nailed to the top and to each other using a generous quantity of nails.

The original survived fairly well. The top isn't split in any meaningful way. And the splash stayed together as well. We all should look so good after 230 years.

But I decided to change the way my dry sink was constructed to use fewer nails and allow more accommodation for wood movement. Building the splash in the old manner was a bit of a gamble; building it as shown in this article almost guarantees it won't split.

Here's what I did: I built the splash like I would a solid-wood drawer. Think of the cabinet's top piece as if it were a drawer bottom and you'll get the idea. The top is glued to the front rail of the splash and floats in $\frac{3}{8}$" x $\frac{3}{8}$" grooves in the side pieces of the splash. And the top tucks under the back piece of the splash. This allows it to float freely without stressing the sides or back of the splash as it moves.

Though a bit of overkill, I cannot resist using a scrap spacer to position my cleats. I clamp the cleat in position as I nail it because it can shift as you beat it.

"Simplicity requires perfection in all its details, while elaboration is easy in comparison."

— C.F.A. Voysey (1857 - 1941)
Arts & Crafts furniture designer

In addition to these joinery details, here are some other important details about the splash: I joined the sides of the splash to the front and back using rabbets, glue and nails.

And in the end, the side pieces of the splash stick out ¼" beyond your side panels. This is a detail on the original dry sink and it also hides any imperfection in the way the sides of the carcase and the sides of the splash come together.

Begin work on the splash by laying out the ogee on the side pieces of the splash. I used trammel points set to scribe a 13¾" radius. Depending on your final dimensions, your radius might be a little different.

With the ogee scribed on your splash pieces, you can cut the rabbet on the ends of the splash pieces that will overlap the front and back pieces. This rabbet is ¾" wide and ½" deep and is on both ends of your side splash pieces. Cut this joint using (what else) a dado stack in your table saw. Then use your bowsaw, jigsaw or band saw to cut the ogee curve. Clean up the curve by clamping the two splash pieces together and fairing them simultaneously.

Now you can cut the ⅜" x ⅜" groove in the sides of the splash pieces that will house the top. I used a dado stack; a slot cutter in a router table would be another safe solution. Then cut the mating rabbet on the ends of the top piece. This rabbet should be ⅜" deep and about ½" wide. That's wider than you need, but it will make sure the shoulder of the rabbet doesn't interfere with your splash assembly.

The outside curve of the ogee begins 7½" from the back edge of the splash. Keep experimenting and adjusting the trammels until your inside and outside curves meet and look good.

Nail the backboards in place. No glue. For each backboard I drove two nails into the rail, two into the shelf and two into the bottom. Keep the pairs of nails close to the center of your backboard to allow for more wood movement.

Fairing the two splash pieces simultaneously saves time and produces more consistent results. I used a cabinetmaker's rasp and card scraper to do the job.

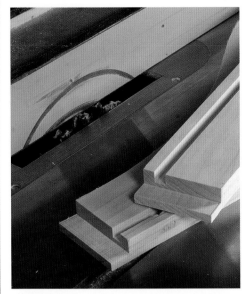

When all the joinery is cut on the sides of your splash pieces, this is what it looks like. Because the rabbet is deeper than the groove, you can allow the groove to run the full length of the splash.

Here's how the top, splash and front rail all come together. You will nail the side to the front rail. The top will float in the groove.

Here's a tip: Leave your top a little wider than you need. That makes it easier for your clamps to grab the back edge of your top when gluing it to the carcase.

Assembling the Splash

Because you want to force the seasonal movement of the top to the rear of the carcase, you should glue the front edge of the top to the back of your face frame's rail.

Place the side pieces of your splash in place as a reference and then glue the top to the rail. While the glue is curing, adjust the side pieces of your splash so they intersect the rest of the splash. I used a spokeshave for this.

Glue and nail the side pieces of your splash to the front and back. I used two nails at each joint up front and four nails at the rear. Set the nails. When the glue has cured you should screw the top

to the rails from inside the carcase. Then smooth plane the outside of your splash.

The Enormous Door

The door to this dry sink terrifies me. At almost 26" wide, it should move about $1/8$" every year, maybe a little less if I'm lucky. I considered making it a frame-and-panel door, but our digital models of that project looked wrong – like putting an Alfa Romeo's front grille on a Pacer.

So I selected boards that had as much rift-sawn figure as possible. Rift-sawn wood moves less in width than plain-sawn. And I also made another small adjustment as I fit the door: I beveled the

It's easier to adjust the sides of your splash before you glue and nail them in place. A spokeshave or rasp makes this simple work.

Plow the ¼" x ¼" groove in the middle of the long edge of the door. Then reset the plow's fence to cut the two rabbets on its mating piece that form the tongue.

It's easier to mould wider stock and then rip the moulding from it. Though not exactly according to Hoyle in the tradition department, it works.

Shift the door in position and then clamp it to the carcase. Then screw the strap hinges to both the door and carcase.

long edge of the panel where the latch is.

So if this door swells and contacts the face frame, there will be only a wee bit of wood wedging the door shut. Then I (or some other poor sap) should be able to pry the door open to adjust the door a tad.

Begin building the door by flattening all the boards that will make up the panel. You could use a simple edge joint to glue the panel together, but the original used a tongue-and-groove joint. So that's what I used.

Use a plow plane to make the groove and its mating tongue; then glue up the door panel. When the glue has cured, flatten the assembled door panel with a jointer plane or belt sander.

One of the nice details on this piece is there is an applied bead moulding on the inside of the door's frame. You'll want to cut and apply this moulding to the face frame before you cut your door panel to its finished size.

I own a ³⁄₁₆" beading plane, though the original bead on this dry sink was likely a ¼" or something slightly bigger. Use what you have on hand and adjust your door to fit.

I cut my bead moulding on a piece of wide stock and then ripped that piece of moulding from that board using my table saw. Then I mitered the three pieces and attached them to the inside of the face frame using glue and pins.

Now fit the door to its opening. Cut it close using your table saw and fit it with a plane. Don't forget to bevel the long edge of the latch side of the door. Now attach the hardware to the carcase and the door. Once you get the hinges in place, remove the hinges from the door and attach battens to the inside of the door. The battens will help keep the door flat.

I attached the battens after installing the hinges because the screws for the hinges were longer than the door was thick. So I wanted them to bite into the battens as well. By attaching the hinges first, I knew exactly where to place the battens.

I chamfered the long edges of the battens. It's a period detail, though the original dry sink didn't have the chamfers. Then I screwed the battens to the backside of the door.

Finishing Details

Break all the sharp edges of your piece using #120-grit sandpaper. Then clean things up for finishing. After much experimentation, we decided to paint this dry sink using two coats of Olde Century Colors' "Yankee Blue."

If you are painting your pine and have some knots or sap problems, you should coat the project first with shellac to prevent the sap from bleeding through your paint. Then reassemble everything and figure out how to put this vanished furniture form to good use.

— *Christopher Schwarz*

The clearance holes for the screws should be reamed out to accommodate the cross-grain construction of the door. I ream out my holes by wiggling my spinning drill bit back and forth. You don't have to get too fancy about it.

Enfield Shaker Cabinet

Casework built with dados and glue alone is troubling. We uncover one old-school solution that ensures your work will endure real life.

Building reproductions of antiques can be like unraveling a mystery. This cabinet from the small Shaker community in Enfield, Conn., has yet to reveal all its secrets. For one, I'm not entirely sure what it was used for at the colony. A couple places refer to it as a jelly cupboard, but most sources prefer the following less-than-helpful label: pine cabinet.

But here's what we do know about the piece and where it comes from. The cabinet was built in the first half of the 19th century (some sources cite circa 1830) at the Enfield colony for the use of its members. Unlike other colonies, some sources state that the Enfield Shakers did not produce furniture for sale to the outside world (although some sources claim they did). Instead, the residents at Connecticut's only Shaker colony ran a thriving seed business. (Shakers are credited with the innovation of selling seeds in envelopes.)

Enfield was founded in 1782, hit its membership peak in 1855 with about 200 members, and then declined like all the other Shaker colonies – with the last eight survivors selling the land and retreating to other remaining colonies.

The cabinet passed into the hands of Edward Deming Andrews and Faith Andrews – two of the most influential collectors and chroniclers of the Shakers. Sometime in the 20th century, the cabinet passed through the workshop of Ejner Handberg, a Massachusetts cabinetmaker who repaired and restored a number of pieces from the Andrews collection. While these original pieces were in Handberg's shop, he made full-size drawings of them on cardboard he scavenged from refrigerator and stove boxes.

Those drawings became "Shop Drawings of Shaker Furniture and Woodenware" (Berkshire House), three volumes of books that are illuminat-

When people first see this cabinet, their instinct is to call it a jelly cupboard, chimney cupboard or pie safe. We're not so sure what its original purpose was, but it does have nice lines.

ing and frustrating. They're illuminating because they're one of the few sources of measured drawings of Shaker originals. And they're frustrating because some specific construction details aren't present. So the books, which I still recommend highly, leave me with many questions.

A Joinery Problem

One area that concerned me with the cabinet was the joinery as drawn. The shelves are housed in dados in the sides. This is a well-accepted way to build a cabinet, but it has always troubled me.

If you think about it for a minute, the dado joint is a poor glue joint in solid wood. Every mating surface in a dado joint puts a long-grain surface against an end-grain surface. In other words, chances are your dado joints are going to be weak because the end grain in the shelf and sides is going to soak up the glue and starve your joint. If the glue weakens and fails, the cabinet will be held together by the glued-on face frame (don't forget that the glue could fail there, too, if stressed or wracked) and the back of the cabinet. If you use a solid-wood shiplapped back, that's not going to offer much support compared to a screwed-in plywood back.

So if you're a woodworker who is concerned about the long-term survivability of your furniture, dados alone might not be a good option. But what do you do?

Avoiding the Overly Fussy

The logical solution would seem to be the sliding dovetail. It's an all-wood mechanical joint that will hold forever, even without glue. But have you ever tried cutting and fitting a whole case of these with 13"-wide shelves? How about 20"-wide shelves? It's a challenge. If you cut the joint square and tight-fitting, it won't go together because of the friction involved. So you have to tweak the male part of the joint to make it sloppy. But how sloppy? And how do you make it perfectly sloppy reliably and repeatedly? Personally, I've found the sliding dovetail better suited for joining smaller widths – think 3"-wide drawer dividers at the front of a chest of drawers.

Instead, I've come to rely on dados that are reinforced by a mechanical fastener – usually a nail but sometimes a screw (think pocket screws). There's a snobbery in woodworking that nails are low-class wood-butchery. Don't believe it. If you've inspected much antique furniture, you'll find nails used extensively. But you have to look close. Though the nails might be easily spotted in mouldings and carcase backs, some of the others are harder to find. Look inside a piece and you might find nails that toenail the shelves or drawer runners to the sides. Lots of the interior guts of a piece can be (and were) nailed. It's a fast way to build. The nails will be there if the glue gives way. And the correct nail will wedge the joint tight for decades, maybe centuries.

I always prefer to have my router template below my work whenever possible. This allows me to use a pattern-routing bit with the bearing on the bottom and limits the amount of spinning carbide exposed to the area below my waist.

Accurately paring this corner is easy if you do it right. First score the end grain of the waste with your chisel, then come back and pare it out to your lines. Place the chisel flat against the flat section of your foot's shape. This guides the tool for a perfect cut – and is why chisels need their unbeveled face to be truly flat.

A survey of Shaker pieces in books and in person reveals that they also used nails in their furniture – sometimes hidden and sometimes not. So even though Handberg's book doesn't show a single nail in his drawing of this cabinet, I took a leap of faith and decided to use both glue and nails in construction. I also took other small liberties. I used cherry instead of pine and made the mouldings easier to fabricate and attach. To ease assembly I also tweaked the back so it's visible at the top of the cabinet. These are but minor sins. When I compare my versions of this cabinet to Smithsonian photographs of the original, I know that I got this one right.

Sides and Feet

Because 13"-wide cherry boards are uncommon, you're likely going to have to glue up at least a couple boards edge-to-edge to make the side panels. You should of course pay close attention to the grain at the mating joint in the middle of the

panel – try to match the grain patterns so that the joint becomes almost invisible. One good strategy here is to try to find some 9'-long boards, crosscut them in half and join them edge-to-edge to make a single side piece. Usually the grain and color are easier to match up when the two pieces come from the same board.

But there's another detail to watch. As you prepare your panels for glue-up, also pick out the wood for the face frame. Do your best to match the grain where the sides meet the face frame stiles. This is a highly visible part of the cabinet and a poor grain or color match will be jarring.

After you've glued up the side panels, glue up the panels for the shelves. This is where you can use your knotty, sappy odd-looking stuff with abandon. Just make sure the front edge of each shelf looks good – that's all anyone will ever notice. Trim your sides and face frame stiles to size and then prepare your router templates that will be used for the feet.

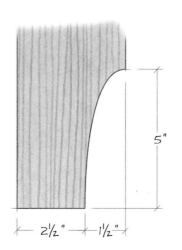

FRONT LEG DETAIL

5"

2½"   1½"

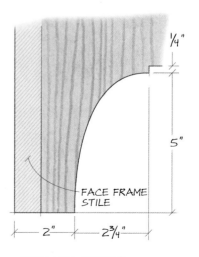

SIDE LEG DETAIL

¼"

5"

FACE FRAME STILE

2"   2¾"

The right-angle dado guide here was designed specifically for ½"-wide dados. Make the jig large enough to clamp it easily to your work and bench without interfering with the router or your hands. When building this jig, be sure to consider the clamping job ahead.

Make the template from ½"-thick plywood, trace the shape on your sides and cut about ¹⁄₁₆" shy of that line with your band saw. Then follow up by routing the shape with a router. You could clean up your saw cuts with hand tools, such as rasps, files and a spokeshave. But because there is so much end grain in this shape, the router is the superior choice if you have the equipment.

If you go the router route, you'll have to clean up the step between the curve and the flat section of the shape – the router will leave a rounded corner. This is quick work for a wide chisel.

The next step is to cut the dados in the sides. There are two paths to follow here. You could rout ¾"-wide x ¼"-deep dados and fit the shelves into these by tweaking the thickness of the shelves with a bench plane until you get a good fit. The other alternative is to cut ½"-wide x ¼"-deep dados and then cut a ¼" x ¼" rabbet in the ends of each shelf. Then you can tweak the fit of the shelf with a shoulder plane or bullnose rabbet plane by planing the rabbet on the shelf – rather than the entire shelf.

I built one of these cabinets with the wider dados and one with the narrow dados. There is little difference between the two approaches. With the wider dados there was less joinery involved, but you have to be careful when sizing each shelf to fit. It's easy to overshoot and get an ugly gap and a loose fit between the shelf and side. With the narrow dados, you have more joinery setups to deal with, but even if you overshoot the mark when fitting your shelf, you won't create that gap because the shoulder of the rabbet will hide it. Either way is fine; pick one that appeals to your skills and the tools at hand.

I milled the dados with a router, straight bit and a shop-made right-angle guide. We covered this process in great detail in Issue 3 of *Woodworking Magazine*. One detail worth mentioning: I milled the dados before milling the rabbet for the backs. This was on purpose. When you mill

Install enough dado cutters on your table saw's arbor to make a cut that is slightly wider than ¾". Then clamp a zero-clearance auxiliary fence to your fence as shown. The key to an accurate rabbet with this method is to keep the work pressed firmly to the saw's table during the cut. The dado stack will try to lift it off the table. For added insurance, repeat your pass on the part to make sure you have a rabbet of consistent depth.

dados with a router, you will usually get some grain blow-out when the bit exits the work. Cutting the rabbet after the dados will clean up any blow-out on your back edge.

The ¾"-wide x ¼"-deep rabbet at the top of the case sides can be cut in two passes – both cuts guided by the right-angle guide.

Now cut the ¾"-wide x ½"-deep rabbet on the inside back edge of both sides. Cutting big rabbets is a task best suited for a dado stack in a table saw, a conclusion we reached after cutting dozens and dozens of rabbets for Issue 1. The zero-clearance auxiliary fence shown in the photo above is a must for this operation.

I clean up my rabbets with a shoulder plane after cutting them with a dado stack. Is this necessary? Perhaps not – this rabbet for the back will not be a glue joint. But a couple passes with a shoulder plane ensure that the corner of the joint is clean, which ensures the back will fit tight.

With the joinery in the sides complete, plane or sand the interior face of the side pieces to prepare them for finishing. Planing and sanding reduces the thickness slightly, so you should do this before fitting the shelves. If you plane after you fit the shelves, that can loosen your joinery.

Fitting Shelves

Now you should turn to fitting your shelves in your dados. If you've opted for the narrow dados, you'll need to mill mating rabbets in the shelves – use the dado stack already in your table saw. You'll have to adjust the settings for a good fit.

After cutting the rabbets, clean them up and tweak their dimensions so that each shelf fits in its dado. Each shelf might need a different number of passes to fit. Don't be alarmed by this. The rabbet on your shelf could be a little off because you didn't use as much downward pressure when cutting it on the table saw. Or perhaps your stock is cupped slightly. That's what the shoulder plane is for – it can correct a great number of ills that some people would try to fix with a mallet.

If you own a narrow shoulder plane or router plane that can fit into the width of the dado, it's a good idea to clean up the bottom of the trench. A smooth bottom will glue better. And this joint needs all the help it can get.

If you opted to make the carcase with the wider dados, use a plane set for a fine cut to tweak the thickness of the shelf until it seats firmly in the

Enfield Shaker Cabinet

	NO.	PART	SIZES (INCHES)			MATERIAL	NOTES (DIMS IN INCHES)
			T	W	L		
Carcase							
❏	2	Sides	¾	13¾	51¼	Cherry	
❏	5	Shelves	¾	13	19	Cherry	in ¼-d. dados & rabbet
❏	2	Face frame stiles	¾	4	51¼	Cherry	
❏	1	Face frame rail	¾	2½	14½	Cherry	1¼-l. tenons, both ends
❏		Backboards	¾	19½	45½	Cherry	shiplapped, beaded
❏		Top cap moulding	¾	1⅞	60	Cherry	½ x ½ rabbet, ³⁄₁₆-r. astragal
❏		Cove moulding	¾	⅞	60	Cherry	⅝-r. cove
❏		Astragal moulding	⅜	⅜	60	Cherry	⅛-r. astragal
Door							
❏	2	Door stiles	¾	2¾	43	Cherry	
❏	1	Top rail	¾	3	9	Cherry	1¼-l. tenons, both ends
❏	1	Middle rail	¾	5	9	Cherry	1¼-l. tenons, both ends
❏	1	Lower rail	¾	4	9	Cherry	1¼-l. tenons, both ends
❏	2	Panels	⅝	7¼	16¼	Cherry	⅜-t. x ½-l. tongue, all edges
❏	1	Door stay	⅜	¾	1⅝	Cherry	⁵⁄₁₆ wedged dowel as pivot

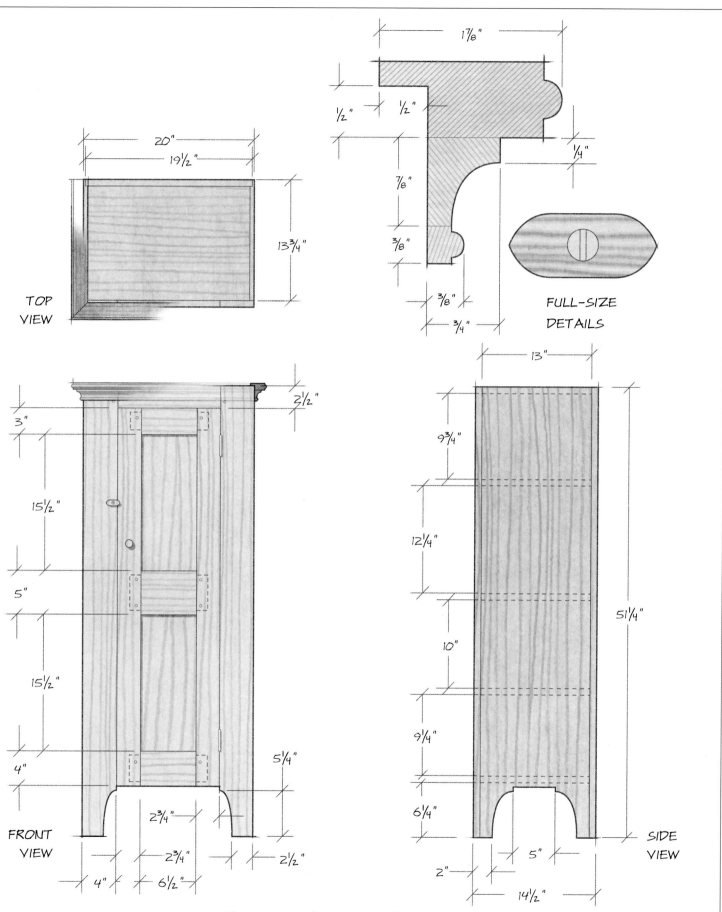

TOP VIEW

FULL-SIZE DETAILS

FRONT VIEW

SIDE VIEW

ENFIELD SHAKER CABINET

A gimlet has myriad advantages when making pilot holes for nails. There's no chuck or drill body to interfere or strike your cheater block. And it gets into tight places that no drill can go. Note that the hole and nail are installed at an angle – mine slope toward the center of the side panels by 7° or so – like a dovetail. This increases the wedging action of the nails.

When toenailing, you quickly run out of room for your hammer's head and need to turn to the nail set to finish the job. Resist the temptation to strike the nail head at an angle in lieu of the nail set. The nail will usually bend.

When installing cut nails, do what you can to keep them away from the ends of the board. Cut nails are little wedges and if they are installed too close to the end, they will split the work. These are installed ⅜" in from the end. I used four nails in each side.

---

dado. When I go down this path, I rely on my dial caliper to speed the work and make it predictable. Use your dial caliper to measure three things (this is when you should use its decimal function). Measure the width of the dado. Measure the thickness of your shelf. Then measure the thickness of a shaving from your plane. Now you know approximately how many passes you'll need to make with your bench plane. Here's a typical example: My dado is .750" wide. My shelf is .756" thick. And my plane is set to take a .001"-thick shaving. So I know that if I take three passes with my plane on each face of the shelf I will be close to a close fit.

I know this sounds fussy, but it is surprisingly fast and easy to do. And it works – I've been doing it for years. Plus, once you make your three passes with your plane, the surface is ready for assembly and finishing.

Once everything fits, clamp up the project without glue. Then take everything apart and reassemble it with glue. Although this isn't a particularly complex assembly, I would choose a slow-setting glue (Such as Titebond Extend) or perhaps a liquid hide glue (such as Old Brown Glue), which is both slow-setting and reversible with heat and water. You also could use a poly-

"My eyes have been filled with the endlessly changing patterns of the grains. I have felt the warmth of a thousand suns in my hands every day. I have smelled the rich, tangy odors of the freshly hewn chips. These are the things that have made my life so fine. These are the most precious things I can leave for you, my son."

— Jonas Wainwright, carpenter from a letter to his son in 1832

urethane glue, which sets slowly, but there can be some foamy squeeze-out problems if you're not an experienced user of this adhesive.

Toenailing for Tenacity

Once the glue has cured and you can take the project out of its clamps, toenail the shelves to the sides using cut nails. All cut nails require a pilot hole, and these cut fine finish nails require a ³⁄₃₂" pilot to ensure the wood won't split during nailing. I have a little cheater block shown in the photo above that guides my pilot bit. This little block guides my gimlet at the correct angle. A piece of tape on the gimlet indicates when I should stop turning. To make your own cheater block, simply draw on your project the path you want your nail to take through the shelf and side. Transfer that angle to a piece of scrap and cut the scrap to that line. There's no science to it. My cheater block starts the pilot hole ¼" up from the inside corner and at a 35° angle.

Installing cut nails is straightforward. Start the nail with the cross pane (if your hammer has one). Cut nails will sometimes twist in their holes. If they twist too much, they'll split the work. A cross pane helps you keep the nail oriented correctly as you start it. Then sink the nail as deeply as you dare with the face. Finally, sink the nail ⅛" below the surface of the wood with a nail set.

Place a nail at each corner where the shelves meet the sides. But don't toenail the top in place. Because that area of the sides will be covered by moulding you can nail the top in place from the outside of the case. This also adds to the overall strength of the case. Note that the nails on the outside of the case should be angled, much like dovetails, to increase their wedging power.

An Unusual Face Frame

The face frame for this cabinet has two stiles and one top rail – no bottom rail. This configuration makes it easier to assemble the face frame but more challenging to install. All of the joinery for the face frame is the same as the joinery for the door, so you should cut everything at the same

time. One word of advice: Cut the stiles for the door and face frame ¹⁄₁₆" wider than the finished width. This will give you some room to trim the face frame flush to the carcase after assembly and extra meat to trim the door to width.

If you are going to mill the mortises in the stiles by machine – a drill press or hollow-chisel mortiser – then I recommend you make the mortises ⅜" wide and the tenons a matching ⅜" thick. The ⅜" mortising chisel removes waste very effectively. If, however, you are going to mortise these by hand, I recommend a ¼"-wide mortise – your mortising chisel will be less likely to destroy your work during the sometimes-brutal mortising process. There are many ways to cut mortises by hand, and I've been experimenting with five methods (some ancient; some modern) for several months now for a future issue. I haven't reached an ultimate conclusion, but I right now am

If you mill your mortises by machine, use a ⅜" hollow mortise chisel, as shown above. Be sure to skip a space between each plunge on your first pass. Then come back and clean up the waste between the square holes. This prevents damage to your tooling.

favoring an approach where you drill a hole at one end of the mortise and then pop out the waste by angling the chisel toward the hole. You can see this technique in action at Jeff Gorman's website (go to www.amgron.clara.net and click on "Mortising and Tenoning").

For cutting the tenons, you have many choices. You can saw them by hand or mill them using a router – both techniques were covered in Issue 2. A third option is to use your table saw and a dado stack in a manner similar to that described with a router table. I chose the table saw for this project to keep the number of tooling setups to a minimum – the table saw was already set up for this operation from the previous two operations.

And though there is but one rail in the face frame, make an extra rail and cut the tenons on it as well. During assembly you can clamp this extra rail between the stiles at the foot to keep your face frame square.

I recommend you make your tenons 1¼" long. This length will allow you to successfully draw-bore the joint, a technique explored in Issue 4. If you have no wish to drawbore the joint you can drive a peg through the joint after assembly to achieve the same look – but not the same mechanical integration. Now plane or sand your face frame parts and assemble the frame. Draw-bore the joints or peg them after assembly. I used a 5⁄16"-diameter peg.

Glue the face frame to the carcase and clamp the extra rail between the stiles as shown in the photo at right. The face frame should extend proud of the sides a bit, which is correct. I find it easier to prop up the project on low beams on my bench so I can clamp across the face frame and sides with the project lying on its back. Once the glue is dry, trim the face frame flush to the carcase. I prefer to use a bench plane for this operation, but an electric router equipped with a flush-trimming bit will also do the job. I prefer the bench plane because it will produce a surface ready for finishing – the router-cut surface will need sanding or planing.

Now you have a couple details to decide on. The original Enfield cabinet had a bead cut into the front edge of the frame. You can add this bead if you like. I milled a ⅛"-radius bead onto the second version of this cabinet I built (not the one on the cover). One nice aspect of the bead is it gives you a perfect trench on the face frame for nailing the face frame to the carcase.

Solid-wood Shiplapped Back

As mentioned earlier, a solid-wood shiplapped back is not going to add as much rigidity to your carcase as a plywood back. But it does look nicer every time you open the door of this piece.

You can make your backboards random or regular in width. Either way, you need to cut a ¼"-wide x ⅜"-deep rabbet on each long edge of your backboards so they overlap one another and hide any seasonal expansion and contraction. I

Cutting tenons on the table saw requires you to follow all the same protocols when cutting a rabbet. Keep firm downward pressure on the work – the dado stack wants to lift the work. Varying pressure will result in thicker tenons. Cut your face cheeks and face shoulder first.

Cut the edge cheeks and edge shoulders next. First raise the dado stack to make a ⅜"-deep cut. Then pass the work over the blades. Use consistent downward pressure when cutting tenons this way to ensure your joints are identical in their dimension. This makes fitting each joint easier.

Again, a slow-setting glue can be your friend in this situation. The joint between the face frame and carcase is highly visible. Clamp it until it looks tight all around.

The long edges of the stiles are easily trimmed flush with the carcase with a bench plane – it's soothing work, actually. However, trimming things up at the top of the cabinet is more of a challenge. There's a lot of end grain to deal with. Use a sharp low-angle block plane and wet the end grain with mineral spirits to soften the wood.

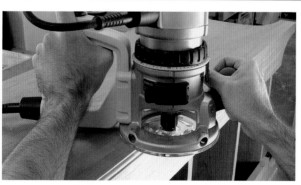

A D-handled router is designed for edge routing such as this. It adds stability and makes it easier to get a superior cut. Another option is to cut this bead with a moulding plane (side-bead planes are fairly common on the used-tool circuit). Those are next on my (long) list of hand planes to buy.

I used 8d headless cut brads to attach the face frame. Unlike the other brads in this project, these require a 1⁄16" pilot hole. The nail set drives the brad's head below the bead and out of sight.

again turned to my table saw with the still-set-up dado stack to do this job. With the rabbets cut, I planed all the backboards to prepare them for finishing. Then I used the ⅛"-radius beading bit in a router in my router table to mill a bead on the long edges.

Installing shiplapped backboards isn't hard. I used a shoulder plane to tweak the rabbets to get everything fitting tight. Then I attached the backboards one by one. The boards on the ends can be fastened to both the carcase sides and the shelves. But the boards between them should be fastened with a row of screws (or nails) down the center of each board only. If you attach a board with more than one row of screws, you are asking for a split when the wood starts to move (and it will). Don't forget to leave a small gap between the boards to allow for seasonal movement.

Doors: Building and Fitting

Almost all the joinery for your doors should be complete. All you need now is a groove for the panels and a mating rabbet on the panels. The mortises in the stiles allowed me to cut stopped grooves easily with the plough plane.

Make your groove match the width of your mortises. If you cut a ⅜"-wide mortise, cut a ⅜"-wide groove for the panels. Now cut a mating rabbet on your panels. Use your table saw and stack dado set (again) to cut this ⅜"-deep joint. Fine-tune the results with a shoulder plane.

One fine point about wood movement: When trimming your panels and cutting the rabbet, many woodworkers simply overlook the fact wood expands and contracts mostly across its width. They give the panel expansion room all around the panel in the rails and the stiles. That's not necessary. You can allow your panel to bottom out in its groove in the rails and allow for expansion and contraction in the door's stiles only.

These panels will bottom out in the groove in the rails and float in the groove in the stiles. Once the door is assembled, I like to drive a single brad through the groove and panel at the top and bottom of each panel. This brad keeps the panel centered in its frame.

Fit the rabbets on your backboards with a shoulder plane. Once they sit flat, screw them in place (you can replace the screws with nails after finishing the cabinet if you like).

Here's how I do this: Cut your panel and its rabbet so it bottoms out in both the rails and stiles. Then trim the long edges of your panel to get the expansion room you need in the stiles. This prevents you from cutting rabbets of two different widths. This strategy will also help prevent your panels from rattling in their grooves.

Plane or sand all your door components and then prepare for assembly. If you are drawboring your joints you can assemble this door one joint at a time if you please. This could allow you to fine tune the panel's fit and tweak the fit between the rails and stiles. Or you can glue it all at once.

Remember this: It's easy for all assemblies to end up out of square after clamping and gluing. A little bow here and there can add up. By squaring up your frame-and-panel assemblies after gluing and before final fitting, you'll make a lot less work for yourself. The door took less than 30 minutes to fit and install in the face frame.

Fitting the Door

This door is easy to fit because you have only three edges that are critical – the stiles and the top rail. There's no bottom rail to worry about. If you followed my advice then your door should be oversized for the opening that it has to fit into. Joint one stile of the door and rip the door down so it's ³⁄₃₂" smaller than its opening. Remove the same amount of material from each stile – this will require a couple cuts. Clean up the saw marks from the stile that will receive your hinges. Use your longest plane for this task.

Install the hinges on the doors. Be sure to line up the hinge barrels with the door's rails, as shown in the photo on the cover. Now you can fit the door with the hinges in place. It should be a tight fit. Prop up the door in place from below (as shown in the photo below) so that the top of the door presses against the face frame's rail. Remove one of your back boards and screw the hinges to the carcase from inside the case. Be sure to press the hinge leaf for the carcase up as you drill your pilot. This removes the slop from the barrel of the hinge, so the door will hang right where you intended it to. Remove the prop from below the door.

Now get out a straightedge, ruler and marking knife. I mark out the gap or "reveal" directly

These non-mortise hinges from Amerock used to be my favorite. Now these hinges are made in China and I've found some quality problems. Amerock officials insist the problem is being fixed. All I can say is that no matter what hinge you buy, make sure it swings precisely and isn't sloppy.

I cut a scrap to a close size and then added a few strips of tape to hold the door right where I wanted it from below. If there had been a lower rail, I would have shimmed the door in place from below with thin wooden wedges.

on the door and plane to those lines. This allows me to ignore whether the door is square or a parallelogram. It will fit and look good in the end.

When you tweak the top of the door, you are going to be again planing end grain. Soak the end grain like you did when trimming the top. And work from the outside to the center to prevent chipping at the ends. You can plane the long edge of the stile with your longest plane.

Once your door fits, you can work on the shop-made cabinet stay that holds the door shut. The stay is made from ³⁄₈"-thick scrap, a small wedge and a dowel. First take your scrap and bore a ⁵⁄₁₆"-diameter hole through it for the dowel. Then trace the shape of the stay on the scrap and cut and shape it to your satisfaction. Now take a 2"-long section of ⁵⁄₁₆"-diameter dowel and cut a thin kerf through its end grain. The kerf should be made with your finest saw (Japanese pullsaws work quite well here). And the kerf should be about ½" deep into the dowel.

Make a small wedge from hardwood. The wedge should be ¹⁄₈" thick, ⁵⁄₁₆" wide and about ½" long. Put glue on the dowel and wiggle it into the hole in the stay. Now put a little glue on your wedge and tap it into the kerf until the dowel is wedged into the stay. When the glue is dry, trim the wedge flush with a saw.

Now drill a ⁵⁄₁₆" hole in the carcase stile for the dowel. Inside the case, mark on the dowel where

it first emerges on the inside of the stile. Drill a ¹⁄₈"-diameter hole through the dowel tangent to that point. When the cabinet is finished, you'll install the stay by putting it in its hole and gluing a ¹⁄₈" dowel through that hole inside the case.

The door's knob is an off-the-rack ⁷⁄₈" Shaker-style knob from Rockler Hardware.

Authentic Moulding

This moulding profile was taken directly from Handberg's drawings. He shows it made in two pieces. The top, overhanging piece with the astragal is one piece; the lower half with the cove and bead is a second piece. Suffice it to say that I couldn't find a router bit that would mill this lower profile. So I made the moulding from three pieces: The top overhanging piece, a coved piece and a beaded piece. With some careful wood selection, it will look like one piece.

There was one other change I made to the moulding. The original moulding was flush to the top edge of the cabinet. This meant that you had a lot of joinery showing up there, and if your joinery isn't perfect, you'd be showing it off. So I cut a ½" x ½" rabbet on the underside of the top cap moulding. This does several things (all good): It hides a lot of end grain on the top. It conceals the fit (good or bad) between the moulding and the case. And it adds a lip to the top of the cabinet. I like the lip, which helps keep objects from spilling to the floor.

The moulding can be milled using three common bits (see the Supplies box for details). Once you get the router work complete, mill the rabbet on the top cap moulding. Install the moulding by fitting the front piece first. It's the most critical length of moulding on the whole piece.

With that piece of moulding sized perfectly, you can glue and nail it in place with the spacer scrap supporting the moulding on one end. Then things get easy. Miter the front ends of the mouldings that travel across the sides of the case, commonly called the "returns." When the miters are tight, mark where they meet the back edge of the carcase. Trim them square, then glue and nail them to the case (watch out for the nails in

Although I really like my hammer and cut nails, I like my headless 23-gauge pinner just as much for installing small mouldings such as the beading on this case.

the carcase). Turn the case upside down on your bench and install the cove moulding using the same strategy.

The rest is just finishing things up. Break the edges with sandpaper and decide on a finishing strategy. If you're going to putty your nail holes, I recommend you do this after finishing. There's putty designed just for this (commonly available at every home center) and it allows you to mix and match the color closely.

Both of these cabinets are in my home now awaiting their final owners. What's curious about them is that building them actually created a few mysteries rather than unraveling them. The shelf arrangement is quite curious. The irregular and unexpected spacing makes me wonder what was stored in the original. Most people take one look at this cabinet and say "jelly cupboard" or "pie safe." But I'm not so sure.

— *Christopher Schwarz*

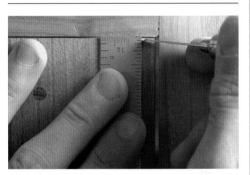

I like a ¹⁄₁₆" gap or reveal. Here I'm marking that directly on the stile with a marking knife. Do the same at the other end of the door. Connect the marks and plane to that line.

Whenever possible, rest your doors on your shop floor when planing the top. Good support, a sharp iron and a little mineral spirits will make the end grain fly off your plane in unbroken ribbons.

To install the length at front, first cut a scrap piece of moulding with perfect 45° ends as shown. Butt the front moulding against this scrap at one corner and mark at the other end where the moulding touches the corner of the carcase. Miter at that mark. Then attach the front piece.

Supplies

Freud
800-334-4107 or freudtools.com

Freud router bits
- ³⁄₁₆"-radius half-round bit #82-104 (cuts large astragal)
- ⁵⁄₈"-radius cove bit #30-107 (cuts cove)
- ¹⁄₈"-radius half-round bit #82-110 (cuts small bead)
- ¹⁄₈"-radius beading bit #80-122 (cuts bead on stiles and backboards)

Rockler
Rockler.com or 800-279-4441
1 ■ Cherry Face Grain knob 1" # 61665, $6.39 ea.

Prices correct at publication deadline.

Adding Age to Cherry

Growing old gracefully is one of the signature features of this sometimes-finicky wood.

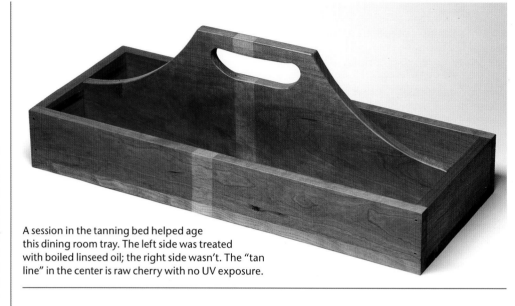

A session in the tanning bed helped age this dining room tray. The left side was treated with boiled linseed oil; the right side wasn't. The "tan line" in the center is raw cherry with no UV exposure.

My favorite piece of furniture in my home is the antique library table that serves as my desk. There's nothing particularly impressive about the design, but the wood is gorgeous cherry that glows with inner fire. In fact, after intensifying for more than a century, the color is much closer to rich sherry than raw cherry. And that's one of the qualities that makes cherry such a popular choice among American hardwoods – its looks improve with age. But therein lies the problem: New pieces of cherry furniture can appear anemic, especially with just a clear finish on them. Instead of a warm rust-red, you're more likely to see washed-out pink or even a gray cast. It takes years for cherry to age into a natural beauty.

If you've worked much with cherry, you know how finicky – not to mention expensive – it can be. Not only is it prone to sudden grain reversal – and thus tear-out while working it, you can't always tell by looking if a board is going to finish well. The last thing you want is a blotchy mess after you've spent hours in the construction process. A board that appears clear and straight grained may soak up stain in an unpredictable (and unattractive) pattern.

It's Worth the Wait
That's why some woodworkers contend that the best finishing method is to simply wait a few decades and not try to fake what it takes nature years to create. But because most of us would prefer to have our projects looking good from day one, we experimented with a number of methods designed to mimic the aging process, then lined up the sample boards side by side to determine which we liked best.

Our decision was based purely on the personal preferences of our editorial and art staff, taking into consideration that the wood's color would continue to deepen over time.

In the book "Understanding Wood Finishing" (Reader's Digest), Bob Flexner writes that, "old cherry that has darkened naturally is actually quite impossible to match with stains or toners.

The color can be matched well, but neither the stain nor toner can recreate the translucence of naturally aged cherry."

That's why, with one exception, we eschewed stains and toners – we had no wish to cover the beauty of the natural wood, or produce a finish that would be compromised years from now after the wood has aged gracefully. Our goal, in effect, was to create a good fake I.D. – something that will fool people until the wood's chronological age catches up to its stated age.

The Contestants
After first selecting sample boards similar in appearance then preparing each for finishing in the same way, we tried exposure to sun, exposure to sun after a coat of boiled linseed oil, natural Danish oil, a mixture of natural and dark walnut Danish oil (the exception), clear shellac, orange shellac, garnet shellac, lye, and potassium dichromate. For each method, we followed the instructions on the container. When dry, each sample board was top-coated with an aerosol spray lacquer so that the sheen on each was as similar as possible.

The clear shellac looked little different than the naked board, which is to say not very pleasing or even worth the effort. The other two types of shellac resulted in finishes of remarkably similar appearances, which, while not unpleasant, did not resemble aged cherry. Instead of bringing out the natural beauty of the wood, they merely reflected

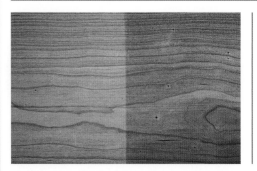
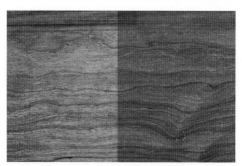

The left sides of both of these pieces of cherry were covered while the right sides were exposed to full sun for eight hours. The difference: The sample board on the right was first treated with boiled linseed oil, which we decided gave the most pleasing results.

the color in the flakes. In addition, each type of shellac resulted in a fair amount of blotching – obviously undesirable but something that can appear in cherry with any film finish.

Like the natural shellac, the natural Danish oil created little appearance of aging. The mixture of the natural and dark walnut Danish oils resulted in a color that while pleasing, was lacking in red tones. One of our editors has in the past achieved good results on cherry with the mixture; it's possible that the boards we selected were simply recalcitrant – a not uncommon problem with the species.

When working with both lye and potassium dichromate, it's important to follow strict safety precautions. Lye can cause serious chemical burns to your skin, and potassium dichromate is considered a carcinogen, so wear a mask to avoid breathing the powder. Also, it's important to neutralize the lye by washing the wood afterward with a weak white vinegar solution – otherwise, the reaction could be re-started should water get through your topcoat in the future. Both cause chemical reactions with the wood, the results of which will vary depending on the strength of your solution. Because results will vary, you may wish to experiment. We tried both methods twice, the first time combining the powders with tap water, the second time using filtered bottled water.

With the lye, the results were similar in both instances. Combining approximately ½ teaspoon of powder with one quart of water, then brushing it over the wood resulted in a rich red color that developed overnight. While it looked nice, it also looked much like mahogany. In addition, because the wood will continue to naturally darken in color as it ages, if the initial treatment is too dark, it may eventually be unrecognizable as cherry, which would defeat our purpose here.

Unlike the lye, the two mixtures of potassium dichromate looked completely different. Combining approximately an ⅛ teaspoon of powder with tap water produced overnight results that resembled dirty walnut more than aged cherry, while the bottled water mixture produced a color just a shade darker than the clear shellac – which is to say little color at all.

And the Winner Is …

What we think produced the best result was boiled linseed oil and a day in the sun. Or, lacking a sunny day, a session at the tanning salon. Of course, you're unlikely to find a tanning bed with the capacity to hold your highboy, so you'll simply have to wait for the clouds to clear. On the sample boards pictured on the "Contents" page, we simply placed the boards on sawhorses outside our workshop on a sunny day. While it's relatively easy to produce an even tan on a flat piece of wood or a small piece that creates few shadows, it's likely to be a little trickier with a large project. The good news is that repeated

> *"Take a piece of wood — plane, sand and oil it and you will find it is a beautiful thing. The more you do to it from then on, the more chance that you will make it worse."*
>
> — Tage Frid (1915-2004)
> professor, Rhode Island School of Design,
> and author of the landmark
> *"Tage Frid Teaches Woodworking"* (Taunton)

sun exposure over several days didn't result in a noticeably darker tan than what we achieved for our dining room tray with one tanning-bed session, so if you face a different side of your piece into the sun on subsequent days, you should end up with even coloring.

Why? The color change that takes place in cherry exposed to the sun is a continuous thing that's going on, explains USDA Forest Products Laboratory expert Mark Knaebe.

"It's a logarithmic rate of change, kind of like a nuclear half-life. It starts out fast and then slows down," which gives the "untanned" area time to catch up, he said.

While all wood is in some measure chromophoric (meaning it changes when exposed to light), cherry has a more immediate and noticeable reaction to ultraviolet (UV) light than do most other domestic hardwoods. But, says Knaebe, moisture and oxygen are also necessary for the reaction to occur. If you were to build in a vacuum, the color of your wood wouldn't change.

A more practical way to keep the color of your cherry constant, if that's a look you like, is to use a pigment stain, says Knaebe, which in effect acts as a blocking agent. Unlike dye, which is made from organic chemicals that break down over time in the light, pigments are basically bits of ground up rock, which lasts a lot longer. But as Flexner argues in his book, while you may be

able to achieve a pleasing color, you won't be able to mimic the glow that comes from within naturally aged cherry.

Achieving the 'Perfect' Results

To achieve our "perfect" results (which we decided were the best balance of current beauty and expectation of future good looks), here's how to proceed. First, prepare the surface to be finished using progressively finer sandpaper, up to #220-grit, or plane it smooth. Then, mix two parts boiled linseed oil with one part mineral spirits (try to mix only enough for each application). The mineral spirits thin the mixture and make it easier to apply.

Apply a generous amount to the raw wood using a rag, foam brush or one-use bristle brush, and allow it to soak into the surface for five to 10 minutes. Then, wipe off the excess oil with a dry rag. We placed our sample board in the sun immediately and left it there for eight hours. The dining room tray cured overnight before its 20-minute tanning session. Both resulted in almost the same amount of color change, and additional sun exposure had no noticeable added effect. After waiting a week for the oil to cure, we sprayed on a top coat of lacquer.

Dispose of excess oil/mineral spirits by soaking up the remainder with a rag or rags, then set the rags out in a single layer to allow the oil to cure. We generally set the rags out on the rim of our garbage can. If you bunch up the rags when they are soaked in oil there is a danger of spontaneous combustion as the oil cures. Once the rags feel dry (usually overnight in a warm room), it's safe to throw them in the garbage.

Bask in the Sun

In the end, we agree with current dermatological wisdom – lazing around in the sun adds age to your bits and pieces. But for the purposes of making your cherry look nice, that's a good thing. So go ahead and slather on the oil.

— *Megan Fitzpatrick*

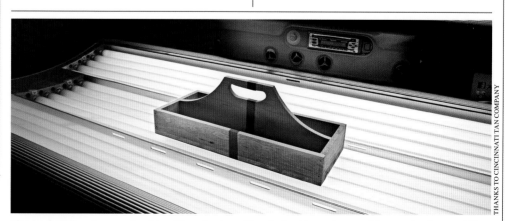

The weak Midwest sun makes it hard to get a decent tan during November – not to mention it gets chilly with nothing but a piece of tape around the midsection. So we decided to take our tray for a tanning-bed session to help speed up the aging process.

THANKS TO CINCINNATI TAN COMPANY

Understanding Wipe-on Finishes

The moment of truth for many projects comes long after the shop is cleaned, the tools are put away and the work is sanded. Applying a finish stops many woodworkers dead in their tracks.

Finishing is the chore almost all woodworkers fear most because it has the greatest potential for spoiling the project. So it's only natural that woodworkers would seek a risk-free finish. For this reason, many choose a finish that's wiped on. Finishing manufacturers have capitalized on this fear and have developed rag-on finishes – that's the good news about many products today.

The bad news is that the finishes you find on the shelves at your home centers have similar names but aren't alike – and you can't figure out what each one does by simply reading the can.

This is what they all have in common: You wipe them on, allow them to dry and then add more coats for additional protection.

But the real questions for us are: Just how many coats do you need? And how much protection can you expect? To get these answers you first have to have some knowledge of the finishing product's contents. Because the actual contents aren't listed on most products and the names can't always be trusted, you can do a simple test at home to get some answers.

With the exception of pure oil finishes (such as boiled linseed oil) most wiping finishes are either a varnish that's thinned with a reducer (like paint thinner or mineral spirits) or a combination of oil and varnish. To see which one you have, pour a small amount on a hard surface like glass or metal to form a small puddle. Let the puddle

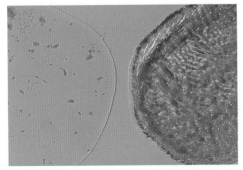

When a thinned or wiping varnish dries on a non-porous substance, such as this piece of glass, it is smooth and hard (left). Oil/varnish blends, on the other hand, will cure soft and wrinkly on a non-porous surface (right).

dry for a couple of days. If the puddle dries hard and smooth, you have a thinned, or true, wiping varnish. If the puddle dries wrinkled and soft, it's an oil/varnish blend.

Why is it important to know what kind of wiping finish you have? When it comes to protecting the wood, varnish wins because it dries hard.

The reason has to do with the way the products are manufactured. A typical oil-based varnish is made by cooking alkyd resins with an oil (usually modified soybean oil). To make a wiping varnish, the finish is simply thinned with paint thinner or mineral spirits. Oil/varnish blends go further, adding more oil and thereby further reducing the quantity of varnish in the finish.

Still confused about what to do? Well, the sure-fire way to get what you want is to make your own wiping varnish. It's easy. Buy a can of oil-based varnish and thin it with paint thinner or mineral spirits. Add either one part thinner to four parts varnish or, for a slightly thinner mix, one part thinner to three parts varnish. If you make your own, select varnish with the sheen you prefer. Usually a mid-level sheen such as semi-gloss or satin is best for furniture finishing.

With your finish mixed, actually applying it is mostly foolproof. First, make sure you have adequately sanded the project. I prefer to use a random-orbit sander for flat surfaces. Start with #120-grit sandpaper. Sand out all the imperfections: scratches and marks left by your tools and glue. Then move progressively through finer sandpaper grits: #150, #180 and #220. Brush or blow off the dust between each grit. Remove as much dust as possible before applying the finish.

To apply the wiping varnish, use a clean cloth rag. T-shirt material works well, rivaling cotton cheesecloth, which is touted as being especially lint-free. You can purchase cotton cheesecloth at most home centers or paint stores.

Wipe on the finish equally on all surfaces. The surface should look wet but it should not pool. This is especially true for the first coat, which soaks into the wood. The subsequent coats don't penetrate and will look wetter.

After the first coat has dried, lightly sand using either #320- or #360-grit coated sandpaper. The coating helps prevent the finish dust from clogging the sandpaper. Norton Abrasive's 3X brand and 3M's Tri-M-Ite are good options. This light sanding should substantially smooth the finish surface. Wipe clean all the dust and recoat. In all, three to four coats should be enough.

If you colored your project beforehand with an oil-based pigmented stain, you need to be careful. The application of a wiping varnish using a rag could cause the stain to redissolve and smear. Instead, lightly brush on two coats and don't brush over areas with wet finish. After the second coat dries, sand the wood to smooth the surface. Be sure to sand lightly, however, especially near edges or on moulding details. These areas are susceptible to sanding through the finish and then through the stain color, which will expose the natural color of the wood.

— *Steve Shanesy*

A Finishing Experiment

We conducted a couple of simple experiments with five wiping varnishes readily available from local home centers, plus our own homemade version and a full-strength varnish. Two products (Minwax and General Finishes Arm-R-Seal) are wiping polyurethanes, which technically are varnishes but use urethane resins instead of alkyd resins.

In the first experiment, we applied all the finishes to a walnut plank and compared the looks, as seen in the photo. We applied four coats, with light sanding after the first coat.

For the second experiment, we placed equal amounts of the finishes (measured to the thousandth of a pound) in identical open containers and allowed the finish to evaporate, leaving the dried resin on the bottom. We then weighed the dried material. The result told us how much of each finish was solids (which protect the wood) and how much was solvent (a carrier of resins that evaporates, leaving a dry, solid film finish on the wood). The dried samples also gave us a better understanding of the hardness, flexibility, clarity and color of each finish when cured.

As a reference, these characteristics can be viewed in a variety of ways. For example, an amber color in the dried film could be good if you want to add warmth to the look of your wood. But a finish with little color may be preferred if you're finishing a white wood such as maple or ash. Hardness is a good attribute but it's a trade-off with flexibility, an equally important attribute that allows the finish film to move with the wood during seasonal expansion/contraction cycles.

Of the seven samples tested, only one dried notably differently – Waterlox. All of the other products showed minor differences.

■ General Finishes Arm-R-Seal and Sealacell looked about the same. Both were among the clearest with a mild yellow color – Arm-R-Seal

We tested seven wiping varnishes to see how they performed when rubbed on a walnut plank, shown here. At the bottom are the dried films that remained when the liquid dried in the open containers.

was a bit more orange. Arm-R-Seal's film was less flexible and harder. In measured characteristics, it had the highest percent of solids (34 percent) of all the commercial products except unthinned regular varnish. Arm-R-Seal is considered a sealing coat, with Sealacell used as a finishing top coat. Sealacell tied for the lowest percent of solids (29 percent).

■ The Minwax Wipe-On Poly sample dried to a tough, brittle, clear film that was amber in color. On the board, it produced an attractive protective film without appearing thick or plastic-looking. It was less clear than other products and had a 32 percent solids content.

■ Formby's Tung Oil produced one of the most pleasing-looking finishes of the group. While it tied with Sealacell for the lowest solids rating (29 percent), the film on the wood had a more natural look. The dried film was yellowish and flexible, yet tough. It was almost as clear as the two General Finishes products.

■ Waterlox, as previously noted, appeared as a dried film more orange and far less clear. The dried sample actually was translucent and had a solids content of 31.5 percent. On the board, it appeared duller and slightly less clear than any other product. The dried film was softer and more flexible than the other products, making us wonder about its suitability for use in demanding circumstances such as tabletops or countertops.

■ The unthinned varnish, a McCloskey product, and our home-brew wiping varnish made from it produced clear, flexible yellow-tinted films that were as tough as any in the group. As expected, the varnish directly from the can had the highest solids content at 39.5 percent. Our thinned wiping version equalled the highest of the commercially prepared products at 34.5 percent. On the wood, the straight-from-the-can varnish was too thick to produce a smooth finish by applying with a rag. The thinned version did not appear to produce a thick-looking finish. Rather it appeared clear and natural, but was a bit more dull than the others in the group.

— Steve Shanesy

Look through the shelves at your local home center and you'll see many products with similar names. But how do you know what the products really are? Our list will help.

Common Wiping Varnishes

- Daly's ProFin
- Formby's Tung Oil Finish
- General Finishes Arm-R-Seal
- General Finishes Sealacell
- Gillespie Tung Oil
- Hope's Tung Oil Varnish
- Jasco Tung Oil
- Minwax Wipe-On Poly
- Val-Oil
- Waterlox
- Zar Wipe-On Tung Oil

Common Oil/Varnish Blends

- Behlen Danish Oil
- Behlen Salad Bowl Finish
- Behlen Teak Oil
- Behr Scandinavian Tung Oil Finish
- Deft Danish Oil
- Maloof Finish
- Minwax Antique Oil Finish
- Velvit Oil
- Watco Danish Oil
- Watco Teak Oil

Shaker Hanging Cabinet

If you own any books about the Shakers or their furniture, you probably have seen a small storage cabinet like this one hanging in the background behind the more celebrated pieces.

I first spotted a close relative of this cabinet in William F. Winter's "Shaker Furniture" (Dover). After a long and glowing description of the chairs shown in the same photograph, Winter notes only: "This small, pine, wall cupboard (from the North family, New Lebanon) is a typical convenience of the sisters' shops."

When I visited the Shaker Village of Pleasant Hill (shakervillageky.org) in Harrodsburg, Ky., I saw a similar cabinet hanging on a peg in one of the second-floor rooms. While eating sweet-potato casserole in the Trustees' Office Inn that evening, everyone else at the table was raving about the built-in cabinets; I was smitten with the little hanging cabinet (and the casserole).

Then, years later, I noticed that Thomas Moser published a more refined version in his seminal "How to Build Shaker Furniture" (Sterling).

The way I see it, this small cabinet has what few woodworking projects can truly lay claim to. It is both simple to build and exceptionally well-proportioned. For that, it deserves center stage.

4 Important Lessons

When building this hanging cabinet there are four important things to pay attention to:

■ Rabbet joinery: This cabinet – in one way or another – is built using mostly rabbets. Become familiar with this joint before you attempt this project.

■ Wood selection: This cabinet will not look right if you choose the wrong boards for the front. The rails and stiles must have the straightest grain possible. Curvy, diagonal or irregular grain will distract from the simple lines of the piece. Save the most dramatic grain patterns, such as a cathedral grain, for the door's panel.

One common mistake many beginners make is that they try to make a project with as few boards as possible. While no one likes to waste wood, the bigger sin is to build a project that could have looked a lot better in the end. So buy some extra wood and save the scraps for the interior pieces that won't show on a future project.

When picking boards for the two side parts, choose pieces that have straight grain at the edges. This grain pattern will match the straight grain on the case stiles, making the sides look pleasing and – if you're lucky – almost seamless.

■ Fitting a door: Beginners hate fitting doors. Experts know there is a trick to making them right with little fuss. Follow the directions carefully and you'll see how straightforward it can be.

■ Wood movement: The back is made from a solid-wood panel, so it will expand and contract about ⅛" with changes in humidity. This means you have to attach the back in a special way to prevent it from splitting or wrenching your cabinet apart as it answers nature's call.

Making a Strong Case

Once you select your boards and joint and plane them down to the correct thickness, you should mill all the parts for the carcase. Joint one long edge of each board, rip them to width and then crosscut them to finished length. Leave the door parts and frame stiles long for now – you will cut them to fit the assembled carcase.

The first joints to cut with this project are the three rabbets in each side piece. Set up your table saw to cut a ¾"-wide x ¼"-deep rabbet using the instructions provided in "Cut Accurate and Clean Rabbets." Make a test cut in some scrap that's the same thickness as your sides. Check your work with a square and some care. If this joint does not have a dead-on 90° corner, your carcase won't have one either. If it is square, check the dimension of the rabbet using a dial caliper. This might sound like overkill, but it's not. Here's why: If this joint is just a little off, then all the joints that follow it will have to compensate for this small error – especially when you start building the door and fitting it to the case. Small errors like this tend to add up during the course of a project.

When you're satisfied with the setup of your dado stack and rip fence, lock the height of the arbor. This is important for a couple of reasons. With some less-expensive table saws, you can actually force the arbor to creep downward during a cut with a dado stack. I've seen it happen – your dado will look like a ramp for skateboarders instead of a properly made joint. Also, you will be keeping this exact height for the next two joinery operations, so locking in your setting is a good idea. With your saw set, cut this rabbet on the ends of the two side pieces. This joint holds the top and bottom of the case in place.

Next, cut the rabbet in the sides that will hold the back panel. To create this rabbet, you need only adjust your rip fence to make a ½"-wide x ¼"-deep rabbet and cut that rabbet on the long back edge of each side piece.

After that, cut the dados in the side pieces that will hold the two ½"-thick shelves in place. To make your life easier, make sure you do not change the height of the dado stack you just used to cut the rabbets. Remove the dado stack from the arbor and install the correct number of wings, chippers and shims to produce a perfect ½"-wide dado.

The dados for the shelves are ¼" deep. By leaving the height of the blades alone, you ensure that the shelves, top and bottom will keep your case square. If you change the height of the blades even a tiny bit before cutting the dados, one of two bad things will happen. If your cut is too deep, your shelves won't seat all the way down into the bottoms of the dados without some extraordinary clamping pressure. (If you manage to close this joint, your carcase will end up with an hourglass shape and the rabbets at the top and bottom will be gappy and weak.) If your dado cut is too shallow, the shelves will cause the sides to bulge out

in the center and the rabbets at the top and bottom will be gappy, unattractive and weak.

To make the dados in the sides, use your table saw's miter gauge (set to 90°) and a gauge block clamped to your rip fence, as shown in the photo below. Mark on your side pieces the locations of both dados. Sure, it will take an extra minute, but it prevents mistakes. Also mark the top and bottom of each of the sides so you don't get the right and left sides confused – a common mistake that even professionals make.

With the dados cut, you are almost ready to assemble the basic carcase. It's always a good idea to prepare your interior surfaces for finishing before assembly. Finish-sand the inside faces of your pieces (start with #100-grit paper and work up to #220), or plane and scrape the surfaces to your liking.

Test the fit of the joints and clamp the case together without any glue. Do not skip this step. A rehearsal is worthwhile for several reasons: You'll figure out exactly how many clamps you need so you don't have to go rushing across the room for more as the glue sets up. You'll also figure out the best procedure for clamping the case without your parts flopping around. And you'll make sure your rabbets and dados fit soundly.

As you make this milk run, make sure you keep the front edges of the top, bottom and shelves perfectly flush with the front edge of the side pieces. The top, bottom and shelves, if you haven't noticed, are ½" narrower than the sides.

Before you take the clamps off, pay particular attention to the squareness of the case. Measure the case from corner to corner and compare the two dimensions. If they're the same, everything's square. If they're not, put a clamp across the two

I recommend using a dado stack for cutting rabbets because it requires only one setup. The featherboard makes the operation safer and more accurate by keeping your work pressed firmly against the saw's table.

corners that produced the longer measurement and apply the tiniest bit of clamping pressure. Compare the corner-to-corner measurements again. Repeat until everything is perfect. I like to check the squareness now because the cabinet usually behaves the same once you add the glue.

Now add glue in your rabbets and dados. If you are new to woodworking, I recommend a slow-setting glue for casework. There are several varieties, the most common being Titebond Extend. The glue's extra "open time," which is when the glue is wet and your parts can move

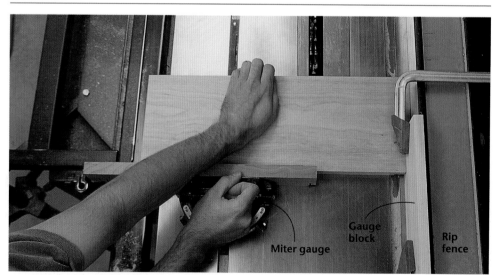

The gauge block, which is clamped to the rip fence, sets the location of the dado on the side pieces. But because the gauge block sits in front of the saw blade, there's no danger of trapping your side piece between the rip fence and the blade while making this cut – a major source of kickback. If you have a stock miter gauge, this would be an excellent time to add a piece of adhesive sandpaper (I prefer #100-grit) to its smooth metal face to improve grip during this operation.

Angled nails wedge the joint

Stile

Mind the gap

This is a highly visible joint, so make extra sure you watch out for gaps between the stiles and the sides.

Nails are not an act of the devil. Someday the glue will fail, and it's the nails that will hold everything together. Make sure you angle your nails (18-gauge brads are good) as shown so that the fasteners wedge the side piece against its mates.

around, will allow you to tweak the position of your parts. When applying the glue, a thin but consistent film will bond your joints without making a big mess. When you apply the clamps, a little glue squeeze-out is good – it means you haven't starved your joints of glue.

After 45 minutes, take the case out of the clamps and nail the sides to the top and bottom pieces, using the above photo as a guide.

World's Simplest Face Frame

Traditionally, face frames are built using both vertical pieces (stiles) and horizontal pieces (rails). Not so with this project, which has only stiles. This makes things a lot easier.

Cut your stiles to finished width and length, and finish-sand or plane them. If you're handy with a block plane, it's wise to cut your stiles about $1/32$" long and trim them flush to the case at the top and bottom after affixing them to the carcase. If you're not so confident, just take extra care in cutting your stiles to length.

Attach the stiles to the carcase using glue and clamps. Nails aren't necessary here. Make an effort to ensure the long edge of each stile is perfectly flush with its mating side piece; otherwise the opening for your door will not be square.

To complete the opening for the cabinet's door, you need to attach the additional $1/2$"-thick top and bottom pieces that have the decorative cove cut milled on them, which is easy to do.

As you study the cutting list below, you'll notice that the outside top and bottom are different widths – the top is $1/2$" wider than the bottom. That's not a mistake. It's actually a clever way to create a notch in the back edge of the outside top piece (cutting stopped notches is no fun). Let me tell you what you're going to do to that top piece:

Shaker Hanging Cabinet

	NO.	PART	T	W	L	MATERIAL	NOTES (DIMS IN INCHES)
Carcase							
❏	2	Sides	$3/4$	7	19	Cherry	$3/4$"-wide x $1/4$"-deep rabbets on ends
❏	2	Inside top & bottom	$3/4$	$6^{1/2}$	17	Cherry	
❏	2	Shelves	$1/2$	$6^{1/2}$	17	Cherry	In $1/2$"-wide x $1/4$"-deep dados
❏	2	Stiles	$3/4$	$2^{1/2}$	19	Cherry	Glued to carcase
❏	1	Notched outside top	$1/2$	$8^{3/4}$*	19	Cherry	
❏	1	Outside bottom	$1/2$	$8^{1/4}$	19	Cherry	
❏	1	Back	$1/2$	18*	$24^{1/2}$	Cherry	
Door							
❏	2	Door stiles	$3/4$	$1^{1/2}$*	20*	Cherry	$1/4$"-wide x $1/2$"-deep groove on one edge
❏	2	Door rails	$3/4$	$1^{1/2}$*	$11^{1/4}$	Cherry	$1/4$"-wide x $1/2$"-deep groove on one edge, $1/2$" TBE
❏	1	Door panel	$1/2$	11	17	Cherry	$1/2$"-wide x $1/4$"-deep rabbet on four back edges

* Dimensions listed are oversized. See the text for details. TBE = tenon both ends

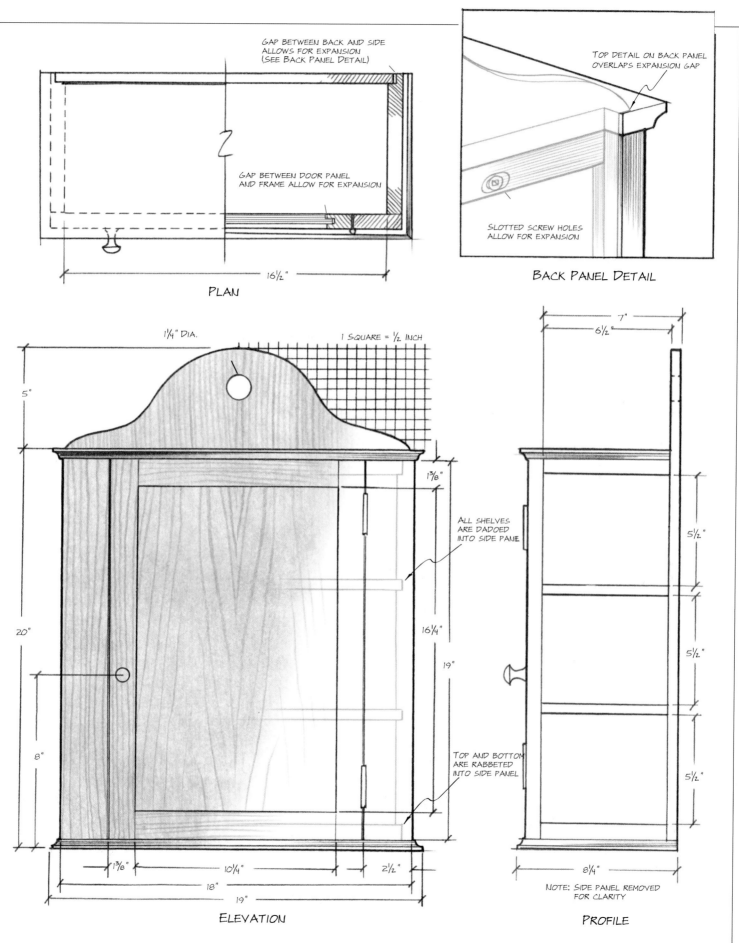

GAP BETWEEN BACK AND SIDE
ALLOWS FOR EXPANSION
(SEE BACK PANEL DETAIL)

GAP BETWEEN DOOR PANEL
AND FRAME ALLOW FOR EXPANSION

16½"

PLAN

TOP DETAIL ON BACK PANEL
OVERLAPS EXPANSION GAP

SLOTTED SCREW HOLES
ALLOW FOR EXPANSION

BACK PANEL DETAIL

1¼" DIA.

1 SQUARE = ½ INCH

5"

1⅜"

ALL SHELVES
ARE DADOED
INTO SIDE PANEL

16¼"

19"

20"

8"

TOP AND BOTTOM
ARE RABBETED
INTO SIDE PANEL

1⅜"   10¼"   2½"

18"

19"

ELEVATION

7"

6½"

5½"

5½"

5½"

8¼"

NOTE: SIDE PANEL REMOVED
FOR CLARITY

PROFILE

SHAKER HANGING CABINET

Cutting an accurate stopped notch like this is a pain. By ripping the oversized top down and regluing smaller blocks on the ends of the top, you create the perfect notch for the back piece.

Centering grooves on your work is child's play if you cut them in two passes. Here you can see that I milled one half of the groove and have turned the piece around to mill the other half.

Make the tenons by cutting a rabbet on both sides of the rails. Use your miter gauge and fence to make this cut. It's a safe operation because you can't trap your work between the blade and fence.

First you're going to rout the cove detail on three edges of both the top and bottom.

The best way to do this operation is on a router table that's set up with a ⅝" cove bit, though you can do it hand-held in a pinch. Either way, make sure you rout the detail on the ends first, then come back and rout the long edge. This will clean up a good deal of splintering that occurs when you exit the cuts on the ends.

Next take only the top piece to the table saw and rip the back edge off the board so it's 7¾" wide. Take the fall-off strip and rip it so it's ½" wide. Crosscut 1" off each end of that falloff piece and reglue each end to the back edge of the top piece, making sure the cove detail matches. Voilà! You have an instant stopped notch in your top.

Attaching the top and bottom pieces to the carcase is easy if your case is square and your joints are flush. Before you attach the top and bottom, check their fit against the carcase itself. You want a tight joint at the front and the sides. If you don't get a seamless fit with only hand pressure, you'll need to tweak the carcase until you do. Relying on your clamps to close an imperfect joint is asking for trouble.

Sometimes this process takes a bit of detective work to figure out what's wrong. For example, the top of my carcase had an inexplicable but

slight bulge in the center, so the top piece would rock back and forth on it. A sharp block plane made short work of the problem. As you remove material, try to stay away from the edges of the carcase. That's where you can create problems that will show in the finished piece.

When satisfied with the fit of the top and bottom pieces, apply a liberal amount of glue to the carcase and position the top and bottom in place. When you've got them where you want them, nail them in place through the inside of the cabinet. Use only a couple of nails in each; their job is to hold the top in place as you clamp it. Apply clamps around the cabinet to secure the top and bottom to the carcase and check for gaps.

The Stub-tenon Door

Because this is a light-duty door, we can build what's called a "stub-tenon" door. Essentially, it's a traditional mortise-and-tenon door that uses short (some would say "stubby") tenons that are only ½" long. A bigger traditional door would use tenons at least 1" long. We've included a tutorial on this style of door starting on page 37.

The advantage to these short tenons is they allow you to build the door without having to cut mortises in the stiles. The ¼"-wide x ½"-deep groove you cut for the door's panel also serves as the mortise for the tenons on the rails.

While stub-tenon doors are a good trick, the real trick to making perfect doors is to learn about "horns." What are horns? Again, take a look at the cutting list and you'll notice that the stiles are 1" longer than they need to be to fit in the door's opening. And both the rails and stiles are ⅛" wider than called for in the drawing.

This extra length and width create what look like horns on the assembled door. These horns allow you to make a door that is slightly oversized when compared to the hole in the cabinet. Once

the door is assembled, rip and crosscut it square to fit perfectly in the door opening. There is no easier way to fit a door.

So let's build the door. Cut your stiles, rails and panel to the sizes listed in the cutting list. Now mill the ¼"-wide x ½"-deep groove in one long edge of the rails and stiles. The best way to do this is with a rip blade set to make a ½"-deep cut. A rip blade is best because the top of its teeth are flat, so the bottom of your groove also will be flat. Crosscut teeth will leave "V"-shaped channels in the bottom of the groove. Position your saw's rip fence so there's a ¼"-wide gap between the teeth and the rip fence.

Cut the groove first with one face of your work against the fence, then turn it around and make the cut with the other face against the fence. This method ensures that the groove is perfectly centered on your rails and stiles. If there happens to be a thin scrap hanging in the middle (as shown in the photo above center), you can adjust the fence and make a third pass to eliminate it.

Next get your rails and prepare to cut the tenons on the ends. These tenons are made by cutting a rabbet on both faces of the board. Two rabbets make a tenon, as shown in the photo above right.

Set up your dado stack with an accessory fence just like you did when you cut the rabbets on the side pieces. Bury the dado stack in the accessory fence so that you're making a cut that is exactly ½" wide x ¼" deep.

Use your miter gauge to guide your rails across the spinning dado stack. Make a couple of test cuts on scrap that is the same thickness as your door stock. Test the fit of your scrap tenon in the grooves you cut in the rails. Fine-tune your fence setup and cut the tenons on the ends of both rails.

Now fetch your ½"-thick panel. To fit this panel in the grooves in the rails and stiles you must first cut a rabbet that is ½" wide x ¼" deep on the panel's four back edges. Coincidentally (OK, it's not really a coincidence), this is the same setup you just used to make your tenons.

Now finish-sand your door parts and dry-fit the door. You'll notice how the stiles extend past the rails. These are the horns I told you about earlier. The tenons must close tightly with only minimal clamping pressure. If you are straining to close the joint you are almost certainly twisting your door so it's not flat. Take the joint apart and investigate the problem. Usually there's gunk that's preventing a good fit, or the tenon is too long for the depth of the groove.

Once you have a seamless door frame clamped up, take the whole thing apart and glue the tenons in the grooves. (Never glue a solid-wood panel in place in a door. It has to expand and contract with changes in humidity.)

After about 45 minutes, remove the clamps from the door. Measure your door opening and temporarily screw the hinges to the carcase. Now true one stile of your assembled door by running it over the jointer. Rip the door to its finished width on your table saw, trimming evenly from the left and right stile. Then crosscut it to the

You can see here how the stiles stick out past the rails of the door. These are the so-called "horns," which you then trim off to make the door the perfect size.

A Better Hinge

Installing hinges for an inset door can be a brutal lesson in precision. Inset doors, as their name implies, sit inside the cabinet or the cabinet's face frame. The space between the door and the cabinet – called the "reveal" – has to be perfectly equal all the way around the door or it won't look right. Overlay doors, on the other hand, are much more forgiving to install because a rabbeted lip on the door covers up the gap between the cabinet and the door. If you're a little off – or sometimes even a lot – no one will ever notice. But overlay doors don't generally have the look of a fine and refined piece of furniture. They say "kitchen cabinet" instead of "prized possession."

So if you want to install inset doors, you're going to have to wrestle with mortising a butt hinge into both your cabinet and door, right? Wrong. During the last five years we have become huge fans of a hinge made by Amerock that is remarkable for three reasons: One, it lets you install the hinge without cutting a mortise. Two, once you install the hinge you can tweak its position until the door is perfect and then lock in your final setting. And three, these hinges look great on traditional cabinets.

The secret to these remarkable hinges is that they have oval-shaped holes for screws that allow you to shift the door slightly up and down in its opening and even cock it deliberately out of square to match a door opening that's not perfect. Once you get the door just right, you secure the hinge permanently with either a final screw or a brad – depending if the hinge is designed for a face-frame cabinet (which uses what Amerock calls a "full back-to-back wrap-around hinge") or a frameless cabinet (which uses a "partial wrap-around hinge").

In the hinge pictured at left, you can see the holes for the brads in the leaf that attaches to the case. Curiously, you have to supply your own brads to lock this leaf in place; my only gripe with this hinge is that they aren't included.

On the leaf that attaches to the door you can see the two screw holes that lock in that setting. (One of the holes has a screw in it; the other does not.)

The Amerock hinges are available in a variety of finishes, including wrought iron, brushed nickel, dark antique brass, antique brass and polished brass. Plus they are available in a variety of styles that match many styles of furniture with a finial tip, a ball tip or just a plain button. These hinges aren't cheap – about $6 per pair no matter where you go. But that price includes high-quality screws for installing them. Once you try these hinges, we don't think you'll go back to traditional mortise hinges unless you have to.

— *Christopher Schwarz*

Amerock Corporation
4000 Auburn Street, P.O. Box 7018,
Rockford, IL 61125-7018,
800-435-6959 or amerock.com

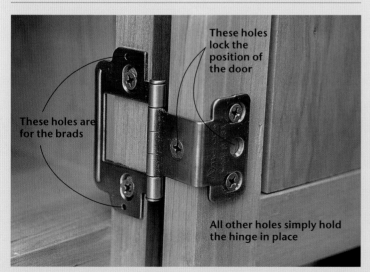

These holes lock the position of the door

These holes are for the brads

All other holes simply hold the hinge in place

If you struggle with installing hinges for inset doors, this can make it easier.

correct length. Test the fit in the door's opening and fine-tune things until the door has a perfectly consistent gap all around. You can use a table saw to do this, but I prefer a hand plane because I mess things up in a much slower fashion than with a power tool. Once your door fits, you can tweak its position in its opening if you use the hinges we recommend in the Supplies box below. Add the knob of your choice and a catch (the magnetic ones are the easiest to install).

More Notches in Your Back

As I designed this project, I tried different ways to make it so the back was not one piece of $17\frac{1}{2}$"-wide solid wood. The solutions were more complex than I liked or they didn't look right, so I decided to stick with the original wide back.

To make this work, I first had to calculate how much the back would expand and contract in a typical Midwestern environment (which has some pretty radical humidity fluctuations, I can tell you). Using the formulas in R. Bruce Hoadley's "Understanding Wood" (Taunton Press), I figured out how much movement to expect. According to Hoadley's formulas, the panel will expand about $\frac{1}{8}$" when the humidity fluctuates between 8 percent and 14 percent. This is a reasonable range to expect in our climate.

So now you need to measure the space between the two rabbets on the backside of your assembled carcase. It should measure 17". So the lower part of the back piece should measure $16\frac{7}{8}$" wide. That's simple enough. The real difficulty comes when dealing with the curvy top part of the back. It's $17\frac{1}{2}$" wide. That extra width overhangs the top of the cabinet. Once again this means you have to create a stopped notch on the two long edges of the back.

The simplest procedure is to use the same trick you used for creating the notch on the top piece: Gluing small pieces on the back to make a notch. And that's a fine way to do it as long as you pay close attention to matching the grain. This is a very visible part of the cabinet.

Make your back piece a bit wider to start with: 18" is about right. Rip two strips off each long edge so the back ends up $16\frac{7}{8}$" wide. Keep track of which edge each strip came from because that will make it easier to match the grain when regluing the blocks in place. Now take those narrow strips and crosscut 5" off the top of each. Reglue these blocks to the back.

After the glue dries, mark the curvy shape on the back and cut to that line. A band saw, scroll saw or coping saw will do. Just make sure it's a fine-tooth blade. Clean up the rough saw-cut edges with sandpaper, files or a spokeshave. Then drill the $1\frac{1}{4}$"-diameter hanging hole in the location shown in the drawing. Finish-sand your back.

Attaching the back is easy if you pay attention to the issue of wood movement. The back is attached by screwing through it into the top and

To make this notching operation go smoothly, make sure you rip the narrow strips from the back using a sharp rip blade. This will ensure that you'll get a clean cut and the blocks will be easier to reglue and get a seamless joint.

bottom pieces. You want to secure the back in the center of the cabinet so it expands equally on either side. Here's how to do that: Drill six screw holes in the back, three along the top and three along the bottom. The middle hole should be a standard round clearance hole. But the holes to the left and right should be elongated left-to-right. It's these elongated holes that allow the back to expand and contract with changes in humidity.

I've seen people make a template to rout perfect elongated ovals. Then they make the countersink using a template and a chamfer bit. This is not necessary. All you really need to worry about is allowing the shaft of the screw to pivot as the back moves. The screw's head can remain basically in the same place.

Here's how I make elongated holes: Drill a standard clearance hole for your screw that allows the screw's shaft and threads to pass through without biting into the wood. Next, angle your drill 45° one way and drill out a bit of one side of your clearance hole. Then angle the drill 45° the other way and drill out the other side of your hole. Finally, come back with your countersinking bit and countersink your clearance hole. Once done, then you can screw the back to the case using some #8 x 1"-long screws.

Finishing Cherry

Before you apply a finish to this project, take a few minutes to break the sharp edges with #120-grit sandpaper. This will make your project more enjoyable to touch and less likely to get damaged. Now remove the back and door.

Because cherry darkens nicely with age, I prefer not to add much coloring. In any case, staining cherry can be difficult because it blotches.

But new cherry with a clear finish looks a bit anemic until it gets a couple of years of coloring, so I like to help the process along. Begin by wiping on a coat of boiled linseed oil that's thinned down

This elongated hole allows the back to expand and contract and still stay tightly secured under the screw. I make these holes by wiggling my drill bit. The other option is to drill a round hole and elongate it with a small rat-tail file.

to a water-like consistency with paint thinner. Wait about 30 minutes and wipe off the excess. Then take your project outside and let it bask in the warm sun for an afternoon or two. This will jump-start the coloring process.

After a couple of days of letting the oil cure, you can add a protective top coat. The simplest finish for this is a wiping varnish – essentially a thinned-down off-the-shelf varnish. For more details on mixing and using this finish, check out "Understanding Wipe-on Finishes" on page 30.

If you want to hang this project like the Shakers did, you'll need to build and hang a board with Shaker-style pegs. The length of the board is up to you and the scale of your room. We've included a supplier of cherry Shaker pegs below.

The last trick is to find a place in your home that really shows off the proportions and workmanship of this fine piece. You don't want this project to ever languish in the background.

— *Christopher Schwarz*

Supplies

Rockler
800-279-4441 or rockler.com
2 ■ Amerock ball-tip, full wrap-around hinges in antique brass, #31300, $8.99/pair
1 ■ Cherry Shaker $1\frac{1}{8}$" knob, $\frac{3}{8}$" tenon, #78469, $9.49/pair. (Also available in oak, walnut and maple.)
1 ■ Narrow magnetic catch, #26559, $2.49 each
   ■ Cherry classic Shaker pegs, #23382, package of eight/$8.99 (Also available in oak and maple.)

Prices correct at time of publication.

Shelf Support Basics

Storage doesn't do you much good if you can't divide it to suit your needs. That's what shelving is all about and there are a number of ways to put your shelves in just the right position. We've gathered the best of the pack here with quick explanations of their best applications.

Though there are a number of good choices listed, the most common support with the best price and function is the spoon pin, with or without the sleeve. We also appreciate the invisible application found with either the low-profile pin or the hidden shelf wire. When using any of the supports that require carefully located holes in your cabinet sides, we recommend cutting a piece of ¼" hardboard or plywood to about 3" wide and nearly the height of your opening. Drill a single line of shelf holes in this piece and use it as a template for all the holes.

– David Thiel

Standard with Clip

One of the most common, inexpensive, versatile and ugliest shelf supports ever manufactured. While you can easily adjust shelf locations in 1" increments, the metal track is always visible and requires a groove machined in the sides. This support looks best in office furniture – not a project you spent hours building. Available in ugly nickel or zinc plate, ugly white and uglier brown.

Reinforced Support

An economical option, this plastic support slips into a hole (or multiple holes to allow for adjustment) that you drill in the cabinet sides. Like the metal track above, these are also common in office furniture and are not attractive. They also hold the shelf away from the side by as much as ⅛".

Locking Support

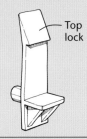

Top lock

This support also fits into holes drilled in the cabinet sides. As an added feature, it locks the shelf in place from above, avoiding accidental tipping. Economical, but still rather unsightly, it also holds the shelf away from the cabinet sides. Use this for commercial furniture or for shop cabinets where you don't want a shelf to ever come crashing down – not for that Queen Anne highboy.

Right-angle Support

Slightly less unsightly, this support is almost invisible (with the shelf in place). The optional rubber pad keeps the shelf from sliding off, but it still leaves an unattractive gap between the cabinet side and each shelf. This is a good choice for furniture in a child's room or in a rumpus room.

Adjustable Support

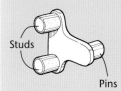

Studs

Pins

This support compensates for sloppy drilling. By trapping the shelf between the studs, the pin can rotate in the hole to find a balance between the four holes. A nice feature, but the ugly gap is still there, and now you've got a stud showing above the shelf. Save this support as a last option if (or when) you've messed things up.

Straight Pin

This is a true pin. Although low visibility, it has some problems. If the hole is slightly oversized, the pin can work loose, dumping the shelf. If the holes are not drilled perfectly, the shelf will wobble. On the other hand, if small notches are cut on the underside of the shelf, the pin can nestle in the notch, holding the shelf firmly.

Spoon Pin

Optional sleeve

A refined version of the straight pin, this pin can be used with or without the sleeve. It's then slipped into a hole or holes drilled in the cabinet side. The pin allows the shelf to fit all the way against the cabinet side without any visible gap, but still has a shoulder to hold the shelf in place.

Screw-in Spoon Pin

Taking the pin and sleeve concept a bit further, this pin screws into its sleeve. It's a nice idea, but ultimately a little like gilding the lily, and best reserved for high-end glass casework. These pins are pretty darn expensive because you have to buy a threaded sleeve for every shelf-pin hole.

Low-profile Pin

The most invisible and still very economical, this support requires a little extra machining. The plastic pins are still slipped into holes drilled in the cabinet sides, but the shelves themselves have stopped saw kerfs along the ends that accept the blade of the pin. The shelf fits around the pins (in place) and the support disappears.

Hidden Shelf Wire

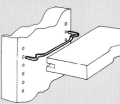

Another invisible variation is a hidden shelf wire. Rather than using two independent pins that slip into grooves in the shelves, this system uses a wire support. Essentially requiring the same amount of machining and drilling, this actually provides a more stable support and puts less stress on the shelf. The wire spreads the support over the depth of the shelf rather than focusing it on two bearing points.

Smart Ways to Hang Cabinets

Once you've completed the Shaker Hanging Cabinet, you can sit back and enjoy it. Well, almost. You still need to hang the cabinet – and it's been our experience that this final step can take minutes or hours, depending on your planning.

The hanging process should actually begin with the design phase of the project. With the cabinet shown here, we've followed the Shaker tradition and mounted a peg board to the wall, with the cabinet hung from a peg.

Other methods (more common today) are to mount the cabinet to the wall through the back of the cabinet (either with just the back or with a hanging strip) or to use a French cleat, which is invisible and convenient.

Screwing Through the Back

Depending on the size of your cabinet, you may have used a ¼"-thick back or thicker (½" or ¾"). With a thicker back, mounting the hanging cabinet to the wall is simply a matter of finding a stud and marking that stud location on the inside of the cabinet. Then you drill a clearance hole for the screw (usually ³⁄₁₆" diameter), hold the cabinet in place and level on the wall, and screw the cabinet to the stud with a #10 x 3"-long screw. If the cabinet is wider than 16", you'll be able to put a second screw through the back and into a second stud. This should be enough to support most cabinets that aren't going to be holding your grandmother's fine China.

If your cabinet is less than 16" wide, you'll need a drywall "molly" to reinforce the second screw. Mollys are sold in the picture-hanging section of your local hardware store and allow you to put a screw almost anywhere in a wall. There are half a dozen different kinds of mollys that are suited to hold different weights. Check with your local hardware store for a good selection.

If you're hanging a large cabinet and want to use a ¼"-thick back (to make it less expensive and lighter in weight), a hanging strip will make mounting the cabinet easier. This strip (shown below left) can be built into the design of the cabinet or simply applied to the back. It goes inside the cabinet and below the top. Actually building the strip into the sides adds some strength, but it also adds an extra step or two to the project.

Screwing through this strip instead of just the thin back will give you more strength and reduces the chance of tearing through the thin back material with the screw.

Using a French Cleat

French cleats offer invisibility and incredible strength, but they do steal some storage space from the inside of the cabinet. These cleats can be purchased (made from aluminum or steel) for the truly lazy, or made from simple ¾"- or ½"-thick scrap. The cleat is in two pieces, each with a 45° bevel on one long edge. One goes on the back of the cabinet; the other attaches to the wall. When you nest the 45° bevels together, the cabinet hangs firmly on the wall. You should be able to do pull-ups on your cabinet if it is properly installed this way – no kidding.

To use a French cleat, you have to design a gap behind the back of the cabinet to house it. Essentially the cabinet is built with the back recessed into the cabinet, so the top, sides and bottom still touch the wall.

Beyond the strength gained by using a cleat (as long as you catch a stud or use mollys), cleats are easy to level. The wall section of the cleat is attached with one screw and that section is leveled and fixed in place. Then the cabinet is simply slipped in place over the wall cleat. It's pretty cool.

– David Thiel

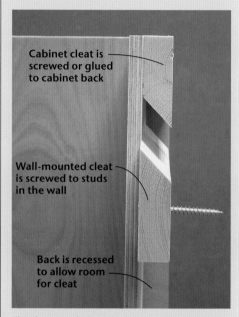

Cabinet cleat is screwed or glued to cabinet back

Wall-mounted cleat is screwed to studs in the wall

Back is recessed to allow room for cleat

The shop-made French cleat in action. This French cleat is made for a board ripped at a 45° angle, but the cleat also could be made with interlocking rabbets. Either way, you get some amazing strength and convenience.

Back is recessed to allow room for cleat

This store-bought version of a French cleat takes up less room behind the cabinet and is priced at about $13 for 10 sets. Place one hanger every foot to hold heavy cabinets.

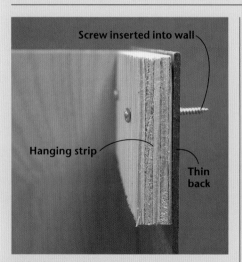

Screw inserted into wall

Hanging strip

Thin back

With a larger cabinet, a thin back makes more sense but will not be sufficient to secure the cabinet to the wall. By adding a hanging strip, the weight of the cabinet is more evenly transferred to the cabinet box.

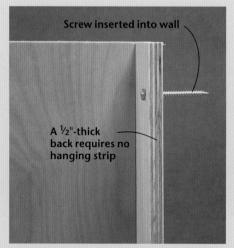

Screw inserted into wall

A ½"-thick back requires no hanging strip

With smaller cabinets, a thicker back (usually ½" or more) can be used without any major weight concern. This thicker back also allows you to simply screw through the back of the cabinet directly into the wall and stud.

Making Stub-tenon Doors

The stub-tenon joint will never be the super-hero of your joinery arsenal because it doesn't have the stuff necessary to be a strong joint. The mating parts are short (hence the "stub" moniker) and it's housed on only two sides: the face cheeks of the tenon. There is sufficient glue surface, but the cross-grain orientation compromises the glue joint. In the pantheon of woodworking joints, the stub-tenon joint may be more accurately described as a 90-pound weakling.

But even so, this can be sufficient for smaller, lightweight doors that don't take a lot of abuse. For example, you wouldn't choose this joint for kitchen cabinet doors or built-ins for the kids' playroom. But it's OK to use a stub-tenon door for a vanity cabinet or for a project that's built as much for looks as it is for service.

Once a door weighs more than four or five pounds, or is larger than 18" x 24", you must abandon the stub-tenon joint for a more substantial one. Mortise-and-tenon construction, dowels, loose tenons and even biscuit joints are superior choices for larger, heavier doors.

So why use a stub-tenon joint? Well, it's easy to make because it requires a minimal amount of setup time regardless of the method you choose to cut the joint. It's usually cut with a router in a table or on the table saw using a stack dado set.

The ease of setup is because the same groove that's cut to receive the panel doubles as the groove for the stub tenon. Plus, the same cutter that makes the groove can be used to form the tenon after an easy adjustment, which I'll tell you about later.

Other advantages of the stub-tenon joint include the ability – make that the requirement – to make either flat or raised frame-and-panel doors, and the relatively low cost and multipurpose use of the tooling required. For the router, all you will need is a ¼" spline-cutting bit; for the table saw, all you will need is a stack dado set (both of which you will end up using in countless future projects).

A disadvantage, along with joint strength, is the inability to add a moulded detail, such as a roundover or an ogee, on the inside frame edges. Only a square edge works because of how the stile, or vertical part of the the frame, comes together with the rail, or horizontal part of the frame. The use of moulded edges requires special tooling to produce a cope-and-stick joint (where identically opposite male/female shapes nest together). Tooling for this joint can be expensive

and usually quite fussy to set up.

Making the stub-tenon joint is straightforward regardless of which method you select. The method you opt for will be dictated by what equipment you have in your shop. If you have a table saw and stack dado set (a wobble dado is not recommended for this operation), you're equipped for that method. Choosing to use the router table may depend on what type of router and table you have available in your workshop.

If you use a router (one that is either fixed-based or plunge-style) that requires you to adjust the height of the bit from below the table, you may find that making fine adjustments to your bit's height is a problem. We'll cover this process later in this article. But if you have one of the so-called router-lift mechanisms, or if you own a newer router that allows you to adjust the bit height from above the table (which makes these fine adjustments a snap), you'll find very precise height adjustments a breeze.

Which method is easiest? My vote goes to the router-table method as long as you have a router lift (which is expensive) or a router with through-the-base adjustment. This method allows the user to raise or lower the bit by inserting and turning

a tool right through the base. It's the ability to make fine adjustments easily that tips the scales in favor of the router for me.

Getting Started

Regardless of which method you use, start by preparing the wood for the stiles, rails and panels. To the best of your ability, use stock that's flat and of uniform thickness. And be sure your saw or jointer fence (if you use one) are set exactly 90° to the table. Any cut that is out of square will lead to a door that is cockeyed or twisted (also known as "in wind").

When preparing your stock, cut out a few extra pieces that can be used for making test cuts when setting up the router or table saw. Make your stiles and rails about ⅛" wider than your project plan calls for. Additionally, add about 1" extra length to the stiles so they have what are called "horns" when the door is assembled.

The extra width and length give you a fudge factor when it comes time to fit the door to the cabinet opening. Should the opening be slightly larger than planned or out of square, the extra width and length will help you accommodate. Also, if the door itself is out of square, the entire piece can be fixed after assembly.

Now choose stock with the best grain pattern for the door parts. Select straight-grain material for the stiles and rails. This grain pattern usually is found toward the outside edges of boards. Then select the wider grain material for the panel stock. This grain pattern usually is found in the center of a board. Make sure you select pieces that are uniform in color for all the door parts.

Arrange the straight-grain stile and rail stock so that any curves or bows "frame" the panel appropriately. Generally, this would mean the grain should "curve out" at the middle points of the rails and stiles. When satisfied, mark each piece to identify its location. Be sure you note which side will face out after assembly.

Stub Tenons with a Router

With ¾"-thick stock, you'll want to use a ¼" spline-cutting router bit. It should be equipped with a guide bearing that allows the bit to make a cut that's at least ⁷⁄₁₆" deep.

Mount the bit in the router and then mount the router in the router table. Next, set up the fence so it is in line with the front edge of the bearing. This is easy to do by using a straightedge held against the bearing and then bringing the fence forward (to the straightedge) until everything is in line. Lock the fence in place. If your fence allows you to adjust the infeed and outfeed wings, move them as close to the cutter as possible without impeding the cutters.

First up is to cut the groove on the long edges of the stiles and rails. The groove should be centered on the edges. Make a series of test cuts on scrap stock that's exactly the same thickness as your good material. When satisfied, run the stile and rail parts, making sure you always place the outside face up and the designated inside edges along the fence. By running all the parts this way any minor error in centering the groove in the board's edge will be minimized.

Next, form the tenons on the ends of the rails. The thickness of the tenon must match the width of the groove to make a good joint. The length of the tenon will match the depth of the groove automatically because, like the groove, the depth of cut is dictated by the bearing on the router bit.

First lower the router bit so that the top edge of the cutter is just a whisker below the groove. Before making a test cut, though, you'll need a back-up block to support and guide the narrow rail ends safely past the cutter. A back-up block also prevents "blow out" on the backside of the stock where the cutter exits.

The back-up block can be a piece of ¾" plywood. But take care that the plywood you choose has truly square corners. If it is out of square, you will likely make your tenon cuts out of square, which will cause your door to become out of square when glued together. A handle for the back-up block, as seen in the top photo on page

Every step of making stub-tenon doors requires square cuts, whether on the table saw or router.

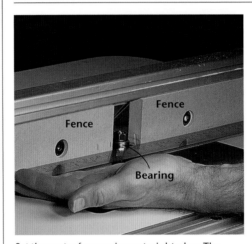

Set the router fence using a straightedge. The fence face should align with the front of the bearing.

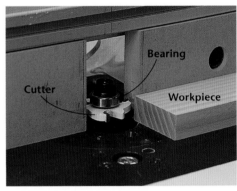

The first step is to cut the grooves in both stile and rail edges. To set the proper height of the ¼" spline-cutting bit in your router, center it on the width of the stock as closely as possible. The depth of cut is determined by the bearing above the cutter – ⁷⁄₁₆" to ½" is ideal.

39, is optional, as is the adhesive-backed abrasive sandpaper I added to help prevent the work from slipping during the cut.

To make the cut, place the back-up block against the fence and move the rail into position. Keep the face up and place the long edge of the rail against the back-up block and the rail end against the router-table fence. When moving the piece into the cutter, keep pressure on the rail down and against the back-up block. At the same time, be sure the block remains against the router table's fence. If it's your first time, make a couple of practice cuts on scraps to get comfortable.

To form the tenon, the rail must be run past the cutter twice. Rather than readjusting the router bit height, just flip the part over and run the second side. This is where the centering of the groove becomes important. Test-fit the tenon and continue adjusting the bit height until the tenon slips

After making test cuts for the groove location, run grooves on the inside edges of all parts. It's important to keep the parts organized and marked so that the good face is up. By doing this, you'll minimize any problems caused by minor inaccuracies in centering the groove precisely.

into the groove using only slight pressure. When satisfied, run both ends of each rail. (The stiles do not get this cut.)

Stub Tenons with a Table Saw

Much of the process used for making stub tenons with a router apply to the table saw as well. In this case, however, a rip blade and stack dado set are used instead of the spline cutter.

Install the rip blade (used because of its flat-topped tooth grind) and adjust the saw fence. The fence setting will establish the width of the groove in the stiles and rails. You will make the groove in two passes, each pass with the opposite side of the piece against the fence. This ensures the groove will be centered on the edge. If the panel is 1/4" thick, adjust the fence so that 1/4" of space is between the blade and the fence. Now set the

height of the blade to slightly less than 7/16". Make a test cut and check the depth of cut.

In setting the blade height, sneak up on the final height by adjusting upwards in small increments. You'll find that moving the blade down is not very precise – a function of the way a table saw works. When the blade height's set accurately, lock the adjustment, then make the groove on the inside edges of the stiles and rails.

To form the tenons you need to install a stack dado set that will cut at least 1/2". You also need to clamp a strip of wood, called an accessory fence, to your table saw's fence. This is to make sure part of the dado cutter is buried in the accessory fence. To bury it, lower the cutter below the table, move the securely clamped accessory fence slightly over the cutter, then slowly raise the cutter into the fence until it is about 3/8" high.

Now you can set the fence to make the cut that establishes the length of the tenon, in this case 7/16". Measure carefully and compare it to the depth of the groove you just cut. If the tenon is too long, it will bottom out in the groove and the joint won't close. It can be fine-tuned once the dado-stack height is properly set.

Just like you did when cutting the groove, start the height adjustment below the desired height and sneak up on the correct height. Make test cuts of both face cheeks of the tenon, then check the fit. When raising the dado stack, remember every amount of adjustment is doubled because you're taking material from both sides.

To make the cuts, use your table saw's miter gauge. Make sure the miter gauge is set square to the blade and fence. Place the rail against the miter gauge with the end tight against the fence. Push the rail over the blade with enough pressure so you can easily hold it down and against the fence. Check your tenon for proper fit and make adjustments to the fence and/or cutter height as needed. When satisfied, cut all the tenons.

A shop-made back-up block (with an optional handle shown here) helps you steady the rails when you're cutting tenons. It supports the part when the narrow width passes over the cutter. It also helps you make square cuts on the ends, an important aspect of making square doors.

When cutting the tenons, hold the part down firmly against the edge of the back-up block and tight to the router table fence. Guide the part using the edge of the block held firmly against the router table fence as well. After cutting one side, flip the part and cut the opposite side.

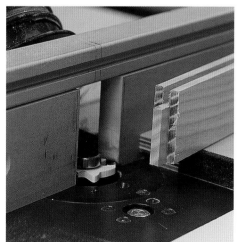

Three simple passes over a spline-cutting bit form the completed stub tenon and panel groove.

Stub-tenon Door Panels

You can use flat or raised panels in stub-tenon doors. But remember, raised-panel doors add more weight because they require a thicker panel, usually ⅝" thick. With flat panels, you can make them ¼" thick to match the width of the groove exactly, or you can make them a bit thicker and cut a rabbet to fit the ¼" groove.

With flat panels, you can substantially increase the size of the doors and not worry about the weak stub-tenon joint by using plywood for the panel and gluing it in the grooves. By doing so, you gain tremendous strength and the stub-tenon joint does none of the work in supporting the door. With solid-wood panels, however, gluing all around is not an option because the panel will expand or contract with changes in humidity. It's acceptable to add glue at two places on a solid-wood panel – the top and bottom in the center of the panel. The panel will grow or shrink at its edges but not at its center.

When sizing the panel be sure to allow for wood movement as well. About ⅛" all around the panel is a good rule of thumb.

Before gluing the doors, you should dry-fit the doors without glue. You also should sand the panel before glue-up. Don't sand the stile and rail edges after assembly – do it before. Likewise, sand the inside stile and rail edges everywhere except in the joint location. This is very important to remember because sanding inside the joint can ruin the fit.

If you want to stain or color your project, you should do so before assembly. Not only is it easier, but you can stain up to the edges of the panel. If you don't stain up to the edges, it is likely that an uncolored part of the panel will be exposed when the panel eventually shrinks.

When it's time to assemble the project for real (called "final assembly"), add glue to the joint sparingly. You don't want squeeze-out to inadvertently glue the panel at the frame corners. Remember, the panel will need to move.

Clamp with moderate pressure, just enough to close the joint. Too much pressure can distort the door. Place the clamps in the center of the joint across the panel width. Also remember to place the rails in their proper locations, allowing for the extra-length "horns" at the ends of the stiles. Lastly, check the door for square.

Used in the appropriate situations, stub-tenon joints can be an easy and painless way to make attractive cabinet doors.

— *Steve Shanesy*

When making grooves on the table saw, a rip blade is used. With ¾" stock, set the fence ¼" from the blade. Make a ¼" groove in two passes, each with the opposite side to the fence to guarantee the groove will be centered on the edge.

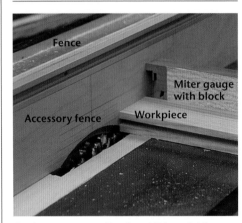

Cutting tenons requires the addition of chippers to the dado stack and an accessory fence added to the table saw fence. Instead of a back-up block, the slot miter gauge is used. Sizing the tenon is done by adjusting the blade height and saw fence.

Proper alignment of the fence and saw height produces a tenon that's exactly as long as the groove is deep. The thickness of the tenon matches the width of the groove. Inserting the tenon in the groove should require just a little pressure.

"When I'm working on a problem, I never think about beauty. I think only how to solve the problem. But when I have finished, if the solution is not beautiful, I know it is wrong."
— R. Buckminster Fuller (1895 - 1983)
inventor, architect and engineer

Test the fit of the tenon and groove. The right fit will have both faces perfectly flush and the shoulders of the tenon should seat.

Select straight grain for the frame parts. The grain direction should sweep inward. Select "cathedral" grain for the panel. Note how the points, or "cathedrals," point in the same direction.

American Wall Cupboard

We set out to design a piece that would be at home in the 18th or 21st century. The work with a pencil proved to be as important as the work with a plane.

When you design a piece of furniture to build, there are three well-worn paths (some might call them ruts) to follow.

The first path is to design a piece in a wholly original style. This actually happens about once or twice a century, and its rarity is why we don't have furniture styles such as "Early Bill," "Middle Chuck" or the "Late Butch Period." Few people alive can claim they have successfully launched a style, but don't let that stop you from trying.

The second approach is to build replicas, either spot-on or with mild alterations, such as an additional drawer, or substituting a square ovolo moulding for a bead. This is a good way to learn the vocabulary of different styles, though it is time-consuming to learn everything by the doing. Some woodworkers (even professionals) might build only six pieces in a year.

The third approach is to design a new piece with vintage parts, like rebuilding an old car. With this approach, you expose yourself to hundreds of images of the form. You could look at tables, cabriole legs or Arts & Crafts desks, for example. Then you select your piece's dominant element from the library – say a leg, a door or a bonnet – and design your piece around that. (However, you can't easily mix parts from different genres. It might seem like a good idea to put a Honda push rod in a Chevy, until you hit that metric barrier.)

When asked the secret to good design, Steve Hamilton, a builder at Mack S. Headley & Sons (headleyandsons.com), boiled it down to two words: "Picture books," he said. "Get a bunch. Look them over."

What I like about this cabinet is that it doesn't hide all the contents when you close the door. You can set one precious object in the right spot (a plow plane, perhaps), that will be the center of attention when you lock the door.

PHOTOS BY THE AUTHOR

Design on the Run

Designing a suitable early American wall cupboard for *Woodworking Magazine* began with a day in our collection of books and images. You don't need to spend a lot of money to build a book collection, most of the resources you need are at the public library and on the Internet.

My first stop was Wallace Nutting's "A Furniture Treasury." This book is available in many different forms, and it's common to find copies for about $25. The book is as-advertised. It's hundreds of pages of images of early American stuff that has been organized into categories such as "chests" and "Windsor chairs."

The second source was auction catalogs from Christie's (christies.com) and Sotheby's (sothebys.com) auction houses. The catalogs these houses publish for their Americana auctions are outstanding. Good images. Good overall dimensions. And good history lessons as well. These catalogs can be pricey at $50 or more, but you can usually browse the catalogs on the Internet for free, though sometimes you have to register with the auction house (registration is free).

The third source was an old favorite of mine from my grandparents' library: "Fine Points of Furniture: Early American" (Crown) by Albert Sack. This common book can be had for about $10 – the new revised edition is much more expensive and rare. Sack's book compares different kinds of pieces and ranks them as "good," "better" or "best." This book helps hone your tastes in mouldings, proportion and turnings.

After a day of reading, I chose a fetching tombstone door from Nutting's book and found many tall and skinny shapes for wall cupboards that looked like pieces I had seen at Winterthur, the DuPont's Delaware estate and museum.

My design firmed up when my doctor got too busy for me one Wednesday. After showing up for my appointment, I was told there would be an hour delay. So I sat in my car and sketched about 10 wall cabinets. I didn't worry about dimensions or joinery, just the overall look and feel of the piece. Each sketch took about five minutes and tried out variations on the door (one or two?), the drawer (one, two or none?) and the width of the stiles and rails (chunky or light?).

After those sketches, I chose the best two designs, sketched them again and showed them around to woodworkers and friends. It sounds like a lot of work, but I have found that good design is like making stir fry: You first chop vegetables and mix sauces for a long time. The active cooking time is real short – if you've done your prep work.

From Face to Back

This cabinet is built using the techniques outlined in "Build a Better Cabinet" on page 48 of this issue. So if you want to know why I began with the face frame, read that story first and decide how you are going to proceed.

This wall cabinet begins with a face frame that's joined with mortise-and-tenon joints. Then you build and fit the door. Then you build the carcase around those established dimensions. The rest – mouldings, the back and the drawer – are the final details.

"We construct and construct, yet intuition is still a good thing."
— Paul Klee (1879 - 1940)
Swiss painter

Using a dado stack to make tenons allows you to use one setup for the face cheeks and a second assembly for edge cheeks. Other approaches use four setups or more. Test each tenon in a sample mortise (below) for best results.

The leading cause of errors is measuring. Use your tenons to lay out your mortises, and you will make fewer mistakes where a rail ends up too high or low. Even if you goof, you still can recover by adjusting the door and carcase.

To keep all my door rails oriented I draw a large triangle across the face of all three parts using a grease pencil. That way I'll be able to determine where each piece goes with just a glance.

After you dimension your stock, the face frame and the door begins with cutting ¼"-thick tenons on the ends of all the rails. Test the results in a sample mortise, though you can tune up the tight-fitting miscreants before assembly.

With all the tenons cut, you can use them to lay out the locations of your mortises on the stiles of your face frame (don't lay them out on the door's stiles yet). Then cut your mortises. A hollow-chisel mortiser is the typical choice in our shop, though a mortise chisel would be a good choice if you were building only one of these cabinets.

Then assemble your face frame and confirm (twice) that the openings for the drawer and door are as you planned them. If you make a mistake, you can adjust your drawing to accommodate your door and drawer. This sort of mistake is why I usually mill my door stiles an inch longer than the cutting list states – sometimes you need a slightly bigger door.

Go for a Tight Fit

When you make your door, the temptation is to build it so it drops right into the face frame with a perfect 1/16" gap all around. As that is unlikely to happen in such a complex assembly, the better bet is to shoot to build the door to the same size as the opening in the face frame and shave the door down when you hang it.

Lay out the mortises on your stiles and cut those. Then lay out the 5"-radius arc in the top rail (the centerpoint of the 5"-radius arc is 1½" below the bottom edge of the rail). Remove the waste using a band saw, bowsaw or jigsaw and smooth the arc's saw-blade marks.

The lower rails require a groove that is ¼" wide and ¼" deep to house the door's panel. These grooves can run the entire length of the rails. However, you need to cut these same grooves in the lower section of the stiles only. The section of the door that holds the glass doesn't need a

Lay out the arc with a board butted against the top rail to give the compass' point a place to bite into. Then you can clean up the curve with a spindle sander (below left) or rasps and scrapers (below right).

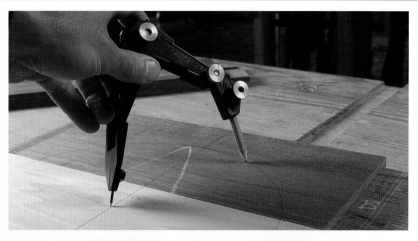

groove – it needs a rabbet instead. (You'll cut this rabbet after assembly.)

The stopped groove in the stiles is troublesome. You can make it on power equipment, but only with some risk – you'll have to drop the piece onto a spinning router bit or saw blade.

So I made my grooves by hand. It's safer and not a burden on time when it's just one door. First I plowed out as much as I could with the aptly named plow plane. This left a ramped area where the groove stopped. So I broke that up with a mortising chisel and cleared out the waste with a router plane. It takes longer to write the sentences above than to do the act, so give it a whirl.

The tenons on the bottom rail will have to be haunched to fill the groove you just cut. Yes, you could rig this on the table saw, but two short cuts with a fine-tooth saw also will fill the bill (and the groove).

Perilous Panel; Pounding Pegs

Then comes the part of any casework project that I dislike: The raised panel. I don't own the router bit for this profile, and I don't own the right kind of panel-raising plane. So I have to do it on the table saw. Use a zero-clearance insert for maximum support of the thin edge of your workpiece and a high accessory fence to keep your hands away

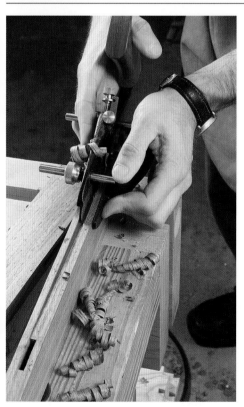

A plow plane can be used to make a stopped groove. Begin making short strokes where the groove stops, and then make longer and longer strokes until you are plowing the whole length of the groove.

A ¼" mortise chisel breaks up the waste in the ramp left behind by the plow. This is why metric and Imperial tools don't play nice together.

A small router plane zips out the waste with little effort – leaving a perfect stopped groove behind. It takes more tools to do than with a plunge router, though not much more effort.

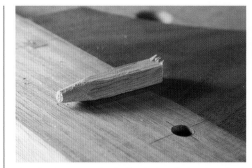

Here's what a peg looks like before being knocked in. The sharp corners of the peg will cut the round hole into a square and create a tight fit and neat appearance.

Tilt the sawblade to 12° and sneak up on the cut until the panel fits your groove. Then remove the inevitable tool marks with a rabbeting plane (right) followed by sandpaper.

from the blade.

Now you can assemble the door and peg all the joints in the door and face frame. I used $\frac{1}{4}$" x $\frac{1}{4}$" white oak stock for the square pegs. First drill a $\frac{1}{4}$"-diameter hole through the tenon (its centerpoint is $\frac{3}{8}$" from the shoulder of your tenon). Then whittle one end of your peg round, drip in a little glue and pound the peg home.

Now you can cut the rabbet for the glass. I used a $\frac{1}{4}$"-wide rabbeting bit in a router table and took small bites until I reached the final $\frac{1}{2}$" depth. Chisel the rounded corners square; and round over the square corner up by the tombstone shape – that will make the glass easier to fit.

Fitting the Door

Now you can trim the door square and decide how thick the cockbead moulding needs to be to fill the gap between the face frame and door. This is another place you have some built-in forgiveness for errors. If you made your door correctly, it should be $\frac{3}{8}$" smaller than the hole in the face frame, which means you need $\frac{3}{16}$"-thick cockbeading for the face frame.

Make the cockbeading with a beading plane or router on a wide board, then rip the resulting bead free of the mother piece. Miter, glue and nail it in place all around the door and drawer opening. Then fit and hang the door in its opening.

And Now the Carcase

With the face frame and door complete, you use those as a guide for building the carcase behind. Lay the face frame directly onto the sides and lay out the locations of the divider and shelf. You cannot miss now.

With your joints laid out, you can cut the $\frac{1}{4}$"-deep x $\frac{3}{4}$"-wide dados for the shelf and dividers – plus the $\frac{1}{2}$" x $\frac{1}{2}$" rabbet for the backboards. Then dovetail the carcase. Mark out the tails on the side pieces; the pins are on the top and bottom. This allows the case to better resist gravity.

Remember: These dovetails are for structure only. You will cover them all with moulding. So you can practice your speed rather than go for

Traditional cabinets have this moulding incorporated directly into the stiles and rails. Applying it after assembly allows you to adjust the door and drawer opening to suit your situation (if an adjustment is necessary). Don't forget to glue the miters.

Here the sides of the case are on edge on my bench and I'm marking the location of the divider directly on the front edge of the sides. When I cut the dado for the divider I'm going to shoot for the middle of this mediary rail, which will make fitting everything even easier.

a joint you can flaunt. Save that compulsion for when you are building the drawer.

Clean up your dovetails and the exterior of your carcase and glue the divider and shelf in place. Then attach the face frame with glue (and cut nails, if you please). Let the glue dry overnight, then trim the face frame flush to the carcase with a plane or a flush-cutting bit in a router.

The Drawer and Back

The drawer runners are simply leftover pieces of

I cut a shallow $^1/_8$"-deep x $^5/_8$"-wide rabbet on the ends of the sides to assist with the dovetailing (top photo). It makes it easier to transfer the tails to the pin board and it helps when chopping the waste (above).

When I have a lot of material to hog off, a router is the right tool. Here I'm trimming the face frame close to the carcase. Then I follow up with a scraping plane to level the joints without worrying about grain direction.

American Wall Cupboard

NO.	PART	T	W	L	MATERIAL	NOTES
Face Frame						
☐	2	Stiles	$^3/_4$	$2^5/_{16}$	$36^7/_8$	Walnut	Each is $^1/_{16}$" over-wide for trimming
☐	2	Rails	$^3/_4$	$2^5/_{16}$	$18^7/_8$	Walnut	$1^1/_4$" TBE, and over-wide
☐	1	Mediary rail	$^3/_4$	1	$18^7/_8$	Walnut	$1^1/_4$" TBE
☐		Cockbeading	$^3/_{16}$	$^3/_4$		Walnut	$^3/_{16}$" d. bead
Door						
☐	2	Stiles	$^3/_4$	2	27	Walnut	Add 1" to length at rough milling
☐	1	Top rail	$^3/_4$	$5^1/_2$	$14^1/_2$	Walnut	$1^1/_4$" TBE
☐	1	Mediary rail	$^3/_4$	$1^1/_2$	$14^1/_2$	Walnut	$1^1/_4$" TBE
☐	1	Bottom rail	$^3/_4$	2	$14^1/_2$	Walnut	$1^1/_4$" TBE
☐	1	Panel	$^5/_8$	$12^1/_2$	$8^1/_2$	Walnut	In $^1/_4$" x $^1/_4$" groove
Carcase						
☐	2	Sides	$^3/_4$	8	$36^7/_8$	Walnut	
☐	2	Top and bottom	$^5/_8$	$7^1/_2$	$20^7/_8$	Walnut	
☐	2	Shelf and divider	$^3/_4$	$7^1/_2$	$19^7/_8$	Poplar	In $^1/_4$"-deep dados
☐	2	Drawer runners	$^3/_4$	2	$7^1/_2$	Poplar	Rabbeted to fit drawer
☐		Backboards	$^1/_2$	$20^3/_8$	$36^7/_8$	Poplar	In $^1/_2$" x $^1/_2$" rabbet in sides
☐		Top moulding	$^7/_8$	3	50	Walnut	1" r. roundover
☐		Top cove	$^5/_8$	$^5/_8$	50	Walnut	$^1/_2$" r. cove
☐		Base moulding	1	3	50	Walnut	Square, no profile
☐		Base cove	1	1	50	Walnut	1" r. cove
Drawer						
☐	1	Drawer front	$^3/_4$	$3^5/_8$	16	Walnut	
☐	2	Drawer sides	$^1/_2$	$3^5/_8$	8	Poplar	
☐	1	Back	$^1/_2$	$3^1/_8$	16	Poplar	
☐	1	Bottom	$^1/_2$	$15^1/_2$	$7^3/_4$	Poplar	In $^1/_4$" x $^1/_4$" groove

TBE = Tenon both ends

Rat-tail Hinges: Easy to Install

Traditional rat-tail hinges are a nice touch to an early American piece, and we're fond of the handmade ones from Horton Brasses. These look like the real deal, hammer marks and all. But the great thing about them is they are easy to install.

Begin by positioning the hinge where you want it on the face frame — we think it looks best to line up one of the flags on the leaf so it is in line with a door's rail. Then you bore a $^1/_8$"-diameter hole for the hinge's through-bolt. This hole pierces the face frame. Place the center of this hole $^1/_2$" in from the edge of your door opening.

Now bolt the hinge in place and screw the tail piece to the face frame. The rest is simple. Thread the leaf over the hinge's post and screw it to the door. You're done.

What's nice about rat-tails is that you can easily lift the whole door off its hinges, which is handy for fitting the door to its opening.

— CS

Rat-tail hinges are my favorite surface-mounted hinges. With a little care and planning, they are also a snap to install.

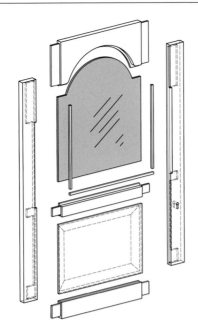

DOOR
EXPLODED VIEW (SHOWN FROM BACK)

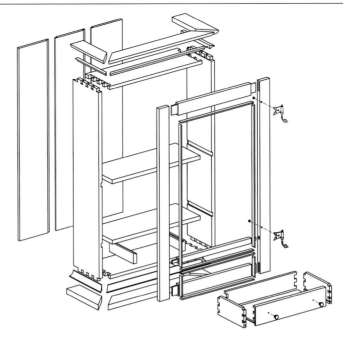

FACE FRAME, CARCASE AND DRAWER
EXPLODED VIEW

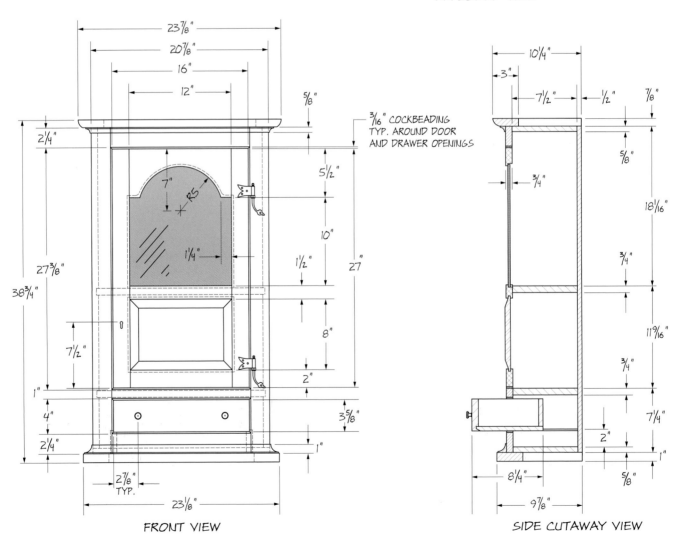

3/16" COCKBEADING TYP. AROUND DOOR AND DRAWER OPENINGS

FRONT VIEW

SIDE CUTAWAY VIEW

AMERICAN WALL CUPBOARD

poplar that I scooped off the floor and rabbeted. The "L" shape at the top captures the drawer. I glued these in place to the bottom of the carcase. When the glue was dry, I drove in some nails from below to further secure these essential cabinet guts.

You can build the drawer in any manner you please. I went full-on traditional. That meant that the sides join the back with through-dovetails. The sides join the front with lapped dovetails (sometimes called half-blinds). And the bottom sits in a ¼" x ¼" groove in the sides and drawer front. The underside of the drawer bottom is like a raised panel.

With the drawer complete, you can add the moulding. Each profile consists of three pieces: the part that crosses the front of the case and the two that run back along the sides, commonly called the "returns." All the moulding is attached in the same way. Glue and nail the front pieces firmly to the case. When you attach the returns, add glue at the miter and the front 3" of the case. Then nail the moulding in place. This will allow the case sides to move with the seasons.

The back is merely shiplapped pieces of poplar that are nailed into the ½" x ½" rabbet in the side pieces. Nail them in place after finishing. The finishing process is covered in detail on page 30 of this issue. Using a clear finish alone on walnut is not advisable – it gives the wood a cold cast. We're proud of the simple process and warm color that results from our dye-tinted shellac.

After finishing, secure the glass with water putty or by nailing in strips of ¼" x ¼" walnut around the sides and bottom of the glass's opening. Putty is the more traditional touch.

Design vs. Construction

I keep a log of my shop time for every project, and for this wall cupboard I logged only about 23 hours of active construction time (I don't log the time I'm waiting for glue to dry). What might come as a surprise is that I spent at least 12 additional hours in the design phase of this project. Though that seems excessive, it pays off.

I'd rather have a great-looking piece with a few cosmetic issues than a technically perfect piece with awkward proportions.

As a result, the most important tools for completing this wall cupboard were an eraser, a chewed-up ink pen and a small notebook that I carry everywhere I go.

— *Christopher Schwarz*

Apply glue to only the front 3" of each drawer runner. Then use a combination square to position the drawer runner while the glue is still wet. Clamp the runners in place, let the glue dry, then nail them in from beneath. The nails will hold the runners and bend as the case expands and contracts with the seasons.

I've borrowed this small drawer-bottom plane from Philly Planes (phillyplanes. co.uk). As they say in England: "It works a treat."

Supplies

Horton Brasses
800-754-9127 or horton-brasses.com
1 pair ■ right-hand rattail hinges
    #RT-R, $98.00/pair
2 ■ ¾" black iron knobs
    #BK-1, $13.50/ea.

Lee Valley Tools
800-871-8158 or leevalley.com
1 ■ 25mm surface-mount lock
    #00N2925, $6.30
1 ■ plain key
    #00N2990, $5.90
1 ■ old brass 1¹³⁄₁₆" vertical escutcheon
    #01A5003, $2.80

Prices correct at time of publication.

The moulding is in three pieces and is attached with glue and nails – I used 23-gauge headless pins. It's easier to attach the smaller cove mouldings with gravity assisting you, as shown here.

Build a Better Cabinet

Many methods to build cabinets invite error. We distill several systems into a process that eliminates measuring and mistakes.

Woodworking magazines and books are cluttered with explanations of how to do the small stuff: cut an accurate joint, prepare a surface for finishing or build a door or drawer. What is mostly absent is a discussion of how to put those small steps together into a system of building that makes sense.

I've been in shops all over the world, and each has a different way of gluing boards together to make cabinets, doors and tables. All of the systems work. But some waste time. Some require precise measuring. And some curry simple, obvious and disastrous errors – such as making a door that is 1" too small.

About 10 years ago, I started spending time with Troy Sexton, a cabinetmaker in Sunbury, Ohio, who builds early American pieces in his one-person shop. Troy is unusual in that he has spent lots of time compressing the procedures to make a cabinet so that he reduces error at every turn, and he arranges each step in building a cabinet so the process flows smoothly.

Many people would say that Troy builds cabinets backward. He starts with the face frame, then he builds the doors and hangs them in the face frame. Then he builds the carcase and fits the drawers. In other shops, they typically start with building the carcase of the project, then they build the face frame and attach it to the carcase. Then they hang the doors in the openings and finally build the drawers to suit.

After adopting Troy's "face frame first" method years ago, I found other professional woodworkers who also work that way, and I started tweaking this method to incorporate handplanes into the system (Troy uses power equipment almost exclusively). What follows is the result of lots of trials, errors and cabinets.

If you build the face frame of a cabinet first, you can save construction time and reduce mistakes caused by measuring. Plus, this technique works well in a shop that uses both hand and power tools.

The 'Face Frame First' Approach to Cabinets

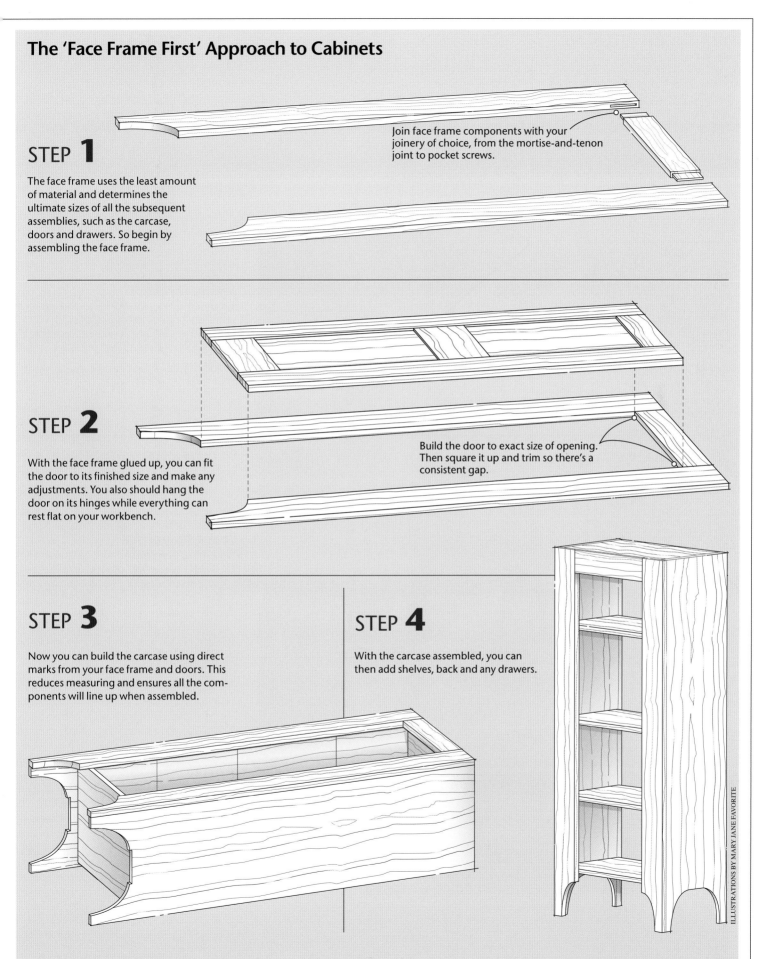

STEP 1

The face frame uses the least amount of material and determines the ultimate sizes of all the subsequent assemblies, such as the carcase, doors and drawers. So begin by assembling the face frame.

Join face frame components with your joinery of choice, from the mortise-and-tenon joint to pocket screws.

STEP 2

With the face frame glued up, you can fit the door to its finished size and make any adjustments. You also should hang the door on its hinges while everything can rest flat on your workbench.

Build the door to exact size of opening. Then square it up and trim so there's a consistent gap.

STEP 3

Now you can build the carcase using direct marks from your face frame and doors. This reduces measuring and ensures all the components will line up when assembled.

STEP 4

With the carcase assembled, you can then add shelves, back and any drawers.

ILLUSTRATIONS BY MARY JANE FAVORITE

Why Build the Face Frame First?

Not every cabinet uses a face frame. If you live on the West Coast or prefer modern furniture, chances are you aren't going to attach a face frame to your cabinet. If you build these so-called "frameless" cabinets, move on to the next section.

But if you build American furniture in historical styles from the 17th to mid-20th centuries, chances are that your cabinets will have a face frame – a framework of ¾"-thick wood that defines the openings of your doors and drawers and strengthens the carcase behind it.

Building the face frame first has several advantages. First, it uses less material than any other step in the process. So if you make a serious goof, you're not out a lot of material.

Second: The face frame determines the size of your doors and drawers. So once those are fixed by the construction of the frame, you can then build your doors with confidence.

Third, you can hang the doors in the face frame more easily with the face frame detached from the carcase. Most woodworkers hang their doors after the face frame is on the carcase. So they are fighting gravity all the way home. Either the cabinet is upright and they are balancing the door on its skinny bottom edge, or the cabinet is on its back and the door is prone to droop into the carcase. This is a problem particularly if the doors are inset into the frame instead of doors with edges that lip over the face frame.

It's far easier to fit a door when everything is flat on your workbench or assembly table. Plus you have easy access to both the inside and outside of the face frame – something you give up when you attach the face frame to the carcase.

Also, you do less measuring. You can use your assembled face frame and door to directly lay out the dados in your carcase sides. So there's less opportunity for a measurement error.

And finally, building the face frame first allows you to make mistakes from which you can easily recover. Say you place a rail at the wrong position when you build your face frame. No problem. You simply adjust the size of your doors and change the position of your shelves and dividers to suit. If you build the carcase first, a mistake on the face frame usually means that the face frame is headed for the scrap pile.

The Frameless Variant

If your cabinet is a frameless one, you should begin with building the doors. The doors will then determine where the dividers will go in the carcase. Once you build your doors, you can lay them directly on your case sides to mark out where the dados should go for shelves and dividers – this also reduces errors.

Incorporating Handplanes

The face-frame first system works great with power tools, but many beginning hand-tool users might be confused about how to incorporate planes into the system. Here's how:

Most woodworkers know that the jointer plane is for flattening stock and the smoothing plane is for preparing it for finishing, but some get confused as to when these planes should be used in construction. Is the jointer plane used before or after assembly? Do you smooth plane the finished assemblies or the individual pieces?

Part of the answer is contained in the names of the planes. The jointer plane flattens the stock before the joinery. The smoothing plane is used when assembly is complete and you get to a point where the next step won't allow you to use a plane. For example, you should smooth plane the side of a carcase right before you attach the moulding. After you attach the moulding the smoothing plane can't access that entire area.

So let's walk through the three types of assemblies in furniture construction: frames, slab boxes

Here I'm thinning down the rails a bit more than the stiles with a jointer plane that is set up like a smoothing plane. Then I'll assemble this frame and smooth plane the long stiles to finished thickness.

If you look closely at this photo you can see the stiles are slightly proud of the rails. Thinning the stiles is easier than thinning the rails with a handplane because most face frames are vertical and so they fit on your benchtop better that way.

With the face frame and door flat on my work surface, it's much easier to position the door so there is a uniform gap all around. Plus adding the hinges is a great deal easier.

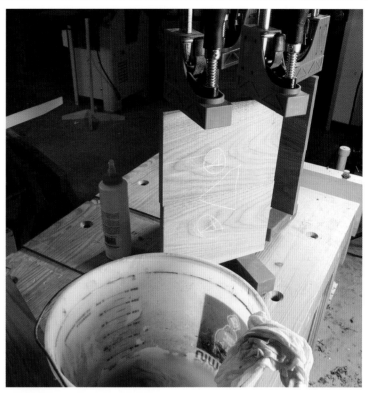

The individual boards in these panels have been prepped with a jointer plane. Then I glued up the panels and will be able to go right to the smoothing plane because the seams are tidy and flush.

and tables/stools to see how planes can be incorporated into the "face frame first" approach.

Frames: Face Frames and Doors

After preparing all the stock with my power jointer and planer for my face frame, I'll flatten all the boards with a jointer plane before cutting the joinery on them. The jointer plane removes the milling marks, twists, cups and bows left over from the power equipment.

Then cut your joints and plane the rails only with either a smoothing plane or a jointer plane set up for a fine cut. This will make the horizontal rails a bit thinner than their adjoining vertical stiles. If there's a panel that goes into this frame, flatten it with a jointer plane, cut the joinery on it and smooth plane it before assembly.

Then assemble the frame. When the glue is dry you have a frame where the rails and panel are ready for finish, but the long stiles are slightly proud. So use a smoothing plane to reduce the stiles in thickness to the same thickness as the rails. This takes some practice to do well, but you'll be an expert after a couple attempts.

Then build the doors, fit them and hang the doors on their hinges.

Dealing with Panels and Boxes

Most solid-wood carcases involve some sort of slab sides or slab shelves. As a result, you need to glue up several boards into wider panels. Here's

how you do that with handplanes: First arrange the individual boards for best appearance when you plan your panel, but try to get the grain running in all the same direction in the slab. This makes it easier to plane after assembly.

Then use the jointer plane on all your individual boards to flatten them. Now you can cut any joinery on the boards' long edges. Some woodworkers use splines, some use biscuits, many use nothing but the glue. When you glue things up, make every effort to keep the boards flush at the seams. If you struggle with this step, switch to a slow-setting glue, such as liquid hide glue.

When the glue has cured, remove the panel from the clamps and evaluate it. If you kept your seams flush, you should be able to clean up the panel with a smoothing plane to remove glue and dress the panel to go in a frame.

If you have misalignments at the seams (more than $1/32$"), you need to attack the panel with a jointer plane – first diagonally to the grain and then with it. This gets the panel back to a flat state in an efficient manner (a jointer plane takes a cut that is about three or four times thicker than that of a smoothing plane).

With the panel flat and the glue removed, you can cut the joinery on it. Cut your dados, grooves and rabbets. Then assemble the carcase with your flattened slabs. Or if you are making a raised panel for a frame, cut its moulded edge, and then prepare it for finishing with a smoothing plane.

With the carcase assembled, you can then attach the face frame (if you have one) and then smooth plane the entire carcase for finishing.

Tables, Stools, Post-and-rail

The other kind of assembly is similar to a stool or table. You have stretchers or aprons running between thick legs or posts. These are treated much like a frame construction with a minor variation. Use the jointer plane to dress all the surfaces, then cut your joinery. Then smooth plane everything before assembly.

The reason you do this is that the legs will likely be too fragile to smooth plane after assembly. After assembly, you might have to clean up some spots with a plane, scraper or sandpaper, but you want to minimize this because the assembly is awkward to secure to your workbench.

After assembly, you will need to level the top edges of the aprons so they're level to the top of the legs. Do this with a jointer plane. Then you can go on to build your table or stool's top using the procedures above for slab panels.

The techniques above don't account for every single situation in the shop, but the principles are sound. Use your jointer plane to get your stock flat at the first. Assemble your cabinets by first tackling the assembly that uses the least amount of wood and is the most critical. And keep your mind open for new ways to work.

— *Christopher Schwarz*

Fitting Inset Doors

Achieving a good fit with consistent gaps is a hallmark of craftsmanship. The hard part may be convincing yourself that you can do it.

When I worked as a professional cabinetmaker I was always surprised at the number of so-called professionals who would go to any length to avoid making inset doors. Most of them just won't do it. The excuse was usually along the lines that it is too difficult and takes too long.

Nice work isn't possible if you talk yourself out of it before you begin.

But if you simplify the problem, it comes down to making a square piece of wood fit inside a square opening, and that is a basic skill in woodworking. It shouldn't be a terrifying experience, and with a systematic approach and a bit of practice it will become second nature. Achieving a good fit on an inset door or drawer begins long before the assembled door goes into the completed frame.

It begins with making good parts. Learn to prepare stock with square corners, straight edges and flat faces. Throw out the notion of "close enough," and replace it with seeing how close you can get. The temptation to let something a little long or a little wide go, with the hope that it will all work out later, is strong. Little mistakes don't work themselves out as a project nears completion; they gang up and accumulate, most often in the most visible spot they can find.

I begin fitting doors to their opening by doing some surveying. I check the corners with a large square. At this point, someone is likely to chime in with the advice to measure the diagonals of the opening to see if it is square. It's OK to do that, but the only thing it usually proves is that you'd like to put off really fitting the door to its opening for a few more minutes.

It isn't easy to get an accurate measurement from corner to corner, and even if the numbers are the same, there are several other conditions

Fitting doors to their openings can be intimidating, but with a systematic approach it is nothing beyond cutting one piece of wood to an exact size and shape. The first thing to tackle is accurately determining the parameters of the opening.

that will yield equal numbers but crooked corners. A short rail will create a trapezoid instead of a rectangle and slightly bowed pieces can create any number of odd shapes that will pass the corner test but still fail to fit.

One of the cruel yet effective ways that woodworking teaches us is this: You don't know how well you have performed one step until you are halfway through the following step. If your opening isn't right, you may not realize it until it is too late to correct. Next time around, you'll be more careful, but this time you'll need to do extra work. If the frame is out of whack you can still fit the door, but it will take longer and won't look quite as nice as it could.

"If you think small things don't make a difference, try spending a night in a room with a mosquito."

— Tenzin Gyatso (1932 -)
the 14th Dalai Lama, exiled leader of Tibet

The same thing holds true for doors: Check them to see if the edges are straight and the assembly is square. If something is amiss, it can usually be corrected, but you need to know exactly what is wrong in order to fix it. I'm relatively confident, so I build doors to the size of the opening and ideally trim an equal amount off all four edges in fitting.

Some people will make the doors larger than the opening, but I think this encourages sloppy work, and it complicates matters when you need to decide exactly how much to trim and where you need to trim it.

Nobody is Perfect

Systematic fitting has to start somewhere, and the first decision is how large to make the gaps. As seen in the picture above, a dime or a piece of plastic laminate is a good starting point. Smaller than that is possible, but it raises the chances of something binding or sticking.

The laminate and the dime are each less than $1/16$" thick; standard-grade laminate is .048" thick, and a dime is about .049". This presents a challenge and a choice. The choice is to become comfortable working with fractions that small, or to set a lower limit of numbers you can work to.

With a set of fractional dial calipers you can easily measure small fractions. If creating nice work is your goal, it doesn't make sense to start guessing when you're trying to achieve a nice fit. Knowing how much to remove, and how to remove a predictable small amount, is critical.

Either machines or hand tools can be used. Measure a plane shaving with calipers, and with a little division and multiplication you will know how many plane swipes it will take to remove just enough. The jointer is the tool of choice for a powered approach, and the picture at far right shows how to set up the machine to remove a predictable amount of material with each pass.

The ruler on the infeed table is $1/32$" thick. With a long straightedge across the outfeed table, position the infeed table until the ruler meets the bottom of the straightedge, then lock the infeed table in place. You can double-check how much is removed in one pass by measuring the width of a piece of scrap with the calipers, making a pass across the jointer and measuring again.

One Edge at a Time

All of the fitting work is fussy, and this is an area where it's a real advantage to complete the face frame first, then fit the doors and drawers before assembling the frame and cabinet. If you put the door and drawer fitting off until after assembly, you won't be able to work on a nice flat surface. You'll be floating in space, trying to judge critical distances while balancing a door in mid-air.

The hinge stile is the best place to start for fitting a door. It's usually the longest edge, and for the hinges to function, the stiles on the cabinet and the door need to match. When fitting a drawer front, start with the longest edge. It's too late at this point to do much to the cabinet stile if it isn't straight. Corrections to the door are far easier to make than corrections to the opening.

If the cabinet stile is bowed into the opening in the middle, you may be able to get a block plane in the opening to remove it. If it is bowed in the other direction, material must be removed in the corner – not an easy task. Tool catalogs promise that a chisel plane will work for this, but this is a clumsy tool and the chances for success are slim.

If you can get away with it, taking a slight amount off the corners of the door to match the frame is a better choice. If conditions are really bad at this point, reworking or remaking the frame might be a less painful way to cut your losses. Once again, this is another good reason to leave the face frame and cabinet separate entities as long as possible.

It's also important to keep opposite components of the door as close to equal in width as possible. After running the hinge stile over the jointer, I compare its width to the other stile. When I trim to the finished width, I'll leave the hinge stile alone, and remove stock from the lock stile only to keep things equal.

An Opportunity to Ruin Everything

Getting the hinge stile straight, or at least a decent match to the frame stile, is only the starting point. The door is still too large for the opening. For the power-tool woodworker, the temptation is strong

Good fitting begins with knowledge of what you are fitting to. A large drafting square is ideal for checking corners.

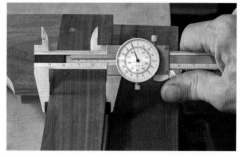

When trimming parts on opposite sides of a door, it's important to keep them as close as possible to the same size.

to head to the saw and cut the door to length. This is the next step, but it pays to make sure of two things: that a square cut is needed and that the saw setup is correct.

I think this one operation is a good reason to invest in a sliding table for the table saw. Lacking a sliding table, having a crosscut sled or panel-cutting jig are good alternatives. Unless the door

Set the jointer to remove a predictable amount of material. The steel rule on the infeed table under the straightedge is $1/32$" thick.

Dial calipers that read in fractions enable you to measure small distances precisely.

Squaring up a door is quick work with a table saw, but you must be able to make an accurate cut. There is no second chance.

is narrow and short, the standard miter gauge likely won't be up to the task.

I like to establish the bottom edge as the second step. This is a good time to recheck the corners of the frame and the door. If the opening is square, and the hinge stile straight, a crosscut will do. Some woodworkers will use the jointer, but care must be taken to avoid blowing out the end grain as the last stile passes over the knives.

Begin making the cut, but back the door out from the cutterhead after an inch or less. Reverse the position of the door, keeping the uncut portion flat on the infeed table until the previously cut area is on the outfeed table. Continue to feed the door, keeping it against the fence with downward pressure on the outfeed table. This tends to leave a rough cut on the end grain, so leave some extra material to be sanded or planed smooth.

If the opening isn't quite square, the bottom of the door must be trimmed to match. If you forged ahead and made a straight cut, the door won't fit – or if it does there will be a noticeable difference in the gaps at each side. To determine how much to remove, place the bottom end of the hinge stile in the corner of the frame and place the door across the opening. The opposite corner will either overlap the frame or show a gap.

If it overlaps, make note of the distance, and mark the edge of the lock stile. If there is a gap, that distance should be marked on the hinge stile. With one leg of a framing square, or some other straightedge, mark the bottom of the door. A pencil line will work, but clamping the straightedge and cutting in the line with the knife will give a better reference.

The knife line becomes essential if you're using hand tools to trim the bottom edge. The same issue that causes problems with the powered jointer will also make trouble if you're handplaning – the end grain will likely tear out as the plane exits the cut. The solution is also the same. Begin by cutting in on the widest part of the cut, working in from the end. Then work from the opposite direction until you reach the knife line.

Trimming the end with a plane allows you to make adjustments progressively. Mark the desired end result with a straightedge and a knife.

Begin the process by planing the end grain on one stile, working from the outside in to prevent tear-out.

Continue trimming by planing in the opposite direction until you reach the marked layout line.

Check frequently for square as you plane. It's easy to tilt the plane as you concentrate on reaching the line.

As an alternative to a plane, a shim behind one end will allow you to quickly make a slight adjustment to cut an angle slightly out of square using your table saw.

Some woodworkers put the door in a vise or otherwise clamp it so the edge to be trimmed is horizontal. I find it awkward to balance the plane on a narrow edge, especially if the edge is far above the benchtop. I work with the edge vertical, and the door clamped flat to the bench. Other planes will work, but I prefer a low-angle block plane because it works well at cutting end grain, and it is easy to reverse it in my hand if I want to cut on the pull stroke. With either method, check frequently that the edge is square.

The table saw is also a viable option for making these odd cuts. Instead of trying to make a tiny adjustment to the angle of the fence, or if you're using a sled with a fixed 90° fence, insert a thin shim between the corner of the door and the fence as seen in the photo on page 54, bottom right. Start with a shim that's thinner than the gap, and make the first cut removing as little material as possible. The angle can be changed in miniscule increments by moving the shim laterally.

On Top of the Situation

The procedure for trimming the top is the same as the bottom. A shim equal in thickness to the desired gap can be placed between the bottom of the door and the top of the lower cabinet rail to better gauge how much material ought to be removed from the top. The same cautions for matching the opening and methods for making the cuts apply.

The amount removed from the top will determine the sum of the gaps at both the top and bottom of the door. It pays to check the fit as you go. Even though the door will likely be too wide for the opening, the up-and-down fit can be checked directly by holding the door at a right angle to the frame and sliding it into place.

The big advantage of using a plane for this fitting is the ability to remove controlled amounts of material in smaller increments than can be reasonably achieved with power tools. The second-best reason to use a plane is that you can arrive at a ready-to-finish edge at the same time as you reach a good fit. When using power tools, sanding the edges to remove tool marks can easily widen the gaps, or knock them out of square.

With three of the four edges complete, the last long edge can be trimmed. If the opening and the door are both square, this is simply a matter of reducing the width of the last stile. If things are off slightly, I work to get the door to fit within the opening, shim the top and bottom gaps equally, then scribe the edge of the door to the edge of the frame. A pencil can be run along the edge, marking the high and low points.

It All Hinges on This

At this point, the hinges can be set. Because we used surface-mount hinges in this project, the door was placed in the frame opening with shims wedged in place to hold the door in position. If butt hinges are used, mark the locations on both the frame and the door. Go ahead and mount the hinges.

If all goes well, the even gaps at the top, bottom and hinge stile will remain as they were before placing the hinges. If not, you will need to choose between adjusting the hinge placement or readjusting the door gaps. Readjusting the door gaps will result in making them larger than originally planned and repeating steps already taken. This is where the lessons of carefully setting hinges are learned.

With butt hinges, make the initial setting using only one screw per hinge leaf. If the door needs to be relocated up or down, a second attempt can be made, fastening the hinge with a screw in an unused hole. When the fit is good, fill the first hole with a whittled scrap of wood; then fasten the hinge using all the screws.

If the gap between the door isn't even at the hinge stile, thin shims can be placed between the hinge leaf and the wood. Only a small adjustment can be made with this technique, as any but the thinnest shim will begin to show as a curious gap between the hinge and the wood it attaches to.

After the hinges are set, the final gap between the lock stile and the cabinet can be finished. If the gap is small, a square edge on the back stile will prevent the door from closing. Make a pencil mark on the door where the back edge of the lock stile hits the opening at both the door top and bottom. Connect these two marks with a line.

If the marks are the same distance from the edge, an adjustable square or a marking gauge can be used to place a line along the back face of the lock stile. If there is a variation, use a straightedge to connect the two marks. In an ideal world, the long edge should be square to the top and bottom edges, and the gap should be consistent. If both can't be achieved at this point, an even gap is the better option.

If the gap was even before setting the hinges and didn't change, a slight bevel can be planed on the back of the door. With the door flat and the back facing up, begin planing by knocking off the corner. Hold the plane away from vertical a few degrees to establish the angle.

The angle can be established by eye, comparing the gap between the lower edge of the door stile and the sole of the plane with the distance marked on the upper face of the door. As the plane strokes become wider, stop and look at the end of the door to ensure that the angle is close. Stop planing just before the bevel reaches half the thickness of the door and reattach the hinges.

The last few light strokes can be made with the door on the hinges. The edge should not come to a sharp point, as this will be likely to chip or tear at some point in the life of the door. On a ³⁄₄"-thick door, the flat area from the front of the door coming back should be between ⅛" and ¼" wide.

— *Robert W. Lang*

After the door has been hinged, the other stile will need a bevel to allow it to open and close. Mark directly from the cabinet opening.

Work from the back side, planing a bevel until the line is reached.

Correct the angle to take wider shavings, leaving ⅛" to ¼" of flat area at the edge.

BOXES

The 1839 School Box

A nearly forgotten tale of an English apprentice offers up an excellent lesson in hand-tool joinery.

In 2007, a lightweight box showed up on my desk from Joel Moskowitz, who runs the Tools for Working Wood store in Brooklyn, N.Y. Inside was a short book that has yet to give up all its secrets and tricks to working wood by hand.

Called "The Joiner and Cabinet Maker," this book – first published in 1839 – was one of a series of short hardbacks written to introduce young people to the basic knowledge needed for a trade, such as baking, coopering, printing or joinery.

What's amazing about this particular little book is that it is an engaging work of fiction that tells the tale of young Thomas, a lad who is apprenticed to a joiner's shop in a rural English town. Thomas begins his apprenticeship by sweeping the shop, managing the hide glue pots and observing the journeymen.

Then, thanks to a plot twist, Thomas is tasked to build a rough box for a customer who is leaving on a journey that same day. The book follows Thomas every step of the way, from stock selection through construction and finally to delivery, when Thomas brings along an envelope of cut nails for the customer so he can secure the lid shut before his trip.

Thomas goes on to build a school box and finally a large chest of drawers, all the while picking up different joinery skills and the right attitude to become a competent and trusted journeyman.

It's an idyllic tale, and likely a bit sugar-coated compared to the reality of an apprentice's life in early 19th-century England. But that detail aside, the book is extraordinary. Not only is it fun to read, but if you build the three projects shown in its pages, you will get an excellent course in working wood with hand tools.

And so since January, I have been constructing these three projects by following the instructions in "The Joiner and Cabinet Maker." And as I followed the text, I learned a great deal about the

The plan for this box came from an 1839 book of fiction about an apprentice in a rural shop in England.

fine details of English-style hand work, which relied on skill and cunning as much as sharp tools.

When I read it for the fourth or fifth time, I still picked up tips I'd missed during previous readings.

This fall, Moskowitz and I are republishing "The Joiner and Cabinet Maker" complete, and we're including a section from Moskowitz that explores historical England and woodworking during this period, and a section from me that will include detailed descriptions of the opera-

> "When tools were rude, great precision and nicety of finish could not be expected. To return to the crude joints of our ancestors would be a distinctly retrograde move."
>
> — David Denning
> "The Art and Craft of Cabinet-making" (1891)

tions and complete construction plans.

(The original book had only two pages of illustrations without any dimensions, so the three projects had to be created in Google SketchUp using the advice in the text.)

All three of the projects have a lot of lessons for modern woodworkers who want to incorporate hand tools into their workshops. The second project in the book, the school box, is probably my favorite. Young Thomas is asked to build this box for a boy he befriended while building a rabbit hutch. The box will travel with the boy to boarding school (I presume) and is designed to hold his books, personal effects and snacks.

The school box project introduces the readers to gluing up panels, making them flat and joining them with through-dovetails. There's also a fair amount of interesting detail on stopped dados and installing hardware.

About the School Box

The joinery methods used in this project might make a modern woodworker cringe. Some joinery seems overkill; other joinery seems like a cross-grain wood-movement nightmare.

Despite my misgivings, I built the project as Thomas did (for the most part). We'll see how the project fares in the future.

Here, in a nutshell, is how it goes together: The front, back and ends are joined with through-dovetails. The bottom of the box is glued and nailed to the case. (An interesting detail here is the grain runs from the front of the box to the rear.)

After the case is assembled, you cut the stopped dados for the till, which slides into place and rests on cleats. The lid is attached with hinges (which you have to bend yourself). All the moulding is attached with nails and glue.

Here's the Deal

Young Thomas was told to build the box using "deal," a term that might be unfamiliar. In England and in Colonial America, deal was a generic term for a softwood that was nominally 9" in width (however the sources disagree on what the standard thickness was).

To create the panels needed for the school box using deal, Thomas glued up the panels with the material in the rough using hide glue and a "rub joint." This is when the glue is applied to the jointed edges and the pieces are rubbed together until the glue cools and sets up. You can then, if you wish, put a clamp across it. Or merely set the panel aside for the glue to set up overnight.

Dress all the panels using a fore, scrub or jack plane. Work across the grain to remove material and flatten the panel. To avoid spelching on the outfeed side of the board, bevel the far corner using your plane.

Once you get one panel flat, the book advised that you use that as a reference surface for checking the other panels as you worked. Place the true panel on top of the questionable one then check for twist by pressing at the corners. I was skeptical about this procedure, but it worked – I confirmed my results with winding sticks.

Finish dimensioning your panels to width then thickness. Then cut them to length. If you are following in Thomas's footsteps, you'll use a sash saw and a bench hook. Then clean up the ends by shooting them with a plane.

Pins-first Dovetails

The dovetail layout in "The Joiner and Cabinet Maker" was surprisingly specific, including the size of the pins. The book called for pins that were $\frac{1}{8}$" wide on the narrow side and $\frac{1}{4}$" wide on the wider side. This results in dovetails that are fairly mild in appearance in $\frac{3}{4}$" material.

As I wasn't planning to paint this box, I decided to make a subtle alteration. I used the book's suggestion for the number of dovetails and the $\frac{1}{8}$" spacing. However, I used a 14° slope, which resulted in a bolder dovetail. Feel free to follow the path of Thomas or your own eye. The historical record supports many slopes, both mild and wild.

Use a marking gauge to scribe your baselines on your pieces. Thomas set his gauge to the exact thickness of his work.

Thomas cut his pins first then chopped out the waste with a chisel. No sawing out the waste or other intermediate step was involved. Those of you who have watched me cut dovetails know that I prefer a tails-first approach and use a coping saw to remove the bulk of my waste.

But I'm just as comfortable cutting the pins first. It's all just sawing, chiseling and transferring the shape to the mating board. You can get

A "rub joint" is easy to execute in short panels such as needed for the school box. It's surprisingly easy to do. Use enough pressure to close the joint, but not so much that all the glue squeezes out.

Use strokes across the grain to remove the material. Then use diagonal strokes across the panel to get the board as flat as you can. Small softwood boards are easy to process this way.

Use one flat panel to check another. If your bench is truly flat, you also can use that as a reference surface. However, a freshly flattened board is likely the more reliable barometer.

Cut the panels to length using a sash saw, then clean up the results with a plane. I use my shooting board for both operations.

Mark the pins out with a pencil (or a knife if you please). Saw down to the baseline.

Chop halfway through the waste. Then flip the board over and chop through the remainder.

One of the advantages of cutting the pins first is that it's easy to reach in to mark out the mating tails with a sharp pencil. The disadvantage is that you have to balance the pin board on end while you do this.

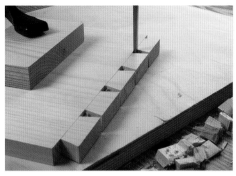

After sawing out the tails, remove the waste with a chisel using the same method. Some people will put an additional kerf down the center of the waste so it breaks up more easily as you knock it out with a chisel.

The easy way to plane up the assembled box is to sleeve it over a piece of scrap that hangs off your benchtop. In this case, I also have the box wedged against the jaw of my leg vise, which allows me to work the carcase without ever clamping it to anything. Gravity and the force of the tools do all the work.

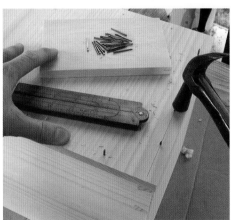

The book calls for the grain to run from the front to back – and for the bottom to be glued and nailed. While this might cause some problems down the road, it might also be a MacGuffin – I calculated that the quartersawn Eastern white pine bottom will move a little more than $1/32$" in our Midwestern environment.

Plane up the bottom flush to the case with a smoothing plane. I'm keeping most of the tool's sole on the carcase to reduce the chance that my bottom's edge will have an odd slant. When my plane takes a shaving that is the full width of the bottom piece, I'm done.

worked up about the different approaches to the joint, or you can ignore that noise and spend the effort becoming a better dovetailer.

Once you've chiseled out the waste, mark your tails from your pin board. Place the tail board flat on your bench and balance the pin board on the end. Reach in with a pencil and mark the tails. Then saw out the tails. Be sure to leave the entire pencil line behind.

After completing all four corners, tweak your joints for assembly. The dovetail elite will work right from the saw and chisel with no testing or dry-fitting of the joint. If you aren't able to do this, don't fret. Thomas couldn't, either.

"The really good workman, by long practice, will make even a large dovetail so exactly in the first instance as to have none of this fitting to do, and to be able to drive the joint up at once. But for a young hand like Thomas, it is very well to make a good dovetail at last, after some trouble in easing and fitting; much better than either to cut the pin-holes too large at first, or too small, and then to split the wood by driving the joint tight in a hurry."

When applying glue, paint it on all surfaces of the joint. While end-grain surfaces don't offer as much strength as long-grain surfaces, they do add strength to the assembly. Knock the box together. If your joints are tight you shouldn't need clamps.

One interesting piece of advice from the book is to hammer the pins after assembly to tighten up the joints. You can over-do this, but it will mushroom and compress the wood a bit and improve your fit.

"Some careless workmen look to this hammering to fill up all the spaces which their bungling has left, but it is impossible to hammer a bad dovetail into a good one, though a good one may be made better by this means."

With the glue dry, plane the box all around.

A Questionable Bottom

The bottom piece is planed up so it is oversized. Then it is glued and nailed to the carcase. It sounds simple enough, but "The Joiner and Cabinet Maker" specifies that the bottom piece should have its grain running from front to back, not end to end. Why? For strength.

I've seen this approach in old tool chests especially, but I was surprised to see it in such a small piece of work. Running the grain as the book suggests introduces more wood-movement problems than running it end to end.

With the grain running from front to back, the bottom will push the moulding away from the ends of the school box. Were the bottom's grain running from end to end, you could encourage the movement to push out the rear of the box, where there is no moulding to hinder it. Plus, the bottom wouldn't move as much because its width would be narrower.

To work around this "problem" I came up with

a couple other wild ideas, but then I decided to just do what I was told and see what happens.

So I glued and nailed on the bottom using cut headless brads and set them below the surface of the wood. (Be sure to file or grind your nailset so it is rectangular in section. This helps your accuracy with cut nails.)

Moulding for the Bottom

The moulding that wraps around the front and sides has a small chamfer on the corner. (Thomas wasn't quite ready for the moulding planes I suppose.) No matter how you stick this profile, I recommend that you cut the chamfer on one long board then miter the board into your three lengths.

I'm using a chamfer plane attachment for my block plane, but small chamfers such as this can be easily freehanded by striking a couple gauge lines or pencil lines and working down to those.

This keeps the grain and the profile consistent at the corners – even if you aren't consistent.

Lay out the miters on your moulding and cut them with a handsaw (use a miter box if you have one). Then clean up the mouldings with a plane. If you've never tried this, give it a whirl. It's much

If you lay out your miters with knife lines, planing down a miter is fairly simple work. I like using a block plane because it balances easily on the sawn miter.

easier than you think – especially if you don't have to fit the moulding on all four corners.

Keep working the corner miters until they look good. Then you can attach the moulding with glue and nails. Be sure to glue the mitered surfaces because those are critical.

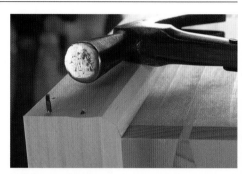

Nail the moulding to the bottom of the carcase and nail through the miters as well. I'm always surprised how few people glue and nail their miters, but I'm not surprised by the resulting gaps.

1839 School Box

	NO.	PART	SIZES (INCHES) T	W	L	MATERIAL	NOTES
❑	2	Front & back	3/4	10	15	Pine	
❑	2	Ends	3/4	10	10	Pine	
❑	1	Bottom	1/2	15	10	Pine	Nailed and glued to case
❑	1	Till wall	1/2	3 1/2	8 3/4	Pine	In 1/8" dados
❑	1	Till floor	1/2	4	8 1/2	Pine	Rests on cleats
❑	2	Till cleats	1/2	1/2	4	Pine	Nailed and glued to case
❑	1	Lid	3/4	10 1/16	15 1/8	Pine	
❑		Base moulding	1/2	1 1/2	40	Pine	Chamfer on top edge
❑		Lid moulding	1/2	1	40	Pine	Chamer on bottom edge

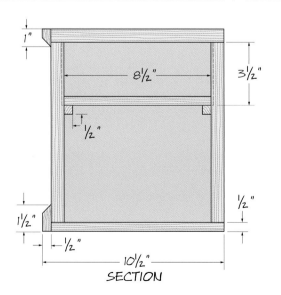

SECTION

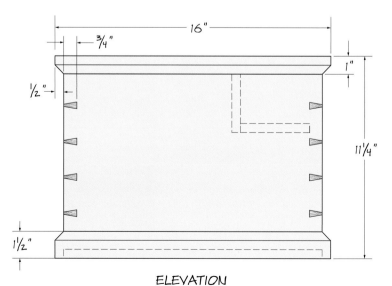

ELEVATION

ILLUSTRATION BY ROBERT W. LANG

SCHOOL BOX

Handmade Stopped Dados

The till inside the box is an interesting piece of work. The wall slides into stopped ⅛" x ½" dados in the front and back pieces. The bottom of the till rests on cleats that are nailed to the front and back. The wall and the bottom are nailed at their corner and the whole assembly slides out.

What's the till for? Snacks for the student.

Begin work on the till by cutting the stopped dados in the front and back piece. Saw out the walls and then remove the waste with a chisel (or a router plane).

When you saw out the waste, you can work against a fence – a traditional technique. Also, feel free to saw past the line where the dado will end. No one will ever mind those kerfs. That will make chiseling out the waste quite painless.

Chisel out the waste to a ⅛" depth. Use a small block of wood with a ⅛" notch as a depth indicator.

Now nail the cleats to the front and back that will support the till's bottom. Nail and glue the bottom and wall together and slip the assembly into the dados.

Install the Lockset

Before you put the lid on the box, install the lockset in the carcase. The key to installing the lockset is a single hole that is the same size as the lock's pin (the round cylinder that the end of the key sleeves onto when working the lock).

Mark out where the pin should be and bore a hole through the case. I used a birdcage awl, which has a tapered tip. Once the pin can be press-fit into the hole, stop boring.

Press the lockset's pin into the hole through the front of the box. Put a clamp on it to keep it in place. Then use a knife and a square to mark the extents of the mortise you require on the top edge of the front. Then connect those two knife marks with your cutting gauge. Waste away the material. Score it with a chisel and pry it out with a small router plane set to the thickness of your lockset's top plate.

Sorry about the period-inappropriate MDF in the photo. I use a scrap to guide my saw as I saw out the extents of the stopped dado. Push your fingers gently against the sawplate – don't worry, you won't get sawn.

Use a cutting gauge or a butt chisel to define the square terminus of the stopped dado.

Use a chisel to remove the waste between your sawcuts. You can use a small block of wood with an ⅛"-long nub to determine when you are at your final depth.

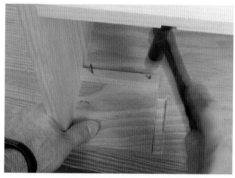

A couple nails are enough to keep the cleat in place. Be sure to orient the wedge shape of the nail so it bites into the end grain. Otherwise your cleat could split.

Now press the lockset's pin into the hole from the inside of the carcase until the works of the lock rest on the inside face of the carcase. Use a pencil to trace around the works.

Use a saw to define the left and right edges of the lockset's works – then lay in a bunch of kerfs to make it easy to remove the waste between those two initial kerfs. Waste away that area with a chisel and a router plane. You'll need to use a short bench chisel or a special lockset chisel, which has a very low profile.

Then fit the lockset's pin back into the hole and mark out the shape of the back plate. Remove the lockset and waste away that area until the entire piece of hardware fits flush to the carcase. This gradual process ensures you remove only the material necessary, which maintains the strength of the front piece.

This is the most critical part of the entire operation. Once the hole is marked out, ream out a hole that is the same size as the pin in your lockset. Take your time here.

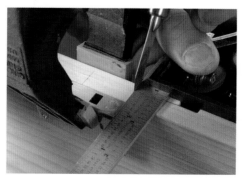

Pressing the lock's pin into the hole this way allows you to mark out the mortise without danger of running your knife into the metal of the lock.

A cutting gauge makes a deeper mark than a pin gauge. Take a couple light passes at first to ensure the knife doesn't wander.

The Lid and its Hinges

Like the bottom piece, you should leave the lid slightly oversized as you fit it, so that if you make a mistake, you can trim things to fit. The first step is to mortise the hinges into the case and mark where you want the lower leaf to bend. Then bend the steel hinges to the correct shape and screw them in place.

The mortise in the case needs to be deep enough to accommodate both the hinge leaf and the thickness of the barrel. According to the book, the location of the hinges is key. It uses a proportion common in old furniture. Take the length of the lid and divide it in half. Then space the hinges so their centerlines are this dimension apart from one another.

Cut the mortises by sawing the walls and removing the waste with a chisel. Screw the lower leaf to the case as shown. Then mark where the bend should occur.

As far as bending hinges go, the ones in the Supplies box are a snap to manage. Secure the hinge in a metal-jawed vise then bend it with your hands and finish the job with a hammer. (If you are worried about mucking it up, buy three hinges instead of two.) Then screw the upper leaf to your lid piece.

Trimming and Adding Trim

With the lid secure you can plane the lid so it has about $1/16$" overhang on the front and ends. Then you can add a chamfer to the lid moulding and miter it. Attach it with glue and nails.

When you attach the moulding to the ends of the lid, there is a cross-grain wood-movement problem to overcome. One common strategy is to add glue to the miter and the front third of the moulding. Then nail the moulding in place along the entire edge. The glue will hold the miter tight at the front. The nails will let the lid move at the rear.

Once the moulding is secure, trim it flush to the lid. Then attach the strike plate for the lock to the underside of the lid.

You can guess where the bend will happen or mark it directly. Keep in mind you need to accommodate the thickness of the leaf in your bend. So you want your bend to begin on your line.

I'll attempt to attach my lid moulding so it is either dead-on flush with the top of the lid or a little proud. Then it's a simple matter of trimming it down to the lid.

The easy way to attach the lid is with the case on its back. A small spacer under the case makes it easy to line up the hinges on your lid.

Finish the School Box

The finish Thomas used on this school box isn't discussed in "The Joiner and Cabinet Maker," though several finishes for pine objects are mentioned in its pages, including boiled linseed oil and wax, straight paint or even grain-painting.

I ragged on a thinned oil finish with a little varnish added to give the piece a little protection. Six coats gave me an acceptable sheen and build. Then I waxed the piece. To keep the lid from opening too far, I screwed a small strip of leather to the inside of the lid and the case.

I was so pleased with the proportions of the completed school box I did something I've never done before with a project: I started another school box immediately. This one in cherry.

— *Christopher Schwarz*

Be careful tracing around the works of the lock. Modern locks have curved corners so your pencil can go deeper than it should because of these curves.

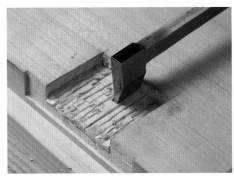

A lockset chisel (this one is from Lie-Nielsen Toolworks) is a handy specialty tool. You can also do this work with a stubby chisel.

Supplies

Lee Valley Tools
800-879-8158 or leevalley.com
2 ▪ Unequal strap hinges $7^1/2$" x $3^1/2$"
   #01H2127, $10.20/ea.
1 ▪ $2^1/2$" box lock
   # 00P2325, $14.20
1 ▪ Horizontal pressed old brass
   escutcheon
   # 01A1971, $1.90

Prices correct at time of publication.

Drawer Primer: Sliding-lid Box

We discovered that our drawer-building technique is an ideal method to make sturdy storage boxes.

This simple box uses the same saw setups and rabbeting techniques for building the drawer shown in the "Simple Shaker End Table" on page 112.

However, there are a couple of differences. Unlike a drawer, this box has a sliding lid that's cut using the same joinery we used to make the bottom. We also added a notched piece of wood inside to organize the box's contents (for us, it's chisels). And there is a small amount of detailing anyone can try: The lid's bevel and thumb pull are made with a chisel, rasp and small gouge.

To make the box, first choose wood with straight grain for the sides, front and back, and wood with nice figure for the lid. We built ours from a hybrid called Lyptus. Dress (joint and plane) your lumber, then cut the parts to finished size, except for the tool holder.

Cut the rabbets on your side pieces next, then cut all the grooves. These grooves capture the box's bottom and guide the sliding lid. Finally, cut the rabbets on your bottom and lid.

Lay out the $^{11}/_{16}$"-wide x $^{1}/_{4}$"-deep bevel on the lid and shape it using a rasp. Once you get close to your layout lines, finish the job with a block plane or #120-grit sandpaper and a sanding block.

Lay out the location of the thumb pull on the lid. Define all the edges using a straight chisel and a gouge for the curved area. Chop out the straight section with a chisel and use the gouge to remove the waste. Hand plane or sand all the parts. If you wish to make a tool holder, do so now. To make the slots for our chisels, we drilled five evenly spaced $^{1}/_{2}$" holes, then cut out the remaining material with a hand saw or a band saw.

Dry assemble the box. Once satisfied, glue the sides to the front and back. The bottom floats in its groove and the lid (obviously) slides. Reinforce each joint with $^{5}/_{8}$" brad nails. We finished our box with garnet shellac.

— *Christopher Schwarz and Kara Gebhart*

PHOTO BY AL PARRISH

Sliding-lid Box

	NO.	PART	SIZES (INCHES)			NOTES
			T	W	L	
❏	1	Front	$^{1}/_{2}$	2	$6^{7}/_{8}$	$^{1}/_{4}$" x $^{1}/_{4}$" groove on bottom
❏	1	Back	$^{1}/_{2}$	$2^{1}/_{2}$	$6^{7}/_{8}$	$^{1}/_{4}$" x $^{1}/_{4}$" groove on top and bottom
❏	2	Sides	$^{1}/_{2}$	$2^{1}/_{2}$	15	$^{1}/_{2}$"-wide x $^{1}/_{4}$"-deep rabbet on ends; $^{1}/_{4}$" x $^{1}/_{4}$" groove on top and bottom
❏	1	Bottom	$^{1}/_{2}$	$6^{7}/_{8}$	$14^{1}/_{2}$	$^{1}/_{4}$" x $^{1}/_{4}$" rabbet on all sides
❏	1	Lid	$^{1}/_{2}$	$6^{7}/_{8}$	$14^{3}/_{4}$	$^{1}/_{4}$" x $^{1}/_{4}$" rabbet on sides and back
❏	1	Tool holder	$^{1}/_{2}$	$1^{1}/_{2}$	$6^{3}/_{8}$	Varies depending on your usage

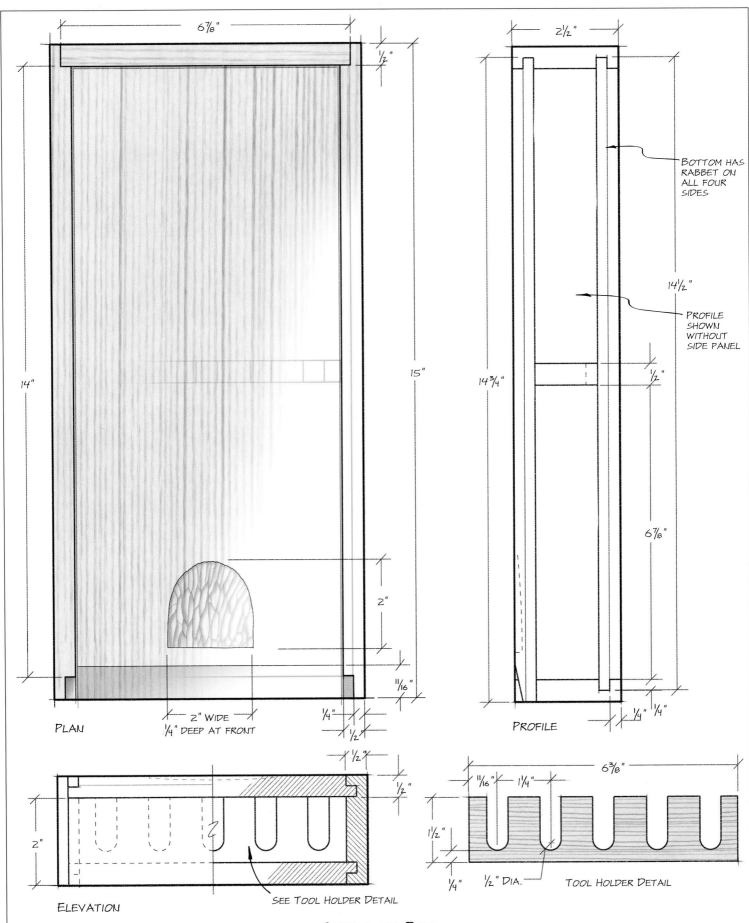

6 7/8"

1/2"

14"

15"

2"

11/16"

PLAN

2" WIDE
1/4" DEEP AT FRONT

1/4"

1/2"

2 1/2"

BOTTOM HAS
RABBET ON
ALL FOUR
SIDES

14 1/2"

PROFILE
SHOWN
WITHOUT
SIDE PANEL

14 3/4"

1/2"

6 7/8"

1/4" 1/4"

PROFILE

1/2"

1/2"

2"

ELEVATION

SEE TOOL HOLDER DETAIL

11/16"

1 1/4"

6 3/8"

1 1/2"

1/4"

1/2" DIA.

TOOL HOLDER DETAIL

SLIDING-LID BOX

CHESTS

A Better Blanket Chest Design

Many common designs for chests make construction far more difficult than necessary.

Though the chest is one of the oldest forms of furniture, that doesn't mean that the human race has settled on the best way to build it.

There are, in fact, many ways to build chests that make the process fussy, challenging and time-consuming – and the results look identical to a simpler chest.

To find the best way to build a chest, we surveyed plans and historical photographs of hundreds of examples from 1600 to the present. And then we boiled all that down to find the simplest way to build the complex chest shown here, which is an adaptation of a blanket box from the Shaker's Union Village community.

This may not actually look like a complex chest. But compared to historical examples, this chest was fancy in many ways. To understand why, let's look at the development of the form.

Community Chests

The first chests had all the joinery you'd find in a dugout canoe (that is, none at all). Early chests were made from one block of wood hollowed out with tools, fire or other forms of gumption.

Later, when riven boards became common, chests were built with two ends that also served as feet (the grain of these ends ran vertical). Then the front and back were fastened to the ends. This grain ran horizontal.

There were some other common variations as well, including assemblies where the ends, front and back became frame-and-panel constructions – and the stiles ran to the floor. Another type of chest was a simple box propped up on feet that were turned or were slabs of wood (such as with the Sea Chest on page 81.

On all forms of chests, moulding typically appears as a transition point between the box and the base or the box and the lid.

From there it was a short hop to make the chests out of two separate assemblies: the box itself and the base, which we call the plinth.

How to join the box and the plinth is the focus

Three common forms of chests that show different strategies for the base.

of this story. It doesn't have to be difficult for the chest's maker, but it sure can be.

Two Trying Designs

Traveling down the more difficult design path when building a chest begins with one assumption: That the plinth is merely moulding and should be applied to the box as such.

Once you make this assumption, here's one difficult (and common) way to make a chest: You cut a moulding profile into the top edge of the plinth pieces, join the plinth pieces at the corners and wrap them around the box. If you use a miter joint at the corner, it's fussy to fit the plinth exactly to the box – errors are easy to make and hard to hide. If you use dovetails, it is even fussier to wrap the plinth pieces because you'll have to cope the moulded edges at the corners.

Oh, one more thing – the plinth is like Atlas. It supports the whole chest, so you should use some fairly thick stock when making it, at least ¾" for a sizable chest. Or you need to add some glue blocks at the corners to support the box.

But what if you don't want that big ¾" step between the plinth and box? Well, you can cut a rabbet into the top edges of the plinth pieces, but then you are rabbeting, dovetailing and coping all your plinth pieces, and any error is going to result in a noticeable gap.

A variation of this particular design is supposed to make some of this easier. You wrap the plinth pieces around the box, and then you apply mitered moulding to the top edge of the plinth pieces. This hides any errors and makes the moulding easy to join at the corners.

And this does improve things. But it's still more work than necessary.

A second common way of building a plinth is to use bracket feet below a mitered frame that has its edge moulded. The mitered and moulded frame supports the box above. The bracket feet below support the frame. What's the downside? You need to get the fit between the box and the

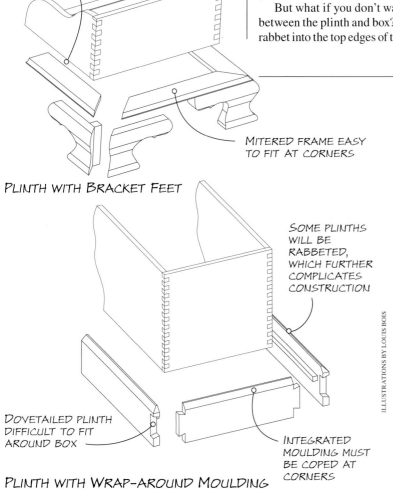

TRANSITION BETWEEN BOX AND FRAME MUST BE PERFECT

MITERED FRAME EASY TO FIT AT CORNERS

PLINTH WITH BRACKET FEET

SOME PLINTHS WILL BE RABBETED, WHICH FURTHER COMPLICATES CONSTRUCTION

DOVETAILED PLINTH DIFFICULT TO FIT AROUND BOX

INTEGRATED MOULDING MUST BE COPED AT CORNERS

PLINTH WITH WRAP-AROUND MOULDING

When setting out all your joinery for the plinth (and the box above it), it's critical to mark your parts. I use a cabinetmaker's triangle to orient my front, back and end pieces.

frame dead-on – or add another layer of moulding to hide any gap between the box and frame.

The above method is easier than wrapping your moulding around the box, but we think there's an even better way to build this chest.

Detach Your Plinth

Though it seems counter-intuitive, it's easier to get a more accurate result with a chest like this if you build the plinth separate from the box so it acts as a platform for the box. Then you set the box on the plinth, drive a few fasteners and run moulding around the transition point to hide errors or irregularities.

Why is this better? For starters, you don't have to be as fussy with your joinery to make the outside dimension of your box match the inside dimension of your plinth. If your box or plinth end up a little bigger or smaller than intended, then you can size your moulding to accommodate the difference. It's a lot easier to trim 1/16" off a skinny piece of moulding than it is to remove that off the front and ends of a 16"-tall chest.

The other distinct advantage is that you don't have to jump through hoops if you want to use a delicate transition moulding. It's just as easy to make the transition large as it is small.

Plus, making the plinth separate doesn't require much more wood (it can be as little as two sticks). And the extra material is hidden so it can be an inexpensive or ugly species.

Finally, making a separate plinth allows for easier repairs, should that ever be necessary. You can easily detach the plinth or even replace it.

About the Union Village Chest

The Union Village Shaker community is near our offices in Cincinnati, Ohio, but it doesn't figure large in the world of Shaker furniture like the eastern Shaker communities do. Union Village was the first and largest Shaker community west of the Allegheny Mountains, and it was the parent community for the western Shaker communities in Ohio, Kentucky, Indiana and Georgia.

Founded in 1805, more than 4,000 Shakers lived at Union Village during its peak, selling herbal medicines, seeds and brooms. The community declined until it was sold in 1912, and the structures are now a retirement community.

One of the artifacts from the village is a walnut blanket box with fine lines and tight dovetails. The box is similar to many Shaker chests that are extant, but this one has always been a favorite.

We chose to adapt this design because it highlights the advantages of our preferred chest-building method. The fine bit of transition moulding around the plinth is easy to accomplish with this construction technique.

While we retained the proportions and lines of the Union Village original, we used finger joints instead of dovetails. And we used figured maple instead of walnut. These alterations give the box a contemporary feel without looking like a pack of cigarettes with cabriole legs, or some such post-modern nonsense.

Begin the Building

Unless you possess wide boards (as the Union Village Shakers did), you need to glue up narrow boards into wider panels for the lid, front, back and ends of the box. The plinth and bottom are made from narrow stock. So while the glue in my panels was curing, I worked on the plinth.

The plinth has a front, back and ends that are joined with finger joints. Plus there are two "carcase supports" sunk into the plinth pieces. The carcase supports are housed in 3/8" x 1/2" rabbets that run the full length of the front and back, plus 3/8" x 1/2" stopped rabbets in the ends.

Cut the finger joints on the corners of the plinth pieces. After much experimentation, we found the best results came from plowing down the middle

Don't try to clamp your work in our finger-joint jig vertically. Gravity will fight you the entire time. Lay the jig flat and let gravity lend a hand as you position your pieces for routing.

When routing between the fingers, try to stay clear of the jig as you plow through the workpiece, as shown above. Then clean up the walls of the joint. This makes tighter joints.

Be sure to plan your plinth's finger joints so that the top of the front and back pieces can take a through-rabbet as shown.

The two keys to a successful glue-up: A slow-setting glue and small plywood blocks that press the fingers together.

of the joint with a straight bit and then routing the sides. This eliminated the risk of our router shifting the parts around.

Once you get the corner joinery cut, plow the ⅜" x ½" rabbet on the top edge of the plinth's front and back pieces. Note that if you lay out your finger joints correctly, this rabbet runs through the entire length of the front and back pieces.

To cut this rabbet, I used a dado stack that was buried in an accessory wooden fence on our table saw. This method allows you to cut the joint with the work flat on the table, not on its edge.

Before you cut the curves on the plinth, assemble it. The corner joints will strengthen the feet as you cut the dramatic curve. To glue the joints, you can choose cyanoacrylate, as explained in this issue, or use a slow-setting polyurethane or liquid hide glue. Yellow glue sets up too fast.

To clamp the finger joints, I made a bunch of small blocks of wood that I taped to the fingers.

These little blocks allowed my clamps to put pressure right where it was needed.

After the glue has cured, remove the clamps, trim the end grain bits flush and make the ⅜" x ½" stopped rabbet in the ends of the assembled plinth. First cut a bunch of kerfs with a handsaw, then chisel the waste.

Then fit those carcase supports into the rabbets in the plinth. Glue and nail the carcase supports into the plinth's rabbets. Then get ready to cut the curves on the assembled plinth.

To cut the curves, first remove the bulk of the waste with a jigsaw, then clean up the curves with a plywood pattern and a router equipped with a pattern-cutting straight bit.

The curves on the ends, front and back are identical, so one short plywood pattern handles all the curves. To rout the straight run between all the curves, I clamped a straight piece of stock to the plinth and used that as a pattern.

Build the Box

The box above the plinth is fairly simple. Here's how it goes together: The corners are joined with finger joints. The bottom boards are shiplapped and nailed into rabbets in the front and back of the box. The till wall slides into a dado in the front and back. The till's bottom is nailed to cleats below.

The hinges are let into notches cut into both the back and the two hinge blocks, which are glued to the outside of the box's back. The hinge blocks support the hinge out to its barrel. And finally, the chest's lid is screwed to the hinges.

Begin by ensuring the front, back and ends of

A little alcohol and a block plane make light work of the proud end grain from the completed finger joints. The alcohol softens the tough end grain.

After you saw out the extents of the notch for the carcase supports, chisel the waste with some light chopping.

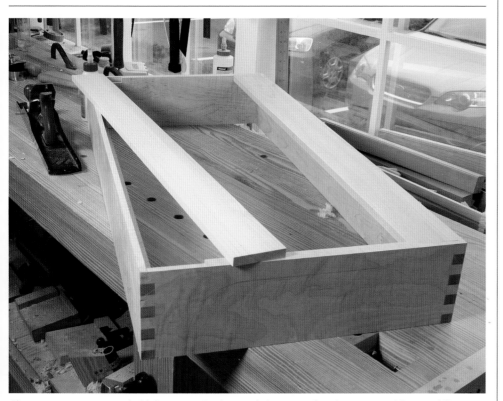

The two carcase supports hold the carcase in place and give you a place for your transition moulding.

Saw the curved shape of the plinth after assembly. If you do it before, the corners will be too fragile to clamp up without fussy cauls.

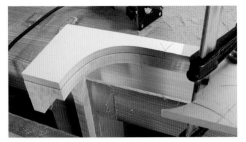

Normally, I would shape these curves with a rasp, but at the encouragement of our power-tool expert, I used a pattern-cutting bit and our trim router. I still like my rasps, but this is a very close second.

Union Village Blanket Chest

NO.	PART	SIZES (INCHES) T	W	L	MATERIAL	NOTES
Carcase						
❑ 1	Top	³⁄₄	18	39	Maple	Edges radiused by hand
❑ 2	Front & back	³⁄₄	15⅝	37½*	Maple	³⁄₈" x ½" rabbet, bottom edge
❑ 2	Ends	³⁄₄	15⅝	17¼*	Maple	
❑ 2	Hinge blocks	³⁄₄	3	6	Maple	½" x ½" chamfer, one end
❑	Case bottom	½	36	16½	Poplar	Several shiplapped boards
❑ 1	Till wall	½	6½	16¼	Poplar	In ¼" x ½" x 6½" dados
❑ 1	Till bottom	½	8	15¾	Poplar	Nailed to till cleats below
❑ 2	Till cleats	³⁄₄	³⁄₄	7	Poplar	Nailed to front & back
Plinth						
❑ 2	Front & back	³⁄₄	5	38½*	Maple	³⁄₈" x ½" rabbet, top edge
❑ 2	Ends	³⁄₄	5	18¼*	Maple	³⁄₈" x ½" notches, top edge
❑ 2	Carcase supports	½	3	37¾	Poplar	Fit in rabbets & notches
❑	Cove moulding	½	½	130	Maple	½" r. cove, nailed to plinth

* Cut these parts slightly longer and trim to final length after assembly

the carcase are indeed square. If they are out, you need to correct them before you rout the finger joints. Otherwise your carcase will go together all cockeyed. I prefer to shoot the ends of panels with a shooting board and a heavy plane. This is slower than making one mighty cut on the table saw, but it is unlikely to make things worse.

Cut your finger joints for the box. Then mill the ³⁄₈" x ½" rabbet in the front and back pieces. Don't cut stopped rabbets in the ends – that's more trouble than it's worth. The dado stack set-up you used for the plinth's rabbets will do the same yeoman's job in the carcase.

Before you assemble the carcase, rout the ¼" x ½" x 6" dados for the till wall. This job is handled by a right-angle jig we developed for the router, shown in the photo below right.

Preparing for Assembly; Pulling the Trigger

Assembling finger-jointed carcases used to be one of the most stressful glue-ups in our shop. It usually involved every clamp in the shop, a helper and a bottle of Mylanta. That was back when we used yellow glue for the job. No more.

Yellow glue is probably the last glue you should use for this job. It sets up entirely too fast, leaving you with open joints and a sinking feeling in your stomach. Either use polyurethane or liquid hide glue. These two solutions will give you an hour of assembly time. If you are still unsure of your skills, use liquid hide glue, which is reversible with a little heat and water.

The easiest way to glue the corners together is to get them semi-assembled, then wipe glue on the long-grain surfaces inside the joint with a flat little scrap. Then apply the little blocks like you did with the plinth and turn on the clamping pressure. After the glue has cured, level all your joints and get ready to fit the interior parts.

Thinking Inside the Box

The bottom boards are shiplapped on their long edges, then nailed into the rabbets on the bottom of the carcase. Cut the shiplap rabbets on the table saw like you cut all the rabbets for the plinth and carcase. Cut the bottom boards to fit snugly, then space them out by inserting a couple quarters between each board. The 25-cent space allows the boards to swell during the wet months. Then nail the boards into the carcase's rabbets. No glue.

My shooting board and jack plane ensure that all my panels are dead square. These needed tweaking even after a ride on the sliding table on our table saw.

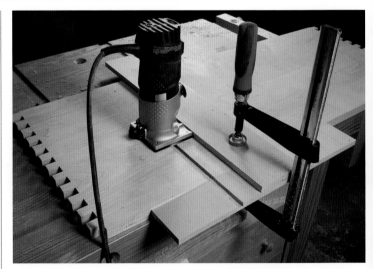

The router dado jig from *Woodworking Magazine* Spring 2005, Issue 3, is a favorite in our shop. (Any jig that lasts more than a few weeks in our shop is to be admired.)

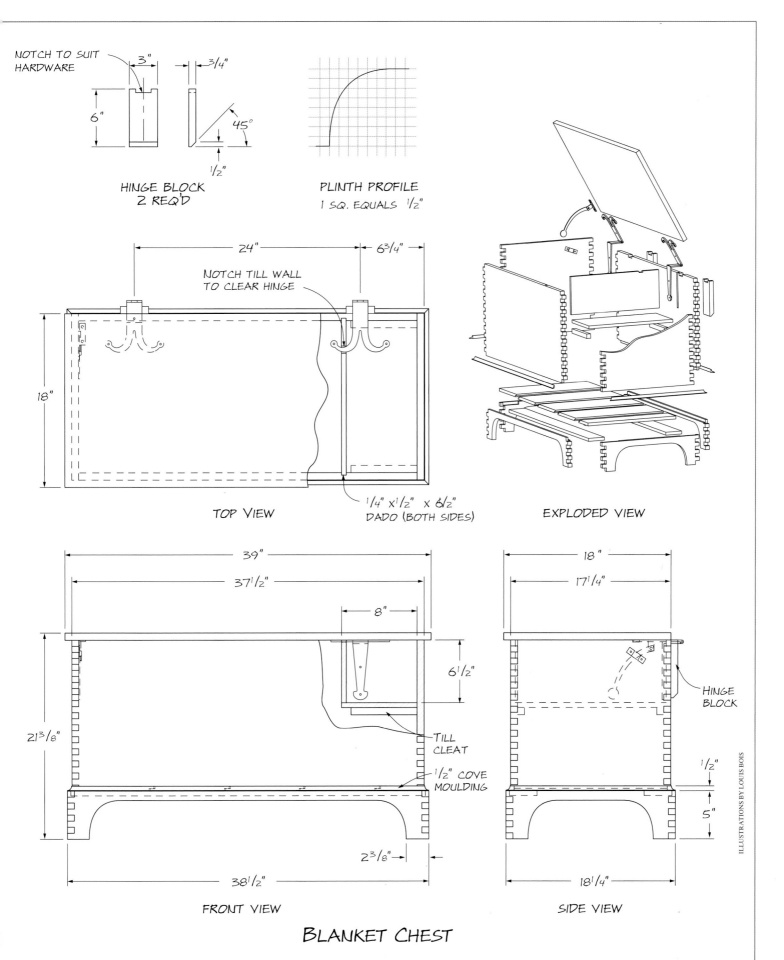

NOTCH TO SUIT HARDWARE

3"

3/4"

6"

45°

1/2"

HINGE BLOCK
2 REQ'D

PLINTH PROFILE
1 SQ. EQUALS 1/2"

24"

6 3/4"

NOTCH TILL WALL
TO CLEAR HINGE

18"

1/4" x 1/2" x 6 1/2"
DADO (BOTH SIDES)

TOP VIEW

EXPLODED VIEW

39"

37 1/2"

8"

6 1/2"

21 3/8"

TILL CLEAT

1/2" COVE MOULDING

2 3/8"

38 1/2"

FRONT VIEW

18"

17 1/4"

HINGE BLOCK

1/2"

5"

18 1/4"

SIDE VIEW

BLANKET CHEST

Here the corners are nearly fitted and I'm smearing an oh-so-thin layer of polyurethane glue into each joint.

The till is simple. Fit the till wall into the dados in the front and back. Glue it in place. Then trim the till bottom to size. Glue and nail two till cleats below the bottom. Then nail the till bottom to its cleats. Again, rely on gravity and nails – not glue.

Carcase, Meet Plinth

Now you can join the plinth and carcase. Put the carcase upside down on the benchtop and center the plinth on the carcase. Screw the plinth to the carcase by driving through the carcase supports

and into the bottom boards. About four screws in each carcase support will do the job.

Now you can figure out exactly how big your transitional moulding should be. Make your moulding (I used a ½"-radius cove bit and left a 1/16" fillet at each edge). Then miter it, tweak it, glue it and nail it.

Shape the hinge blocks, attach them to the back of the carcase and then cut the recesses for the iron hinges. Screw the hinges to the carcase and then clean up your top piece for the last important detail.

Shaping the edges of a lid is something I always enjoy doing by hand with a plane. First shape the ends (which will blow out the long edges). Then shape the long edges to clean up the previous step's mess.

To shape the edges, I first mark the curve using a quarter, then I worked to that line with a traditional hollow moulding plane. A block plane will do the job, but it will leave a faceted surface that you should fair with hand sanding.

Then it's just a simple matter of screwing the lid to the hinges and adding some sort of stay to keep the lid propped open.

The Finish is Simple and Easy

This blanket chest was built during the winter months, so I had to use a hand-applied finish instead of spraying it in my driveway.

Supplies

Van Dyke's Restorers
800-558-1234 or vandykes.com
2 ■ black iron chest hinges
    #02018071, $12.99 each

Lee Valley Tools
800-871-8158 or leevalley.com
1 ■ pair 8⅝" steel stays
    # 01A62.20, $31.40/pair
2 ■ pkgs. #7 x ¾" pyramid screws
    pkg. of 10, #01X38.76, $1.95/pkg.

Prices correct at time of publication.

I've built a fair number of chests during the last 15 years, from tool chests to toy chests to other blanket chests similar to this Union Village version. Each had its charms, but each also had its rough spots, especially when massaging the transition between the base and carcase.

Not so with this chest. The only real challenge will be to decide which room of the house it belongs in.

— *Christopher Schwarz*

Clamp the corners and then across the corners to pull the carcase into square. One clamp squared the entire carcase. You might need a clamp on the bottom as well.

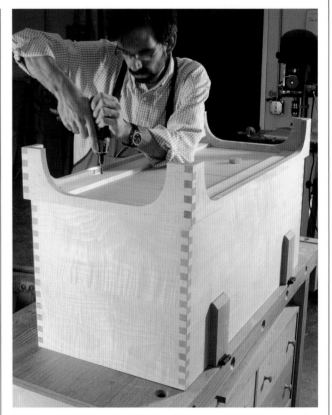

With just eight screws, you'll keep the bottom rigid, the carcase in place and have a delicate step for the transition moulding.

Better Finger Joints

The dovetail's machine-age cousin is fussy to cut and assemble. We've fixed both those faults.

Most woodworking joints can be traced back in time for centuries. Ancient Egyptians excelled at dovetails and the Romans relied on mortises and tenons. Joinery was all handwork until the Industrial Revolution mechanized most processes in the middle of the 19th century. Mortisers, table saws, tenoners and dovetailing machines were all in common use in furniture factories well before 1900.

In addition to new ways to make old joints, machinery and tooling were developed to create joints that weren't common at the time, but became popular because they could be made quickly. The finger joint, also called a box joint, is an example of this development.

Before the machine era, this joint was used only to form a wooden hinge. When first developed, and until recently, it was strictly utilitarian, used mainly to make strong shipping boxes and crates. With our current infatuation for visible and decorative joinery, the finger joint has moved from utility to visibility.

The effort to cut a finger joint entirely with hand tools is at least equal to the effort to hand cut dovetails. In many ways it takes more effort, and the return for the effort is dubious. It is a more demanding joint to make, and it lacks the inherent mechanical advantage and aesthetic appeal of the dovetail. But it is significantly easier and faster to make finger joints by machine, if one is willing to work precisely to set up the tools.

For example, the jig used to build the Blanket Chest on page 16 in this issue was intended to have slots and fingers ⅝" wide. When completed, the overall width of the jig was ¹/₁₆" bigger than planned. That translates to an error in each component of .0025", about half the thickness of the average human hair. Because the parts are all the same size, the joints produced fit together nicely, and if I hadn't told you about the variation, you wouldn't notice it in the finished piece.

If you're trying to cut finger joints with a fixed-width cutter such as a dado stack or router bit, that half-a-hair is about the outer limit of tolerance. If you can't set up, measure and adjust in those teeny increments, you'll be dependent on luck alone to make a nice finger joint. But working to that degree isn't as hard as you might think.

A shop-built router jig can make large, accurate finger joints. The solution for making a better jig proved to be finding a better duct tape.

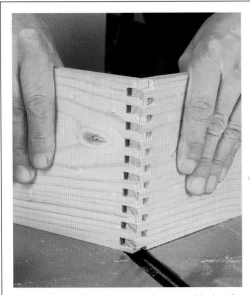

A good fit on a finger joint can be assembled with hand pressure only. If you need to beat on it or clamp it to get it to close, it is too tight.

A Rout of Passage

Making finger joints is a good opportunity to develop skills. Even if you abandon finger joints after one or two tries, the exercise will expand your woodworking vocabulary. You may decide to move on to more attractive joinery, or you may decide that this is a worthy method for much of your work. In either case, the effort will make you a better woodworker. The lessons learned in finger joints will serve well in other areas.

Finger joints are very strong. The amount of interlocking surface area makes a corner with a large area of long-grain to long-grain glue surface and good mechanical strength. The only weak area is the way the joint resembles a hinge. A sharp impact directly on the corner can cause the joint to unfold or come apart. Except for that disastrous scenario it's as strong as a joint can be, and a good choice for small boxes and drawers.

The type of wood used will make a difference in how forgiving the joint is to put together. Softer woods, such as pine or poplar, will compress when assembled. White oak or maple aren't as cooperative, and may require more force to assemble, and more finesse to make the joint. This is a place where the science of the machinist and the art of the woodworker converge. The tolerances are close, but the joint should be made so that it can be assembled without resorting to clamps or hammer persuasion.

The location of the sweet spot for fitting will also vary with the width of the joint or the number of fingers. It's a matter of compounding errors, and like compounding interest, a number that seems insignificant can grow large enough to defeat you. A handful of finger joints for a drawer is fairly easy. A finger joint the size of those used on the blanket chest (especially in a hard, unfor-

An attachment to the miter gauge shows the exact location of the cut, allowing you to make irregularly spaced joints.

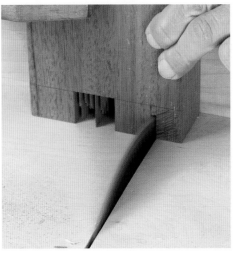

Clamp the work securely to the miter gauge and make certain the cut is within the waste area.

Confidence in cutting is the key to a successful joint, whether it is cut by eye or by jig.

giving wood) is pushing the limits, but not beyond possibility for the careful craftsman.

Consistency and repeatability is the key to finger joints. If you can cut accurately (and stay on the right side of the line) you can line up each cut individually. Attaching an L-shaped backer to the table saw's miter gauge shows the exact location of the cut, and this can be used quite effectively to make precise cuts on the table saw.

If the spacing of the fingers varies as shown, and you're only making a few joints, this is a faster method than making a dedicated jig.

Regularly sized and spaced fingers shout for a jig. It's fussy work, but repetitious. The secret is to use a method that builds consistency into the process. If the work is small enough to safely travel vertically over the saw blade, the jig pictured above is an old standby that works well.

Time-tested Method

This is the classic method of producing a finger joint with a jig that attaches to the table saw miter gauge, and it works very well for small pieces. It's reasonable to run a drawer side vertically over the table saw, but longer or wider work becomes unwieldy. If you're uneasy about holding the work on the table saw, try the router jig on page 77.

Because the table saw jig requires the saw to be set up with a dado head, cut all the parts you need before changing over to the stack dado set. You should prepare the parts for the jig, the parts you intend to join, and several extra pieces of stock for making test cuts.

You'll need a piece of plywood, at least $\frac{1}{2}$" thick and about 6" x 12". In addition, you'll need a piece of hardwood the exact thickness of the width of the cut and about 12" long. I rip the hardwood a little thicker than necessary, then use a handplane to sneak up on a good fit in the slot. It doesn't hurt to have an extra piece on hand in case you go too far with the plane.

Simple Concept – Precise Execution

After installing the stack dado head (we used $\frac{1}{4}$", but the fingers can be any width) make certain the head of the miter gauge is square to the blade and adjust the height of the blade to the thickness of the parts to be joined. Hold the plywood vertically against the miter gauge and make a cut near the end. The exact location isn't critical, but leave at least $\frac{3}{4}$" to 1" beyond the cut. From here on, you need to be as precise as you can be.

Reduce the thickness of the hardwood guide block until you can press it into the slot in the plywood. You need only worry about the thickness, not the width, as long as the width is less than the height of the slot. A set of calipers will help in letting you know how close you are. If you measure your plane shaving, you will be able to predict the size as you work, and you should check the fit of the actual piece in the slot frequently.

When the piece fits, cut a couple inches off one end and glue it in the slot. I use cyanoacrylate (Super Glue) so I don't have to wait too long

for the glue to dry, but any wood glue will work.

After letting the glue dry, place the longer piece of hardwood against the edge of the dado stack. Slide the miter gauge into position, then move the plywood laterally until the two hardwood sticks are touching along their lengths.

Don't throw the longer piece away; you'll need it again in a few minutes. Clamp the plywood to the miter gauge and secure it with a couple pan head screws. If all went well, you'll be in the right position. If not, the flat areas under the screw heads will let you move the plywood side to side for a fine adjustment.

First Cut – Testing, Testing

Both halves of a joint are cut at the same time. One piece is held against the hardwood protruding from the plywood, and the other piece is offset by the width of the slot. The extra piece of hardwood is used as a spacer to align the parts for the first cut.

Clamping the two pieces together, and to the

Table Saw Finger Joints

Jig construction for the table saw method starts with cutting a notch in the plywood backer that attaches to the miter gauge.

The hardwood guide block must match the width of the slot exactly. It's right when you can feel some resistance as you press it into the slot by hand.

An extra piece of hardwood is used to set the distance between the blade and the other block. Make it long enough to be held against the blade front and back.

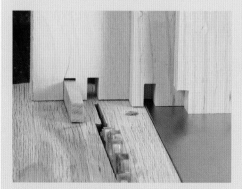

One half of the joint is cut against the guide block, forming a notch. The other half is held away by the spacer, cutting out the corner.

Both pieces are cut at the same time. After the first cut, the pieces are placed with the notches over the guide block.

As the cuts continue, each cut registers the next cut, and if the setup is correct, the work proceeds quickly.

plywood attached to the miter gauge, allows you to make the first cut safely. You won't have to worry about the pieces slipping, and you can concentrate on moving the miter gauge smoothly forward with your hands away from the dado stack.

After making the first cut, set the spacer aside. Each succeeding cut is made by placing the notch just made over the hardwood, as seen in the photos on the facing page. The spacer will keep the work from slipping sideways, so you don't need to use a clamp after the first cut. You can pause after the first few passes to see if the fingers and slots fit together, but it goes fast enough that I prefer to cut the entire width of the joint before making a test fit.

There are three possible outcomes. In the best case, the two parts of the joint will come together with hand pressure only and have no visible gaps. If the joint won't go together at all, the fingers are wider than the slots. To correct this, loosen the screws holding the plywood to the miter gauge, and move the plywood so that the hardwood guide is closer to the blade.

If the fit is sloppy, the fingers are too small, and the plywood needs to be moved in the opposite direction. When adjusting either way, use the extra hardwood spacer as an aid. It's easy for something to slip a little as you hold things in position and tighten the screws. When you're happy with the fit, making the joints goes quickly, and as long as the parts are the same width, there aren't many things that can go wrong. A similar jig can also be used on a router table.

Better Way for Bigger Boxes

On larger work, a better approach is to build a jig for moving the tool across the work. The first choice for this is the router instead of the table saw. Our solution is the shop-made jig on page 77. Equal-width material for the fingers and spacers is the key element to this jig. It is quick to assemble, adaptable to any practical width, and with a bit of tweaking is incredibly accurate.

Although finger joints look complex, the whole idea is that the cuts be made efficiently. With many joints, the bulk of your investment in time will be in tweaking the fit after machining. The opposite is true of finger joints; take your time getting set up to make the cuts so they will fit nicely directly from the machine.

This may look crazy, but it works. Thin cyanoacrylate glue will wick into the joint after it is clamped together and hold as well as any other method of gluing.

Make extra pieces to test your jig, your setup and your technique. I start with two pieces of stock, and if the first test isn't quite where I want it, I trim a couple inches or so off the ends and try again. This leaves enough to have assembled joints to see if I'm really making progress, but doesn't waste material unnecessarily.

A Crazy (Glue) Solution

The downside to the finger joint is that it takes some time to apply glue during assembly. Water-based glues will swell the fingers and that can keep the joint from going together. Or the glue can begin to dry on one end before you have finished spreading the glue.

One solution is to partially assemble the joint, and apply the glue with a brush. If it's a large assembly, use a slow-setting glue such as liquid hide glue or polyurethane glue, and clamp the corners one at a time.

An alternative we found is to assemble and clamp the joint without glue. Thin cyanoacrylate is then applied along the outer intersections of the joint and allowed to wick into the joints. Set one side of the joint horizontally, apply the glue and wait about five minutes before turning the work and gluing the opposite side.

With this technique the glue won't dry instantly, but if left for a few hours it will become as strong as a conventionally glued joint.

We tried this method with some other glues, including thin PVAs intended for fixing loose joints in chairs. The "Chair Doctor" produced a strong joint, but sealed the end grain enough that it showed when the joint was finished. The cyanoacrylate left no visible traces after the completed joint was trimmed with a block plane.

— *Robert W. Lang*

The final step is to trim the surfaces of the joint flush. Close cutting will mean little trimming.

A New Way to Rout Finger Joints on Large Pieces

When we began to plan this issue, the emphasis on finger joints was a given, but the specific techniques weren't. We knew we would feature the table saw and dado method for small parts, but we weren't comfortable milling larger pieces that way. Our first thought for large case pieces was to use a commercially made router jig. That is indeed a workable solution, and many well-made jigs are on the market.

But it didn't seem right to offer no other alternative than sending readers out to make an expensive purchase for a joint they will likely make only on an occasional basis.

Being of frugal stock, I decided there must be another way. The key to finger joints is equal sizes, and I realized that by making fingers and spacers from stock ripped at the same time, I should be able to put together a jig that would perform as well as anything available on the market. In less than an hour I had a working prototype of the jig we used.

Rip the Strips

We were after joints with $\frac{5}{8}$"-wide fingers and slots, so I began by ripping $\frac{1}{2}$"-thick Baltic-birch plywood to that dimension. The reason for using the plywood was to eliminate wood movement from the equation. I made a couple test cuts and measured the results with calipers to get as close as possible to the proper size.

Ripping carefully from a wide piece of plywood stock yielded enough material to cut the $5\frac{1}{2}$"-long fingers and the $2\frac{3}{4}$"-long spacers. After cutting these parts to length, I attached the parts to a $2\frac{3}{4}$"-wide, $\frac{3}{4}$"-thick plywood backing strip with yellow glue and 23-gauge

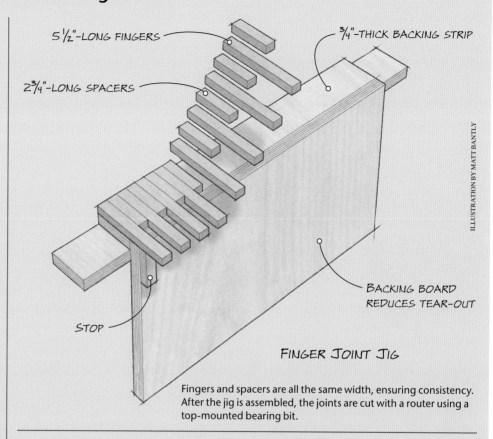

5 ½"-LONG FINGERS

2¾"-LONG SPACERS

¾"-THICK BACKING STRIP

BACKING BOARD REDUCES TEAR-OUT

STOP

FINGER JOINT JIG

Fingers and spacers are all the same width, ensuring consistency. After the jig is assembled, the joints are cut with a router using a top-mounted bearing bit.

ILLUSTRATION BY MATT BANTLY

pins. I laid a few beads of glue on the strip, started with a long piece, and made sure the first piece was squarely placed then butted the parts against one another one at a time and nailed them down. A longer $2\frac{3}{4}$"-wide piece was added below to stiffen the jig and provide a place for clamping the jig to the bench.

A larger piece of plywood was glued and screwed at a right angle to the backing strip. I placed the screws below the fingers so that I wouldn't cut into them with the router later on. This piece prevents the wood from tearing out on the back of the cuts, and provides a way to attach the work to the jig. One edge

Stop

The first workpiece is placed with the end tight against the bottom of the fingers, and the left end against the stop.

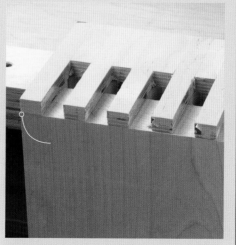

The second piece is placed over the first, with the left side flush against the outer edge of the first finger on the jig.

Dial calipers will help you zero in on the exact measurement you need.

of the backer piece is aligned with the edge of the first finger, and a small piece of scrap is attached to the edge to act as a stop.

Both panels of the joint are cut at once. The edge of one piece is placed against the stop with the show side out. The edge of the other is aligned with the opposite side of the first finger, offsetting the joint one finger's width.

Making the fingers of the jig the same size as the finished parts simplified construction and reduced the chances of making an error in calculating the difference between the diameter of a router bit and a template guide. A 1/2"-diameter flush-trimming bit with a bearing mounted above the cutter would trim the work exactly to the edges of the jig.

Or so I thought. The pieces from my first test cut went together too easily, leaving visible gaps at each joint. My quest for perfection was almost foiled by router and router-bit behavior. My measurements showed the bit and bearing to be the same diameter, and the width of the fingers and spacers to be equal. But the act of making the cuts produced slots a few thousandths of an inch wider than the fingers.

This wasn't entirely unexpected. To get a bit with a 1/2"-diameter cutter and bearing, I had to use one with a 1/4"-diameter shank. Even with a pretty good router and a quality bit, enough runout existed to increase the width of the slots by a few thousandths of an inch. This error was consistent, and rather than seek perfection where it didn't exist, I looked for an easy way to make an adjustment to the jig.

The fingers of the joints were undersized, so either the long fingers of the jig needed to be wider, or the spacers in between narrower. Either solution would mean taking the jig apart and starting over. The first step was to see how much change was needed, and answering that question led to a fast and simple solution.

I put blue masking tape on the sides of each finger. My guess was the thickness of the tape would move the router bit enough to obtain a good fit. My instincts were good, but the bearing on the router bit destroyed the tape while cutting the first test joint.

I headed down the street to the local hardware store in search of something thin, sticky and durable. The solution proved to be aluminum duct-sealing tape. This is not to be confused with common duct tape. Duct-sealing tape is much better.

This tape is a thin metal foil with a very sticky back. I cut small pieces off the roll with an X-Acto knife, peeled off the backing paper and placed a piece on the side of each finger. I pressed the handle of the knife over the tape to press it firmly in place. It held up well during routing, and the $9 roll of tape is likely a lifetime supply of an excellent shim material.

Using a router bit with a smaller diameter than the fingers is an advantage. As we experimented with different techniques, we found we achieved the best results by pushing the spinning bit straight in between the fingers to start each cut. This removed most of the waste without putting pressure on the fingers of the jig.

We then made two more passes, holding the bearing against each finger to make a light, clean cut. Both sides were cut by pushing the router into the jig instead of coming in on the left side and out on the right. This reduces tear-out that otherwise might occur as the router bit exits the work on the right-hand side of the slot. This may seem like extra work, but the final two cleanup passes take little time and produce cleaner edges.

With the large pieces of the blanket chest, it was easier to place the backing piece of the jig flat on the bench, clamp the work to the jig, then turn the jig and the work together to a vertical position before clamping the jig to the bench and routing the joints.

This was far easier than trying to hold the workpieces upright while aligning and clamping them to the jig. Fitting the end of the workpieces tight against the bottom of the fingers is critical to obtaining a good joint.

Ideally, the width of the work should be some multiple of the finger width. This leaves the joint with a whole finger or whole space at either side. The stop can be positioned to leave a partial finger at each end, as long as the second piece is offset by the width of a finger.

I considered buying some aluminum bar stock to make a permanent version of this jig – one that would last forever and be incredibly adjustable for any size of box or finger configuration. Luckily, I was talked out of that notion by a co-worker who pointed out that it was so fast and simple to put together this jig that it made more sense just to build a new iteration whenever the need occurred.

— RL

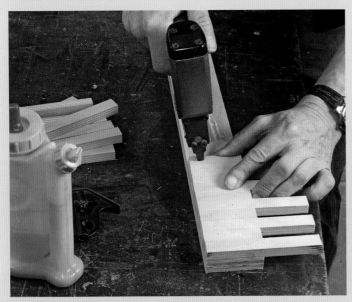

Assembly is simply a matter of gluing and nailing the fingers and spacers to a plywood strip. After making sure the first finger is square, butt one piece against another and nail in place.

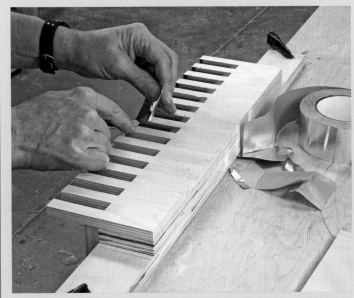

Aluminum duct-sealing tape closes the gap caused by router and bit runout, and holds up well in use.

Best Crackle Finish

Create an authentic crackle finish with a product that's straight from a home center. It's fast, cheap and easy.

Crackle finish on antique or nearly antique pieces is not something that happens overnight. It takes years to evolve. But, being part of an "instant gratification" age, we're asked to replicate a crackle finish in short time. But how?

In the past when adding a crackle finish to my work, I turned to an HVLP (high volume, low pressure) system and lacquer, but I also have a method of producing a crackle effect that involves hide glue. And, it's been suggested that other glue types will work as well. In addition, I found a crackle-finish product at a home center. Which products work and which don't?

I purchased a fresh bottle of liquid hide glue (hide glue ages, so look closely at the date on the bottle) and classic white glue. I almost always have yellow glue (aliphatic resin) in my shop and we had a small jug of American Traditions "Faux Weathered Crackle Glaze" already in the shop.

I had been told the crackle glaze did not work when previously called upon, but I decided to try it for myself. So one afternoon, prior to actually beginning with test pieces, I loaded the glaze onto a slab of poplar and waited for the layer to reach a stage that was dry enough to add paint, but not too dry.

When that stage was reached, I added a layer of flat, water-based paint. A crackling effect was not instant, but developed nonetheless. My outcome was obviously different from the earlier attempt. I figured that I must have the touch for producing a crackle finish.

With at least two viable products to produce a crackle finish not involving a sprayer, I ducked back into the shop to begin testing.

Why This Process Works

Because the glues and the glaze are water-based products, the crackling process works only when water-based paints are used. The glue is dry or nearly dry when the paint is added on top. Due to

Achieving a crackle effect for your painted furniture can be complicated if you make it that way. But in this case, simple is best. Hide glue, a paintbrush and water-based paint is all that's needed for a finish that appears aged – but is completed in less than a day.

the water in the paint, the glue surface is reactivated and stretched. The paint dries more rapidly than the glue or glaze, then as the glue and glaze dry, the paint layer is separated to form small, and sometimes not so small, cracks.

On to the Test

I began the testing by milling several pieces of poplar for painting. The plan of attack was to coat the #150-grit sanded surfaces with a layer of crackle medium, be it glue or crackle glaze, then apply a coat of paint on top to watch the crackle come to life.

First up was the crackle glaze. I knew this would work and I anticipated a good start. With the glaze in place and tacky, but not dry to the touch, I spread on a layer of paint. I waited. And waited. Nothing happened.

How strange to have great results with the first try and less-than-adequate results the next day. What changed?

I went back to look at the paint that was used in my coworker's unsuccessful effort. That paint was a semi-gloss. My perfect-result paint was dead flat, and the paint I selected for testing had a slight sheen. I had found the reason for the inconsistencies with the crackle glaze. This product works, but you need to keep a keen eye on your choice of paint. A flat sheen works best.

Glue Would Work

With one product shot down due to its specific sheen requirements, I moved on to glue – knowing that hide glue was sure to work. But how would the other more common types of glue perform? That's something to discover.

In order to brush out any of the glue products, I found it necessary to thin the adhesive; otherwise I had to smash the brush into the wood's surface. I added enough water to the glues to be able to spread them with a paintbrush. Look for a small amount of brush drag, but keep the thinning to a minimum. Too thin equates to no crackle.

I went to ordinary white glue straight away. If this grade-school favorite worked, then the effect would be a snap for just about any woodworker. White glue might be found in a closet or junk drawer somewhere in your home or workshop.

After the white glue was spread on the wood and allowed to reach a tacky state, I added a layer of flat paint, the one with a low sheen, then waited. This time there was a small amount of movement in the paint layer. Slowly, the crackle appeared. But it was nothing like what I wanted to achieve. I decided to move on.

The Last Two Glues

Aliphatic resin glue is a product most woodworking shops have at hand. I again thinned the glue with a small amount of water, brushed it onto the poplar board and allowed the adhesive to become tacky.

Next, I loaded my flat paint onto the glue and watched with anticipation for the cracks to come forward. This time the crackle was non-existent. I had a much better result using white glue. It's best to leave the yellow glue for woodshop uses – assembling panels and furniture joints.

I felt confident that liquid hide glue would give me the crackle finish results I wanted. I mixed water into the glue so I could brush it easily, then layered the mixture onto another board. When the coat became tacky, I slathered on the paint to await the results.

The action kicked in so quickly I barely had time to paint the entire board. The finished crackled surface was everything I was looking for – a clear-cut winner. And, hide glue produces a crackle finish with any water-based paint I've tried. That's easy to work with.

Fine-tuning the Crack

Here are a couple pointers I discovered along the way. To make crackle paint using hide glue an easy task, don't panic after you apply a glue layer to the project; the layer looks terrible, then levels as it becomes tacky. Also, for the best results, work on horizontal surfaces if possible. And, if you apply the paint to a glue layer that is especially wet, the crackle that comes about is extremely wide and not so pleasing to the eye.

Occasionally, it looks better to crackle small areas as opposed to an entire façade. If the majority of your painted area is at eye level, too much crackle can be overpowering. But the lower to the ground the painted area is, the less intense the crackled finish appears.

In addition, make sure to apply the paint layer with variations in film thickness to provide variations in the crackle lines. And while you're able to apply a glue layer with brush strokes going in all directions, you need to apply the paint in an orderly fashion. Brush only in one direction, horizontally or vertically.

However, the most important tip I can convey is to try the process on scrap pieces before loading it onto your project.

— *Glen D. Huey*

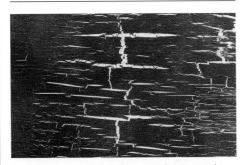

It's important to watch the type of paint used with store-purchased glazes. Flat paint worked with the glaze, but the crackle finish was a "no show" when the paint was glossier.

You'll find that thinning the glue products helps greatly when you brush on a layer. Look for a bit of drag on the brush as you work.

Ordinary white glue did show cracked lines, but if you compare this finish to that of the hide glue process, you'll notice a big difference in the design of the crackle.

Hide glue is "tried and true." Crackling a painted finish using hide glue is easy and the look is authentic.

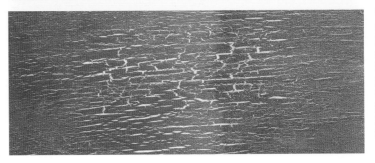

Variations in the thickness of the paint layer helps vary the design of the crackle finish. In the middle of this sample, the paint was on the thick side; around the perimeter of the block, you'll notice a finer, lighter effect.

A Simple Sea Chest

Whether you're a polished skipper or a certified landlubber, you'll find many reasons to build this canted-side sea chest.

I**f** you were a sailor who sailed deep waters prior to 1870, you packed your belongings into a sea chest. (Coastal sailors, those who returned to port often, used a sea bag.) Sea chests – banned by the United States Navy in 1870 due to the lack of space for each sailor to have his own chest – are simply six-board chests.

Designs range from straight-sided chests, to those that are canted or angled on the front, to examples with both the front and back canted.

Why are the sides angled? That was to help protect sailor's shins from knocking the lid as the ship rocked with the swells of the water.

While most sea chests feature dovetailed corners, we've simplified the construction of this example and maintained the design to build a chest with basic joinery.

Set Sail on the Project
To begin construction, mill the four case panels – both ends, the front and back – to size and thickness. With the two ends front and center, establish the chest's shin-saving angle. Mark a point along the top edge of the panel that's 2" in from each end. Next, use a straightedge to draw a line connecting those points with the nearest bottom-edge corner. Bingo: the angle is set.

Because this type of cut doesn't work well at the table saw, I think it's best to use an alternative method. Cut close to the line at your band saw

---

"We must free ourselves of the hope that the sea will ever rest. We must learn to sail in high winds."

— Aristotle Onassis (1906 - 1975)
shipping magnate

While the angled panels make this chest look difficult to build, the construction is actually quite simple. It's a great introduction to angled work for the beginning woodworker.

then finish the cut with a router and a pattern bit. Use the bottom edge of the opposite end panel for a simple straightedge.

The most important measurement you'll use in building this chest is that angle created on the end panels. Use a bevel gauge to find the angle.

Take the gauge to your table saw and tilt the blade to match the setting of the bevel gauge and remember that degree setting.

With the blade tilted, cut one edge of the previously squared front and back panels with the face side up. You just want to remove material to create the bevel, not much more. Next, move the fence closer to the blade, flip the face side down and cut the opposite edge of the panels. If you cut both panels at the same setting, you ensure the front and back panels match in width.

Both ends of the front and back panels receive rabbets on the interior face. Install a dado stack at its widest setting in the table saw, attach an auxiliary fence and bury some of the stack into the fence, but leave ¾" exposed. Set the blade

height to ½" then run the panels against the auxiliary fence to cut the four rabbets.

Fit, Trim and Nail
When the angle is cut on the edges of the front and back panels, the widths of the pieces diminish slightly. As a result, the ends need to be trimmed. Position one end to either the front or back panel then mark the amount needed to restore the match. Trim the ends at the table saw.

Assemble the box one end at a time. With the pieces aligned and in position, remove one end panel then add glue along the entire rabbet – the grain on all panels runs the same direction so there are no concerns with cross-grain construction. Replace the end panel on the box then add clamps as shown in the photo at right.

Tap the ends to make sure they seat into the glue and are tight to the other panels, then you're ready to nail the joint together. That's right, nail. Building a chest couldn't get much easier.

There is a secret to nailing this chest without

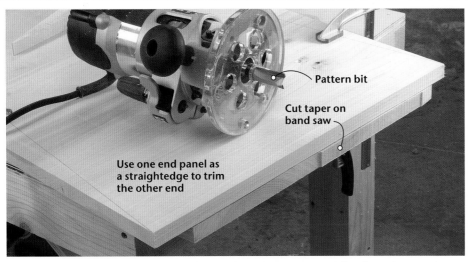

Use one end panel as a straightedge to trim the other end

Pattern bit

Cut taper on band saw

A router with a pattern bit is a perfect method of obtaining a square, straight edge – given you start with a straightedge as your pattern.

Transfer the angle of the canted front and back from the chest to the table saw with a bevel gauge. Set the angle dead-on to make the cuts accurate.

Drawing pencil lines along the board's edge allows you to sneak up on the cut without removing too much material. Due to the angle of the saw blade, you'll nibble the bottom of the edge and work your way to the top. When the pencil lines are gone, you're at the top edge.

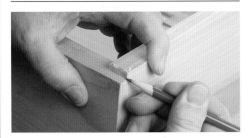

Look for ⅛" shrinkage once the front and back are trimmed to match the angle of the end pieces. The ends need to be trimmed to an exact match.

Thanks to the rabbeted corners, clamps positioned at the top and bottom hold the case square and are away from the corners to make nailing the corners a simple task.

incident. If you're using reproduction cut nails, it's necessary to align the widest part of the nail with the grain direction of the wood. That, along with drilling a proper-sized pilot hole, keeps the grain from splitting. Nail both corners of the first end, then repeat the steps for the second end.

Board Number Five

The fifth board of this six-board chest is the bottom. The bottom of the chest is actually a series of three boards affixed onto a rim that encompasses the entire box. Begin by milling the long rim pieces to size, then angle-cut their edges just as you did on the front and back panels – again the

angle measurements are important.

The long rim pieces are fit to the front and back on the interior of the chest, flush with the bottom edge. The end cuts are square and made with a miter saw. I used a thin bead of glue and nails to attach the rim.

Because the width of the long rim pieces change when cut, as did the panels, you also have to adjust the width of the short rim pieces. The short rim pieces run from side to side, between the installed long rims. Make the end cuts at a miter saw with the blade angled to the correct setting. The cut is across the end, not along the edge. Add glue, then nail the short rims to the chest.

A guaranteed way to split the grain of the front and back panels is to attempt to install a reproduction fine finish nail into your chest with the head of the nail positioned across the grain.

Mill the three pieces for the bottom to thickness. Then, at the table saw, create one angled edge with the blade once again set to match the bevel gauge.

The opposite edges of the two outside bottom boards receive rabbets. It's important to cut the rabbets on the top edge of the boards, or on the narrow face. The angled edge has to fit against the chest sides with the rabbeted edge showing as you peer into the chest.

Cut the outside bottom boards to length then position them inside the case. Push the pieces against the front and back of the chest then measure the distance between the two rabbeted edges. The distance measured is the width of the third board that completes the bottom.

Once that piece is sized at the table saw, create rabbets that match those on the outside boards. Cut the middle board to length then slip it into the chest. A couple screws at each end of the middle board keep the bottom in place – but it wouldn't hurt to add a fastener to the outside boards too.

Add a Little Lift

This chest is raised off the floor with four feet. One edge of the feet, the 4" edge, is cut at an angle to match the chest, while the edges facing the ends are square cut.

Mill the stock to size, then cut the matching angle at the table saw. Next, move to the miter saw and cut four pieces to the final size (3¼").

With the chest upside down on its top, position the feet so both show edges are flush with the chest. Drill countersinks into the feet, two into the front/back panels and one into the end panels.

To add a nice touch to an area of the chest that's seldom seen, clip the interior corner of the feet. Position the foot to the chest, mark the foot at the inside edge of the rim pieces then use a miter saw to cut between those two points.

Add a thin bead of glue to the foot, orient the foot to the chest and attach the two using #8 x 1¼" wood screws.

Last But Not Least

The base of the chest is finished in paint, but I chose to stain the lid, battens and cleats. Mill the

Supplies

Lee Valley Tools
800-871-8158 or leevalley.com
2 ■ unequal strap hinges,
  #01H20.12, $8.40 each

Horton Brasses, Inc.
800-754-9127 or horton-brasses.com
1 ■ pkg. fine furniture nails, N-20,
$4.00/¼ lb.

Prices correct at time of publication.

The outer bottom pieces cannot lift up due to the angle of the chest. To keep the opposite edge in position make sure the rabbets are cut into the face of the bottom pieces and get the center board rabbeted to fit.

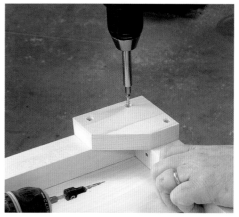

Add feet to the base of the chest to raise the bottom off a floor (or a ship's deck). These feet are cut to the appropriate angle to match the slope of the front and rear faces.

material necessary for the stained parts, then size the lid according to the cut sheet.

Work begins at a router table. The edge profile is not a true roundover, but it is made with a ½" roundover router bit. Adjust the bit height so only the upper portion is being used (see photo at right.) Shape the ends first then the front edge. Flip the panel and repeat on the opposite face to finish the complete profile. The rear edge of the top panels is left square.

Battens, found on most sea chests, are a snap to create. Cut the stock to size then lay out the cut lines. Mark the halfway point on both ends of each batten (¾"), move in along the bottom edge and place a mark at 2½". Connect those points. Cut close to the lines with a band saw then smooth to the lines with a sander.

The battens are screwed to the lid. Make sure your screws hold firm, but be careful – if you drive the screw too far, the face of the lid is damaged.

Use a drill press to countersink three ⅝" holes (one centered along the length and one 1¼" in from each end). Set your depth stop at ¾" off the drill press table – leaving the material that thickness works perfectly for #12 x 1¼" pan head screws. Once the countersink is drilled, continue through the batten with a ¼" drill bit.

Position the battens just inside the moulded edge, ¼" from the outside edge of the chest. Add a bead of glue along the front 4" and use clamps to hold the pieces firm. Drill a small pilot hole prior to installing the screws, cinching them tight.

The ¼" hole is a larger diameter than the screw, which affords a small amount of compensation for wood movement while the glue at the front forces movement toward the rear of the top.

Strap hinges used for chests are most often crooked to fit inside the chest back and under the lid. The hinges selected for this chest require some simple bends to fit that profile. These bends can be easily accomplished with a vise and ham-

Nowhere is it written you have to use the entire router bit. Use only a portion of the roundover router bit to create the edge profile for the chest.

mer. Install the hinges but remove them prior to finishing the chest.

Get a Handle on It

Handles on many antique sea chests are considered works of art. The cleat is only part of the story for top-quality chests. A second important aspect is the rope pulls or "beckets." Many beckets are extremely fancy. This chest is basic and the beckets are grommet style – rope tied through holes in the cleat.

The cleats, one on each side of the chest, begin as pieces that are as thick as can be garnered from rough 4/4 stock, or ⅞" at minimum. Arcs cut at the ends of each cleat are decorative. To match the look on this chest, remove ¾" of the width and 1½" along the length at each end. Make the cut at a band saw then smooth the area with a spindle sander.

The beckets are attached through two holes drilled into each cleat. Draw a line across each cleat that's centered from top to bottom, then equally space and drill two ⁵⁄₁₆" holes along that

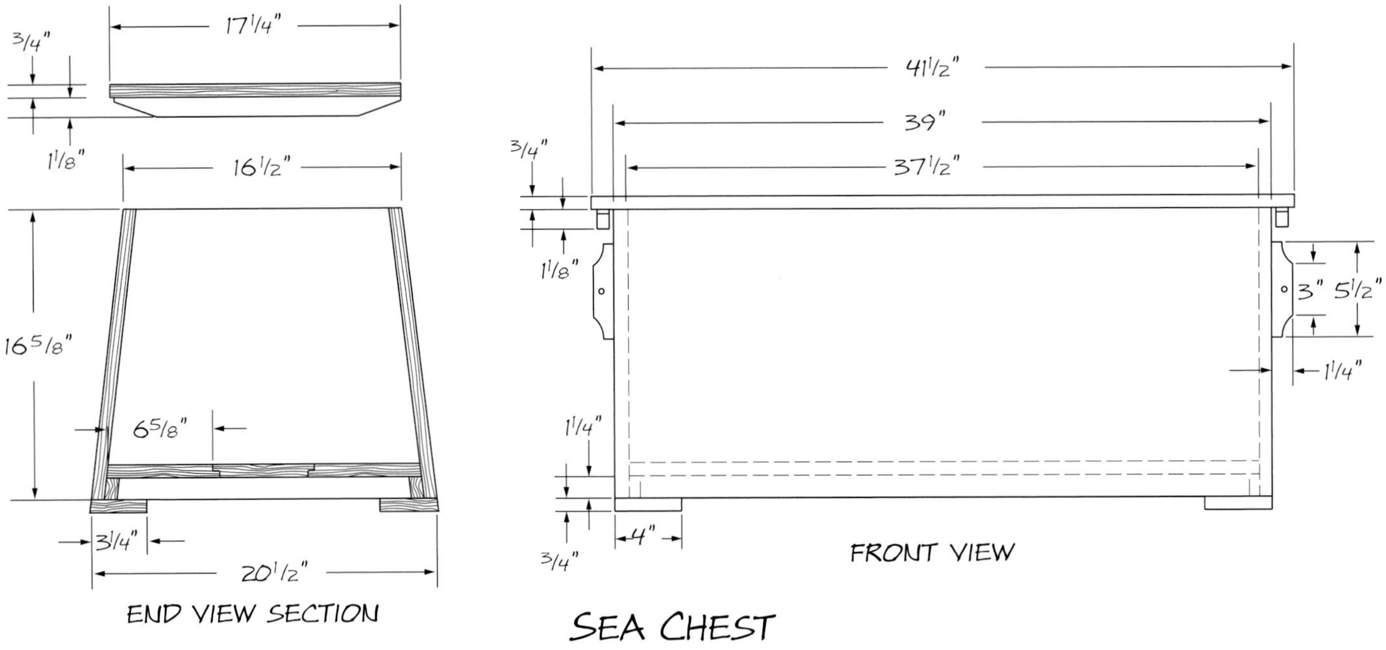

ILLUSTRATIONS BY ROBERT W. LANG

line. Slightly oversized holes allow easy installation of the ¼" rope.

The cleats are attached with two screws through the interior of the chest. Position the cleats prior to any finishing steps, then drill and countersink holes for the screws. Install the cleats, but remove them prior to finishing the chest. Note which side of the chest each cleat fits so installation after finishing is less frustrating.

When the chest is completely finished and the cleats are once again installed, on goes the rope or beckets. Start with a 27" piece of rope, tie one end in a figure-eight knot then slide the opposite end into the rear hole of the cleat. Loop the piece through the front hole to form a handle, and tie a second knot to secure the handle near the end. Each pull of the beckets squeezes the knots tighter.

About the Finish

Sand the entire project with #150-grit sandpaper and prepare to paint and stain. The finish on this sea chest base is a painted crackle finish. (Learn how to "Crackle Finish" on page 79 in this issue.) The crackle effect adds age to any project as well as an interesting look. A few products available at most home-center stores are all you'll need.

The stain finish is a coat of Olympic Interior "Special Walnut" oil-based stain with a layer of Watco "Dark Walnut" Danish oil, topped with a layer of shellac. For further explanation of this finish, see "Authentic Arts & Crafts Finish," *Woodworking Magazine* Spring 2007, Issue 7.

— *Glen D. Huey*

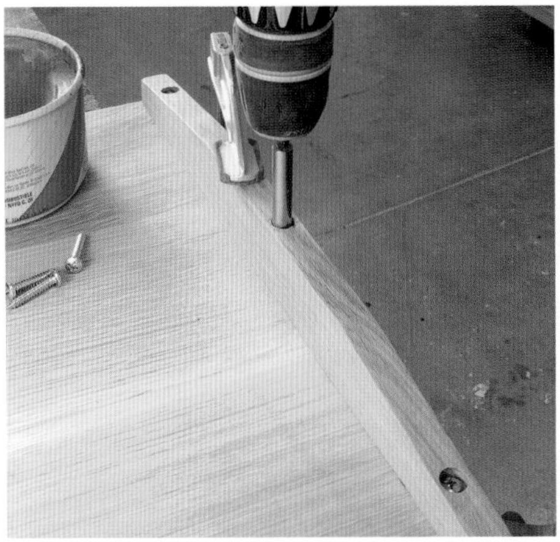

Seasonal-adjustment stress is relieved by mounting the battens with pan head screws through slightly oversized holes. Drill a pilot hole then add wax to the screw to reduce chances of splitting the lid.

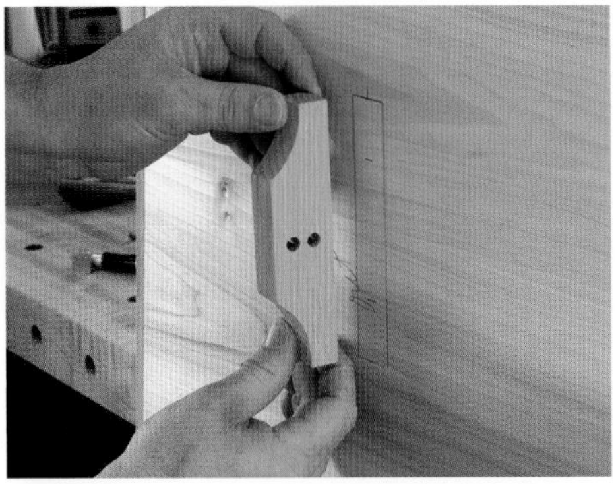

Position the cleat to the case sides, mark for screws then drill small pilot holes from the outside in. This establishes a precise interior location for countersink holes.

Sea Chest

	NO.	PART	SIZES (INCHES) T	W	L	MATERIAL
❑	2	Front/ back panels	¾	16¾†	39	Poplar
❑	2	End panels	¾	16¾†	20	Poplar
❑	1	Lid	¾	17¼	41½	QSWO*
❑	2	Battens	¾	1⅛	17	QSWO*
❑	2	Long rims	¾	1¼†	38†	Poplar
❑	2	Short rims	¾	1¼†	18†	Poplar
❑	4	Feet	¾	3¼	4	Poplar
❑	2	Outer bottom	¾	7	37½	Poplar
❑	1	Center bottom	¾	5¼†	37½	Poplar
❑	2	Cleats	⅞	1½	5½	QSWO*

* Quartersawn white oak; † Trim to fit

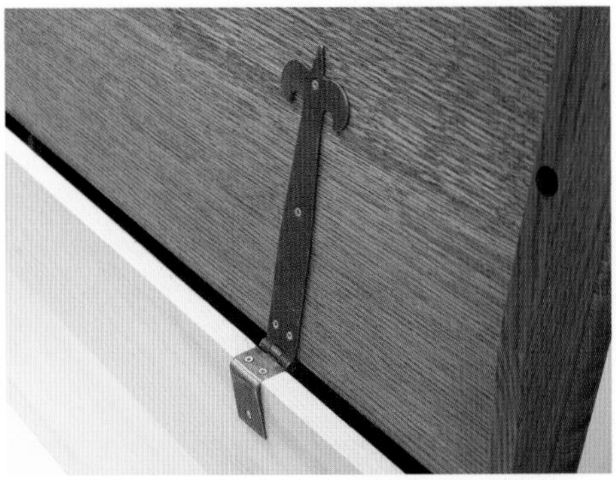

The softer metal of the strap hinges affords an opportunity to bend the hinge to a "proper" design for trunks and chest. Matching screws to the hardware improves the aesthetics of the project.

TABLES

American Trestle Table

One of the oldest designs for a dining table is also one of the most highly engineered and contemporary. But will its unusual dimensions work in a modern home?

Traditional trestle tables have a bit of an austere reputation. They show up in Gothic churches, prim pilgrim homes and in severe, stripped-down Shaker meeting halls. They are a form of furniture that has been boiled down to its bare bones – take any one part away, and a trestle table will surely collapse.

Once you build one, you will also realize that they are an engineering marvel and a clear precursor to the invention that built our skyscraper cities: the I-beam. Still, despite their spare charm and long history, there are some things about the dimensions of trestle tables that don't conform to our typical expectations for tables.

For starters, they are shockingly narrow. Most furniture-design books insist that the top of any dining table should be 36" to 42" wide – and 48" wide isn't out of the question. But when you look at the historical record, the widths of trestle tables are, quite literally, in your face. One of my favorite early 17th-century trestle tables in Millis, Mass., is a slim 25" wide. By comparison, Shaker trestle tables seem positively luxurious with 27" and 31¼" widths.

And the trestle form frequently looks quite fragile, which seems at odds with the fact that these tables are typically the centerpiece of a casual dining area. They show up in taverns, meeting halls and other communal dining rooms, and the surviving examples exhibit the marks and scars of heavy use.

For many years, I've wanted to build a trestle table to replace the store-bought, white-pine apron table my wife and I got after college. The pine apron table was a testament to everything I disliked about commercial furniture: The top was

Trestle tables are comfortable in any style home, from early American to Bauhaus. And like the timeless styling, the engineering is a remarkable combination of old world and new. The wedged through-tenons are as old as ancient Egyptian furniture, and the resulting form is much like a modern I-beam.

To speed the acclimation of your lumber to its environment, cut it to close width and length. Stack the pieces to allow airflow through the wood, and check its progress with a moisture meter.

Begin your joinery by marking out the location of the mortises in the feet. Clamp all four boards together and mark the joinery simultaneously to reduce measuring errors.

Before face-gluing boards together, I dress the mating surfaces with a jointer plane. A few swipes remove imperfections left from the planer. At the end of each stroke, you want to reduce pressure on the toe of the plane to make the surface truly flat. Here I'm removing my right hand from the tool during the stroke to illustrate the point.

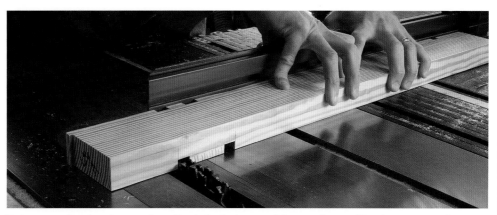

To keep your hands as far away from the dado stack as possible, use a fence with a stop on your miter gauge to set your cut. Your setup does not have to be fancy: The fence can be a piece of plywood screwed to your miter gauge. The stop can be a scrap of wood clamped to the fence.

pieced together using narrow, knotty and poorly matched boards. (A monkey could have done a better job of planning the tabletop.) The legs had bulbous turnings that were sloppily sanded. And the hardware that joined the legs to the aprons had to be snugged up regularly.

But if I hated our dining table, then I was equally afraid of the trestle table I wanted to build, which looked narrow, tippy and ready to collapse, so I put it off for 15 years. But during a recent day trip to the Shaker Village at Pleasant Hill, Ky., I sat at the tables there. They were indeed narrow, but that made them more intimate for conversation. They were lightweight, which allowed them to be moved with ease. And after 150 years of use, they were still rock-solid.

I left Pleasant Hill that evening during a spectacular thunderstorm, but the fireworks over Harrodsburg, Ky., didn't catch my eye. I was too wrapped up in working out the details of my table in my head.

An Economy of Materials

After a few hours of CAD work on my laptop, I had another small revelation: These tables require remarkably little material. For the prototype, I had planned on using Southern yellow pine for the base. For the tabletop, I had set aside two flitch-cut cherry boards from a local farm that were each about 18" wide, if you measured the bark. I had purchased these cherry boards green for about $90 and had been drying them in my shop – I thought they were quite the bargain. But when I made my shopping list for the base, I was pleased to discover that the base required only three 10'-long 2 x 12s – about $37 of yellow pine.

There is a definite downside to using yellow pine – it can be wet. And a check with a moisture meter pointed out the problems in this pine. Fully acclimated yellow pine usually reads about 9 percent moisture content (MC) in our shop. This stuff ranged from 12 percent to 16 percent MC.

So I began by marking out all my parts and ripping and crosscutting them to rough size – about 1" longer and ½" wider than their finished dimensions. If your wood is fairly straight, this is a safe operation for the table saw. If your wood is quite twisted, plan B should be a band saw or handsaw. Cutting up the 2 x 12s wet does two things: First, it speeds their drying by exposing end grain – most of the moisture enters and leaves wood through the end grain. Second, it helps squeeze the maximum thickness out of the parts – bows, cups and crooks are minimized by

cutting a larger board into smaller pieces.

After a week of waiting, the boards were all within a couple points of equilibrium and construction could begin. The first step was to mill all the yellow pine to 1¼" thick using a jointer and planer. The joinery in surviving trestle tables is remarkably robust: usually wedged or pegged through-tenons. And so I followed suit.

Each end of a trestle table has a foot, leg and brace. And these end assemblies are joined by a long stretcher. In this table, the leg and foot are joined by a wedged and pegged through-tenon. The brace and leg are joined by a bridle joint. And the two end assemblies attach to the stretcher with a big pegged and wedged through-tenon.

The feet, legs and braces are each made up of two pieces of pine that have been face-glued together to create 2½"-thick pieces. To ease con-

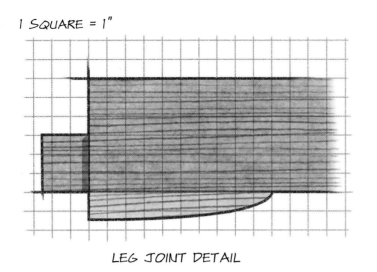

1 SQUARE = 1"

LEG JOINT DETAIL

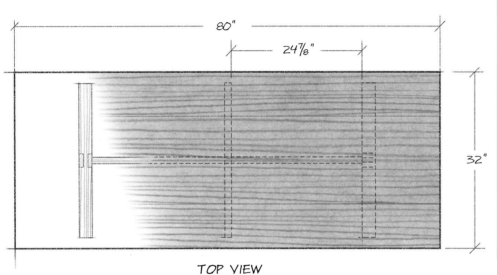

80"

24⅞"

32"

TOP VIEW

struction, I milled the mortises in the feet and legs before face-gluing these components together. This technique allows you to mill the mortises with a saw (such as a table saw, band saw or handsaw) instead of a boring machine, and it results in more accurate joinery.

Mortises With a Saw

The mortise in each foot measures 1¼" thick, 2" wide and 3" deep. So each foot piece requires a notch that is ⅝" x 2" x 3". The mortise in each leg is ¾" x 3" x 2½", so each leg piece requires a notch that is ⅜" x 3" x 2½". With the joinery marked, cut your notches. I used a dado stack in my table saw, which is only one of the many options available. I've also done this step with a band saw or a handsaw plus a coping saw. Let your tools be your guide.

To assemble the legs, feet and braces, apply an even coat of glue to one part and place its mate in position. If your joint is good, it should take only three or four clamps to snug everything up. The glue will allow your parts to slip around as you apply pressure. Do your best to keep the notches lined up for the mortises, though small misalignments (as much as ¹⁄₁₆") can be remedied by wedging during assembly (wedging atones for a variety of sins).

Allow the glue to dry. If you use yellow pine, keep the assemblies in the clamps for five hours. (This was the advice of the technical specialist at Franklin International, which makes Titebond.) Yellow pine's resin can resist the glue's absorption. Once the assemblies are liberated from their clamps, you need to square them up and even out any misalignments in the parts. A jointer plane can do this, as can light passes with your powered

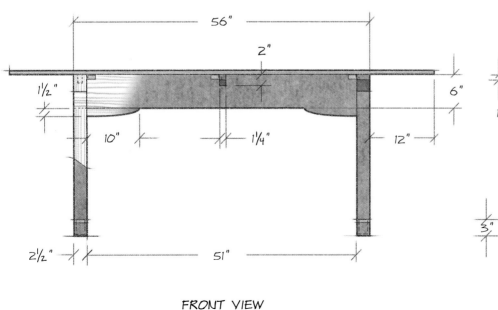

56"

2"

1½"

6"

10"

1¼"

12"

2½"

51"

FRONT VIEW

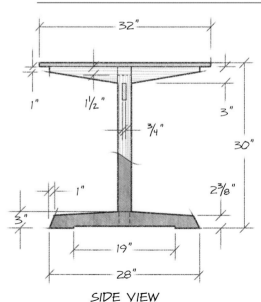

32"

1"

1½"

¾"

3"

30"

1"

3"

2⅜"

19"

28"

SIDE VIEW

AMERICAN TRESTLE TABLE

After the joinery is cut, match up the pairs again. Note the cabinetmaker's triangles I've scribed on each piece. These triangles, which I mark on every assembly, help keep like parts together and pointing in the right direction. They remain on the work until the very end.

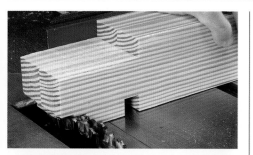

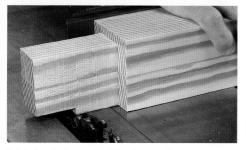

With the dado stack still in the saw from cutting the notches, it was the logical choice to form the tenon. The same rules apply: Use a fence and a stop to achieve accurate results safely.

To fit the tenons to the mortises in the feet, use a rabbet plane, shoulder plane, rasp or chisel. I used a rabbeting block plane, which is ideal for long tenons such as these.

Four clamps were more than enough to glue each leg. During these glue-ups, I wipe off the oozing glue with a damp rag so I can see what the joint line looks like. Just because you have squeeze-out does not mean your joint is closed tight.

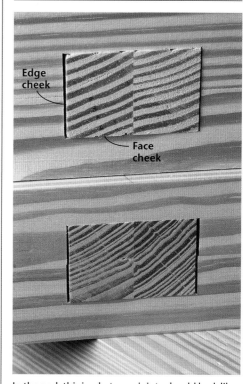

In the end, this is what your joints should look like: The face cheeks of the tenons are tight against the mortise walls; the edge cheeks have a little slop for wedging.

American Trestle Table

NO.	PART	SIZES (INCHES)			MATERIAL	NOTES
		T	W	L		
❑ 1	Top	3/4	32	80	Cherry	
❑ 2	Feet	2 1/2	3	28	Pine	
❑ 2	End braces	2 1/2	3	28	Pine	
❑ 1	Mid-brace	1 1/4	2	28	Pine	
❑ 2	Legs	2 1/2	2 1/2	29 1/4*	Pine	1 1/4" x 2" x 3" tenon, one end
❑ 1	Stretcher	1 1/4	6	56 1/4*	Pine	3/4" x 3" x 2 5/8" tenon, both ends
❑ 2	Corbels	1 1/4	1 1/2	10	Pine	

* includes extra length for trimming

The band saw makes simple work of the notch in the top of the leg. Define the straight walls of the joint, then cut diagonally to remove the waste between. Nibble the waste at the bottom of the joint up to your layout line.

jointer and planer. (I like to use the jointer plane because it leaves a nicer surface; but then, I really like using jointer planes.)

Now you can cut the tenon on the end of each leg that will join it to the foot. This is a big tenon – 1¼" x 2" x 3". You can cut this using the same tool you used to make the notches: a dado stack in your table saw, a band saw or a handsaw. In the end, you want it to fit snugly where the tenon's face cheeks meet the mortise walls. The tenon's edge cheeks can be gappy. Wedges will tighten everything up; so focus on the face cheeks.

A Puzzle Joint at the Top

The point at which the leg joins the brace is a bit of work. There's a lot going on at this three-way intersection. Not only do you have the leg and brace coming together, but you also have to get the stretcher in there and keep all the joints balanced and strong. You could cheat and lower the

location of the table's stretcher near the floor. But this will weaken the overall strength of the table. Placing the stretcher flush against the tabletop supports your top and tightens up the entire table by giving you that I-beam construction.

So in the end, it's worth the extra fuss.

To join the brace and leg, I chose a bridle joint secured with a peg. The female part of this joint is a 1" x 2½" x 1½" notch that's centered in the top of the leg. The male part of the bridle joint consists of two complementary notches on the sides of the brace and one big notch on the bottom of the brace.

Begin cutting the joint by making the notch in the top of the leg. The band saw is the logical machine for this operation; stay away from the dado stack for this one – you would have to stand the leg on end during the cut, which is quite a dangerous thing to do.

The notches on the brace can be cut on either the band saw, table saw or by hand. I've done it all three ways in building the prototype and finished example of this table. The table saw is more accurate, though you have to raise the dado stack up pretty high to make that notch on the bottom

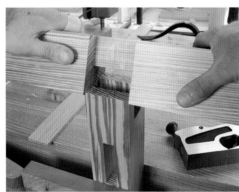

Measuring might mess you up here. Instead, lay out this joint by first striking centerlines on the leg and the brace. Line up the parts using a try square and mark the location of the joint on the brace. When the joint is complete, the leg and brace will nest together, with the tough end grain on the brace against the edge grain of the leg (to resist racking). Plus there's a fair amount of face grain in the joint to help gluing.

Note how I'm steering the cut from the far end of the leg. This actually improves control and makes your cut smoother. Guiding the work up by the blade results in a choppy cut.

The long sole of the jointer plane allows it to true both individual boards and assemblies, such as a door or the ends of this table. Don't be afraid to work across the grain with this tool; a power sander or smoothing plane will clean up the work later.

This looks like hot-dogging, but it's not. The work is under control at all times and it's easy to keep your digits away from the knives. It's far safer than some tapering jigs I've seen on the table saw.

The Veritas Chamfer Guide on my Veritas block plane is one of my handiest tools. In fact, I rarely take the guide off the plane. It cuts nice and even chamfers up to $\frac{1}{2}$" x $\frac{1}{2}$". When you reach the desired chamfer, the plane simply stops cutting to let you know you're done. Brilliant.

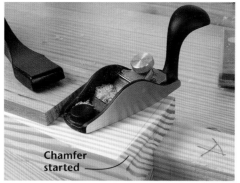

Chamfer started

The chamfers on the brace are short and simple. Lay them out, then work from both ends to the middle, which will eliminate blowing out your grain. Takes but a minute.

A few good taps on a chisel will open up the mortise's exit point. You also can use this opportunity to square up any misalignments when you glued up the two blanks to make the feet.

A Japanese flush-cutting saw is a marvel at cleaning up these wedged joints. Use light sawing pressure and work around all sides of the joint to keep the saw cutting true.

of the brace. The band saw and handsaw options are much safer, though they require more hand skill to execute. In the end, I recommend the band saw or handsaw.

When you dry-fit all these joints together, don't be dismayed if the assembly seems twisted. There is a lot of joinery surfaces coming together in this assembly. Here's how I deal with the problem: a jointer plane. (Do you sense a pattern?) Dry fit all the parts and then level the joints and remove twist in the assembly by working across the joints with your jointer plane.

With your joints flush and your assemblies flat, take everything apart and add the details of this table that will transform the ends from a simple "H" into something interesting to look at. The first order of business is to cut tapers on the feet and brace. First crosscut the ends of the feet and braces at 23° using a miter saw. Now lay out the tapers using the construction drawing as a guide. You could rig up a tapering jig to make these cuts using your table saw, but it is far simpler to use a band saw and then clean up the cut on your power jointer (or use a jointer plane).

This also is the time to cut the relief on the bottom of each foot. This is easily accomplished on the band saw. The $\frac{3}{8}$" x 19" relief cut creates two pad feet on each foot. After making your cut on the band saw, a little work with a chisel and block plane tidies things up.

Once your tapers are complete, the remaining details are optional. On the prototype trestle table (which is now in my dining room), I moved straight to assembly from here. With the version shown here, I decided to add a few chamfers to dress up the design and add shadow lines, which will appear more graphic with a coat of paint.

The chamfers on the legs are $\frac{3}{16}$" x $\frac{3}{16}$". You can lay them out and cut them in any way you please: router table, table saw or (my favorite) the chamfer plane. I also cut matching chamfers on the brace where the leg and brace meet.

Kerfs and Wedges Work Together

Wedging a mortise-and-tenon joint locks it permanently together (if that's your desire). For this table, I decided to cut two kerfs in the tenon and wedge each one. The kerfs are located $\frac{1}{4}$" in from the edge cheeks of the tenon and run about three-quarters of the way down to the tenon's shoulders. Choose a saw based on how much of a gap you need to wedge. A full-size handsaw is best if you have a tight fit. A dovetail saw is best if your fit is sloppy.

Now you need to make some wedges. Look for stock that can take a beating without splitting. Ebony would be a terrible choice. Try white oak or hickory or even ash. We had some jatoba in our offcut pile that was the perfect thickness for this job. I took some small blocks of the stuff and beat it with a hammer to see if it split easily. It resisted my hammer, so I used it for the wedges.

I make my wedges with an 8° taper. It's a simple thing to do with a little sled I built that has the fence cocked 4° (see the story on wedges on page 100 for more details). This method is fast, so make lots of extra wedges: some with fine points, others with blunt ones.

A wedged joint is far more effective if the mortise has a slight trumpet shape. The wedges will spread the tenon at the wider opening, locking the joint permanently. I create this trumpet shape by simply chiseling away a little (say $\frac{1}{16}$" to $\frac{1}{8}$") from the two ends of the mortise where the tenon exits. You don't need to be precise about it; just make the mortise wider where the wedges go.

Assemble the Ends

After all this work, assembly is fast and simple. I chose to drawbore both the bridle joint and the mortise-and-tenon joint. Drawboring is a pegging technique we covered in detail in the Autumn 2005 issue. If you don't wish to drawbore the joint, simple $\frac{3}{8}$"-diameter pegs will do. However, if you are going to drawbore the joint, you should drawbore the tenon first and then wedge it – not the other way around.

To assemble, paint glue in the mortise and the notch in the top of the leg. Add your wedges and pegs to the joints. If you want some extra insurance, add a couple clamps across the foot and brace to snug things up. When the glue is dry, cut your pegs and wedges flush.

A Solid Stretcher

The long stretcher between the end assemblies is what will keep this table from racking along its length, so this joint needs to be carefully fit. The stretcher's length adds some extra challenge to the process. At almost 5' long, it's too lengthy to wrestle over the table saw (without special equipment). For the prototype table, I used a tenon saw, but because the joint and stretcher are both huge, securing the work and sawing to the line was a challenge. I tried a couple other techniques that combined hand and power tools, but in the end, the best solution was to use a router with a straight bit, followed by a handsaw.

The trick is to define the shoulder of the joint accurately with the help of a fence clamped to your work. I wouldn't recommend trying this with a router that has a round base plate – a flat area on the base is more accurate. (If your router has a round base, temporarily replace the round plastic sub-base with a square piece of ¼" plywood.)

A piece of fall-off is ideal material for the fence for this cut. I marked out the joint with a knife all around the stretcher and then positioned the fence carefully to cut right up to the knife line.

With the routing complete on this face cheek, this is what you should have. The unrouted area will be cut away with a handsaw in the next step.

Set the bit's depth to ¼" and cut the shoulder. Now waste away the 3" x 2⅝" area that will become the tenon. Don't waste away the area that will be later removed with a handsaw at the top of the stretcher – you need this material to support the base of the router.

Repeat this operation on the opposite face of the stretcher, and then on the other end. Remove the bulk of the remaining waste with a handsaw. I actually found this easiest to do with the stretcher laid on low sawhorses and one knee holding it in place while I sawed. Then clean up the shoulder with a block plane and chisel and begin to fit the tenon in its mortise.

Now shape the corbel and glue it to the bottom edge of the stretcher. If you are not going to paint your base, be sure to carefully match the grain so the corbel and stretcher look like they are one piece.

Adding the corbels to the stretcher greatly simplifies cutting the detail and fitting the tenon. I got this idea from a Shaker example.

One More Brace – and Buttons

A table this size requires one more brace in the stretcher to support the top. For the prototype table (which had an 8'-long top), two mid-braces were necessary. The smaller braces are simple to cut and fit. I attached the mid-brace using a bridle joint. First saw a 1" x 1¼" notch in the stretcher and the mid-brace. Fit them using a chisel. Secure the mid-brace with glue and a dowel.

Now you can assemble the entire base using the same routine you used to join the feet to the legs. Saw two kerfs in the tenons on the stretcher. Make wedges. Peg and wedge the joint.

With the base assembled, there are likely going to be some parts that aren't perfectly aligned. You want the top surfaces of the base to be in the same plane, though that's a challenge to achieve during glue-up. The top edge of my stretcher was a bit proud, so I knocked it down using a jointer plane.

The tabletop is secured to its base using wooden buttons. Each button has a ¼"-thick x 1"-long tongue that fits into a matching notch in the base. Then the buttons are screwed to the underside of the top. Making the buttons is easy: I took some wide ¾"-thick scrap and milled a rabbet on the end. Then I ripped the buttons free from the scrap board.

To make the notches in the base, I used a biscuit joiner. The blade of a biscuit joiner is ⅛" thick, so two overlapping cuts gave me the ¼" groove I needed. If you don't have a biscuit joiner, you can secure the top with screws. Drill clearance holes through the braces and ream them out to allow the top to expand and contract.

The base is now complete and you can turn your attention to the top. For the project shown on the cover, I asked Senior Editor Robert Lang to make the top because he was writing the story on splines on page 94. For details, see his story titled "A Proper Top for the American Trestle Table" at right.

Note that there is no shoulder on the bottom of the stretcher's tenon. The bottom shoulder will be created by gluing on the corbels in the next step. As you clean up the top part of the shoulder, use a square to ensure you are removing all the bumps that could interfere with a solid fit.

Again, this isn't a show surface, so you don't need to worry about planing across the grain; just get everything flush and in the same plane. I secured my table base against my sawbench for this operation.

For the prototype, I made the top using the air-dried cherry boards I mentioned at the beginning of the article. They had to be dressed by hand because they were too wide for the machinery. The challenge of such a top is an article unto itself. Robert's approach to the top is simpler, looks great and is easily executed.

Notes on Finishing (and Feasting)

The base is painted a traditional Shaker green. It might look brighter than what you expect from Shaker furniture, but it's likely dead-on. John T. Kirk, the author of "Shaker World" (Harry N. Abrams), created this green by mixing it according to the Shaker's recipes. The other hues, particularly the red and yellow, were also bright to our eyes. We usually expect muted tones from the Shakers, but those somber colors are probably the result of fading and patina from age.

To get this color, we let our local Sherwin-Williams do the matching work. They came up with a color they call "Shade-Grown" (SW 6188). For details on applying a painted finish, see "How to Paint Furniture Like a Professional" on page 30.

With the table complete, it's a remarkable bit of engineering. I cringe (and then marvel) at how my 5-year-old gymnast can vault herself off its edge while the whole thing stays rooted. It is so lightweight that I can lift the end of the 8'-long prototype with two fingers to vacuum up bits of macaroni and cheese.

And then there's the width. The table here is 32". I made the first version at 28". I like the narrow width; eating and entertaining is a far more intimate affair because of it. There's plenty of room for the place settings, but the narrow width brings an unexpected, welcome closeness.

This is a good thing for both of my families. The table at home knits us tighter together at dinnertime. The version shown here, which now graces our magazine's office, keeps the editors close at hand as we plan the next issue.

— *Christopher Schwarz*

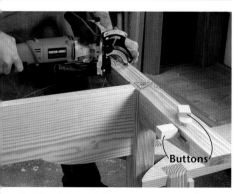

Set the biscuit joiner's fence so that there's ½" between the fence and blade. Make all the cuts in the table base on your braces and mid-brace. Then set the fence so there's ⅝" between the fence and blade and repeat all your cuts.

A Proper Top for the American Trestle Table

One of the things that never fails to impress me about old furniture is the beautiful wide planks that were available. One hundred fifty years ago, a tabletop of this size could have been made from one or two wide planks. The disappearance of old-growth wood has forced us to make tops from narrower pieces, and along the way we've adopted methods based on theories that sound good, but don't always make sense when examined closely.

Old woodworking textbooks barely touch on gluing two boards together edge to edge to make a panel or tabletop. If you had wide enough boards available, why would you want to? None of the methods commonly suggested today, such as ripping wide boards into narrow strips or alternating the direction of growth rings in every other board, are ever discussed. However, these methods appear so often today (passed on by many shop class teachers) that many woodworkers have adopted them as rules. The trouble with them is that if you are working with properly dried wood at equilibrium with its environment you are only making more work for yourself in order to make a top that is less stable and far less attractive than one made from as few pieces as possible.

The most attractive top is a single, wide board. The next best thing is one made from a few wide pieces with the grain and color matched so that it is as close as possible in appearance to the ideal. Any method that puts the appearance of the finished top last is artless. Get your hands on the widest stock you can, let it equalize to the environment of your shop, and get the edges straight and the faces flat. Match the grain on adjacent pieces so that the top looks good and don't worry about anything else.

I spent almost as much time selecting and arranging the boards for this top, as I did in milling, assembling and finishing them. To get the five boards in this finished top, I rooted through a stack of about 50, initially selecting about 20 of the widest, straightest pieces. I lined those up to compare the grain and color and rejected another eight boards before I began milling the remaining dozen. Four more boards either revealed some ugliness, twisted during jointing, or were too warped to mill flat.

My normal procedure is to edge glue boards together using only butt joints. My first attempts at this were more difficult and frustrating than what I am able to do today. Along the way, I've learned to prepare stock that is straight and flat, and acquired equipment to make that process relatively easy. I've learned what can go wrong, and ways to prevent or repair that. If I were starting over, I might take

Even though a single board wouldn't have a repeating pattern of cathedral arches and straight grain, careful attention to matching similar patterns on the edges of individual boards results in an attractive top.

a different approach, and incorporate an aid to align the parts like the splines discussed on page 94.

Matching the grain for an attractive top is more art than science, but it's vitally important, and there are some techniques to make the process easier. One of the secrets I've already divulged – pick through as much lumber as you possibly can to get the boards that belong in the top. Often you will find boards from the same tree, and these will give you the best opportunity of getting a good match.

I look for similar grain patterns, and most of the time flat- or plain-sawn stock will have a cathedral pattern in the middle of the board, with straighter grain along the edges. As I mill the boards and get them to finished width, I try to keep the arches centered, and match the straight grain to straight grain. If the straight grain isn't present on the edges, match one cathedral to another or try to get it to blend with the straight grain on the next board for the most attractive look.

Leaving the pieces long until after the top is glued together allows you to slide them back and forth until the best match is achieved. Some woodworkers will look at the grain direction on the edges while matching so that final smooth planing will be less likely to result in tear-out. I don't bother with this, although sometimes I wish I had. I don't want to be distracted from getting an attractive top, and I think one of the best challenges in woodworking is getting to really know the material and finding an effective way to deal with the tricky spots. Keeping the edges aligned during glue-up minimizes the amount of planing to be done afterwards and with a sharp plane iron there will be a magic angle at which to plane. The challenge is in discovering it.

— *Robert Lang*

Understanding Splines

Edge joints don't need to be reinforced to make them stronger, but the addition of thin strips in the joints serves a more important purpose.

The hard part of making a solid-wood top isn't making it strong enough, or orienting the boards in the right direction, or having the proper mojo to keep it from warping later on. The hard part is lining up the edges of the pieces when you glue them together. If the individual boards don't come together evenly, then a tremendous amount of work must be done once the glue has dried. The high spots will have to come down to match the surface, and what is worse, the entire surface will need to come down to match the low spots.

Splines, thin strips of wood placed in grooves on the edges of the pieces to be joined, are an excellent way to keep the boards aligned. Wood is flexible enough in length that the splines will even out the undulations and hold the pieces straight while the clamps are applied. While they do make the joints stronger, butt-jointed pieces in a tabletop are strong enough without them. Making a strong link in a chain stronger won't add anything to the weak links.

To make a flat top, you obviously need to have flat parts, but when you make a top as large as the top on the American Trestle Table on page 86, you come up against the limits of your tools, skills and the material. Any work you do on a tabletop is easier to do before the top is put together. Flattening a single board isn't that difficult, but reaching over to the middle of a wide top to plane off $1/16$" that's sticking up above its neighbor is. Splines will keep edges aligned to each other even if the pieces have a slight amount of bow or twist, and are well worth the extra effort it takes to employ them.

If the material is planed to finished thickness (or close to it) before gluing up, splines will ensure that cleaning up the glue joints won't leave it too thin. This is especially important if you don't have

Wood splines within the joints of a tabletop add strength to the joint, but that isn't their main function. Keeping the edges of these long joints in line with each other is vastly more important.

a planer, and purchase material that is already surfaced on both sides (known as S2S).

There are two great advantages to continuous splines. Think of it as a tongue-and-groove joint with two grooves and an independent tongue. Because the mating surfaces go all the way along the edge, high and low spots along the edge will

match when you clamp the boards together. You can also register your cut from one face of the boards, thereby eliminating measuring errors and minimizing setup time.

Dowels or biscuits can also align parts, but you can't always predict where they need to be. Boards can dip down and rise up in between the dowels or biscuits, leaving you with a series of spots to flatten out after gluing. Irregularities in the surface can throw off the alignment of your boring jig or biscuit joiner making these methods more of a hindrance than a help.

So why not mill a tongue-and-groove joint? Wouldn't that be less work than making two grooves and an extra piece to stuff in them? If you were making a lot of tops, and had a shaper with a power feeder, you might have a case. If you're only making one top at a time, making two grooves will be faster, and will give you better results.

Take the Tool to the Work
By making the grooves with a $\frac{1}{4}$"-wide slotting cutter in a hand-held router, setup time will be minimal. As long as you run all the parts with the router base on the same face of the board, the grooves will line up to each other. You won't have to match the setup for the groove to a second setup for the tongue (as with a tongue-and-groove bit set). In fact, it's better if the cutter is set slightly off center. That will keep you from putting the top together with one of the boards oriented incorrectly.

If you do this task on a router table, or with a stack dado set in the table saw, keeping the wood pressed flat to the table and fence becomes critical. If the stock has any bow or twist to it, it will likely move away from the fence as you make the groove, destroying your chances for things to line up nicely in the end.

You can set up with featherboards or other hold-downs to prevent this, but in half the time it takes to get set up, you would be finished by using the hand-held router. It's a case where it's easier to move a small tool over large parts than it is to move the large parts over a small cutter.

After laying out the boards for the top for the most attractive appearance, I mark two legs of a triangle across the joints as seen at right. This marks the faces as the top faces, and also keeps them in order. I know that the boards with lines all the way across get a groove on both edges, and that the two outside pieces get one groove on the edge the marks cross.

The $\frac{5}{8}$"-deep groove is a heavy cut to make in one pass, so I make sure to clamp the work securely before routing the groove. Cherry, which we chose for this tabletop, tends to break out along the edges of the groove. To keep the edges clean and make the final cut easier, I first feed the router right to left, making a shallow climb cut. Then I run it left to right to the full depth. When making a climb cut, clamp down the board securely and keep a firm grip on the router. The goal isn't to remove a lot of material; that wouldn't be safe. All you need to do is define the edges of the groove. I leave the boards a few inches longer than needed so I don't need to worry if there is any tear-out at the beginning or end of the cuts.

Not a Material Difference
For the splines to work properly, they need to fit nicely in the groove. I made mine from offcuts from the tabletop, but if this is your first attempt at splines, you might consider a man-made alternative. Medium-density fiberboard (MDF) or tempered hardboard are usually close enough in thickness to fit well in a $\frac{1}{4}$" groove. Use one of these, and you'll only need to worry about getting the width of the splines correct. We'll pause for a moment to let the solid wood purists and myth believers howl, then we'll explain why this is a good choice.

The purpose of the spline is to align the parts. Adding strength to the joint is not really an issue. The most important thing is that the spline fits snugly in the groove. If there is any slop in the fit it won't do the job. If you have trouble sizing pieces within a few thousandths of an inch, using a material with a known, consistent thickness will eliminate one source of frustration.

Some people will tell you that spline material should always be plywood, or that it should be solid wood with the grain running at a right angle to the joint line. While these may be stronger in theory, if enough stress is put on the joint to break the solid-wood edges, the joint will fail no matter what material is inside the groove. The solid-wood edges above and below the spline will always be the weakest part of the joint, and they are more than strong enough to hold the top together without the spline.

Plywood is far too inconsistent in thickness to make a decent spline. The variations will defeat the purpose, and it doesn't make much sense to fuss and fiddle to make an odd-size groove to try to get it to work. Replacing one continuous spline with many short ones to run the grain across the

Using a hand-held router with a slot-cutting bit is a more accurate and efficient way to make the grooves than running the edge of the boards on a router table or across a dado stack.

After settling on the final arrangement for the boards, mark two legs of a triangle across them with a lumber crayon or chalk. This will help keep them in order, and locate where to run the grooves.

joint turns a simple process into an exceedingly complicated one. When the time comes to glue up the top, I don't want to be fooling around with dozens of little pieces.

The only reasonable objection to using hardboard or MDF is the appearance of the spline on the end grain of the top. Although most people wouldn't notice, it would bother me to see it. You can use a few inches of solid wood at the ends of the splines, or if you don't want to see anything at the ends, start and stop the router cuts a few inches from the ends, and taper the ends of the splines to match the ends of the grooves.

The good news about using splines is that they work very well to keep two edges in alignment. The longer the edges of the pieces being put together, the more likely it is that there will be a slight bow or twist in the length of them. In preparing the stock, it's easy to correct problems in the width of any board, but nearly impossible to achieve perfection in the length. Fortunately, the flexibility of the wood allows the splines and

The splines and grooves need to be a close match so measure carefully. A set of dial calipers will allow you to zero in on a perfect fit.

the attachment of the top to the base to correct minor deviations along the length.

Better Doesn't Always Mean Faster

The bad news about splines is that they don't really make building a large tabletop any easier or faster. You're actually adding a few more steps and parts to the process, and they need to be done correctly. In addition, all of the other steps still need to be as carefully done as they would be if the splines weren't being used. The edges of the parts need to be as square and as straight as it is possible to make them. Adding the splines means you have to also pay attention to detail when cutting the grooves, making the splines and assembling the top.

After cutting the grooves, I begin to prepare the spline material by measuring the width and depth of the groove with dial calipers. I mill the spline material to thickness first, and in an ideal world this would be accomplished with rip cuts on the table saw. In the real world, however, thin pieces will bend a little as they pass the saw blade resulting in thin areas. I rip the parts about $^1\!/_{16}$" oversize and then make light passes through the planer, measuring with the calipers (as shown at left) after each pass until the material will slip into the groove with hand pressure only. Material this thin will be more likely to shatter or kick back going through the planer, so wear safety glasses and don't stand directly behind the machine.

If I didn't have access to a planer, I would put a rip blade and a zero-clearance insert on the table saw, and after initially cutting the parts $^1\!/_{16}$" big, I would make a finishing cut to the final size using a featherboard before the blade and a splitter or second featherboard after the blade, as shown below. The surfaces of the splines don't need to be pristine, so minor saw marks won't matter. If,

however, the spline burns as it's being ripped, the glue won't stick to the burned areas. A sharp ripping blade and the featherboards should prevent this. If there is some burning or other irregularity, it can be cleaned up with a card scraper, a plane, or sandpaper on a block of scrap wood. But don't get hung up on making them pretty and make them too thin in the process. It's easier to sneak up on the right thickness of spline using a planer or thicknessing sander than it is to get a good fit directly from the saw.

When the thickness of the splines has been established, I then rip them to final width. I rip them just a bit wide, measure the results with the calipers, and make a test fitting to adjust the saw for the final cut. Because I'm making the splines from scrap, I go ahead and make some extras for test fitting and for insurance. These small pieces of spline material can be hard to control, so use featherboards and a push stick to make the final cuts safely and accurately.

Practice Makes Perfect

With the splines complete, I make a dry run of assembling the top. This is to make sure that I have all the material and clamps on hand, and that all the pieces will fit together. Once I start gluing, there isn't time to go looking for another clamp, or adjust any of the joints. If the top doesn't come easily together with light pressure from the clamps I look at the gaps and try to determine what the problem is. I leave the slot cutter set up in the router until the top is assembled in case I need to deepen a groove, and I have my block plane handy to reduce the size of a spline.

To make a flat tabletop, it needs to be glued together on a flat surface. I cut strips of scrap $1^1\!/_2$" or 2" wide and place them about 18" apart across the grain direction of the top. Adding the splines complicates the assembly process, so glue up in stages. I used five boards of varying widths for this particular top, so I first glued the three middle boards together. After leaving them in the clamps for a few hours, I then attached the two outer pieces and left the entire assembly in the clamps overnight.

With the pieces in their proper orientation, put the pieces on edge, so that the grooves are facing up. I put glue in all the grooves, insert the splines, and then apply glue to the exposed edges of the splines and the boards as shown on page 97. This keeps the glue from running out of the groove as I put the pieces together. I then lay the pieces down and pull the joints together by hand

The thin splines can move around while cutting them to finished size. Using a zero-clearance insert, featherboard and splitter will minimize this. A push block that rides on the saw's fence is a safe way to handle this thin material.

Because the splines make the assembly of the tabletop more complicated, glue it together in stages. I used Titebond Extend, but liquid hide glue would allow even more open time. After the center section has been removed from the clamps, apply glue to the splines and clamp on the remaining pieces.

before clamping the top. I start in the middle and work out toward either end.

When the clamps are in place and tightened, I use a scraper to remove any glue squeeze-out. I wipe the scraper off with a wet rag as needed to keep from smearing the glue around. Letting the glue dry on the surface can cause it to dry improperly, and chipping off dried glue is likely to remove some wood along the glue line. If possible, I leave the boards for the top at least 6" longer than the finished dimension, and trim the ends after the

glue has dried. A top this big is difficult to trim on the table saw, so I use a circular saw guided by a straightedge. I then use a block plane to remove the saw marks from the ends and to put a radius on the edges, as shown below.

With carefully prepared parts, the work remaining to finish the top is minimal. A few strokes with a smooth plane or cabinet scraper along the joints make everything level and ready for final sanding and finishing.

— *Robert W. Lang*

Circular Saw Guide

There are some cuts that even the nicest table saws have trouble making cleanly and safely. Trimming the ends of a table-top this size is a good example, and this jig makes the task much easier. You don't even have to pick the top up and carry it. You lay out the cut, clamp down the jig, pick up your circular saw and make the cut.

I made this one from ½"-thick Baltic birch plywood, but it can be made from nearly any material. The baseplate needs to be a little wider than the base of the saw, plus an allowance for the fence, and about 1" past the fence to allow room for a couple clamps. The fence should be low enough that it doesn't interfere with the motor housing of the saw.

I used a piece 8" wide and 60" long. This gives enough length to easily crosscut a full sheet of plywood. I made the fence 1½" wide. I glued the fence to the baseplate leaving about ½" more than the distance from the edge of the saw's baseplate to the blade. I held the fence in place with ¾" brads every 6" to 8" along its length. After the glue has dried, I use the circular saw to trim off the excess material on the baseplate, as seen in the photo below.

The beauty of this jig is that the trimmed edge of the jig pinpoints the location of where the sawblade will make the finished cut. There isn't any need to figure the offset of the saw, or to remember the distance from the edge of the saw's base to the blade, just make a square layout line, clamp the jig to the line, and you're ready to cut. In addition to locating the cut so easily, the baseplate of the jig will minimize any possible tear-out from the circular saw blade on the finished surface.

— *RL*

After trimming the top to final length, a block plane is the easiest way to remove the saw marks and smooth the ends.

With the splines holding the edges of the individual board together, only a minimal amount of work is needed to finish the faces of the joints.

A simple plywood jig can make accurate crosscuts on very wide panels.

Paint Furniture Like a Professional

This time-honored finishing approach helps highlight – not hide – the beauty of your workmanship.

Painted furniture has a long and storied history, from the rich lacquer work of China and Japan, to the French baroque of Louis XIV, to the simple milk paints of the Shakers. Now, we're not going to teach you to create faux Ormulu detailing in gold leaf, but a quality painted finish can make even the knottiest pine look fabulous (with just a bit of prep work), and as historically accurate – if not more so – than a clear finish.

Painting furniture isn't quite like slapping a new coat of color on your living-room wall (which is an art unto itself). First, you need to make sure you have the correct tools. And it doesn't pay to skimp – spend the extra dosh for top-quality paintbrushes. Assuming you clean them correctly after every use, they'll last for years to come and give the best results, every time.

The Tools

While there are a number of good-quality brushes, Rick Gayle, who's been a professional painter for more than 20 years (and is a woodworker), recommends Purdy – nylon bristles for latex paint and natural bristles for oil-based paints. They're available at most any hardware or paint store.

I've done a fair amount of painting, of both furniture and walls, but it never occurred to me that rollers were appropriate for furniture painting until Gayle introduced me to the concept. While it won't work for turned table legs, a roller is wonderful for laying down an even layer of paint on an apron, tabletop or any other piece with a lot of flat real estate. Look for ¼" or ³⁄₁₆" nap roller covers to match the size of frame best suited to the job. The Premium XL Touch-up Kit (from Sherwin-Williams) comes with its own small roller tray and two extra roller covers, and is easy to clean. Don't go for cheaper foam covers; they tend to bring air bubbles to the surface of the paint film. Also, lay in a good supply of #150-grit and #320-grit sandpaper, some clean lint-free rags

Trim the corners with a small brush and feather the edges of the paint line. Then, roll paint over the flat surface of the same piece, making sure to first pick up the wet edge you just painted with the brush. This will help you avoid unsightly lap lines to produce a professional-looking finish.

and a couple plastic pint containers such as you might find at the deli counter.

Putties, Primers and Paints

Now that you have your tools, it's time to select products, and again, go for the good stuff – it pays off in the long run.

If you have shallow divots or small cracks to fill, Gayle suggests using a lightweight non-shrinking spackle, such as Red Devil One Time,

Dap Fast or Crackshot. For deeper holes, consider an automotive filler such as Bondo (deep pockets of spackle are hard to sand flush to the surface). Then, move on to primer. Look for an easy-sand primer such as Porter Paints 184 Sta-Kil Primer/Sealer, Sherwin-Williams Easy Sand Alkyd Primer, Kilz 2 or Kilz Premium. Avoid "full-bodied" general purpose primers; they're too thick for furniture projects.

Now, select your paint. It used to be that oil-based (alkyd) paints were tougher than acrylics and latex-based products. While that's still technically true, Gayle says that acrylics and latex paints have improved so much in the last several years that now they're darn near as tough as their oil-based brethren. Plus, with mineral spirits running $9 a gallon and unlikely to come down in price, cleanup of oil-based paints is not only more time consuming, it's a lot more expensive. (Latex and acrylics can be cleaned up with dish soap and water.) And then there's the drying time. With latex or acrylics, you can prime and paint the first coat in one day, with at least a couple hours of drying time in between (though we don't recommend two finish coats of paint in one day, no matter what it says on the can). With alkyds, the drying time is a lot longer.

So why wouldn't you choose a latex or acrylic? Well, says Gayle, some people adamantly believe oil is still the better choice for baseboards and doors, and pieces of furniture that get a lot of extremely rough usage. We're guessing you're not going to let your kids use the new table as a jungle gym; eschew the oil.

If you take our advice and decide on a water-based product, our expert recommends Sherwin-Williams Proclassic Waterborne Satin or Semi-gloss. If you insist on an oil-base, consider Porter Paints Promaster 2000 Interior Alkyd.

Now that you have all your supplies, it's time to paint, right? Well, not quite. First you have to select a work site (your shop, which is likely full of dust, may not be the best choice). If your project is relatively small, try to elevate it on a table (covered with a dropcloth) for easier access, and put blocks underneath so you can get at the bottom edge of the piece with your roller or brush.

Whatever site you choose, it should be between 65° and 75°, and protected from the wind. Also, avoid direct sunlight. If paint dries too quickly due to high heat or wind, you're more likely to get unsightly lap marks or obvious brush marks.

Prepping and Painting

Now take a close look at all the surfaces to find and fill any gaps, divots or cracks. Don't count on the primer or paint to fill these. After any filler has had ample time to dry, sand the entire surface with #150-grit sandpaper, beginning with any areas you filled. Of course, if you planed the wood, you'll have to sand only the areas you filled, flush to the surrounding surface. It's of utmost importance to start with a flat, smooth surface so take your time on the prep work.

Once sanding is complete and you're convinced the surface is as uniformly smooth as can be, thoroughly clean all surfaces. First, vacuum the project to remove any dust particles buried in the grain. Then, wipe carefully with a tack cloth or a clean, lint-free rag that has been dipped in mineral spirits. Dry the surface with a clean rag and inspect it for any lint or foreign materials.

We used the Premium XL Touch-up Kit (with roller, roller covers and tray), Purdy Nylox brush, a rag, and Sherwin-Williams Proclassic Waterborne Satin.

Finally, it's time to open your primer. Remove the lid, and punch four to six holes around the lip of the can. This helps excess primer drain back into the can rather than act as glue holding the lid to the can the next time you try to open it. Pour a small amount of primer into the trough of the roller tray. (It's preferable to add more later if necessary rather than transfer unused primer or paint back to the original container; that involves greater risk of contaminating the container with dust particles, shavings or other foreign objects.) Reseal the primer can and set it aside.

Now, mentally break the project into discrete sections, and work separately on each one. Dip just the end of your brush into the paint, and use it to "cut in" or "trim" the areas you won't be able to reach with the roller (the corners, for example). Work in the direction of the surface on which you'll immediately afterward use the roller, and feather the paint at the ends. As much as possible, avoid getting primer onto the adjacent or mating surface. This sounds a bit confusing, but the idea is to always keep a wet edge, because that will help you avoid lap marks and lines. So, you don't want to apply primer to any discrete area you're not immediately prepared to complete.

On the Shaker table, for example, we began on one brace, painting all three sides that would show. Then, we moved on to the leg, because there was a small amount of primer in the crevice that we wanted to work with while it was still wet, and from there to the contiguous foot. Then we moved on to the opposite brace. We saved the large expanse of stretcher for last.

Set your brush aside, resting it in a clean pint container, covered with a damp, clean cloth. The cloth will keep the brush from drying out while you're using the roller. Dip the roller into the tray trough just enough to get a little paint on one side of the roller, then "roll it out" on the textured washboard area of the tray to remove excess paint. Now, roll the paint on to the flat surface of your section, slightly overlapping the brushed area while that's still wet. Work smoothly using long

confident strokes.

When you're finished with the first section, cover the roller in the pint container, pick up the brush and move on to the next section. Repeat the process section by section until all exposed surfaces have been primed evenly with one coat.

Now clean your brush, roller cover and containers while you wait for the primer to dry (make sure you watch – it's very exciting). When you think it's dry, wait a little longer. It will take at least four hours, no matter what it says on the can. After you're sure the surface is completely dry, sand lightly with #320-grit sandpaper and clean the surface thoroughly, as you did before. Water-based primers may raise the grain a bit, in which case you may need to sand more vigorously, and possibly apply another coat of primer. Take a careful look at any knots or sappy streaks to ensure the primer has completely sealed those problem areas. Make any repairs you missed on your initial inspection (primer will highlight them) and spot prime or re-prime as necessary. Eager as you may be to get to painting, it really is a good idea to use two coats of primer on previously unfinished wood. It will further seal and block resin, and keep it from bleeding through what you thought was going to be your finish coat.

When you're finished priming, prepare the surface for the first coat of paint by sanding and cleaning it. Then, follow the same procedure you used in priming. Plan on at least two coats of paint (with sanding in between if necessary), with a full day in between each. And don't be surprised if a third coat is required.

— *Megan Fitzpatrick*

Supplies

Kilz
866-774-6371 or kilz.com
- Kilz 2
- Kilz Premium

Porter Paints Co.
800-332-6270 or porterpaints.com
- 184 Sta-Kil Primer/Sealer
- Promaster 2000 Interior Alkyd
- Advantage 900 Series Acrylic

Purdy
503-286-8217 or purdycorp.com
- Nylox or Nylon series brushes (for water-based pints)
- Black china bristle series brushes (for alkyds)

Sherwin-Williams
sherwin-williams.com
- ProClassic Waterborne Interior Latex
- Premium XL Touch-up Kit

Why Wedge Tenons?

Early craftsmen often drove wedges into their tenons to make the joint stouter. Should you? And if so, how?

The venerable mortise-and-tenon joint allowed the first woodworkers to build furniture that was both lightweight and strong. But it was the simple wedge that ensured the work would last hundreds (even thousands) of years.

A wedge is one of the six "simple machines" of physics and is the reason an ax can split wood and a nail can hold it together.

When a wedge is driven into the end of a tenon, it expands the tenon and forces the end of the tenon to become wider than the joint is near the shoulder. When this technique is used in a mortise with trumpet-shaped walls, the wedge transforms the tenon into what resembles a dovetail. The result is an astonishingly strong joint.

The wedged joint shows up frequently in the historical record in Egyptian furniture, large doors for houses and cabinets, and in chairs. But as glues became stronger, this joint fell into decline. Today the wedged tenon shows up mostly as a decorative motif on high-end furniture or in Windsor and ladderback chairs.

Good-quality chairs probably will always use this joint, no matter how strong adhesives become. In the ongoing battle of child vs. chair, the chair will always need all the help it can get.

And there's little need for this joint in the realm of the commercial cabinetmaker. Kitchens aren't designed to last a lifetime, so there's no need to waste precious time and material on a door or cabinet that's going to end up in the dump before the glue ever gives up its grip.

But for the home woodworker, this joint should definitely be in your arsenal. Make a sample joint one afternoon in the shop and you are sure to be intrigued by its pure cunning. When executed properly, a wedged tenon locks the components together like no other frame joint. And because of this immediate lock, you can reduce your reliance on piles and piles of expensive clamps. Once the

Wedging a through-tenon adds strength, but also complexity. We investigated the various ways to make this joint to find the simplest and most reliable method.

joint is wedged, you can take the clamps off and manipulate the assembly.

Wedging a tenon is, in theory, stronger than drawboring a mortise-and-tenon joint. And while wedging is a bit more work to execute than drawboring, it has some other advantages. Wedging

is remarkably forgiving – your first joint will be stout (if not showy). When done with traditional methods, it is actually a reversible joint. And the result definitely appeals to the modern woodworking eye, which appreciates visible joinery.

Theory vs. Practice

There are a few rules for wedging a tenon, and they all seem to contradict one another; it depends on which book you read or school you attend. And though I have personally wedged hundreds of joints (mostly in chairs and in Arts & Crafts furniture), I've also been flummoxed by the lore that shrouds this joint.

So I made a bunch of these joints in walnut and maple using a variety of common techniques. All the techniques resulted in a stout joint that looked good. Then I sawed them all apart to see what actually happened inside the joint when the wedge entered the picture.

When it comes to the shape of the mortise, there is little disagreement among the pundits. The area where the tenon enters the work should be narrower than where the tenon exits on the far side. In essence, the mortise should have a bit of a trumpet shape. The taper on the mortise walls should start somewhere in the middle of the mortise – you don't have to taper the entire wall of the joint. As you'll see shortly, this trumpet shape is easy to make with a chisel.

When it comes to the tenon, that's where the disagreements begin. One school of thought is that you should do nothing to the tenon before assembly and merely wedge the gaps at the ends of the mortise only. While this works, I found that you don't get as much good wedge-to-tenon-to-mortise contact as with the other methods that I investigated.

Saw Kerfs in the Tenon

Another dominant school of thought is that you should cut two saw kerfs down most of the length of the tenon and then drive wedges into the kerfs. Some sources show using a backsaw (which has a thin kerf) to cut the kerfs. Other sources show a full-size handsaw cutting the kerfs. I've used both methods successfully in my work, and I tried both methods for this article and then sawed the joints apart to see if they offered different results.

The wider kerf of the full-size handsaw allowed the wedges to penetrate more deeply, but there was very little difference in the appearance of the joint on the inside. The joint locked solidly up and down the mortise walls.

So if you go this route, which saw should you choose for the kerfs? I choose a saw based on how close the tenon fits in the mortise when I complete the fitting of the joint. In making chairs, for example, the tenon is usually a close fit, so I choose a handsaw with the bigger kerf (or I use a band saw). If I use a small-kerf backsaw for this job, there is a real risk that I won't get much of the wedge into the kerf and the wedge will snap off when I drive it (as you drive the wedge, the mortise fights back; if your first blow is a mis-strike you can snap off the wedge if there's a tight fit on the tip of the wedge).

When the tenon is a looser fit in its mortise, I

Because this tenon has a loose fit (about $\frac{1}{8}$" on either side), I used a backsaw to make the kerfs in the tenon. Note that the kerfs don't extend all the way down to the tenon's shoulder. There's no need – the wedges will only travel so far.

use a backsaw to cut the kerfs. If I use a full-size handsaw in this instance, I could create too much space that the wedges can't fill.

Saw the Kerfs and Then Drill Holes

Another common variant of this joint is to saw kerfs down the tenon and then drill a hole at the bottom of the kerf. The theory goes that the hole will allow the sides of the tenon to bend outward

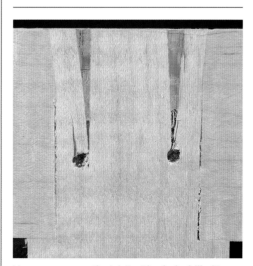

Here you can see the joint with a hole drilled tangent to the kerf (left) and centered on the kerf. In all the samples, the joints with a hole that was tangent to the kerf split back up the tenon as shown – this one filled with glue after the split.

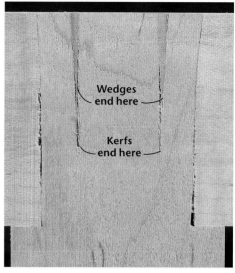

Here's what the joint at left looked like when sawn apart. The wedges didn't make it all the way down to the bottom of the kerf from the backsaw, but the tenon filled the mortise nicely using this method. The joint with the kerf made by a full-size handsaw looked almost identical, except the wedges made it further in.

– instead of splitting the tenon at the bottom of the saw kerf. The other assertion is that the hole will reduce the chances for splitting the part of your project that has the mortise.

This technique always smelled funny to me. I've never had a tenon split on me below the joint's shoulder line, even during my most aggressive moments with a hammer. I suppose a split could happen, but none of the joints I made and then sawed apart for this article showed evidence of significant splitting.

But I decided I should investigate what happens inside the joint when made this way. First I sawed the kerfs as before. Then I drilled $\frac{9}{64}$" -diameter holes at the bottom of each kerf. On half of the sample joints I centered the hole on the kerf. On the other half of the samples I positioned

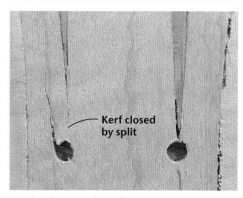

Here's a close-up of another example. Note how the reverse split closed up the kerf and stopped the wedge from entering the joint further.

the hole so its edge was tangent to (just touching) the kerf. Both variations are common.

When I sawed apart these joints, they all behaved exactly the same. For the joints with the hole centered on the kerf, the joint looked fine and solid overall. One of the examples had a tiny split at the bottom of the kerf, but nothing to get worked up about.

However, the examples that had the hole tangent to the kerf performed oddly in my opinion. These holes actually introduced a split that ran back up the tenon. This second split leveraged the kerf closed and reduced the amount of penetration allowed to the wedge. Some of these splits filled up with glue that squeezed in from the mortise wall; others did not.

The bottom line on this joint is that I don't think that the holes are worth the extra steps involved. They don't seem to offer any advantage in a typical joint and they make driving the wedge more difficult. So skip the drill.

No Kerfs, Just a Chisel

There was one more variant I wanted to try that chairmaker David Fleming taught me. He doesn't saw a kerf in a tenon to make room for the wedge. Instead, he assembles the joint with glue and then splits the tenon with a chisel that is the same width as the tenon's thickness.

Introducing a split seemed like a bad idea when I was first introduced to the technique. I was worried that the violent splitting action would ruin the tenoned piece, even before wedging. And the method left even less room for a wedge than the other techniques. Plus it seemed just a bit crude and rash. But I'm always willing to try new things

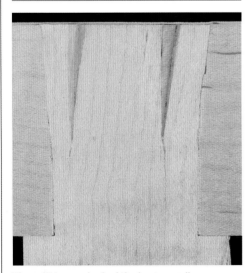

The split tenons looked the best overall, were easy to assemble and had fewer steps. Note how the wedges (and the split) followed the grain lines of the wood. This caused the wedges to enter the joint at a slight angle, but there was no difference in the finished appearance of the joint.

and then saw them apart.

The results were surprising. Splitting the tenon was fast and easy and the wedges slipped into the split without fuss and were easy to drive into the work. But what did the joint look like after an autopsy? Surprisingly good. The wood split along the growth rings of the tenon, which caused the splits to be at a slight angle. But the wedges penetrated deeply and evenly. Time after time, this joint looked better and more solid than the others we tried.

Splitting the tenon isn't always the best way to go, however. If your tenon is a close fit in its mortise, you could snap the wedge prematurely before much of it has entered the joint.

So our recommendation is to split the tenon with a chisel when you have a loose fit (about ⅛" on either side of the tenon) and to use a saw kerf when you have a tight fit.

Making the Joint

Once you have decided how to wedge the joint, the rest of the joint design is straightforward. By using some traditional layout methods, you will make things easier on yourself.

• Add "horns" to your stiles. When you make a frame assembly with rails and stiles, it's traditional to cut your stiles a little longer (¼" on each end will do) than the finished length. The extra length, which is trimmed away later, reduces the chance that the end of your stiles will split when being mortised or wedged. It also gives you a little more surface area you can clamp to get that joint tight.

• Try hide glue. Using either liquid hide glue or hot hide glue makes this joint reversible when you add moisture and heat (a clothes iron and a wet towel do the trick). Hide glue allows you to pull the joint apart if you find misfitting joints after glue-up. It's easier if you do disassemble the joint before you trim the wedges flush. Add the heat and steam, then pull the wedges out with pliers. Otherwise, pry out the wedges with an old chisel. Once you get the wedges out, the joint will be easy to disassemble from there.

• Use white oak for the wedges. White oak is an excellent wood for wedges because it is common and can take a beating. Hickory and ash are also excellent. Using a fragile species for the wedges, such as cherry, increases the chance that the wedge will split. Make your wedges long enough that you will have at least ¼" left to trim after assembly.

Follow the photos at right to see how we assemble this joint. With these techniques (particularly the wedge-cutting sled for the band saw), I think you'll be pleased with this joint and soon ready for its interesting variations: diagonal wedging, which closes a gap around a tenon in all four directions, and fox-wedging, which is a sneaky technique for wedging a blind tenon.

— *Christopher Schwarz*

Assembling the Wedge Join

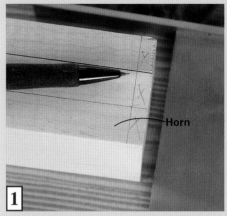

1 When marking out the mortises, be sure to leave some extra length in the stiles, sometimes called "horns." The horns reduce the chance your joint will self-destruct during joinery or assembly.

5 Tip the chisel a few degrees as shown and drive it into the work. You want to stop the taper somewhere in the middle of the mortise. Don't go all the way to the bottom.

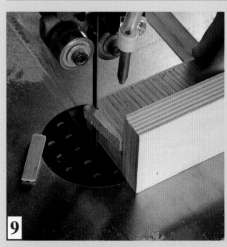

9 With the wedge material flipped and in position, make the second cut. The 4° slope on both edges produces a wedge with an 8° slope.

2
I clamp all my stiles together and mark the joinery simultaneously. Here I'm using the actual tenon to lay out the mortise location. This reduces both measuring and error.

3
No matter how you make your mortise (a hollow-chisel mortiser is shown here), don't try to plunge all the way through from one side. Work from one edge, then flip the work over and work from the opposite edge (keeping the same face against the fence) until the two mortises meet.

4
On the edge where the tenon will exit the stile, mark out about ⅛" from your mortise. Use a chisel to first extend the wall of the mortise out to your layout line. Note that if you used a traditional mortising chisel to cut your mortise, this step might be unnecessary. The natural levering action of the mortise chisel can be used to create the trumpet-shaped mortise.

6
This jig makes wedges better than anything I know. I picked up the idea for it from Lee Valley's web site (leevalley.com, look under the "Articles" section). It essentially is a sled that is skewed 4° and runs in the saw's miter slot.

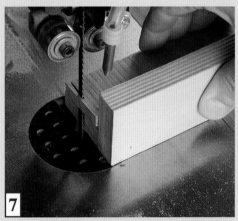

7
To make wedges, you need a board of suitable wedge material that is the same thickness as your tenon. First saw one end off of your blank; discard the waste piece.

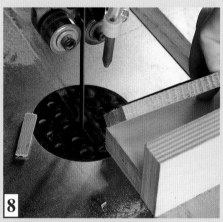

8
Flip the wedge material over and position it so it overhangs the edge of the sled a bit. How much overhang depends on how pointy you want your wedge to be. Experiment.

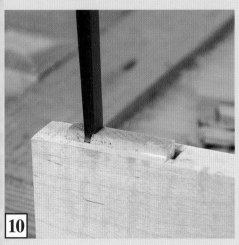

10
Drive a chisel into the end of the tenon to split it. I positioned the chisel ⁵⁄₁₆" from the end of the tenon and drove it straight down until the gap closed up.

11
Add your adhesive, yellow glue or hide glue, and drive your wedges into the joint. Tap them in evenly, alternating one wedge to another. The sound of the hammer hitting the wedge will change when the wedge hits bottom.

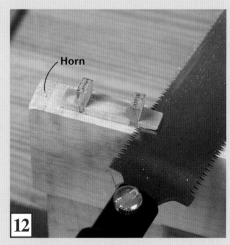

Horn

12
You can trim the joint flush with a flush-cutting saw. I like to use a band saw when I can take the assembly to the saw.

Stickley Sideboard

The hardest part of building this Arts & Crafts classic is choosing just the right piece of wood for each component.

M̲y grandmother – who always wore skirts, never pants – was too polite and proper to roll her eyes when I became enthralled with Arts & Crafts furniture.

Jean West was a die-hard student of antiques. Her library was filled with books about period American, English and Asian furniture. Her home was decorated with these pieces. Her taste in objects, I now realize, was excellent.

When I started collecting and building Arts & Crafts pieces about 17 years ago, she and I would go antique hunting in her haunts in Connecticut and Rhode Island. When I raved about a signed Stickley armchair, she would just shake her head.

"Oh Christopher," was all she'd say.

When Jean was growing up, the Arts & Crafts style was on its way down. All of the cult objects that celebrities now pay thousands of dollars for were – to her – the stuff in student ghettos, beach houses and servant quarters. It was clunky, lifeless and dark.

Though Jean and I never saw eye-to-eye on antiques, I hope she would have approved of (or at least tolerated) this version of Gustav Stickley's No. 802 server. Thanks to the pen of Harvey Ellis, this server has a bold curve that pulls the eye upward. The double taper on the legs lightens its overall structure. And the choice of cherry (my only addition to the soup) also reduces the severity of the original's dark oak finish.

Construction of this piece is surprisingly quick and easy for a major case piece. Like all Arts & Crafts projects, it is a mortising marathon. The aprons, stretchers and web frame all use a mortise-and-tenon joint. Once you get through that, you're just about home.

The Stickley No. 802 server is one of the most graceful pieces from the era. Despite its heavy legs, the piece has a lightness thanks to tapers and a curve.

You can build the drawers any way you please. I dovetailed mine by hand because Jean always poo-pooed anything with machine-cut dovetails. Some family traits are too strong to overcome.

The Heart is in the Extremities

Though the top of this server always commands attention (that's where the food is), the heart of this piece's design is in its legs. Paying close attention when selecting the wood for your legs makes an enormous difference.

While you're at the lumberyard, look for wide 8/4 cherry with rift grain on its edges and cathedral grain in the center. You'll rip off the rift grain from the edges to claim your legs – save the cathedral in the center for another project.

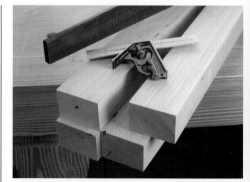

The grain on the legs should be rift-sawn. See how the growth rings run diagonally across the end grain? This ensures your legs will look good from all angles of the room.

The other critical thing to consider is the direction of the grain lines on the front faces of your legs. Because the legs taper at the top and the foot, I look for grain lines that have a gentle curve that mimics this shape. While this sounds artsy-fartsy to beginners, it's something that good woodworkers eventually do on instinct. Develop your instincts now.

Prepare your legs with care. I get mine to both their final thickness and width using the planer. Then I remove the milling marks with a jointer plane and get ready to cut my joinery.

Tips on Tenons

The back apron and all the stretchers are connected to the legs with mortise-and-tenon joints. Selecting your stock for these parts also requires some thought. For the back apron, pick something ugly and sappy but straight. No one will see it.

For the two bottom stretchers, pick pieces with quartered or rift grain. You want straight lines, not curves, down there. And for the curved front stretcher you want to be a little picky. You can use quartered or flat stock here, but I'd look for something that mimics the curve. Remember: People are going to be looking at this part a lot.

All the tenons on this piece are $1\frac{1}{4}$" long, $\frac{1}{4}$" thick and have $\frac{7}{16}$"-wide edge shoulders. Because of the consistency and quantity of the tenons on this server, I like to cut them using a dado stack in the table saw.

The key to accuracy with this method is to use lots of downward pressure during the cut – the blades push your work up. And test each tenon in a sample mortise. If it doesn't fit, run it over the blades a second time.

The tenon for the back apron is too wide for a single tenon. The resulting mortise wall from a

Table saw gospel is that you shouldn't use the rip fence and miter gauge in tandem. This is the grand exception for me. This cut is safe because there is no wood trapped between the blades and the rip fence.

After you have cut all the cheeks, raise the blades and form the edge shoulders. The trick here is to ensure your fence is 90° to your table. If it's not, your shoulders will be mis-cut and ill-fitting.

single tenon would be significantly weakened. So you need to split the tenon. Yes, you could rig up some jig on your table saw. Or you could handsaw the 1"-wide waste out and be done with it.

Now bundle your legs together and mark out where all the stretchers and apron go. Then use your actual tenoned parts to lay out the locations

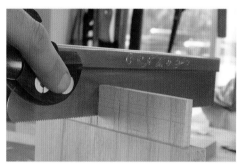

Use a dovetail saw or other rip-tooth saw to first define the edge cheeks of your twin tenons. This is a good way to warm up your sawing skills.

of your mortises. There's no need to measure – that encourages error.

Cut all your mortises. Make them a shade deeper than $1\frac{1}{4}$". This gives you a little room for excess glue, plus the tenons are easier to fit if they don't hit bottom.

A Bit Crazy on the Curve

The curve on the front stretcher has to be perfect. If it's not centered and smooth, it will bug you for the rest of your life. Normally for a broad and shallow curve I'll lay it out using a flexible scrap bent between nails. But for this curve, I built a trammel from a scrap to get a smooth swoop.

Clean up the waste that you couldn't get with your saw by using a chisel. I prefer a narrow tool for this operation because it requires less effort to push forward than a wide chisel.

I mark out my mortise locations using my completed tenons. When I mortise the legs, I remove the pencil line with my chisel. That gives the tenon a little bit of room to move during assembly so I can line things up.

Remove the waste between with some sort of frame saw. This is a bowsaw. You also could use a coping saw – or just bash the waste out with a chisel.

This is quick to do. And it's accurate if you follow these steps. Find a stick long enough for your trammel. Drill a ¼" hole at one end for the pencil. Whittle the pencil just a bit until it fits snugly in the hole.

From the tip of the pencil, measure your curve's radius (45⅞"), and mark that length on your trammel. Drive a screw through the trammel at that point.

Clamp your stretcher to your benchtop and scribe a centerline across its width. The next step is critical: Use a square to shift the stretcher so it is exactly 90° to your benchtop's front edge. Now position the screw's tip so it's in line with the centerline and the pencil's lead is on your centerline. Strike your arc.

Dovetail the Rail

The thin rail above the drawers is joined to the legs with a single dovetail at each end. The dovetails are 1" long and are rabbeted on the underside to make it easy to lay out the mating socket. First cut the sloped edges (I used a 1:6 slope).

Saw the edge shoulders. Then saw a ⅛" rabbet on the underside. This should be no problem for any fine-tooth Western saw or dozuki.

Then lay out the socket on the legs. The rabbet on your rail will allow you to easily hold the piece in position as you trace around it with a knife and pencil. Mark the depth of the socket then saw out its extents.

Clamp the leg down to your benchtop and brace the foot of the leg against a bench dog or a stop. Then chisel out the waste, working down. Pop the waste out by driving the chisel into the end grain.

"If you can't saw a straight line at an angle, then you shouldn't be practicing cutting dovetails — you should be practicing sawing."

— Jim Kingshott (1932 - 2002)
"Dovetails" DVD

Assemble the Base

The end assemblies on this server are odd. The bottom stretchers are tenoned into the legs, but the side panels at the top are not. The grain on these side panels runs vertical, so tenons aren't advised. I joined my side panels to the legs with glue alone. It was easy.

Picking the stock for your side panels isn't as critical as it is for some other parts, but there are some details to think about. On the prototype I built, I glued up each side panel from two narrower boards and went for a bookmatched look. On the second version I built, I found some 14"-wide lumber and made the side panels from

If you've measured your radius correctly there should be a small flat remaining at the ends of your curve. This is intentional. It strengthens the end of the curve, which can be fragile.

Stickley No. 802 Server

NO.	PART	T	W	L	MATERIAL	NOTES
Base						
❑ 4	Legs	1¾	2¼	35⅛	Cherry	2" wide at top; 1⅝" at foot
❑ 2	Side panels	¾	13½	13	Cherry	Glued to legs
❑ 1	Back apron	¾	6¾	36½	Cherry	1¼" TBE; inset ⅛" from legs
❑ 1	Drawer divider	¾	15¾	5	Cherry	Screwed to web frame & top rail
❑ 1	Top front rail	½	1½	36	Cherry	1"-long dovetail, both ends
❑ 1	Curved stretcher	¾	4¹³⁄₁₆	36½	Cherry	1¼" TBE; inset ¼" from front
❑ 2	Bottom stretchers	⅞	3⅝	16	Cherry	1¼" TBE; inset ½" inside of legs
❑ 1	Shelf	¾	12½	35	Cherry	Supported by cleats
❑ 4	Cleats	¾	¾	11	Cherry	Support for shelf, web frame
❑ 2	Top attachment cleats	½	2½	16¾	Wood	Glued to back apron
Top						
❑ 1	Top	⅞	18	42	Cherry	Optional chamfer on underside
❑ 1	Backsplash	¾	3¾	38	Cherry	Glued to top
Web frame						
❑ 2	Stiles	¾	2	33	Pine	
❑ 2	Rails	¾	2	13½	Pine	1¼" TBE
❑ 1	Midrail	¾	4¾	13½	Pine	1¼" TBE
Drawers						
❑ 2	Fronts	¾	4½	16⅝	Cherry	
❑ 4	Sides	½	4½	15	Pine	
❑ 2	Backs	½	4	16⅝	Pine	
❑ 2	Bottoms	½	14¾	16⅛	Pine	

TBE = Tenon on both ends

This dovetail joint is more good sawing practice (and the results will never show). Keep it up, and you'll want to hand-dovetail the drawer, too.

Here's what the joint looks like before you mark out the socket. And people think hand-sawing is sloppier than machine work.

Many woodworkers will saw over the line on the end grain on purpose. It makes chiseling out the waste a tad easier. If you do this, be sure to mark the location of the leg's taper. You don't want to cross that line.

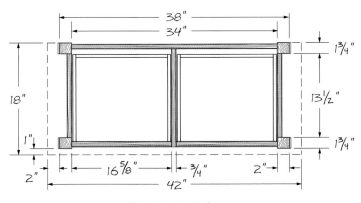

SECTION, PLAN

Here I've clamped a piece of scrap at my socket's scribe line. It helps prevent me from crossing the scribe line when chopping. It's not foolproof, but it is fool-resistant.

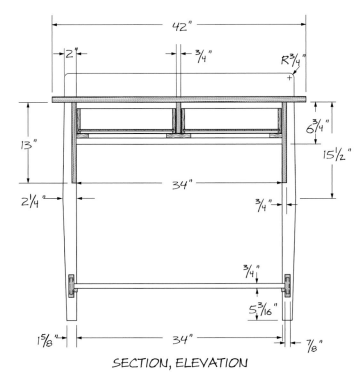

SECTION, ELEVATION

ELEVATION

ILLUSTRATIONS BY ROBERT W. LANG

STICKLEY NO. 802 SIDEBOARD

The point is to make all the legs look the same, not to obey some measurement. You can please your eyes or you can please your ruler. I go for the eyes.

I use a fence on my planes when every shaving has to be perfect. Usually when you joint long edges for a tabletop, you have some extra wood that allows you to correct an off-kilter edge. Not so here.

Here I'm looking for squeeze-out at my seams. Too much squeeze-out will be a nightmare to clean up in this corner. Glue judiciously.

Any sort of soft secondary wood is good for a web frame. I used pine with some blue stain. Here I'm jointing one edge of a stile right before assembly.

Glue up a panel for the drawer divider. I use yellow glue for these joints because it's easy to set up these panels quickly.

that. On the second version, I cut my panels so a cathedral was terminating near the top of the panel. Both servers look good.

Once you have your side panels selected and sized, you can taper your legs. Again, you can make all manner of jigs to make this double taper. Or you can keep it simple. I marked out the tapers on one leg. I cut them on the band saw and cleaned up the results with a jointer plane. Then I used that as a template for the other legs.

If you've gotten this far in the story, you're probably wondering right now if this project is a bomb waiting to go off. I mean, look at those end assemblies. The grain runs horizontal in the bottom stretchers and vertical in the side panels. Won't this piece tear itself apart?

Wood movement aside, it hasn't been a problem in the historical pieces or in the prototype I built two years ago. My guess: The legs bend a bit.

Before you assemble the ends, ensure that the side panels are the exact same size as the distance between the shoulders of your bottom stretchers. A plane is a good tool for this sort of work.

Glue up each end assembly. I used liquid hide glue to give myself plenty of time to shift my parts around just so.

After the glue has dried in both end assemblies, glue up the remainder of the base. You can use the tapered offcuts from your band saw as clamping cauls, but I didn't find it necessary. Do not glue in the dovetailed top rail yet. Drive it in dry during assembly. You'll need to remove it to fit the guts inside the server.

The Guts of It

A web frame supports the drawers and squares up the base. Measure the inside of your base and make the web frame so it fills that space exactly, perhaps even a little too tight.

The web frame is built using the same-size mortise-and-tenon joints as the rest of the server. Cut your joints, assemble the frame, then level all the joints (I used a jointer plane).

The oddest thing about the guts of this server is the divider between the drawers. It is very wide but not very tall – that's because you want it to move in the same direction as your side panels. So glue up a panel for the drawer divider and get the sucker dead flat. Any bow or twist will bind your drawers.

Fine Fitting for Squareness

The web frame and drawer divider are the oft-forgotten culprits with ill-fitting drawers. If the web frame racks the carcase, it's going to be hard to fit your drawers. And if the drawer divider is warped or is installed cockeyed, you are making work for yourself when fitting your drawers.

Once you get the web frame to fit, take ⅛" off one long stile to allow for wood movement at the rear of the base.

Once I get my web frame squared up, I'll fit it to the base. Here I'm tracing how much waste I need to remove to get the frame to fit.

Then I plane down to the line. Just make sure you don't make the web frame into a parallelogram when you do this. Keep it square.

I think it's helpful to clean up as much glue squeeze-out here as possible. This seam is just a tough place to work once everything is glued up.

Some woodworkers go to a lot of trouble to make holes that allow screws to move (router jigs!). Here's all you need to do: Drive your bit through the cleat. With the bit spinning, thrust up $\frac{1}{8}$"; thrust down $\frac{1}{8}$". Done.

Rather than measure the notch you need, use the actual rail to mark your cut. Remember to cut next to the line, not on it.

This is another place I like to work off centerlines. Strike a centerline across the cleat. Strike a centerline on the stretcher. Line them up and nail things in place.

When planing chamfers across the grain, you can easily blow out your corners. With such a visible joint, I don't take chances. I shave the corner with a chisel. Then I work the chamfer from the ends and into the middle. This eliminates any chance of a mishap.

Install the web frame by gluing it to the curved stretcher. Use liquid hide glue if you're skittish about getting this joint just right. You don't want things misaligned, because problems will be a tricky fix.

Once the glue is dry, reinforce the web frame from below with some $\frac{3}{4}$" x $\frac{3}{4}$" cleats. Glue and nail the cleats to the web frame. Screw the cleats to the side panels. To allow some wood movement, use pan-head screws and ream out your clearance holes.

Now you need to get the drawer divider and the top front rail to mesh together to create square openings for your drawers. To position the drawer divider, I like to work using centerlines. Strike the centerline between the legs on the curved stretcher. Then strike the centerline on the thick-ness of the drawer divider. Line them up and that's where the part goes.

Lay the top front rail in position and mark where it overlaps the drawer divider. Cut a notch in the drawer divider, then glue the rail in its dovetails and drive a screw through the rail and into the drawer divider.

Hold the Food; Hold the Napkins

The shelf and top are the easiest parts to install. However, you should spend extra time selecting and preparing the stock for them. They are quite visible on the finished product.

Install the shelf with cleats using the same technique you used to install the cleats below the web frame. Glue and nail the cleats to the bottom stretcher. Screw the shelf in place.

The top is a little more involved, but not much. I planed a $\frac{3}{16}$" x $\frac{3}{16}$" chamfer on the underside of the top. This is not an authentic detail, but it does lighten the appearance of the top a bit.

To complete the top, glue the splash in place. You can use some sort of mechanical fastener to align the parts, but I don't think it's necessary. Apply glue to the bottom edge of the splash and clamp it to the top.

The final detail for attaching the top is to create a way to attach the top to the base. At the front of the server, you can screw up through the front rail and into the top. At the rear of the case, you have a couple options. You can use pocket screws through the back apron (which I used on the prototype) or you can glue in a cleat to the rear and screw through that.

Two important details: Apply most of the glue toward the rear of the top. This will reduce squeeze-out at the front of the splash. Second, I think it's a good idea to clamp this assembly to your bench. Adding your bench's thickness into the equation spreads the clamping pressure along your joint line.

The temptation is to glue the cleats to the sides so they will act as kickers for the drawers. You'll run into some wood-movement problems if you do that. If you are going to install drawer kickers, I'd nail them to the underside of the top once the case is together.

Supplies

Lee Valley Tools
800-871-8158 or leevalley.com
2 ■ 50mm ring pulls
    #01A61.50, $5.10/ea.
Price correct at time of publication.

I use a moving fillister plane to cut the shallow rabbet on the inside of the drawer sides. Each joint takes about 15 seconds to make. Each joint saves me several minutes of fussing around with my tail board to line it up with my pin boards.

And the Drawers

Every woodworker builds drawers differently, so I won't waste too much ink describing my process. I build traditional American dovetailed drawers with sides and bottoms that are $\frac{1}{2}$" thick.

The sides are dovetailed into the drawer's front and back. I use through-dovetails at the rear and half-blinds at the front. The drawer's bottom slips into a $\frac{1}{4}$" x $\frac{1}{4}$" groove in the sides and the drawer front. The bottom, which is beveled on three edges, slips under the drawer's back into its groove.

The one non-traditional thing I do is that I make a shallow $\frac{1}{8}$" x $\frac{1}{2}$" rabbet on the tail boards. This helps me register the tail board against the pin board when I am transferring my layout. I have found that this is worth the time it takes me to cut the rabbet (by hand).

A Finish as Simple as the Piece

Cherry makes its own stain. Sunlight and oxygen do a better job of coloring cherry than a pigment or dye could. To jump-start the natural coloring process, I applied a coat of boiled linseed oil to the project and allowed things to bask in the sun for a day. A little UV goes a long way.

After the oil cured for a couple weeks, I applied a protective topcoat. A wiping varnish or a lacquer finish are both good choices for a server. This piece will take some abuse from heat and moisture, though nothing like your dining table.

After I finished the prototype, I was torn about the hardware. I had planned on using some hand-hammered copper stuff that looked straight out of 1907. But the more I thought of it, the more I thought I needed something lighter. A trip through my grandmother Jean's books (yes, I inherited some of them) convinced me that some Asian-inspired ring pulls would be just right.

Though I don't think she was right about Arts & Crafts furniture, Jean was always right about drawers.

— *Christopher Schwarz*

Simple Shaker End Table

Most joinery for small tables is unnecessarily complex. You can build this icon of good design using simplified (but solid) methods.

When woodworkers first set out to build a project that they designed themselves, the end result is usually overbuilt and chunky-looking. I myself was a victim of just that problem: One of my earliest projects had massive finger joints that were reinforced with #10 screws.

Good craftsmen also must be good designers and good engineers. This mix of sound skills, pleasing proportions and just-right joinery is as difficult to teach as it is to learn.

And so, as my best teachers always said, "It is better to show than tell."

This small Shaker-style table is a perfect blend of traditional joints and delicate lines. Though I'm going to tell you how to build it, my hope is that this article will show you that strong joints don't need to be massive – just well-made. And that good design doesn't have to be flashy – just pleasing to the eye.

This table is adapted heavily from Thomas Moser's excellent book, "How to Build Shaker Furniture" (Sterling). Moser, an English-professor-turned-cabinetmaker, has an excellent eye for design. You can see it in the line of furniture produced by his successful Maine-based business, Thos. Moser Cabinetmakers, and you can see it in this book, first published in 1977.

The first time I built a version of this table, I was stunned by its proportions. The legs are so delicate – just $1\frac{1}{8}$" square. And the detailing is so Spartan – the only ornament is the wide bevel on the underside of the top. But the results are impressive, and I think you'll be impressed, too.

I built the table shown here with a hand-dovetailed drawer. However, if you're not up for attempting that joint yet, don't worry. We've outlined an effective technique for making simple rabbeted drawers on page 125.

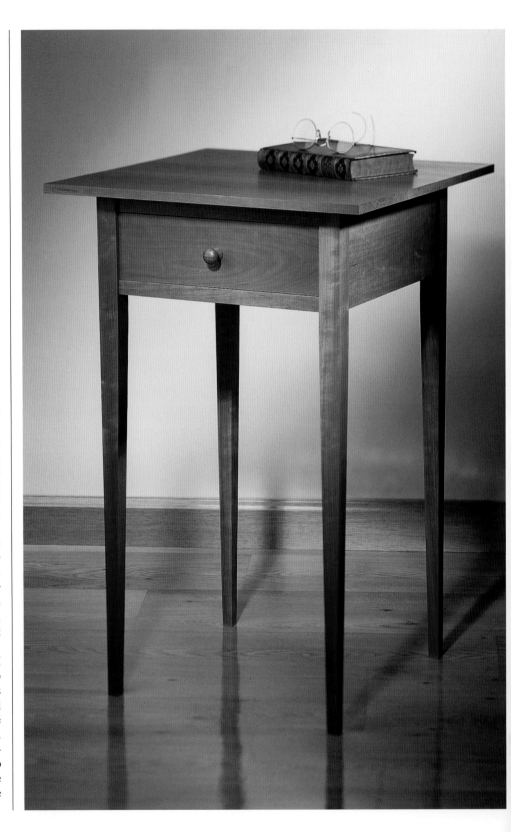

Begin at the Legs

For me, the most difficult task in making this table is choosing the right wood. It sounds ridiculous, but it's true. There is so little wood in this project (only about 12 board feet) that you have to be picky. The pickiness begins with the legs.

Making table legs is more involved than you probably imagine. If you ignore any of the following steps, there's a good chance your legs won't look right and this will bother you when the project is finished. The goal with the legs is to find the straightest-grained boards possible with the end-grain growth rings running from corner to corner. A leg with the growth rings running from corner to corner exhibits what's called "bastard grain" on all four faces.

The reason for this is simple and is shown in the photos at right. If the growth rings do not travel from corner to corner, then each face of your legs will look markedly different than the face adjacent to it. It's distracting and worth avoiding.

If you can find boards at the lumberyard that are cut this way, count yourself lucky, because I never can. So I purchase 1¾" -thick stock (sold in the rough as 8/4 wood) and mill the legs from those over-thick boards.

The legs are 1⅛" thick, so I made a cardboard template with a hole in the center that is oversized, 1⅜" square. I place this template on the end grain and rotate it until I see the grain lines run from corner to corner. Then I trace the shape of the leg onto the end grain using the template.

Next I rip out that shape. Transfer the cutting angle from the board to the blade of the table saw using a bevel gauge and rip one edge of the leg at that angle. Then, rip the leg free of the rest of the waste (you might have to reset your saw blade to 90° to do this) and square up the other three faces of the leg.

With the grain tamed in the legs, you can then joint and plane them to their final thickness and width. I prefer to use my thickness planer for this job. It gives me more consistent results than trying to size the parts on my table saw.

Choose your best-looking boards for the tabletop and drawer front. Your next-best pieces should be reserved for the aprons. The rest of the stuff is useful for the parts inside the case that guide the drawer. Joint and plane all the parts to their finished thicknesses, then rip and crosscut them to their finished widths and lengths.

Tackle the Top

Making a good-looking and flat tabletop is a skill to itself, so we included a primer on gluing up panels on page 118. Even if you have mastered the edge joint used for making panels, you should keep a wary eye when it comes to picking the right boards for your tabletop.

To make the top look as natural as possible, pay attention to the seams. Never join the straight rift-sawn wood edges of a board to the cathedral-

Bastard grain

Flat-sawn grain

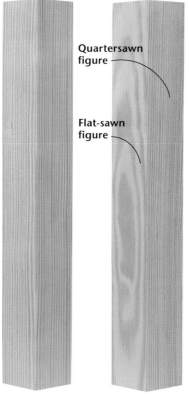

Quartersawn figure

Flat-sawn figure

PHOTO BY TIM GRONDIN

Getting good-looking legs is all in the growth rings. When the rings run from side to side (right), the leg shows flat-sawn figure on two faces and quartersawn figure on two faces. This won't look right. Grain that runs from corner to corner – called bastard grain – creates four faces that all look the same.

Yes, this wastes a little wood, but there isn't much wood in this table to begin with. When the grain lines run from corner to corner of your template, mark that shape and head to the table saw.

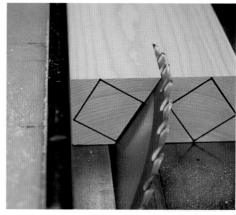

With the shape of the leg drawn on the end grain, it's now just a matter of sawing and jointing to those lines. First cut the angle on the table saw.

Then square things up on the saw or jointer.

The ⅜"-deep mortises are centered on the ends of the legs and are open at the top. This allows you to cut them all with one fence setup. Note that the front legs receive a mortise on only one face. The back legs get mortises on two faces.

The ³⁄₈"-long tenons are cut using the same setup on your router table. Here it's obvious that tenons are nothing more than rabbets that have multiplied.

A ⁵⁄₈"-wide chisel makes quick and accurate work of the small mortises on the legs. If you don't have a mortising chisel, a standard bevel-edge chisel will do the job, though you should avoid wailing on the handle and levering out the chips as much as possible. Work from the center out as shown. Mark the mortise depth on your chisel using permanent marker (believe me, it's not permanent). This works better than tape.

Shave ¹⁄₁₆" of all four faces of the tenons for the lower front rail. Make the same cut on three faces of the upper front rail. Then raise the bit's height to almost ³⁄₁₆" and shave the two larger cheeks on the lower rail. Adjust the height of the bit until the lower rail fits snugly into its mortise.

grain wood you typically find in the middle of a board. This looks horrible. The best arrangement is to join edges with rift grain to similar-looking edges with rift grain. Shift things around until the top looks good. Ignore the adage about alternating the growth rings face up and face down on adjacent boards in a tabletop. The warpage patterns of almost any antique table will quickly point out the fallacy of this approach.

Glue up your top and set it aside for the adhesive to cure. It's time to make mortises.

Simple & Sturdy Table Joinery

Mortise-and-tenon joints are the best ones for a table. Yes, there are metal corner brackets out there, and a couple of biscuits also could do the job. But the simple router-table setup we've devised is so simple, straightforward and inexpensive that there's no reason to cheat here.

Essentially, the mortises are open at the top and milled in the legs using a router in a table and a ³⁄₈" straight bit. The simplified tenons are cut using the exact same tools and setup. There is no reason to buy a pricey mortiser or spend hours learning to make the joint by hand. Both of those approaches are noble; they're just not necessary for this particular table.

It's important to talk about the length of the tenons used for this table. As a rule, you want your tenons to be as long as possible – within reason, of course. An ideal tenon is ³⁄₄" to 1¹⁄₄" long. But when you're dealing with a small project such as this, you need to scale your joinery. The legs for this table are quite delicate, just 1¹⁄₈" square, so full-size joints aren't going to work. And once you set the aprons back ³⁄₁₆", as shown in the illustration on page 115, you get even less room. The maximum length for the tenons in this table is ³⁄₄" with the

tenons meeting in the middle. But making these mortises open at the top makes a fragile shoulder on the inside corner of the leg. Once you glue up the joint, the shoulder is supported just fine, but you risk breaking it before assembly time.

So I opted for ³⁄₈"-long tenons. There is still a remarkable amount of gluing surface and the joint is more than stout enough for a table this small. When you make a bigger table in the future, you can make bigger tenons.

For details on executing this joint, see "Mortises & Tenons for Tables" on page 120.

After milling the mortises and the tenons for the aprons and the legs, you need to join the front two legs with the front two rails. This is a fiddly bit of joinery, but there are some tricks to make

it foolproof. Let's start with the lower front rail.

The lower front rail needs to be mortised into the front legs. The best way to cut the mortises is with a chisel. First lay out the location of the mortises on the front legs. The mating tenon on the rail will be ³⁄₈" thick x ⁵⁄₈" wide x ³⁄₄" long. Next, lay out the mortise wall ¹⁄₄" in from the front edge of the legs.

Chop out the mortises to a depth of ³⁄₄". Work from the center to the ends of the mortise with the bevel facing the center of the hole. Keep in mind as you work that though you want to be as neat as possible, the edge of the mortise will be concealed by the shoulders of the tenon, so the occasional small ding is no harm done.

Now you can cut the corresponding tenon on

Simple Shaker End Table

	NO.	PART	SIZES (INCHES)			MATERIAL	NOTES
			T	W	L		
Table							
❑	4	Legs	1¹⁄₈	1¹⁄₈	26³⁄₄	Cherry	Taper to ⁵⁄₈"
❑	1	Top	³⁄₄	18	18	Cherry	¹⁄₄" x 2" bevel on underside
❑	3	Aprons	³⁄₄	5	12¹⁄₂	Cherry	³⁄₈" tenon both ends
❑	2	Front rails	³⁄₄	³⁄₄	13¹⁄₄	Cherry	³⁄₄" tenon or dovetail
❑	4	Drawer guides	³⁄₄	1	12¹⁄₈	Cherry	Notched around legs
❑	2	Spacers	³⁄₁₆	³⁄₄	11³⁄₄	Cherry	Glued to aprons
Drawer							
❑	1	Front	³⁄₄	3¹⁄₂	11³⁄₄	Cherry	¹⁄₄" x ¹⁄₂" rabbet on ends
❑	2	Sides	¹⁄₂	3¹⁄₂	12¹⁄₄	Poplar	
❑	1	Back	¹⁄₂	3	11³⁄₄	Poplar	¹⁄₄" x ¹⁄₂" rabbet on ends
❑	1	Bottom	¹⁄₂	11¹⁄₄	12³⁄₈	Poplar	In ¹⁄₄" x ¹⁄₄" groove

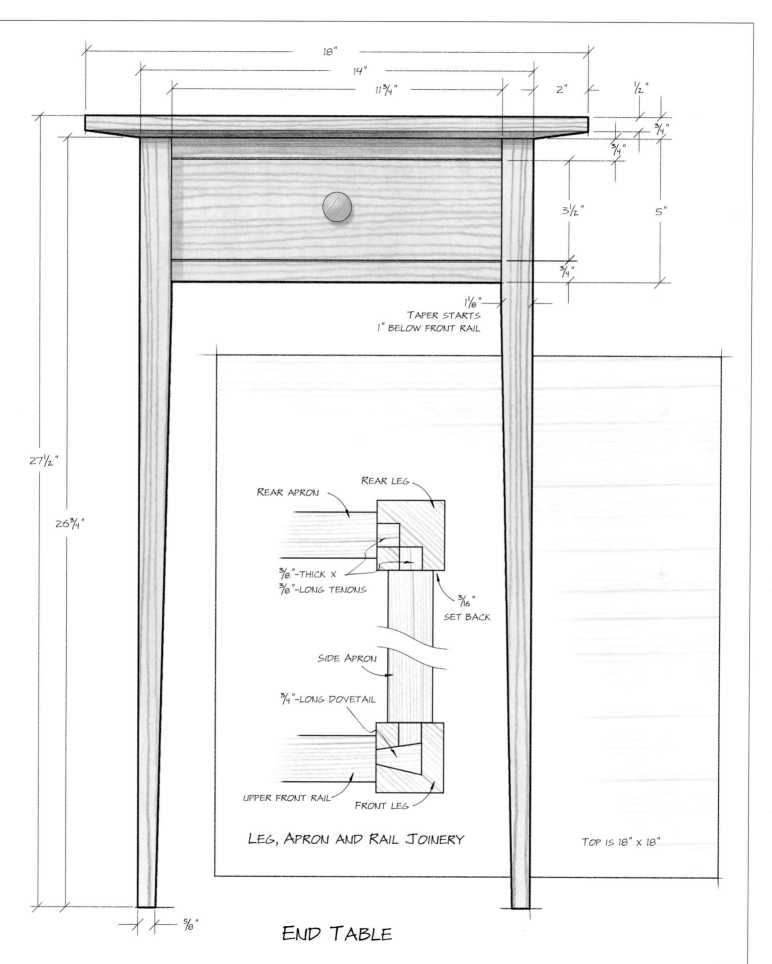

18"

14"

11³⁄₄"

2"

¹⁄₂"

³⁄₄"

³⁄₄"

3½"

5"

³⁄₄"

1¹⁄₈"
TAPER STARTS
1" BELOW FRONT RAIL

27½"

26³⁄₄"

5⁄₈"

REAR APRON

REAR LEG

³⁄₈"-THICK X
³⁄₈"-LONG TENONS

³⁄₁₆"
SET BACK

SIDE APRON

³⁄₄"-LONG DOVETAIL

UPPER FRONT RAIL

FRONT LEG

LEG, APRON AND RAIL JOINERY

TOP IS 18" X 18"

END TABLE

the lower front rail. Use the same procedure as you did for the tenons on the aprons. First set the height of the bit to $1/16$". Then adjust the fence so the tenon will be $3/4$" long. Make a couple of test cuts to confirm your setup.

With the bit at this setting, cut away all four faces of the tenon on the lower rail. Next, get the upper front rail and make this cut on three faces and set it aside. Now increase the height of the bit and shave away material on the tenons until the lower rail fits in its mortise snugly.

The upper front rail is dovetailed by hand into the front legs. Before you despair, take a look at the upper rail, which you just tenoned on three faces. You've cut three perfect shoulders for this joint. So even if your dovetail is the sloppiest one ever cut (which is doubtful), it will still fit tightly against the legs and the joint will never show.

With that knowledge, lay out a $3/4$"-long dovetail on each end of the upper front rail. Its size and slope aren't critical. Lay it out so it's easy to cut

and yet takes away as little material as possible. And make the slope of the angle about 8° or so.

Cut the dovetail on the end of the rail. Next, dry-assemble the table base and clamp up all the joints. Place the upper rail in place (the shoulders should fit tightly between the legs) and trace the dovetail shape onto the top of the front legs and the part of the apron tenon that it overlaps. Disassemble the table and saw out the socket in the legs and on the top of the aprons' tenons.

Now you can assemble the table without glue and take a look at how your joints fit.

Taper the Legs

There are a variety of ways to cut tapers on legs. I don't like the commercial tapering jigs for table saws. They work, but they put your hand too close to the blade. Shop-made tapering sleds are safer, but they require wood, material and time to fabricate. And don't even ask me to explain the math involved in making taper cuts on a jointer.

This table is a great project for practicing your planing. The parts of the base aren't wide, so you don't have to worry about the corner of the plane iron digging into your work. If you're interested in learning to use a hand plane, planing the tapers, rails and edges of tabletops are three good places to begin.

It makes my head hurt.

The most straightforward, safe and foolproof way to cut tapers is to lay them out on the legs, cut them out with a band saw (or jigsaw in a pinch) and clean up the cuts on your jointer or with a hand plane (my tool of choice).

The leg taper begins 1" down from where the aprons end. The legs taper down to $5/8$" square at the foot. That seems almost too delicate a taper, on paper. But when you see the results, you'll be impressed with the strength and beauty of the legs. Don't forget that the tapers are on only the two inside edges of the legs. With the tapers complete, you're ready to assemble the base.

Gluing it up

Begin by sanding or planing all your base pieces so they are ready for finishing. If you choose to sand, I recommend you sand the legs by hand with a small sanding block. A random-orbit sander will give you a bellied surface, which will spoil the fit of your joint. Begin with #100-grit paper and work your way up the grits to #180- or #220-grit.

Start the assembly by gluing a side apron into a mating front and back leg. When this assembly is complete, you can then check the fit of your dovetail a second time and make any modifications necessary for a tight fit. If you're going to peg your joints from the inside (as described in "Mortises & Tenons for Tables"), now is the time to peg those side aprons. Then glue up the remainder of the table base.

Sorting Out the Guts

The rest of the table is simple joinery, but you need to pay close attention to how everything fits so that the drawer slides well. The first order of business is to fit and glue up the four drawer guides. The drawer rides on the two at the bottom. The two at the top have dual functions: They attach the table base to the top and they prevent the drawer from tipping downward when it's pulled out.

Start by notching the corners of all four guides.

Cutting the Dovetails on the Upper Front Rail

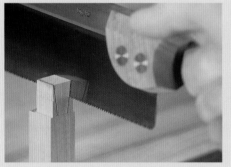

The dovetails are simple backsaw work. Even if you miss your line, you'll be able to fix it when you cut the socket. If you mess up the socket, the result will never show. Saw down to the shoulder and pare away the little waste sliver with a chisel.

Second, mark out the shape of the dovetail on the top of the leg using a mechanical pencil or (even better) a marking knife.

Third, use your backsaw to define the edges of the socket. Saw inside the marked line. You can pare away the extra waste with a chisel once the socket is chopped out.

To remove the waste, first loosen it up by chopping a series of score lines on top of the leg. Then come in from the front of the joint (as shown) to pop the waste out. Keep working down and back. This is good chisel practice.

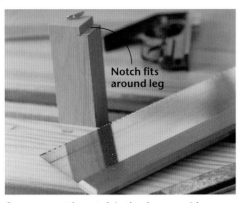

Notch fits around leg

Once you cut the notch in the drawer guide, a sharp chisel can fine-tune the fit with ease. To learn how to correctly sharpen a chisel, see "Sharpening a Chisel" on page 11.

A $^3/_{16}$" x $^3/_{16}$" notch allows the guides to fit around the legs. You can cut it with a band saw or jigsaw if you like, but a backsaw will be just as fast and accurate. When the guides fit around the legs, glue the lower guides to the aprons. Make sure their top edge is flush with the lower front rail. This ensures the drawer won't hang up.

Before you glue on the upper guides, you should drill countersunk holes that will allow you to screw the base to the underside of the top. These holes need to be elongated a bit to allow the top to expand and contract, but please don't get too worked up about this point. There is no need to rout out a slot or drill overlapping holes. Simply drive your drill into the hole, and while the drill is running, pivot it forward and back.

Glue the upper guides in place. Make sure they are flush to the top of the apron (or just a little below) and don't drop below the upper front rail.

You can see details of what the inside of the table base looks like – with all the guides and runners in place – in "Simple & Fast Rabbeted Drawers" on page 125.

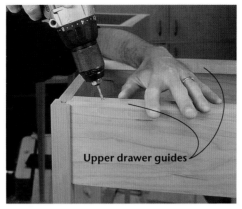

Upper drawer guides

The holes need to allow the body of the screw to pivot. So reaming out the holes as shown is perfectly acceptable.

Return To the Top

You might think that building and fitting the drawer is the next step, but it's not. In a small project, the top will change how everything fits below it. If you tighten the screws between the top and base too much, the drawer will bind up in the case. So really the best course of action is to make the top, attach it, then fit the drawer.

Cut your top panel to its finished size and lay out the bevel on its underside. You can cut this bevel on the table saw much like you would a raised panel for a door. This can be tricky depending on the height of your table saw's fence and the size of the throat opening for the saw blade.

If you choose this route, set your table saw's blade for a 7° bevel and sneak up on the proper cut by making a couple of passes over the blade, changing the height of the blade and location of the fence until you get the bevel you desire.

If that approach doesn't appeal to you, I recommend you mark the bevel on the underside and shape it with a rasp and file. A rasp (I prefer the inexpensive Microplane rasp for this job) can

remove wood in a hurry. A mill file, scraper and sandpaper will clean up your work from there.

Plane or sand the top for finishing. Attach it to the base with #8 x 1" screws. The easiest way to accomplish this is to put the top upside down on your bench. Then clamp the table base in place to the top. Drill pilot holes into the top and then drive each screw home. Now you are ready to construct the drawer.

Drawer Details

When I've built this project in the past, I've made a dovetailed drawer, which is typical of Shaker construction methods. But to make the project simpler to build, I recommend you try out the drawer-building method detailed on page 125 That style of drawer is easy to construct and will be more than adequate for the light duty this drawer is certain to receive.

Note that the sizes in the cutting list for this table assume you will make the drawer using this rabbeted construction method.

No matter how I make my drawers, I usually choose poplar for the sides and bottom. It's inexpensive and machines well. When the drawer is built, I fit it with a jack plane. Plane the top, bottom and outside faces of the drawer's sides until it moves smoothly in and out of the table's base. Then turn your attention to getting the right gap (called the "reveal") around the drawer front, a task suited for a block plane.

With the drawer fit, attach the knob. I like to screw a piece of scrap on the top edge of the drawer back to prevent the drawer from being pulled all the way out of the table (unless you mean to). It's a small detail that I'm fond of.

Cleaning Up

Break all the edges with #120-grit sandpaper and disassemble the table for finishing. With cherry, I think it's worth the extra effort to accelerate its darkening by applying a couple of coats of boiled linseed oil and putting the table out in the sun for a day. Then you can brush or wipe on your favorite film finish. I prefer a satin lacquer.

The first time I built this table, I was going to give it away to my sister as a wedding gift. But when it was complete, it sparked something rare in me: envy. So I kept the table and it sits by my bedside as a reminder of the rewards of good design. My sister can have the next one.

— *Christopher Schwarz*

Supplies

Rockler
800-279-4441 or rockler.com
1 • Cherry Shaker $^7/_8$" knob, $^3/_8$" tenon, #61665, $6.39/pair

Price as of publication deadline.

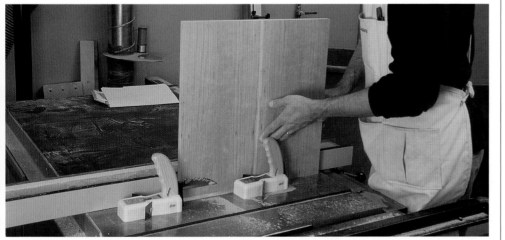

The entire top is riding across the blade on a $^1/_2$"-wide edge, so take care when cutting the bevel.

Gluing up Flat Panels

Three easy steps – joint, glue and clamp – help you create perfect panels.

Wood panels are an essential component in making almost every piece of furniture. While a flat panel less than 6" wide can be made by simply crosscutting a board, a panel wider than that will require gluing a few boards together edge to edge. Keeping those panels flat, straight and attractive is easily learned and will make all of your projects much more successful.

First let's get rid of a common myth: To make sure a panel stays flat, it's not necessary to rip the individual boards to 2" or 3" widths and then reglue them. All this does is create more work and an ugly panel.

Wood moves primarily because of changes in moisture content. After being felled and cut, the wood from a tree slowly acclimates to its environment as the moisture in the wood evaporates. Because of the shape and orientation of the fibers in a board, some will shrink more than others. Even when kiln-dried and assembled into a project, lumber will continue to react to changes in humidity by cupping and warping. The illustration (below) shows how wood will move as it dries and should help you choose the right orientation of growth rings. A trick is to try to leave the wood's heartwood side showing on your panels.

Proper preparation, technique and tools are all required to make a perfectly flat panel.

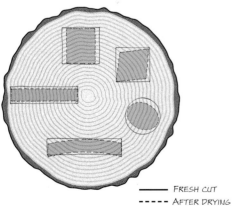

— FRESH CUT
----- AFTER DRYING

The first step in gluing up a flat panel is reading the wood. The end view of a board (or log, as above) shows the different shrinkage pattern for different cuts of lumber. Knowing how your lumber will react to humidity changes will help you with your panel layouts.

Proper wood preparation also can help you avoid warping. When planing boards to final thickness, remove material evenly from both sides to allow grain tension in the board to remain stable.

When you rough-cut your wood, leave the boards a little long and wide (so the panel glueup is 1" oversize in both directions). Cut them to finished size after your glue-up. This lets you cut around imperfections near the edges.

Also, pay careful attention to the appearance of each board. Even though we have to use more than one board to make our panels, we want to make the panels look like they're still one piece. Matching the cathedrals or the straight-grain patterns at the joint (as well as matching the color of the wood) will make for a better-looking finished panel. Try to get all of your panel pieces from a single board length. Color- and grain-matching is much easier then.

Once you've determined where your joints should occur, you must make those edges mate perfectly. The jointer is designed to produce an edge that is perpendicular to the face of the board. But if the fence is slightly off, the edge will be, too. Each board needs to be flat and have at least one perpendicular edge (interior boards need two) to achieve a flat panel. The bottom left photo on page 119 shows a trick to make sure your boards meet flat at the edge every time.

Now let's talk about glue – either yellow or white glue will work fine for a simple edge joint. Glue isn't intended to fill gaps between two pieces of wood, but rather to bond two pieces together. Only use enough glue – about .001" thick – to form a locking layer between the two surfaces. Too much glue creates a weak joint. Insufficient or partially dried glue results in inadequate bonding strength.

Now you're ready to glue up your panel, but there's still lots to know. Let's start with clamping pressure and proper clamp orientation. Clamps are designed to produce tremendous pressure, and that's great, but it doesn't mean you should use that pressure to force an open joint closed during glue-up. If you have to do that then your edges weren't properly joined to begin with. Even with a perfect joint, applying maximum clamp pressure can cause the panel to twist.

You should be able to close the joint using only hand pressure. A slight gap at the center of the joint, called a "sprung" joint, is acceptable (some woodworkers say preferable). This adds tension at the ends of the joint, which can separate as the wood dries. But if the gaps occur at the ends of the panel, problems with the joint pulling open later could occur.

With the glue properly applied, it's time to add clamps. No matter what type of clamp you are using, it's good practice to alternate the bars above and below the panel. You should also space them about 6" - 8" apart on panels made with narrow boards and farther apart (up to 12") on panels made with wider boards. Clamping pressure radiates out from the clamp face at a 45° angle. That radiant pressure should overlap at the glue joint. The order that clamps are applied will help as well. (See photo at bottom right.)

If you're gluing up a panel with many boards (such as a kitchen tabletop with six boards) you can make the glue-up much easier by being a little patient. First glue up three two-board panels, then join those three panels together. Aligning two glue joints is much easier than aligning five.

Another suggestion during clamping is to use your clamps' bars to keep the panel flat. With the panel resting against the bar, the bar adds support (from both sides) to keep the panel flat. But when you use your clamps in this manner, the steel of the bar (if not plated) can react to the glue and leave black marks on your panel. Either slide a piece of paper between the clamp and glue joint or make sure you use clamps with plated bars. Apply enough clamp pressure so the boards don't slide around at the joint. You likely will have to apply some side pressure to slide the boards. If you need extra leverage to level up the joints, twist the unclamped ends of the boards. When the seam is flush between the clamp heads, apply enough clamping pressure to make glue squeeze out of the joint and close the gap to about .001" wide. Again, don't overtighten the clamp. If you're getting good glue squeeze-out and the joint is tight, that's when it's time to stop.

About that excess glue: Before you set the panel aside to dry (that's at least 30 minutes before you can take the clamps off and an hour before you should apply pressure to the joint), take a damp cloth (not wet) and wipe along the joint in short swipes, cleaning off the glue completely.

One myth is that adding water to a glue joint will dilute the glue, weakening the joint – not so. The amount of water involved in the cleaning process will have no affect on joint strength and save a lot of torn fibers if you try to remove the dried glue from the panel later.

Once the clamps are removed, it should only be necessary to plane or sand the joint lightly to smooth it flush on your panel.

And that's all there is to making perfect flat panels. It's the backbone of any woodworking project and when done correctly, it's also one place to let the beauty of the wood show through.
– *David Thiel*

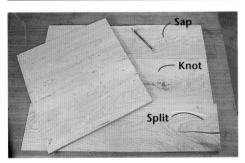

This three-board panel (on top) shows nicely matching grain patterns, making the transition between the boards invisible. The three boards underneath the panel exhibit some problems that can arise in matching grain.

A good glue joint starts with a thin, even coat of glue. Glue will penetrate wood until it starts to cure, then it only lays on the surface of the wood. So for fast glue-ups, putting glue on one surface of the joint is adequate. For multiple or long (24") joints, spread glue on both surfaces.

With your finished faces showing, mark one board with an "I" and the other board with an "O." Also mark the joint on both boards to avoid confusion. Take the board marked with an "I" and place that marked face "in," against the jointer fence, and make your pass. Take the "O" board and set it with that face "out," away from the jointer fence, and make your pass. Even if your jointer fence was out by 2° or 3°, by producing complementary angles at the joint you will have a square joint. And it works for as many boards as necessary to make up your panel. The inset photo shows the flat panel with the 2° offset at the joint.

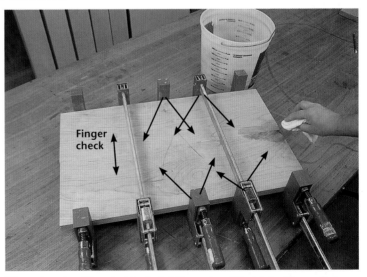

When clamping, it's easiest to start at the center of the joint with your first clamp. As you apply pressure, make sure that the faces are aligned as perfectly as possible by running your finger across the joint. Wipe off the glue with a wet rag. You want to remove the glue entirely, not push the glue further into the grain, so wipe well.

Mortises & Tenons for Tables

We found that all you need to cut this stout joint is a router, a router table and a single inexpensive bit.

To avoid cutting mortise-and-tenon joints, many woodworkers opt to build their projects using simpler rabbets, dados and grooves instead. What many of them fail to realize is that the mortise-and-tenon joint is nothing more than a clever combination of rabbets and grooves.

The mortise is just a stopped groove. And the tenon is just a piece of wood that has been rabbeted on at least one (but usually four) of its faces.

So the real challenge for the woodworker who sets out to make this joint for the first time is actually a set of three manageable tasks:

- Choosing the right tools.
- Setting up the tools for accurate results.
- Choosing a project to practice on.

Why Build a Table?

Without a doubt, the best project to learn how to make a mortise-and-tenon joint on is a table. The typical table has – at most – eight joints to cut. (Compare that to a Morris chair, where you can easily have 75 joints or more.)

Fitting a mortise-and-tenon joint for a table is more forgiving than fitting the same joint for even a simple square picture frame. With a frame, you need to fit the horizontal members (called rails) between the vertical members (called stiles) at the top and bottom of the frame. There can be quite a bit of fiddling to get the rails closed tightly against the stiles at both places.

With a small table, each assembly of two legs and one apron is simpler – you have to fit the joint only at the top of the legs. There is indeed some fiddling when you put these assemblies together into the completed table base, but because the work is done in stages, it's more manageable.

Also, the mortise-and-tenon joint for a small table can be much simpler to execute than the mortise-and-tenon joint for a frame or door. To understand why this is true, you first need a lesson in basic tenon anatomy.

The Tenacious Tenon

Each part of the tenon has a job to do. Once you know this, you'll also know how the joint can be modified or tweaked and still do its job.

All tenons have four cheeks. The wider cheeks are face cheeks and the narrower ones are edge cheeks. The face cheeks are the backbone of the joint. They are the long-grain gluing surface that mates with the long-grain surface in the wall of the mortise. The better the fit between the face cheeks and the mortise, the stronger your glue joint ultimately will be.

The edge cheeks don't provide much gluing strength at all. Though the edge cheeks are also long-grain surfaces, they mate with end-grain surfaces in the mortise, which makes a poor joint. Instead, the job of the edge cheek is to resist racking forces in the assembly. The better the fit between the edge cheek and the mortise, the less likely your project will wobble, even if the glue joint at the face cheek becomes compromised.

Tenons also have shoulders. This part of the joint – which literally looks like a shoulder – can be on one to four of the edges of the tenon. The job of the shoulder is mostly cosmetic: It hides any sloppiness in the mortise opening. It also can be pared in various ways to hide other defects of the joint. For example, if you sanded your mortised piece too much and crowned the surface, the shoulder can be chiseled up near the cheek to eliminate any gap that might appear between the joint's pieces. The shoulder is therefore necessary only on surfaces that show on the final project.

There's something else to consider when making shoulders: If you make them too wide, you can introduce two problems to your joint. First, bigger shoulders means you have smaller cheeks, which reduces the overall strength of the joint. Second, a large shoulder will allow the tenoned board to cup or bow slightly at its edges. Big shoulders can, over time, result in a joint that isn't flush like it was the day you made it.

Fewer Shoulders Make it Easier

With all these parts to keep track of, it's no wonder that some woodworkers shy away from this joint. But tenons for tables can be simpler than tenons for other assemblies. Here's why: The tenons for tables need fewer shoulders. Really, only one face of the apron shows in a table. You definitely don't need a shoulder on the inside of the apron.

A shoulder at the bottom of the apron is optional, though a very small one is easy to fit and prevents the apron from cupping.

And here's the real kicker – you don't need a shoulder at the top of the apron. In fact, I'd argue that eliminating it can make a better joint for two reasons: First, because the tenon is almost the full width of the apron, it keeps your apron from cupping or bowing. This is especially important in a table because a cupped apron can push the tabletop up in places, spoiling its flatness. Second, it makes the mortise easy to cut. Essentially the mortise is stopped only at one end. As you'll see shortly, this allows you to make this joint without a lot of equipment.

Of course, the logical objection to a joint like this is that if the mortise is open on one end then the table won't resist racking. I argue that a properly fitted tabletop takes the place of that mortise wall, constraining the tenon's edge cheek and keeping it from racking. And, as you'll see later, you can easily reinforce this joint with a well-placed peg for added insurance.

Choosing Your Tools

One big objection to mortise-and-tenon joinery is the specialized tools you need to make it. Benchtop mortising machines cost $200; a kit that allows your drill press to serve as a makeshift mortiser costs about $70 (assuming you have a drill press). An option is to cut your mortises with a plunge router and a shopmade or commercial jig ($75 or so). But these jigs take time and money and aren't necessary for this particular joint.

For cutting the tenons, you could buy a commercial jig, build a tenoning jig or get a dado stack ($85 for starters) to do the job on the table saw.

Still other woodworkers insist on cutting the joint by hand. I do a lot of handwork, but making

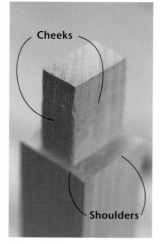

The anatomy of a typical tenon with four shoulders.

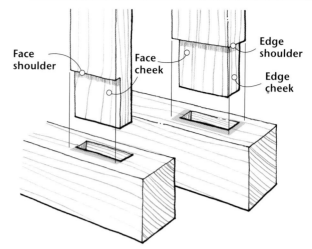

The shoulders cover up any inaccuracy in the mortises of these bare-faced tenons with simple shoulders.

this joint with hand tools requires an investment in tools (tenon saw, carcase saw, mortising chisel and shoulder plane) and practice time. While there is pleasure in cutting this joint by hand, it can be frustrating at first. (See "Cutting this Joint with Hand Tools" on page 122.)

There is an easier way. I argue that you can do all the mortise-and-tenon joinery for a simple table with a router, a router table and a ⅜"-diameter straight bit. All three items are common equipment in even the most bare-bones shop.

In a nutshell, here's how it's done: First mill your mortises in the legs. Set up the straight bit in your router table and set the fence to center the cut on the width of the leg. Cut the mortise out in several passes, increasing the height of the bit with each pass. You'll need a stop on the outfeed side of the router table's fence to stop the mortise in the same location.

To cut the tenons, keep that same bit in your router table and use a miter gauge (or a scrap of wood) to guide the apron into the bit, cutting a rabbet on each end. Adjust the height of the bit until the tenon fits perfectly in its mortise.

The heart of this method is the ⅜"-diameter straight bit. Why ⅜"? There are several reasons. Aprons for small tables are typically going to be made using ¾"-thick wood, and tenons as a rule are supposed to be half as thick as the stock they're

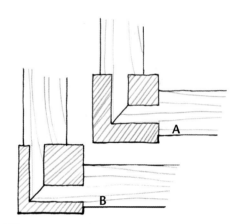

When tenons are closer to the outside of the aprons, as in example "B" above, they can have extra length, compared to the tenons in example "A" that are centered on the aprons.

cut on. This makes a balanced joint: half of it is tenon and the other half is shoulder.

But some woodworkers use ¼"-thick tenons on ¾" stock. For this particular technique, I think that's a mistake. Straight bits that are ¼" diameter are fragile; even quality ones will snap easily if you put too much pressure on them. Similarly, a beefy ½"-diameter straight bit is also a bad idea. You could use one, but then your mortise starts to get so wide that its walls can become more fragile, especially in a small table's delicate legs. I'd save the ½" bit for milling joints for bigger projects, such as dining tables.

The router doesn't have to be fancy – even a low-powered single-speed tool will do this job with relative ease. And the router table doesn't have to be expensive, either. Any table with an adjustable fence will do – even a shop-made version with a simple plywood table and a straight scrap of solid wood for the fence.

Cutting This Joint with Hand Tools

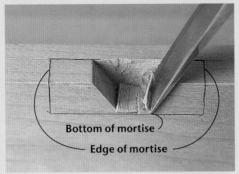

To cut a mortise by hand, use a chisel that's the exact width of your desired mortise. Work from the center out with the face of the tool pointed toward the center of the mortise (left). I sliced open this joint during the process (above) so you can see how you chop out a "V" in the center and then chop to the ends.

To cut the tenons, saw the cheeks diagonally with the piece held in your vice. Seeing two sides simultaneously increases your accuracy.

Once you make the first diagonal cut, turn the work around and saw straight down. The first cut guides your second cut.

The next step is to saw the shoulders. Mark the location of your shoulder with a chisel and straight-edge. This cut will guide your saw. With the shoulders cut, trim them with a shoulder plane (shown above) until the tenon fits the mortise.

Make the Mortises

The first step is to mill the mortises on the ends of the legs. Set up your router table so the bit projects ¼" above the table. Position the fence so the cut will be centered on the end of the leg. You probably won't hit this dimension the first time, so be sure you practice on test pieces.

Clamp a stop piece (a scrap piece is fine) to your fence so your mortises will end at the same place. Where you clamp the stop is determined by the width of your aprons. For example, if your aprons are 4" wide, I'd position the stop so that the mortise is $3\frac{7}{8}$" long. This will give you a small $\frac{1}{8}$" shoulder at the bottom of the apron.

Take some scrap that is the exact size as your table leg and mill a test mortise. Push the leg into the bit with steady pressure. If the bit burns, you're going too slowly; if it chatters, you're going too fast. Check your results. To determine if the mortise is centered on the leg, use calipers and check the length with a ruler.

With your setup just right, you can mill the mortises. First mill all the mortises with the bit set to ¼" high. Then increase the height of the bit to ½" and perform the same operation on all the legs. Finally, raise the bit to ¾" (if that's your final height) and make the last pass. In my book, a 1"-deep mortise would be preferable, but not every project will allow it. The small side table project in this issue uses a ⅜"-deep mortise.

Time to Try the Tenons

Making the matching tenons is surprisingly simple work using the same router-table setup. Set the height of your bit to ⅛" and adjust the fence so that the diameter of the bit plus the distance between the bit and fence equals the length of your tenon. For example, to cut a ¾"-long tenon, position the fence so that the ⅜"-diameter bit is ⅜" away from the fence.

Get some scrap that's the same thickness as your aprons and cut a test tenon. You can use a miter gauge to guide the work, but a simple square back-up block works just as well – and it reduces tear-out as the bit exits the cut. Make the test cut in at least three passes. Start at the end of the tenon and work to the shoulder. This is the safest way to make the cut because you cannot get any wood jammed between the bit and the fence.

Check the length of your tenon and adjust your fence. With the length set, mill the edge shoulders on the bottom edge of the apron.

Next, make the first cut on the face cheek on all the aprons. Do this using the same procedure you followed for the edge cheeks. With that cut complete, raise the bit very close to $\frac{3}{16}$" high and make another pass on all your tenons. Your tenons should almost fit in the mortises.

Getting a perfect fit is just a matter of taking the time to nudge the router bit up until the tenons fit in the mortises you cut. What's a perfect fit? You should be able to fit the tenon in its mortise

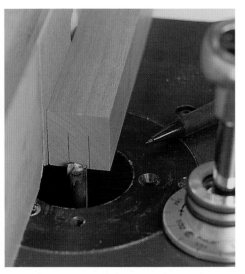

To cut the mortise with the router, first mark out the location on the end of a leg and line up the bit with your layout lines as best you can.

Mark your start and stop points on a piece of tape

Stop

The stop determines the length of the mortise. Don't forget to include the diameter of the bit when determining where the stop should go. Try to get it as close as you can when making a test cut.

using just hand pressure. If you have to use a mallet, it's too tight. If the tenon drops into the mortise and wiggles, it's too loose.

If the tenon is too tight, don't force it. You'll destroy a fragile leg. If it's too loose, you're going to have to beef up your tenon a bit. The best way to do this is to glue hand-plane shavings (for small adjustments) or thicker scraps (for large errors) to the tenon. Once this extra wood is glued in place, you might have to mill down the tenon a bit again. Take your time when cutting your tenons – a little extra care saves you a lot of grief.

When the tenons slide home in their mortises, you're close to completing the joint. Now it's just a matter of squaring the rounded end of the mortise and either mitering or notching the tenons so they fit together, if necessary.

Getting the tenons to fit with each other is simple work with a backsaw. Really, there is nothing difficult about this cut, and even if you mess it up it will never show. If you like, you can cut wide of your line and then pare to your layout line using a chisel.

In small tables (and many large ones), it's typical for the two mortises in a leg to meet at the center. This is easy to deal with; you'll just have to modify your tenons a bit to make them fit. There are two generally good solutions: You can miter the end of each tenon to fit, or you can cut notches on the ends so they interlock, as shown in the illustrations at right.

Both solutions are simple work with a saw. You don't need a perfect fit inside the leg because it will never show. But they are both good ways to get some experience cutting with a hand saw or making a couple of miters.

When your joint is ready to assemble, here are a couple of tips: Don't try to assemble your table base all at once. Glue up one side and then

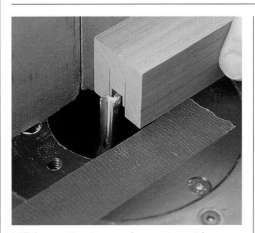

Mill the mortises in several passes to avoid stressing the bit. With your stop and fence in place, the work proceeds quickly.

Walls

A dial caliper ensures that you will have less fussing when you fit your joints. A perfectly centered mortise will result in a table base that is square and not a parallelogram. Check the two mortise walls. When they are equal in thickness, your mortise is centered.

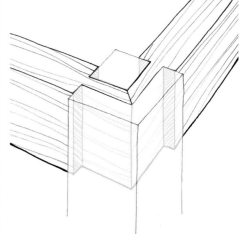

One option to deal with the point where the tenons meet is to miter the end of the tenons.

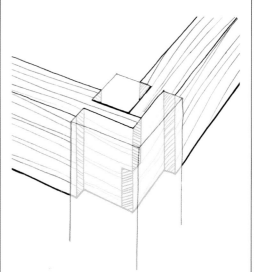

If you don't want to miter the tenons, you can cut notches in the ends so they interlock.

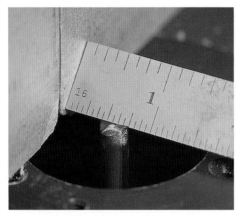

The tenon length is determined by the diameter of the bit and its distance from the fence. Use a ruler to get this setting close. Make a test cut and adjust the fit so it's perfect.

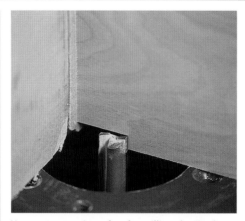

Your test set-up is perfect for milling the single edge shoulder. Make this cut with the apron on edge guided by a back-up block or a miter gauge.

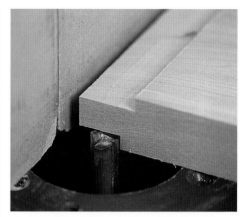

After the second pass, your tenons should be only a hair off. Make this cut on a piece of scrap first to ensure you don't overshoot your mark.

the other. Then glue those two assemblies together. It takes more time, but there are fewer joints to keep an eye on as the glue begins to set up. The glue-up procedure also reinforces the sometimes-fragile mortise wall created by this mortising technique.

Be sure to do a dry fit. If the tenon won't seat all the way into its mortise, shorten your tenon until it does. If there is a gap at the outside shoulder, try paring away some of the end grain of the shoulder at the corner where it meets the cheek – but don't chisel the edge of the shoulder that shows.

During glue-up, add glue on the mortise walls only. Don't glue on the shoulder and don't worry about gluing the edge cheeks or the mortise's bottom. If you get glue there, that's fine, but mostly you want to get the maximum amount of contact between the face cheeks and the mortise wall.

Reinforcements

Finally, I think it's a good idea to reinforce table tenons using a wooden peg driven through the leg. But don't peg your joints until the glue is set up. If you don't want the peg to show, you can peg the joint from inside the table base.

No matter where you put the peg, the procedure is the same. Cut some pegs on your table saw; I like square stuff that's a hair bigger than $\frac{1}{4}$" x $\frac{1}{4}$". I don't use manufactured dowels because they are inconsistent in size. Sharpen one end of your square peg in a pencil sharpener and cross-cut it to 1" long. With a knife, trim off a good deal of the pointiest part of the end you sharpened.

Take a drill with a $\frac{1}{4}$" brad-point bit and drill the hole for the peg. The hole should be deep enough to pass all the way through the tenon but not pass through the entire leg. Usually I like to center my pegs on the length of the tenon.

Put a little glue in the hole and drive the peg in with a hammer. As the peg hits bottom, the hammer will make a different sound when it strikes the peg. Stop hammering. Any more hits could split the peg. As you'll see, this procedure lets you put a square peg in a round hole. The corners of the peg bite into the surrounding wood to keep it from twisting out. Finally, trim the peg flush (or almost flush) using a chisel, a gouge or a flush-cutting saw, as shown below.

With this simplified version of the mortise-and-tenon joint mastered, you can see how a couple of extra cuts can change it. Keep practicing this joint and before you know it, that Arts & Crafts spindle bed or Morris chair will look like an easier (or at least doable) job.

— *Christopher Schwarz*

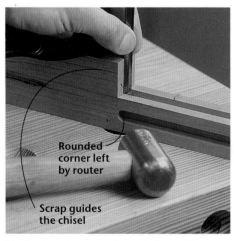

Rounded corner left by router

Scrap guides the chisel

The best way to square the end of a mortise is with a chisel that is the exact width of your mortise. This joint will be concealed by the tenon shoulder, so it doesn't have to be pretty.

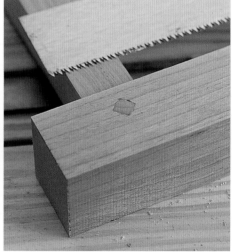

If you've never pegged a joint before, give it a try on one of your test joints. It's actually simple and straightforward work. This extra effort will add strength to your table base.

Simple & Fast Rabbeted Drawers

It takes only one setup on the table saw to cut every joint you need to make a solid drawer. Without a doubt, this is as easy as it gets.

A long the road to comfortably referring to yourself as a "woodworker," there are a few important milestones you must reach. One of these is building your first drawer. For some reason, this project causes more antacid-popping than almost any other project.

A drawer is just a box. The tricky part is that the box must fit accurately into a hole and move smoothly. There are three steps to a successful drawer: precise measuring, accurate joining and careful fitting. This article shows you the tricks we use to successfully complete all three steps.

Measuring Like a Pro

Let's say you're building an end table with a drawer. Knowing the size of the drawer's hole is the first critical piece of information. Seeing how that space is made and understanding how the drawer will "run" in the table is the next step. In traditional case construction, the drawer is just slightly smaller than its hole (which is the technique we're showing here). In modern cabinets, the drawer is considerably smaller than its hole to make room for mechanical slides or glides.

In our traditional case, the drawer hole must be clear of obstructions or corners that the drawer can hang up on. For that reason, the sides of the drawer are traditionally kept in check by "drawer guides," which are simply pieces of wood inside the carcase that are parallel to the sides of the drawer. Essentially, the guides create a smooth sleeve for the drawer to run in and out of.

With the guides in place, you're ready to measure the opening for the drawer. You want to build a drawer that fits the largest part of its opening.

First measure the height of the drawer opening at the left side, right side and in the middle to make sure your case is square. The drawer for the "Simple Shaker End Table" on page 112 is an "inset drawer," which means the drawer front doesn't have a lip that covers the gap between the drawer and case. (Drawers with a lip are called "overlay" drawers, by the way.) Because this is an inset drawer, you should end up with a small gap all the way around the drawer front, called the "reveal." The reveal must be equal on all four sides of the drawer front. Next, measure the width of the drawer opening at the top and bottom. Finally, measure the depth of the drawer space.

Now comes a tricky decision: Do you build the drawer to fit the space exactly and then trim it down with a hand plane to allow for proper movement? Or do you trust yourself to build the drawer so that there is exactly $1/16$" of space between the drawer and its guides?

We like to err on the side of caution. Build your drawer to fit the opening exactly and trim it to fit. If your drawer opening happens to be out of square, trimming the drawer is the easiest way to compensate. So build to fill the space, then work down to a smooth operational size.

PHOTO BY AL PARRISH

One Setup Cuts All the Joints

Now that you know the size of your drawer, you're ready to build it. Mill all your stock to size (see the cutting list on page 18 for the Shaker end table drawer), paying particular attention to its thickness. The thickness of the sides and bottom must be exactly $\frac{1}{2}$" for this operation to work well.

We're going to build our drawer exactly the size of our opening, except for the depth. The drawer's depth will be $\frac{1}{2}$" shy of the depth of the opening to allow us to fit the drawer flush with its opening, which we'll explain shortly.

The drawings on page 127 show how we build simple drawers using one setup on the table saw. You won't have to change the blade height or move the fence as you cut these three joints:

■ The $\frac{1}{2}$"-wide x $\frac{1}{4}$"-deep rabbets that join the sides to the front and back.

■ The $\frac{1}{4}$" x $\frac{1}{4}$" groove on the sides and front that holds the bottom in place.

■ And the $\frac{1}{4}$" x $\frac{1}{4}$" rabbets on the bottom that allows it to slip neatly into the grooves.

It may not be the way you'll build all your drawers, but it's simple and nearly foolproof. The $\frac{1}{2}$"-wide x $\frac{1}{4}$"-deep rabbets at the corners – when reinforced with brads – make the drawer resist racking and tension. While this can't compare to a stout dovetailed drawer, it's more than adequate for most furniture applications.

To make the drawer a one-setup operation, you'll need a dado stack. Dado stacks traditionally have two 6"- or 8"-diameter saw blades that cut a $\frac{1}{8}$" kerf – plus a variety of "chippers" that can be inserted between the two outside blades to adjust the width of the groove to be cut. For our drawer, we're going to use only the two $\frac{1}{8}$"

"Yes, risk-taking is inherently failure-prone. Otherwise, it would be called sure-thing-taking."

— Tim McMahan (1949 –)
international business speaker, author, photographer

outside blades to achieve a $\frac{1}{4}$" groove.

(Note: If you don't have a dado stack, you can use an $\frac{1}{8}$"-kerf rip blade. You'll have to make a few extra passes over the blade, and you will need to move the fence, but only once.)

Now install a new zero-clearance throat insert to be used for this operation alone. (You can buy one from any tool supplier or make one using your saw's stock insert as a template; your saw's manual should show you how.) Without this new insert, rabbeting the bottom using your stock insert can be dangerous, especially with a left-tilt saw. The opening will be too big and your work could tip into the blades.

With the two dado blades installed on your saw's arbor, raise them so they are exactly $\frac{1}{4}$" above the new insert. Set your saw's rip fence so it is exactly $\frac{1}{4}$" away from the dado stack. Confirm your setup with some test cuts and dial calipers.

Use the drawings to walk through the simple rabbeting steps for the front and back, and the grooves for the bottom.

If you use a $\frac{1}{4}$"-thick plywood bottom instead of solid wood, you're done at the saw. If you're using a $\frac{1}{2}$"-thick hardwood bottom, you need to cut the rabbet on its edges so it slides in place.

We've shown two different ways to make a bottom here. In the drawings, we show a bottom

that actually extends past the back. The back is cut $\frac{1}{2}$" narrower than the front. This has several advantages: You can remove the drawer bottom for finishing and easily replace it if it ever gets damaged. It's necessary to build drawers this way when they are deeper than 12" to allow the solid-wood bottom to expand and contract without binding or busting the drawer.

Second, in the photos we've shown a bottom that is completely captured by the groove on the sides, front and bottom. In small drawers such as this one, wood expansion isn't a major concern and this method allows all the drawer pieces to be the same width.

Fine-tuning and Assembly

Before assembling the drawer, dry-fit the parts to ensure everything will go together easily. The rabbets should fit easily, but the bottom needs to slide into its groove without forcing, and you need to make sure the bottom isn't keeping the corner rabbet joints from closing tightly.

If the bottom is too tight you have a few options. You can head back to the saw and move the fence a little closer ($\frac{1}{32}$", or at most $\frac{1}{16}$") to the dado stack and rerun the four edges to thin the rabbet. A couple of passes with a bullnose or shoulder plane will also thin down the rabbet quickly. If the bottom is holding the corner joints open, raise the height of the dado stack ($\frac{1}{16}$" is fine) and, re-run the edges of the bottom. Then keep checking your fit and adjusting until you're ready to assemble.

Use glue and $\frac{5}{8}$" brads to attach the sides to the front and back. Apply glue to the rabbets at the corners. If you're using a solid-wood bottom, don't

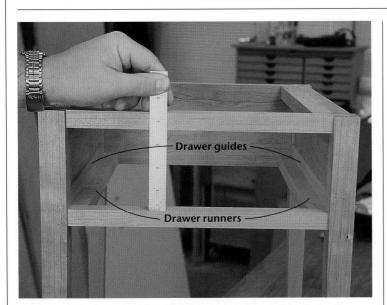

Here I'm measuring the height of the drawer opening near the center. You should also measure the height at both ends of the opening. The width also needs to be measured at top and bottom. Also shown in the photo are the drawer guides and runners in a typical case.

Drawer guides

Drawer runners

When building a drawer with a captured bottom, clamps are placed to apply pressure in both directions with the bottom in place. Note that the clamps are placed just behind the rabbet to apply as much direct pressure to the joint (without interfering with it) as possible. Brads add strength.

Brad location

Build a Drawer with One Saw Setup

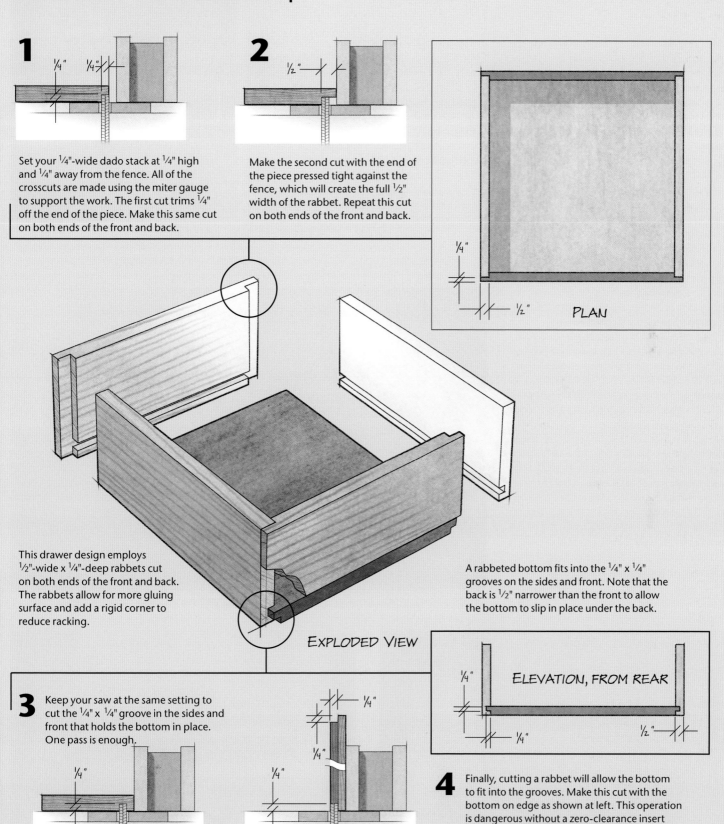

1 Set your ¼"-wide dado stack at ¼" high and ¼" away from the fence. All of the crosscuts are made using the miter gauge to support the work. The first cut trims ¼" off the end of the piece. Make this same cut on both ends of the front and back.

2 Make the second cut with the end of the piece pressed tight against the fence, which will create the full ½" width of the rabbet. Repeat this cut on both ends of the front and back.

PLAN

This drawer design employs ½"-wide x ¼"-deep rabbets cut on both ends of the front and back. The rabbets allow for more gluing surface and add a rigid corner to reduce racking.

A rabbeted bottom fits into the ¼" x ¼" grooves on the sides and front. Note that the back is ½" narrower than the front to allow the bottom to slip in place under the back.

EXPLODED VIEW

3 Keep your saw at the same setting to cut the ¼" x ¼" groove in the sides and front that holds the bottom in place. One pass is enough.

ELEVATION, FROM REAR

4 Finally, cutting a rabbet will allow the bottom to fit into the grooves. Make this cut with the bottom on edge as shown at left. This operation is dangerous without a zero-clearance insert in your table saw. Featherboards help keep the bottom tight against the fence during the cut.

place glue in the grooves. The bottom should be allowed to expand and contract (unless you're using plywood).

Slip your bottom into the groove and clamp the drawer. Place your clamps as shown in the photo on page 126. If you're adding brads to the joints, drive them through the sides into the rabbets in the front and back.

Fitting the Drawer in its Space

When the glue is dry, take the drawer out of the clamps and try to fit it in its opening. It probably won't fit. This is OK. The first step in getting it to fit is to take your block plane and remove material from the top edge of the sides, front and back, checking the fit as you go. You can easily gauge your progress by first marking a $1/16$" line around the outside of the drawer. As you plane, use this line as a reference.

Check the fit of the drawer at the top and bottom by inserting one corner of the drawer in the opening so you don't have to worry about the side-to-side fit. When the drawer fits at the top and bottom, check the side-to-side fit.

Removing material from the sides can be done with a plane or a power sander. If you're planing, remember to work in from both the front and back to avoid tear-out on the end grain that shows on this surface. Remove material slowly and work both sides evenly. It shouldn't take much to get the drawer to slip into place.

You may notice at this point that the reveal around the drawer looks OK at the top and the sides, but the bottom is a tight fit. Here's a little trick: Take your block plane and lightly bevel the bottom front edge to give the appearance of a gap to match the top space. Continue to trim the front with your block plane until the reveal is consistent all around the drawer front.

If you're having trouble planing the end grain on the sides of the front, here's another little tip:

Wet the end grain with some mineral spirits. This will make it easier to slice.

Now it's time to fit the depth. Because we made the drawer $1/2$" shorter than its opening, it will slip in past the front edge of the table. Slide the drawer all the way in, and measure how far in it went. Then predrill and drive two #8 x 1"-long round-head screws (one on either side) in the drawer back. By adjusting the depth of the screws, you can fit the drawer front flush to the table.

With these basic skills in place, you can now use different material thicknesses. And as you become more comfortable with your skills, you can try a new drawer joint on occasion. But you'll always be able to make a simple one-setup drawer that fits perfectly with these rabbets.

– *David Thiel*

The first step in fitting the drawer is to trim the height. A simple block plane can be used to take off a little bit at a time until the fit is perfect.

Next, a larger jack plane removes material from both sides until the drawer slides in smoothly.

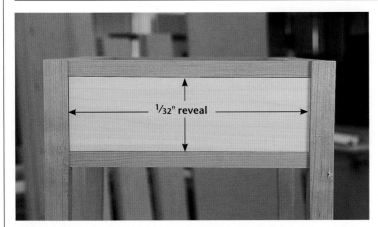

With the drawer in place, you can see the reveal at both sides, on top and on bottom. By beveling the lower edge of the drawer front with a block plane, the spacing appears to match on all four sides.

$1/32$" reveal

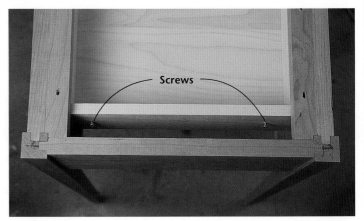

Screws

Another trick to fitting a drawer is to use screws in the back to help adjust the depth. The two screws can be adjusted in and out to fit the drawer front flush in the opening.

A Tale of Two Tabourets

One built by hand. One built with power tools. Well, that was the plan, at least.

When I show these tables to people, I ask them to guess which one was built primarily with hand tools. Everyone gets it right, but none can say why.

Some of the best lessons in constructing cabinets actually come from building small tables.

In many ways, tables are like skeleton versions of complex casework pieces, which stymie beginning woodworkers with their many parts, complex joints and the way the two come together

to make something that's stable and beautiful.

When you build a small table, there is far less wood involved than with a case piece, there are fewer joints and the overall structure is less complex and easier to master. But the real lessons for casework are there. Here are a few examples:

■ The mortise and tenon: This joint is the foundation of table construction – it joins the legs to the aprons and stretchers – and the joint is critical to master when building the frames necessary to make casework. Think: Doors, face frames, drawer dividers and dust panels. When you build one of the tables shown here, you'll use the mortise-and-tenon joint to join the legs and the lower stretchers.

■ The half-lap: Many small tables (such as these examples) have a half-lap joint where the stretchers overlap. Half-lap joinery requires a surprising amount of precision to do well. You are joining two surfaces that have 10 mating surfaces that must be in perfect alignment. If any of those surfaces is off, the joint will show a gap, be unacceptably loose or the parts won't mate flush. Mastering the half-lap – by hand or machine – is a great basic lesson for developing your fine-fitting skills.

■ The dovetail: Many tables great and small incorporate a dovetail where the stretchers meet the top of the legs. And while well-executed dovetails are the foundation of casework carcases and drawers, a table-style dovetail is remarkably forgiving and easy to make. It consists of one tail and one socket. Even poorly executed, this joint is remarkably strong. And here's the nice thing: The joint will be hidden from view thanks to the tabletop. In this table, you'll use a dovetail to join the upper stretchers to the legs.

■ The tabletop: Gluing up an attractive and strong tabletop is key to learning to glue up the wide carcase sides and door panels that are the skin of a typical cabinet. Yet, when you glue up a tabletop, there is much less at stake because the way the top interacts with the base of the table is fairly simple when compared to the complexity of a cabinet's side and its interior parts.

So building a couple small tables with traditional joints will definitely improve your casework skills – no matter what your abilities are at the moment. To prove it, we set out to build two different versions of the Gustav Stickley 603 tabouret – one using power tools and the other using hand tools. The idea was to show you the choices available so you could pick and choose the techniques right for you.

By Hand and By Power

Things, however, did not turn out as planned. I have built dozens of little tables during the last decade for the magazine and for sale. And during the last 11 years I have tried every method imaginable to cut these joints. Plus, with the help of the other woodworkers in our shop, I've refined these methods so they're simple, accurate and don't require complex tooling.

So when faced with the prospect of cutting a joint with a technique I'd set aside years ago, I balked in a few cases and simply refused. Sometimes this meant turning my back on my table saw, and sometimes it meant dismissing my chisels. At almost every step, I found myself forced to justify the tools and processes I employ in the shop. And that struggle to balance speed, simplicity and enjoyment is the heart of the following article.

Stock Selection and Preparation

People ask me all the time to show them how to process rough lumber into boards suitable for fine furniture with hand tools only. I'm happy to show them, and I'm fairly quick about it. It takes longer to explain than it does to actually do when you have the right tools.

But preparing rough lumber for furniture is something I do in the shop only when the boards are too wide for our power equipment. It's not a difficult skill to master, but it requires stamina and physical strength to do well. So when faced with the prospect of preparing the lumber by hand or with a powered jointer and planer, it was no contest.

"I respect a man who knows how to spell a word more than one way."

— Mark Twain (1835 - 1910)
American author and humorist

Stretchers of the Same Length

The four stretchers in the table might not be the most visible parts in the finished product, but they do some critical tasks. They join the legs and top together. And they decide if the base is square or out of kilter. So your first concern should be that each stretcher is the same thickness and width as its mate, and that the distance between the shoulders of all the pieces is the same: $11\frac{3}{4}$".

Note that I didn't say that your stretchers all had to be the same length. They can be, but they don't have to be. For the table with power-tool joints, I crosscut the stretchers to a consistent length with a table saw equipped with a crosscut fence and a stop. Then I marked the shoulders of all the tenons and dovetail joints with a marking gauge pushed along the end grain of the parts.

For the other table, I left the boards at their rough-cut length. Then I grouped all the stretchers together and marked out the shoulders in one

fell stroke using a knife and a square. I found the location of the shoulder by measuring out from the center of the stretchers. After I cut the joinery, I trimmed up any ends that were a little long. The ends are buried in the legs, so their exact lengths are insignificant. Just make them sturdy and to fit.

Both layout approaches are valid ways to work in a modern shop. There are times when you cannot get a really long board on your table saw for an accurate crosscut, so marking out your joinery from a centerline will allow you to skip that machine process.

First Crisis: Cutting Mortises

For the power-tool table, I cut the mortises with a hollow-chisel mortiser using a $\frac{1}{4}$" mortising chisel. The mortises are about $1\frac{1}{8}$" deep to house the 1"-long tenons on your stretchers.

Traditional joint design here would dictate a tenon that's $\frac{1}{4}$" thick and $1\frac{1}{4}$" long (tenon length is typically five times the tenon thickness). But a $1\frac{1}{4}$"-long tenon is risky in a $1\frac{1}{2}$"-square leg. You need to make the mortise a little deeper than necessary to accommodate glue and inevitable junk at the bottom of the mortise, and so there is a real risk of boring all the way through the leg when making the mortise.

So a 1"-long tenon allows you to reduce the risk and maintain most of the strength. Sometimes you have to bend the rules.

After rule-bending and mortise-boring, I picked up my mortising chisel and mallet to cut the mortises by hand for the other table. Now, I'm fairly good at mortising by hand and don't think it's any big deal. But with the mortising machine just sitting there – set up and ready to go as it always is – I put down the chisel.

Most of my hand mortising occurs when the mortiser won't handle the task, such as angled or compound joints, or when the mortises are in a difficult spot, such as the middle of a case side or in a very thick part. But when it comes to straightforward mortising, I choose the machine.

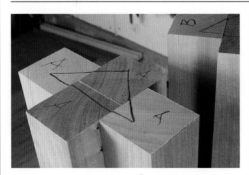

Group your legs together as they will end up in the table (note the diagonal end grain, which ensures the legs will show the same face grain on all four faces) and mark a cabinetmaker's triangle. This triangle ensures your parts will stay in the same orientation throughout construction.

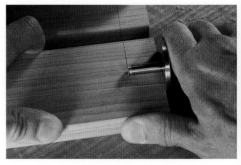

When your stretchers are all the same length, you can mark the shoulders for the joinery from the end grain as shown. This trick works best when you have the precision and repeatability of a machine.

A hollow-chisel mortiser is an essential machine in a shop that constructs traditional (or bulletproof) furniture. There are many methods for making mortises, but none is as simple or effective as a machine dedicated to this all-important joint.

A tenon cheek is a second-class saw cut. Note that I'm advancing my cut on the end grain and the edge grain simultaneously. This helps keep the cut straight. When my kerf touches my shoulder line, I'll turn the tenon around and saw the other edge on the diagonal.

Tenons Two Ways

When it comes to cutting tenons, however, I don't have a dedicated setup on my table saw, so I'll switch freely between hand and power methods. Setting the table saw to cut four tenons is as time-consuming as cutting four tenons by hand.

To cut the tenons by hand, mark out the face cheeks, edge cheeks and shoulders. Saw the cheeks with a tenon saw that is filed for rip cuts then saw the shoulders with a carcase saw that is filed crosscut.

When you cut tenons with power equipment, you have myriad choices. I use a dado stack in my table saw. Here's why I avoid other common methods: I've found that routers don't have the guts to make these cuts in one pass; you're removing ¼" of waste on each cheek and that's a big bite. So you end up making a few passes to make each tenon, and that's a lot of work for the small prize of a perfectly smooth tenon cheek.

I also shy away from tenon jigs on a table saw. They are faster than a router table, but they require a shop-made or commercial jig and they also require two tooling setups for each cheek and shoulder: One setup for the cheek and one for the shoulder. Plus, it can be unwieldy to balance long pieces of work upright on your saw's table.

A dado stack has the advantage of being able to make the cut in one pass (assuming your table saw isn't one of those with a motor that should be measured in "puppy power" instead of horse-power). Plus, there is only one tooling setup for cutting a cheek and shoulder. No special jigs are required. And you can work with your parts flat

A dado stack is ideal for cutting tenons. Work with your piece against a stop and all your tenons will come out the same length.

on your saw's table.

Cut the cheeks and shoulders of the lower stretchers. Then, using the same setting on your fence, cut a ¼"-deep (⅜"-deep if by hand) notch on the underside of your upper stretchers. This notch relieves the underside of the upper stretcher a bit and makes the dovetail easier to cut and fit.

Accurate Half-laps

Making good half-lap joints is a challenge. Years ago I made a series of sitting benches that were based on the work of Nicolai Fechin, and each bench had about 40 half-laps. So I became pretty good at fitting this joint. Here's how.

Begin with components that are the same size. And I mean exactly the same size, especially in thickness. The best way to do this is to handplane the pieces simultaneously on their thicknesses and on their widths. In fact, it's best to do everything you can to get your components nearly ready to finish at this stage. It's a common error to cut the joint and then plane or sand the components, making the joint loose and sloppy.

To lay out the joint, first mark one shoulder with a combination square and knife. Then lay the

Stickley Tabouret

NO.	PART	SIZES (INCHES)			MATERIAL	NOTES
		T	W	L		
❑	1	Top	1	18 dia.		Cherry	
❑	4	Legs	1½	1½	19	Cherry	
❑	2	Upper stretchers	¾	1½	13¾	Cherry	1"-long dovetail, both ends
❑	2	Lower stretchers	¾	2⅞	13¾	Cherry	1"-long tenon, both ends
❑	4	Pegs	⅜ dia.		2	Oak	Oversized, trim to fit

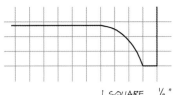

CORBEL STRETCHER PROFILE

1 SQUARE ½"

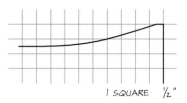

TRUMPET STRETCHER PROFILE

1 SQUARE ½"

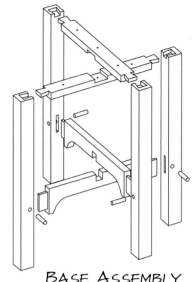

BASE ASSEMBLY

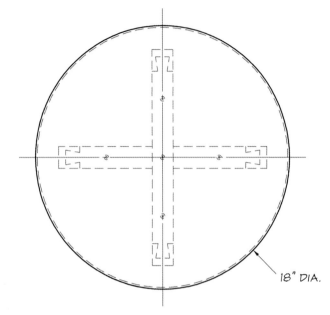

18" DIA.

TOP VIEW

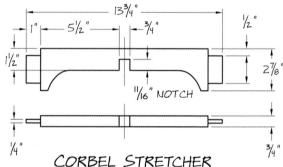

13¾"

1" — 5½" — ¾" — ½"

1½"

2⅞"

¹¹⁄₁₆" NOTCH

¼" ¾"

CORBEL STRETCHER
(2 REQ'D, ONE AS SHOWN AND ONE WITH NOTCH ON TOP)

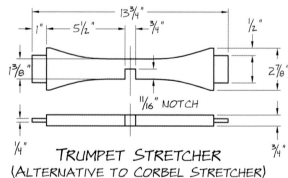

13¾"

1" — 5½" — ¾" — ½"

1⅜"

2⅞"

¹¹⁄₁₆" NOTCH

¼" ¾"

TRUMPET STRETCHER
(ALTERNATIVE TO CORBEL STRETCHER)
(2 REQ'D, ONE AS SHOWN AND ONE WITH NOTCH ON TOP)

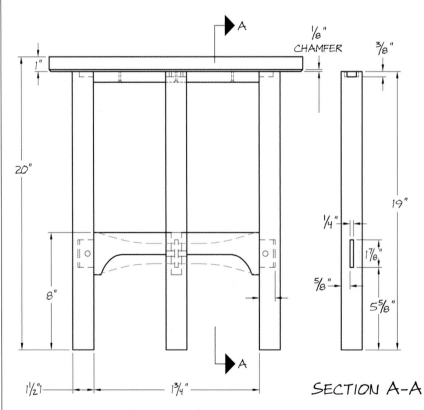

A

⅛" CHAMFER

⅜"

1"

20"

8"

1½"

1¾"

19"

¼"

1⅞"

⅝"

5⅝"

A

SECTION A-A

FRONT VIEW

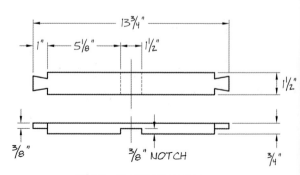

13¾"

1" — 5⅛" — 1½"

1½"

⅜"

⅜" NOTCH

¾"

TOP STRETCHER
(2 REQ'D, ONE AS SHOWN AND ONE WITH NOTCH ON TOP)

Whenever I need parts to be the same size, I "gang plane" them against a planing stop, as shown here. This is a quick way to ensure that the parts are identical in thickness and width. Remember: What's important is they be identical, not some arbitrary number.

Here I'm using the mating piece to mark the shoulder of the joint. Eliminating measuring during operations like this improves your accuracy.

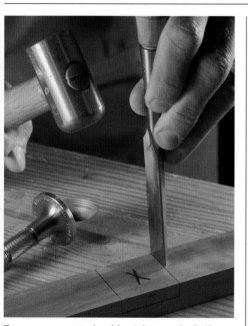

To get an accurate shoulder, I deepen the knife lines with a light tap on my chisel. Note the bevel of the chisel faces away from my waste. This will drive the chisel back into the waste area a bit, which is what you want.

In high-tolerance work I will take the chisel and pop out a wedge-shaped piece of waste to create a V-shaped trench for my handsaw. It works brilliantly.

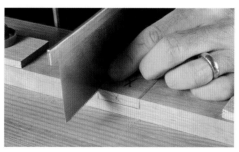

Any fine crosscut backsaw is good for sawing the shoulders. Here I'm using one of my older Japanese dozukis. If this table were made using oak, I'd use a Western saw with more robust teeth.

A router plane can smooth the floor of the joint and prepare it to be fit to its mate. Remember: Router planes don't take a big bite. Small bites will reduce tearing. Also, work from your edges and into the center to reduce tearing.

mating piece up against your combination square and mark the other shoulder of the joint by using this mating part as a ruler. Carry those shoulder lines down the edges and mark the floor of the half-lap, which is half the thickness of the work.

With the joint laid out, you can then decide if you want to cut it with hand tools or power tools. For the power tool-route, I chose a band saw and removed all the waste down to the floor of the joint. Then I cleaned up a little waste with

a chisel. Unless I'm cutting 40 half-laps, I'll use a band saw because it's quicker than a dado stack and doesn't require wasting any test pieces. If you have a lot to do, definitely fire up the table saw.

The hand-tool route is also good for doing just

a couple joints. For the hand-tool table, I sawed out the shoulders, removed the waste with a chisel, then cleaned up the floor of the joint with a router plane.

With one side of the joint prepared you can try to press its mate into the lap. First trim up the shoulders if they are uneven. But if the shoulders are straight and nice, your better bet is to reduce the width of the mating piece with a handplane. It's easier to plane face grain than end grain.

Then press the mating piece into the lap joint. Knock it home. Then use a knife to trace the shape of the mating joint on the workpiece. Take the stretchers apart and cut the other half-lap in the same fashion as you did the first part of the joint. Fit the two pieces until they are flush and tight.

If I have to choose between working end grain or face grain to fit a joint, I always try to choose the face-grain route. End grain is difficult to trim accurately.

With the two pieces pressed together, scribe the intersection of one onto the other. Take the stretchers apart and cut the second half of the joint the same way you did the first.

Easy Dovetails In a Weekend (Really!)

The upper stretchers join the legs in a lapped dovetail joint that will be obscured by the table-top in the completed project. The thickness of the dovetail is not the entire thickness of the stretcher – this makes the joint easier to fit into the leg (and it reduces the amount of brutal chopping).

You can cut the dovetail by hand or with a band saw – I find that a dovetail saw leaves behind a smoothr surface than my band saw (your tools may be different), and so the handsawn dovetails are easier for me to fit.

Mark out your dovetails on all your stretchers. The tails are 1" wide at the top and are the same length as the tenons (1"). The slope of the dovetail

Mark the waste with little Xs (yes, I do this for every joint), then saw the cheek of your dovetail's notch like you would saw out a tenon cheek.

Here I'm sawing out the edges and shoulders of a dovetail joint on my band saw. On a well-tuned machine, this is a pleasure to do with excellent results. If your blade is dull (as ours is), the cut will be rough.

isn't critical as long as it's not too severe. Saw out the edges of the dovetail.

If you are doing this by hand, you'll need to notch out the underside of the dovetail (power-tool users already cut their notch on the dado stack while making the tenons on the stretchers). To make things simple, I cut the notch so it's half the thickness of the work.

The Dovetail Socket: More Failure

With all your dovetails cut, you need to hog out the waste in the top of the leg to make the mating socket. And here again is where I could not do one table by hand and one with power tools.

Cutting one of these sockets is such easy work by hand: Saw out the edges, chisel out the waste and clean up the floor with a router plane. (Note: The router plane is the secret weapon. It ensures the floor is the same depth on all four legs.) Doing this operation with power tools is inefficient.

When I've done these with a trim router, the usual method is to make a quick platform around the top of the leg to support the trim router. (The quickest and dirtiest way to do this is to clamp the leg in your vise with the top of the leg flush to the top of your benchtop.) Then you mark out the

When marking any joint with a knife, resist the temptation to use a lot of downward pressure. You are better off using light strokes and making several passes. The knife is much less likely to wander away.

This bevel-edge chisel will clean out most of the waste, but there will still be a little left that you can tease out with a skew chisel or by simply turning your bevel-edge chisel on its side.

Small router planes don't need a lot of support to do their job really well. The thumb of my left hand is pressing the tool down. The fingers of my right hand are swinging the tool forward to remove waste.

joint and freehand the cut, getting as close as to your lines as you dare. Oh – and be sure to make a couple passes or your trimmer will flame out or your bit will snap.

Then you come back with a chisel and clean out the rounded corners. This entire process is

A card scraper worked quite well on the shallow curve of the trumpet-shaped stretchers. Use a thick scraper and try not to bow it as you work. This will keep your edges at 90° to the face. Bowing the scraper will hollow out the middle of your stretcher sandwich.

If you make the corbel-shaped stretchers, the long flat section can be trued up with a long rasp, as shown here.

An oscillating spindle sander is ideal for the curved section of the corbel shape, but not so good for the flat section. Use whatever combination of tools you have.

For the half-laps made by hand, I cut the shoulders with a carcase saw and chiseled out the waste. For the power-tool version, I did all the cutting and trimming with my band saw.

difficult to do quickly. The visibility stinks while routing. And the clean-up work can be significant if you become a bit chicken while routing.

In the same time it takes to cut one joint with a trim router, I'll have most of the joints done by hand. So let's take a close look at that process.

Place your dovetail on top of its mating leg and scribe around it with your knife. I put the unbeveled part of the knife flat against the dovetail (as shown). Other woodworkers I respect turn the knife around and rub the knife's bevel against the dovetail. Try both approaches; both work.

Mark your waste and chisel a notch for your saw to run in. Define the socket without crossing your layout lines. If you do, it's not the end of the world. Then make a couple extra saw cuts in the waste to make it easy to pop it out.

Then put the leg down on your bench. Brace the foot of the leg against a bench dog and clamp the leg down with a holdfast. Chisel out the waste. Drive down until the chisel stops cutting. Then use the tool to pop out the waste by chiseling into the end grain of the leg.

Chisel out all four sockets. Then use a small router plane to clean up the floor of the dovetail socket. Use a chisel to get any waste in the corners and fit your dovetails in your sockets. Now fetch your lower stretchers and prepare to shape them and cut their half-laps.

A Nice Shape; Another Half-lap

You might have noticed that these two tables have lower stretchers with different shapes. Both the trumpet and corbel shape are historically correct and are taken from Gustav Stickley's drawings. The staff (and my family) was split on which one looked better, so we decided to present both.

I made several extra stretchers to get the shape just right, and I made the shapes with both hand and power tools. For fun, I cut one of the stretchers with a bow saw. It certainly worked, but the band saw is easier (if easy is your thing).

You can refine these shapes using a variety of methods. Rasps, scrapers and sandpaper were a good combination. As was simply firing up the oscillating spindle sander. The real trick, no matter how you do it, is to keep the stretchers adhered together with double-stick tape as you shape them. This makes their appearance consistent.

Now clean up the stretchers as best you can and try to get them to the same thickness. It's time to cut the half-lap that joins the lower stretchers. Make this joint the same way you made the half-lap for the upper stretchers. Make one notch, then use that notch to mark out its mate.

Assemble the Base

There are a couple ways to assemble the base, some of which will turn your table base into an M.C. Escher piece of sculpture. To avoid confusion, assemble the legs first to the lower stretchers alone. Make two separate assemblies.

Then peg the tenons if you like. I used ⅜"-diameter pegs and drilled the hole ⁷⁄₁₆" from the edge of the legs. Then I drove the peg into

Once you put glue on everything, it's going to tighten up the way the joints fit. First get a clamp on those two half-laps. Then worry about the dovetails. I like to drive my dovetails into their sockets with a little scrap of wood.

the hole with a little glue. Always make a couple sample joints before you work on the real stuff. Your drill bits and dowels might not match in diameter. And the run-out on your drill (or your brace and bit) might make the fit even sloppier. Sometimes you need to use a drill bit that is ¹⁄₆₄" smaller or you need to find some beefier dowels.

With the two leg assemblies complete, glue the two assemblies together at the lower stretcher and drive in the upper stretchers. Add a couple small clamps on the half-laps, check your angles with a square and walk away.

These Japanese trammel points were my grandfather's, and I look for any excuse to trot them out, such as a magazine article. Any trammel points will do. Or you can bore a couple tiny holes in a yardstick. Put a nail in one hole and a pencil in the other.

To make the workholding easy, I clamped a block on my bench and affixed the top to that block with some double-stick tape. Note that the face side of the tabletop is getting taped down to the block.

Around the Top

The top is a simple 18"-diameter disc with a small $\frac{1}{8}$" x $\frac{1}{8}$" chamfer on its underside. When gluing up these panels, I made one with edge joints using our power jointer. The other top was made with spring joints made with my jointer plane. Spring joints are edge joints that are a tiny bit hollow in the middle so the top is clamped in tension.

Both techniques worked equally well for me. How will the tops fare in the long haul? Call me in 20 years and I'll let you know.

After cleaning up both panels, I marked out the circle with a pair of trammel points. Note that I did this from the underside of the top so that the hole from the trammel point was hidden.

I cut both tops to rough size on my band saw. There was little point in dulling the blade on my nice bow saw for this rough operation. Then I came to another fork in the road when deciding how to make the top perfectly round.

Making something round by hand is a challenge. I've made a couple tabourets with round tops by hand and spent a long time fairing the top so it looked round instead of blobby and Schmoo-ish. So when Senior Editor Robert W. Lang showed me his router compass, I decided to use that for both tops. The jig is featured in this issue on page 139 and works quite well.

I screwed the arm of the compass to the underside of the top and routed off the ragged waste left by the band saw. This can be a tough cut and your grain might blow out where it changes direction around the edge. My best advice is to take light cuts. I had great luck sneaking up on my final diameter with two light passes.

After routing the top to shape, I routed a small chamfer on the underside. This isn't a historically correct detail. But I like chamfers and these tables look better when the tops look a little lighter.

Then it was time to clean up the edge to make it presentable. I've done this part with power tools (including an ill-fated circle-sanding jig on our disc sander), but I think there's more chance to botch the edge with a power sander. So I turn to scrapers and a little hand-sanding.

The last step is to prepare the top for finishing. Grasping round work can be a trick. Even if you have a fancy dog-hole setup you risk marring the edges of your top. So I converted the offcuts from band sawing my top into clamping cauls that I fit over my bench dogs. This works brilliantly for sanding or for handplaning.

Attaching the Top; Applying a Finish

The top is attached with screws that pass through clearance holes in the upper stretchers. Be sure to ream out the screw holes in the stretchers that extend across the width of the top. This reaming allows the top to expand and contract.

The finish is simple. I ragged on a coat of boiled linseed oil and allowed the tables to sit in the sun for a day. This oil and tan accelerated the aging process in the cherry. After the oil had cured completely I sprayed on two coats of lacquer, though any film finish will do.

Though the experiment to build one table by hand and one by power was a bit of a failure, the resulting tables looked nice, and there was still a lesson buried in there for me about the importance of following your gut. It's captured by a quote from chairmaker John Brown (a quote we published in our first issue in 2004):

"By all means read what the experts have to say," he wrote. "Just don't let it get in the way of your woodworking."

That's good advice – both for the readers and the editors of woodworking magazines.

— *Christopher Schwarz*

Rout the circumference with a spiral bit in your plunge router. Try to keep your motions fluid and quick to create a smooth and burn-free cut. Then get out your rasps and scrapers.

These cauls take a minute to make. Fetch your waste from shaping the top and run it through your thickness planer a couple times. Then bore a hole in each caul to fit it over your bench dogs.

Cutting Circles

Circles are perfect geometric shapes, but perfection in cutting circles is elusive.

Circles are deceptively simple. Their simple perfection is appealing as a shape, but making a perfect circle from solid wood is not a simple task. The eye will easily detect the slightest variation in the finished work, and cutting and smoothing the shape involves dealing with every possible variation of grain direction.

Many methods and jigs promise foolproof results, but in reality, every method has its risks. And no jig will take you from start to finish without additional work somewhere along the line. In preparing this article, the editors compared our experiences with common techniques. In many areas of woodworking, we don't agree on methods, but for once we were unanimous.

None of us ever had any luck setting up a device to cut a perfect circle at the band saw, but we all begin by cutting as close as we can to a circular line using this machine. It takes too much time to build a fixture to spin a blank into a blade. Starting the cut is also a problem and all but the smallest circles need substantial outboard support. And, the surface still requires a lot of work to transform saw-blade marks into a finished surface.

Plan B is to cut the circle entirely with a router. All of us have tried this, but we found it too risky to remove material the full diameter of the bit. We had all experienced a disastrous failure of wood, bit, router or setup using this

---

"A physician can bury his mistakes but an architect can only advise his clients to plant vines."

— Frank Lloyd Wright (1867 - 1959)
architect

This trammel jig makes use of the router's fence attachment to allow you to make fine adjustments to the cutting radius of the jig.

technique. But we all use a router and a trammel jig to trim the band-sawn blank to finished size. And we do additional work after routing to get the edge ready for finishing.

Other obvious methods are setting up a trammel for any saw other than a band saw, or cutting close to the line and cleaning up the saw marks with abrasives. We've heard of people cutting circles on the table saw, but none of us has had success with that. In theory, a jigsaw and trammel setup should work, but cleaning up the sawn surface and starting the cut are problems. Stationary disc and belt sanders can be fitted with a trammel, but as with other trammel methods, starting the work and locking in the finished radius at the same time are easier said than done.

Smoothing sawn edges with a handheld belt sander or a random-orbit sander is possible, as is using a rasp or sanding block. The power-assisted methods are fast but risky – tilt the sander as you move around the curve and you're in trouble. The manual efforts are safer, but not without risk, and will likely take considerably longer.

We don't have a quick and easy solution. Our method is a combination of techniques. We cut close to the line with a band saw, use a router with a trammel jig to remove the saw marks and

create a perfect circle. Then we smooth the edge with a fine rasp and cabinet scraper, or a random-orbit sander. How much cleanup there is left to do depends a lot on the particular wood used.

Testing the Theory
I made several round pieces of solid maple to test our assumptions, and to look for ways to make each step easier. For layout, a compass works up to the tool's limits, which is usually less than 12" in diameter. Beyond that length, trammel points are easier to set and manipulate.

The first choice for making the cut is the band saw. A jigsaw can be used, but it gets awkward keeping most of the blank on the bench, and the cutting action off the bench. Starting and stopping the cut to reposition the workpiece will likely leave a bump or a dip on the edge.

Making the cut in a smooth, continuous motion gives the best results. Start by ripping, aiming for the left-hand quadrant of the circle. When I reach the edge of the circle I keep a smooth motion by spinning the blank into the blade, alternating hands to keep the motion continuous. It's easier to stay outside the line by watching the cut happen rather than trying to make the cut happen.

If a router and trammel will be used later,

the cut doesn't need to be that close. If the cut is within ⅛" of the outside of the line, the router will make it nice without straining. If cleanup is done any other way, the closer the cut to the line the better. Long, smooth arcs can easily be reduced in size. Bumps and dips are hard to remove while maintaining a fair curve on the edge.

With Rasp in Hand

The first method I used to remove the saw marks was a series of three rasps, beginning with a coarse one to bring the high spots down to the pencil line. If at all possible, it's best to work on an edge that is positioned horizontally. I clamped one side of the circle in the bench vise, and used a clamp to secure the other side.

This allows the rasp to be held in both hands. In this horizontal position, the edge can be seen and it's easy to tell when the rasp is flat. When working a curve, as opposed to a straight line, the changing grain direction requires a constant adjustment of pressure on the tool. End grain and transitional grain require more effort to cut than long grain. Make the longest possible strokes, and check the pencil line every few strokes.

Knowing when to stop is important. If the pencil line disappears then there is no reference to work to. It's a funny thing that we can visually see something out-of-round when the work is done, but it is extremely hard to judge a curve while working on it without a reference line.

An exact diameter is rarely as important as having a smooth curve. If the saw cuts are far outside the initial pencil line, you only need to work to the point where there is an even space between the line and the edge. If the line is crossed, either by the saw or the rasp, drawing a new circle just inside the first will give a reference, even if the finished circle ends up being slightly smaller.

After the work with the coarse rasp is complete, removing the marks with a medium rasp will be much faster than the initial shaping, and the final round with a fine rasp will be even quicker. Each grain of rasp will leave a distinctive scratch pattern, and when the old scratches are replaced with finer ones, it is time to move on. The remaining scratches from the finest rasp are removed with a cabinet scraper.

A Powerful Method

A stationary sander is faster than working by hand, but with increased speed comes increased risks. Two things can go wrong: You can burn the wood or you can go too far too fast. Good technique can avoid these problems, but it takes practice. Disc sanders work better than belt sanders because they are less likely to burn end grain.

Most disc sanders have a small table, so it is important to apply downward pressure against the table to keep the edge vertical. Work on the downward-moving side of the disc, and move the work gently into the abrasive. The proper hand

The band saw is the ideal machine for cutting a large circle, but the time spent to make a trammel cutting jig for it isn't worth it. Cut by eye to just outside the line, then use a router trammel jig to trim off the excess and form a perfect circle.

A rasp is the fastest hand-tool method for removing the saw marks. Make long strokes with the tool held flat and keep your eye on the pencil line around the perimeter.

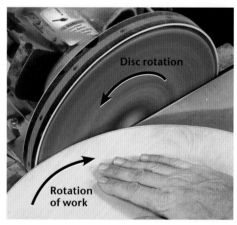

A stationary disc sander is effective, but it needs a delicate touch. Rotate the workpiece into the downhill side of the disc and keep it flat on the machine's table. Otherwise it will jump up on you.

motion is similar to that used at the band saw to make the cut. The work needs to be rotated as it is pushed in. Unlike a flat surface, there is only a small point of a circle's edge in contact at any time. Lingering on a point will either burn the work, or take the edge beyond the line.

Cleaning the disc with a rubber cleaning stick will help to prevent burning, as will keeping the work in motion. It is hard to make a long continuous motion without repositioning the hands, so try to make a comfortable sweep into the disc,

then back off any forward pressure as you switch hands to complete the curve.

During initial smoothing, it is important to use a grit coarse enough to remove material without burning, #80 grit or #100 grit are good starting points. Changing discs involves diminishing returns as finer grits have a greater tendency to burn and will still leave marks on the edge. I don't think it's worth it to change to a finer-grit disc, so after getting the circle down to size, I use another method to remove the scratches left from sanding – usu-

Adjustable Circle-cutting Router Jig

I believe in keeping jigs as simple as possible, but sometimes an extra feature can improve a device by leaps and bounds. Such is the case with this jig. For years I used a simple extended baseplate for routing circles and arcs. A scrap of plywood the width of the router's base and a couple feet long, and a few holes for mounting and a measurement for setting the radius, and I was ready to go.

The problem with this was that there wasn't any room for making a fine adjustment to the radius. I could set the distance to any dimension I wanted, but if something went wrong with the first cut, the option of fixing it by making the circle a little smaller was troublesome. A new hole meant making a fine measurement and drilling again.

The answer, or at least part of it was on the router. The fine adjustment I needed was the same as that of the router's fence. All I needed was a way to attach a simple trammel jig to the router the same way the fence attached. One trip to the hardware store and less than $5 later, and I was ready to go.

A router trammel jig becomes more useful with the addition of a simple method for fine-tuning.

Steel Rods and Scraps

I used a piece of $\frac{1}{4}$"-thick plywood, 6" wide x 22" long. I marked a centerline along the length and cut a piece of $\frac{3}{4}$" x 1" poplar, 6" long. At the hardware store I picked up a piece of $\frac{5}{16}$"-diameter steel rod to slide in the fence-mounting holes of my router. This size will vary with different routers – check the size with a drill bit. It doesn't need to be a piston fit. As long as the rod slides in the fence-mounting holes, and locks down with machine screws, close is good enough.

I used a hacksaw to cut two $8\frac{1}{2}$" lengths of the rod. This length can be varied; I wanted the rod to lock into the router securely and still allow for 3" or 4" of adjustment. At the measurements shown in the drawing, I can make circles ranging in size from 8" to 48". I ground off the rough-cut ends of the rods and mounted them in the router.

With the router base flat on my bench, I put the $\frac{1}{4}$"-thick plywood next to the router, with the poplar across one end. I marked where the ends of the rod met the wood with a pencil, and drilled two holes through the block at the drill press. Then I glued the block of wood across the end of the piece of plywood, using yellow glue and a couple spring clamps.

When the glue had dried, I coated one end of each steel rod with Gorilla Glue (reactive polyurethane) and tapped the rods into the holes until the ends of the rods were flush with the wood on the exit side of the block. I let the glue dry overnight before using the jig.

Swinging Into Action

I purchased two machine screws that fit the threaded holes in the router base to lock the rods in place. I mounted a $\frac{1}{2}$"-diameter spiral-upcut bit, and measured from the edge of the bit along the centerline of the jig and drilled a hole at the desired radius.

What to use for a center pin depends on what type of trail you're willing to leave behind on the bottom of your work. A piece of $\frac{1}{4}$" metal rod, press-fit into a hole in the base of the jig and in a $\frac{1}{4}$"-deep hole in the bottom of the work, is least likely to shift during use but leaves a noticeable hole.

A small brad or finishing nail tapped into the work won't leave much evidence, but can bend, shift or pop out of the hole during use. A short screw driven in a few turns is an effective, middle-of-the-road compromise between the two extremes.

The reason for creating the adjustable trammel jig is that even in the best of circumstances, with a steady hand and good technique, there is still a chance for the wood to tear or the cutter to inadvertently dig in. Be prepared to make the circle a little smaller. Smaller with a clean edge won't be noticed. The intended size with an ugly spot on the edge will be noticed. When you've made a good cut with the router, a few minutes with a card scraper, sanding block or random-orbit sander will finish the work.

— RL

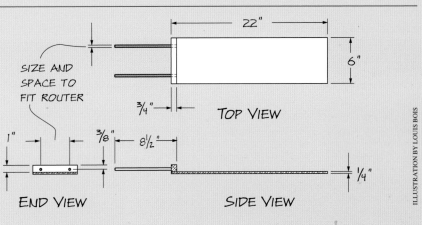

SIZE AND SPACE TO FIT ROUTER

22"

6"

$\frac{3}{4}$"

TOP VIEW

1"

$\frac{3}{8}$"

$8\frac{1}{2}$"

$\frac{1}{4}$"

END VIEW

SIDE VIEW

ally a cabinet scraper followed by a random-orbit sander or I hand sand with a rigid sanding block.

Easier Said Than Done

While it's possible to use a handheld belt sander to remove saw marks and shape the edge down to the pencil line, I wouldn't recommend it. Clamping the work with the edge up means balancing the sander on a narrow edge. It's almost impossible to see what is happening in this position. The alternative, clamping the blank flat on the bench and holding the sander sideways, lets you see what is going on, but it takes finesse to hold the belt sander with the platen vertical.

Random-orbit sanders are effective for removing saw marks and coarse scratches – if the sander can be held with the pad vertical and not tipped. Trying to grind down areas where the saw has strayed from the line with this tool is awkward.

The dedicated hand-tool user might decide that a low-angle block plane or a flat-bottomed spokeshave would be effective at removing the saw marks. While there is some merit to this in theory, in practice it is a slow method with mixed results, especially while working a hard wood. To prevent tearing out the end grain on the perimeter, the blade must be set for a very fine cut, slowing down the work on the long-grain portions.

The changing grain direction will also mean a different direction of attack as you go around the circle. There will be places where tearing out the grain is almost inevitable. In the interest of experimentation, I tried both a block plane and spokeshave, but abandoned the effort in favor of the rasp for shaping the curve by hand.

If you should tear out a chunk somewhere, there isn't any easy fix. On a straight surface you might be able to plane a gentle dip along the length to remove some tear-out, but on a circle the only good solution is to reduce the diameter of the entire circle. That will take time.

Router to the Rescue

A plunge router on a trammel jig is the best solution to cutting a nice clean circle. You don't need to worry about sawing close to a line because the distance between the center and the edge is fixed by the jig. You can control the depth of cut and remove material in manageable steps. But again, theory and reality don't always agree.

In our experience, something will go wrong when trying to make a complete circular cut with the router only. Taking shallow passes in solid hardwood means going around the circle five or six times. Each additional pass increases the chance of something bad happening.

There are several little things that can go wrong; any one of them can mean starting over. The cord to the router can snag, pulling the bit toward the center and creating a divot. Using a small-diameter bit can lead to the bit flexing or chattering. A large-diameter bit can cause a

A random-orbit sander is good for removing coarser rasp or sanding marks, but difficult to use for removing band-saw marks and truing the circle. Keep the sanding pad vertical against the edge of the work and keep the sander moving around the perimeter as you work to the pencil line.

This direction to climb-cut

Routing the circle presents uphill and downhill grain to the router bit. Climb-cutting the entire perimeter will give the best results, but there aren't any guarantees. Starting and stopping the cut to change direction is more likely to cause a problem. Be prepared to make your circle smaller if you need to.

big chunk of wood to tear out where the grain reverses. Leaning in one direction or another as the depth changes or as you shift hands can tilt the router enough to leave a noticeable ridge around the edge of what should be a nice circle.

Cutting the circle to shape before routing, while leaving $1/8$" or less for the router bit to remove, reduces the risk because you only need to run the router around once or twice. Place the rough-cut blank on scraps of wood attached to the bench, so one pass can be made without needing to stop and restart to avoid clamps. The blank can be held to the scrap and the scrap can be held to the bench with double-sided tape or hot-melt glue.

An upcut-spiral bit makes a cleaner cut and is less likely to tear out the grain than a straight bit. When the blank is secure, raise the router motor so that the bit is clear of the work, and attach the jig to the center point of the circle. Drape the cord of the router over your shoulder. Turn the router on, plunge to your cutting depth and move the router around the pivot as smoothly as you can. When the cut is complete, turn the router off and

hold the jig steady until the bit stops turning.

This is the best method we've found, but it isn't without risk. As the router starts, it can jerk or jump so keep a firm grip on the tool. When turning the router off, or when plunging the bit, don't relax your grip and let the cutter move toward the center. And lastly, the direction the router is moved around the circle can cause tear-out in some parts of the circle.

The accepted direction when routing is to go against the direction of the cutter, or counter-clockwise around the perimeter. The exception to this rule is when routing across end grain, or into grain that is running downhill toward the cutter. With a circle of solid wood you will be routing across the grain on opposite sides, and going downhill at two other locations. Even though it is difficult to control, the cut will be cleaner if you go clockwise for the entire cut. And you will need some luck and a firm grip on the tool and jig to get it right on the first attempt.

— Robert W. Lang

STANDS

Stickley Magazine Stand

Furniture built without a back can be alarmingly wobbly. We found a simple and sturdy way to make this open shelving unit stand firm.

Before I began building Arts & Crafts furniture I collected Arts & Crafts furniture, and I came to know two key facts about magazine stands: One, they are surprisingly useful pieces of furniture in the modern home that allow you to store books in any available cranny in a room. And two: All of them wobble like a drunken sailor.

This defect is the result of the fact that they have no back, which actually happens to be one of their most charming features. If you place a lamp on top of any magazine stand, the light will flood behind the cabinet and illuminate the wall behind your books, pottery and most-favored objects. And this backlighting, as any photographer will tell you, is positively enchanting.

So the best way to fix this design defect is definitely not to add a plywood or solid-wood back to the piece. So what do you do? After some contemplation and experimentation, we found the solution: Two narrow strips of wood under the top two shelves. These "shelf supports," as we call them, are then screwed to the sides of the case, making them anti-racking devices that are usually invisible. And with the assistance of the two wider stretchers below the bottom shelf, this magazine stand will stay rigid for a long time.

The other bit of engineering in this project is the joint that attaches the shelves to the sides. Dados are the traditional (and best) way to ensure the weight of your book collection doesn't create enough downward force to ruin the unit. Dados, however, do almost nothing to prevent a case from racking, which is where the shelf supports and stretchers lend a hand.

Every good cabinet is a careful balance of these attributes. If you ignore the engineering when designing a project, you run the risk of it dying an ignominious death at the curb of a fra-

ternity house some day. The other sin – almost as serious – is to overbuild a project with unnecessary reinforcement. When you do this, you could be wasting lumber or hardware that could be used in another project. You also could be adding bulk to a project that would benefit from less weight. And you could be pumping up the visual chunkiness of the project by beefing up parts that would look better when slimmed down.

This harmony between function and form is an important component of any project, but it is something to be particularly mindful of as you build Arts & Crafts furniture. Furniture in this style was intended to integrate itself into the turn-of-the century family home.

Harmony Begins in the Wood

There is very little lumber in this adaptation of Gustav Stickley's No. 79 magazine stand; about 15 board feet of white oak would do the job if you're lucky. But when you have so few parts in a project, you should pay close attention to the quality of the boards that will show. Of the nine parts, you should be concerned with three: the sides and the lower stretcher at the front.

With these three parts you should select boards that show the most dramatic figure. Be willing to waste a few pieces of wood to get it. And be happy to make a couple extra cuts to get the coloring correct and the seams in the right place. To do this, here's what you need to know.

When I started working with quartersawn white oak, I had the fortune of visiting Frank Miller Lumber Co. in Union City, Ind. This huge high-tech mill supplies much of the world with quartersawn lumber. The employees are happy to sell oak by the board foot to the home woodworker and by the train-car load to furniture plants. If you're ever driving through central or eastern Indiana, it's worth a detour.

During my first visit, the guy who was picking our lumber could regularly grab boards with dramatic ray-flake figure on the board's face by looking at the ends of the boards (which were painted brown, by the way).

Bemused, I asked him how he did it. He pointed to the annular ring pattern on the ends of the boards, which was visible under the paint. When these annular rings intersected the face of the board at exactly 90° – in other words, when they were straight up and down – the face of the board was more likely to exhibit the desirable ray flake pattern. Remember this the next time you're at the lumberyard and looking at rough stock.

Once you pick a dramatic board for the lower stretcher, turn your attention to the sides. It's unlikely you'll find a perfect 10"-wide board in quartersawn white oak. They are pretty rare. That means you'll need to glue up two narrower widths to end up with a 10"-wide side piece.

An easy mistake to commit is to make the sides by gluing together a wide board and a narrow

one. This might be more material-efficient, but it probably won't look good in the end. The better solution is to make each side using two lengths from the same board that are $5\frac{1}{8}$" wide each. By gluing up your side pieces from a single board, the result is likely to look harmonious in grain and color. Matching the color is easy; matching the grain is a matter of flipping the boards over and over on your assembly bench until the result looks good.

Personally, I like it when the grain looks like a "Y" that branches up from the center seam of the side piece. Also note that if you're going to hand plane your parts that you need to pay attention to which way the grain is running on the two pieces.

I usually mark an arrow on each face that indicates the grain's direction. These arrows quicken the process of figuring out how to glue the boards together.

Now you can joint the long edges of your boards. But before you crack open the bottle of glue, there is one small detour ahead.

Quicker Cutouts

You can save some work for yourself down the road by roughing out the shape of the cutouts at the top of each side piece before gluing up the panel. The half-moon cutouts at the top are easier to rough out before you glue up the panel.

These cutouts will be routed to final shape after the panel is glued up. So to lay out the shape at the top, make plywood templates using $\frac{1}{2}$"-thick plywood material, a compass and a ruler. See the construction drawing for details. Then

Here you can see three boards. All three are technically quartersawn, which is when the annular rings intersect the face of a board at somewhere between 60° and 90° degrees. As the rings become more vertical, the ray flake becomes more pronounced. The board at left has annular rings at 62°, the middle one is at 72° and the one at right is 90°.

The D-shaped cutouts will be easier to rout to their final shape if you cut them to rough shape before assembling each panel. This step saves you some drilling and some tricky inside cuts. You also can see the arrows I've scrawled on the boards' faces to indicate the grain direction of each piece.

Gustav Stickley No. 79 Magazine Stand

	NO.	PART	SIZES (INCHES)			MATERIAL	NOTES
			T	W	L		
☐	2	Sides	¾	10	40	White oak	
☐	3	Shelves	¾	9⅞	13	White oak	In ¾" x ¼" d. dados
☐	2	Shelf supports	¾	1¼	12½	White oak	Pocket screwed into sides
☐	2	Lower stretchers	¾	2½	12½	White oak	Glued, screwed to case

cut out your shapes using a jigsaw, coping saw or band saw. Sand or rasp the edges of the pattern smooth. Take your time; little bumps will show.

Put your side pieces in place on your bench and pencil in the patterns in the appropriate place. Cut out the shapes on the pieces, but don't get too close to your lines; I'd stay about ⅛" away from your line. Now you can glue up your panels and use the lines from the patterns to help align your parts correctly during assembly.

With a panel of this size, I recommend you apply glue to both faces of the joint and clamp every 12". Begin at the center of the panel and work out. Alternating clamps over and under the panel is always a good idea. When the glue is dry, rip each side to its finished width and cut the ends square. Then it's time to rout the cutouts and shape the curves for the project.

Patterns Make Perfect

Whenever I have to make more than one tricky cutout in a project, I like to make a plywood pattern and then rout the piece to its final shape. For this project I made a pattern for the cutout at the top and the curve at the base of the sides. The pattern ensures that both cutouts will be identical, and you'll be able to clean them up with just a bit of hand sanding. The other option is to cut the shape close and then use an oscillating spindle sander to sand to your line. If you're a whiz with this machine then feel free. I think a router is the less risky route to a crisp execution.

Clamp the pattern to the side piece and then clamp these two pieces to your bench with the pattern sandwiched between your bench and your side piece. You're going to need a pattern-cutting router bit for this operation, and I generally prefer the pattern-cutting bits that have the bearing on the end of the router bit. This bit reduces the amount of spinning carbide that's exposed below the router base (always a good thing), and it allows you to more easily clamp up your work.

Pattern bits that have the bearing above the cutters generally need everything cantilevered off the end of your bench so the bit doesn't cut into your workbench. These bits are invaluable for blind cuts (where the cut doesn't pass through your work) but they're not needed here.

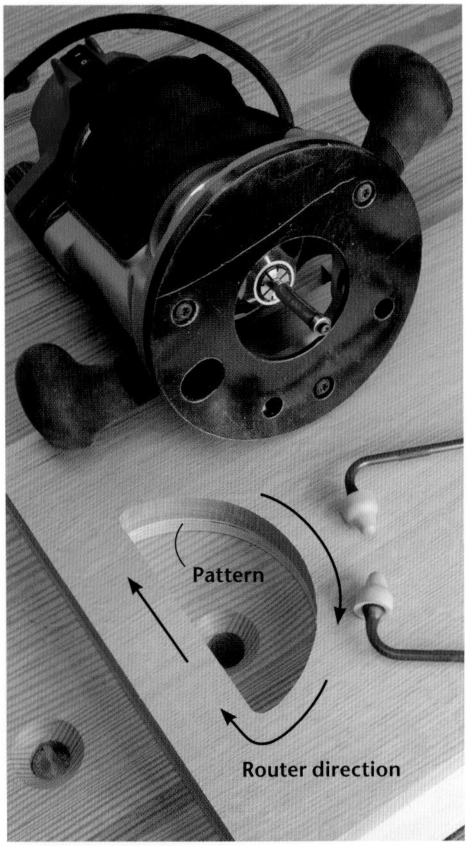

A Bit of Hand Work

Now shape the curve on the lower stretcher. While you could create a plywood pattern and rout this curve, I encourage you to rough it out first using a saw and try using a spokeshave for this operation. A spokeshave with a slightly curved sole makes short work of this shaping operation. And even if you cannot manage to get your tool to leave a perfect surface that's free of tear-out, the edge will never show because it faces the floor.

If you do not own a spokeshave with a curved sole, there are two excellent modern versions now available that I can recommend. The spokeshaves by Lie-Nielsen and Veritas will open curvaceous new worlds for you. (See the Supplies box for contact information.) I would caution you against purchasing inexpensive spokeshaves, such as those from Kunz and Anant. I have found these tools need a great deal of tuning.

Remember to work with the grain with these tools. In the case of a curve such as this, this means you should almost always work from the hill and into the valley, as shown below.

The final bit of shaping is the slight radius at the top corners that is shown in the construction drawing. Lay this out with a compass, cut it close with a saw and smooth the edge with sandpaper. Start with #100 grit and progress to #220.

Here you can see the side and pattern clamped up for routing. When making this cut, move the router clockwise around the opening. Move quickly and smoothly, and try not to hesitate at any point during the cut. This will reduce the chance of scorching the edge.

The two common types of pattern-cutting router bits are shown here. The bit at the top has the bearing above the cutting flutes, which is designed for blind cuts. Below that is a bit with the bearing at the end of the cutter, which I prefer for this operation.

The trick to using a spokeshave is push it in the direction that will push the fibers down, instead of pulling them up, which produces tear-out. Think of the grain as the fur of a cat and the tool as your hand that pets it. It's always best to pet the cat in a manner that smooths its fur.

"Whether made into a wooden pillow or table, wood with excellent grain is a guarantee of splendid poems, and the composition of perfect documents."

— Liu Sheng
from "Ode to Fine Grained Wood,"
a Chinese text from the second century, B.C.

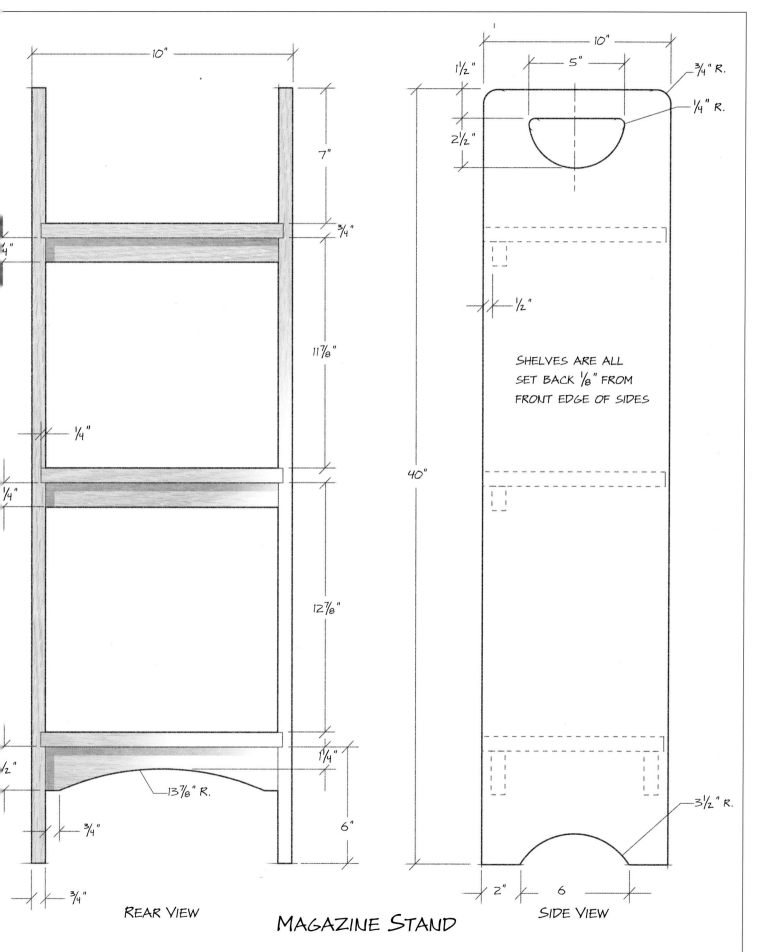

10"

7"

3/4"

1/4"

11 7/8"

1/4"

1/4"

12 7/8"

1/4"

1/2"

13 7/8" R.

3/4"

6"

3/4"

REAR VIEW

MAGAZINE STAND

10"

5"

1 1/2"

2 1/2"

3/4" R.

1/4" R.

1/2"

SHELVES ARE ALL
SET BACK 1/8" FROM
FRONT EDGE OF SIDES

40"

3 1/2" R.

2"

6

SIDE VIEW

Routing Dados

The best way to rout the ¾"-wide x ¼"-deep dados in the sides is to use a T-square jig. You want your dados to begin at the back of the cabinet and stop ¼" in from the front edge. To do this operation consistently six times, I recommend you screw or nail a stop to your T-square jig that will halt the router at the correct place every time. This takes a couple extra minutes of work, but it prevents a careless slip of the hand.

Make each dado in two passes with your plunge router and a ¾"-diameter straight bit: First with the bit set to about ⅛" and then with the bit sent to ¼" below the base of the tool. As always with this tool, move the router swiftly and smoothly for the best results.

Notching the Shelves

Now you need to fit each shelf piece into its dado. If you planed your lumber accurately, it should fit snugly into the dado. If it's a little tight you can either hand plane the shelf to fit, which is my usual method, or carefully send it through your planer for one more light pass – a risky operation. If you overshoot and make the shelf too thin, you can tighten up the dado by gluing a strip of veneer in the dado and fit the shelf again.

Once your shelves fit in your dados, you need to fit the front edges around the rounded routed-out section where each dado terminates. While you could chisel the end of the dado square, any error will show as an ugly gap at the front edge of your shelf. The better option is to saw a notch in each shelf and clean the notch up with a chisel. With a shop-made chiseling guide, your success is almost guaranteed.

The first step is to lay out the ¼" x ½" notches so that the shelves will fit into the dados and sit back ⅛" in from the front edge of the sides. This setback adds another nice shadow line to the project and saves you from having to fit the shelves perfectly flush to the front edge. Lay out your lines with a marking knife and cut the notch, leaving just a sliver of waste.

You can cut this notch with a band saw, but this is an excellent opportunity to instead practice with a hand saw. Sawing to a line is a worthy skill worth developing.

A chiseling guide is a jig that takes about five minutes to fabricate and will make this paring operation a snap. It's made using three pieces of wood: a small scrap of waste wood from the project and two scraps of thin plywood. Nail the plywood to the scrap as shown in the photo at right and clamp the chiseling guide to your shelf.

First Assembly

Now you're almost ready to start putting the pieces together. Before you fit the stretchers and supports, plane or sand your parts so they are about ready for finishing. This is an important point. If you fit the stretchers and supports before sanding or planing, they won't fit as snugly when

Routing the dados in the sides with the T-square jig ensures straight and clean dados that stop exactly where they are supposed to. It is an elegant solution to a thorny problem with case joinery.

you assemble the unit at the end.

Clamp up the shelves between the side pieces and stand the unit up on your bench. Now you want to do the critical fitting. Cut the lower stretchers to their final length so they fit snugly between the side pieces of your clamped-up case. Do the same thing for the two shelf supports.

You can do this fitting operation on your table saw. I, however, like to use my shop-made "shooting board." A shooting board guides a hand plane so it trims off small increments. It's my favorite way to sneak up on a tight fit.

Once you get the stretchers and supports fitting snugly, cut the pocket holes for the screws that attach these parts to the side pieces. Using your pocket-hole jig, bore the screw pockets on

the bottom edge of each shelf support and on the inside face of the lower stretchers. These screws will add a bit of inexpensive insurance.

Dry-fit all the parts of the magazine stand on your bench. Clamp it up like you were going to glue things for real. Now glue and clamp the shelf supports and stretchers to the underside of the shelves. I really recommend you do this with the shelves clamped in place between the sides – even though you'll have to take care and not let

A marking knife or chisel is the perfect tool to lay out the notches on the shelves. Assemble and clamp the case, then use the sides as a guide to mark the notches.

When sawing the notches, the best way to ensure your success is to begin the cut correctly. Use your thumb and index finger to guide the saw blade as you begin the cut.

your glue squeeze out and onto the sides.

Once the glue has dried, you can drive all the pocket screws home. If you are building this project in oak, here's a word of advice: Rub the threads of the screws with a bit of paraffin or beeswax before driving them. Oak is such a dense wood you can easily snap the screw heads off.

After the glue dries, remove the clamps and disassemble all the pieces. Do any final sanding or smoothing at this stage.

Finishing Decisions

Whenever I finish a shelving unit or cabinet, I like to finish it when the parts are disassembled and then glue it up after the topcoat finish is dry. This process is delayed gratification at its best.

Finishing the parts before assembly makes them easier to finish (everything is flat with no vertical surfaces), but it takes a bit more time. You have to tape off all the joints that will be glued so you don't seal them up with the finish. However, the inconvenience is outweighed by the quality results. The inside surfaces of the project end up well finished – a mark of good construction.

Tape off all the dados and their mating edges with masking tape – I prefer the blue painter's tape that doesn't leave a sticky residue behind.

I recommend the finishing technique out-lined in this issue on page 148. It's an improved and faster adaptation of a version we have been refining during the last six or seven years. Once the color is dry, add two or three coats of spray lacquer. This project is small enough that a couple aerosol can of spray lacquer will do the job (though the cans are expensive; about $8 each).

Final Assembly

Once the finish is dry, glue up the case. Put glue in the dados and knock the shelves in place. Clamp everything up. Clean up any squeeze-out; it should be easy to wipe up thanks to the already-finished surfaces. Once everything is clamped and square, drive the pocket screws home. Allow the glue to cure and remove the clamps.

This is the fourth magazine stand I've either built or bought for our home. And it's the only one with real backbone. The system works.

— *Christopher Schwarz*

This chiseling guide ensures the chisel cuts exactly where you want and no deeper. Make this paring cut with a couple passes of your tool to get the hang of the operation.

My shooting board is made from a few layers of plywood that are glued and screwed together. Any plane with the sides ground 90° to the sole can be used for shooting, though I find that planes with more mass are more accurate.

I use a smoothing plane to prepare my parts for finishing. Sandpaper or scrapers are the other logical choices. Which method you select will alter how the color is absorbed by the oak. See the article in this issue on Arts & Crafts finishes (page 148) for details.

If you don't have a pocket-hole jig, you can rig up the jig shown here to do the job with a stepped drill bit. The workpiece is angled at 15°. Set the depth of the drill bit to stop cutting right before it breaks through the end of the workpiece. This will take a little trial and error to set right.

A Simple Arts & Crafts Finish

After experimenting with combinations of dyes and stains, we discover the most authentic look is achieved with one coloring step.

We had a working recipe for an attractive and authentic Arts & Crafts finish. It had all the right elements with a reddish background color that highlighted white oak's medullary rays, the signature look of Arts & Crafts furniture. We had a warm-brown color that collected in the oak's open pores and darkened the rest of the wood to just the right shade of dark brown. But to achieve this dead-on color required time and more than a little finishing experience.

So we challenged ourselves to come up with a faster, easier recipe that would produce the same results – one simple enough that even an inexperienced woodworker could recreate successfully the first time.

Good finishes often require different color applications sometimes using different materials. For example, a "red mahogany" finish produced in a high-end finishing operation isn't achieved by ragging on one brand or another's so-called "red mahogany" stain color. First, a rich red dye or non-grain raising (NGR) stain is applied to the mahogany and allowed to dry. These colors are usually water- or alcohol-based. Once the red color dries, an oil-based brown stain or glaze is applied. This color might be added to a grain filler to close up open wood pores in mahogany. Once this color coat dries, it may be lightly sanded to produce "highlights" in the color, or simply topped with a clear sealer, then coated with a clear top coat, such as lacquer. To adjust the color or simply add more color, a toner color might be added to create shading effects, which is particularly effective around the perimeter of a panel in a raised-panel door.

While our original Arts & Crafts recipe wasn't this complicated, it nonetheless required the base color dye, an application of boiled linseed oil and then a brown glaze. All this was sealed by a top

coat of orange shellac or spray lacquer.

A Series of Tests

Our first attempts at simplification involved either using a brown dye color alone or a combination of a very thinned "wash coat" of amber shellac followed by an application of a brown stain. The hope was that the amber shellac wash coat (a two-pound cut of shellac further cut at a ratio of one part shellac to three parts alcohol) would impart the red background color we wanted but not seal the wood so much as to prevent the stain from "biting" or being absorbed sufficiently.

Our attempts with the brown dye came close to the right color (we used the original Arts &

Crafts child's rocking chair pictured above for comparison), but we colored the "tiger stripe" medullary rays and surrounding wood to such a similar tone that the highlight effect of the rays were compromised. We were also concerned about the dye color fading in time from exposure to sunlight. While some dye colors fade much faster than others, such as red and blue tones, we were not confident the brown, even though darker, would stand the test of time. Dyes used under pigmented stains hold their color better than those fully exposed to light.

The two-step method using shellac and stain failed to produce enough color. The shellac was thinned too much to produce much amber color and it sealed the wood too much to permit the stain to bite the wood sufficiently.

At this point, we concluded that if our journey of discovery for a simple and easy finish was going to be successful, it would by necessity rely on a single color application of a pigmented stain. Pigments are crushed to fine powder, some colors are from real earth compounds, and have long lasting colorfast properties. The fine powder color is suspended in a carrier or medium, usually an oil with other ingredients added to bind the pigment of the wood and others to promote drying. Fading wouldn't be a problem with pigmented stain. By comparison, aniline dye is a synthetic, chemically produced transparent pure color.

While there are many varieties of brown colored stains available, the question became which one and how it would react with the regular grain vs. the medullary rays. We also decided to give Watco's Dark Walnut Danish oil finish a try, thinking that a few wiped-on coats might get us to the color and a total finish we desired. After the third coat of Watco we abandoned the idea because the color wasn't yet halfway home.

Our next experiments included regular oil stains and gel stains. After testing a couple of each, it was clear that gel stain gave us a couple important advantages compared to regular stain. The gel consistency allowed the color to trap in the open pores and it allowed the medullary rays, which are free of pores, to be highlighted. There was more color contrast between these rays and the regular grain.

We tested Bartley and General Finishes' gel stains, and both produced the same results from a performance standpoint, leaving the only remaining consideration being color selection. After sampling a variety of browns from each manufacturer, we settled on General Finishes' Java color (that's right, Java) being closest to our ideal. It was red enough and dark enough to work.

Sanding vs. Hand Planing

When experimenting to find the color finish desired, wood preparation plays an important role. Wood sanded only to #120 grit will accept more stain and appear darker. It will also likely leave sanding scratches that the stain will accentuate when applied. Sanding to the next higher grit, #150, is probably the minimum to avoid sanding scratches. Usually, #180 grit, or at most, #220 grit, is ideal. Grits finer than #220 will begin to diminish the amount of stain color the wood will accept.

Another method of wood preparation is not sanding at all but using a smoothing plane instead. A properly tuned smoothing plane with an appropriately sharp plane iron provides a fine finish surface. And it's arguable that it's as fast as monotonous sanding. But when it comes to staining wood that has been prepared this way, the stain result is considerably different from sanded wood. This is because of the surface of sanded wood being abraded or roughed up is different than a surface of planed wood where the fibers have been cleanly sheared off. Which is more attractive is subjective.

In the magazine stand in this issue, the surface was prepared with a smoothing plane only.

Applying the Gel Stain

The staining method, regardless of wood preparation method, is the same. The gel stain is ragged on fairly thick to a manageable area of about three to four square feet. It's then wiped off, first against the grain, driving the color into the open pores. Next, using a cleaner rag, it's wiped with the grain to an even color. The second wiping requires some care to get an even color. Start with a rag that forms a soft pad with no hard spots (creases) from folds or seams in the material. Hard spots in your wiping cloth apply more direct pressure to the surface than the surrounding soft areas and therefore will pick up more color or leave a streak in the color. This is especially important in your final wiping strokes. These should run the full length of the stained area and require a relatively light touch. Pay special attention to edges and corners where the tendency is to leave

Source

Woodcraft Supply
800-225-1153 or woodcraft.com

General Finishes
Gel stain • Java, #826979, $17.99/qt.

more color behind.

After the gel stain is applied to the entire project, it should be left to dry overnight. The instructions say six hours, so if you have time in the same day, it's possible to stain and topcoat in one day. Overnight is always a safe bet.

We finished the magazine stand project by spraying a clear lacquer from an HVLP sprayer. On a project this size, lacquer could be applied from an aerosol can. Regardless, spray in a very well-ventilated area free of any open flames such as from a furnace or water heater. Lacquer is a highly flammable material. After spraying two wet coats, let it dry for at least 20 minutes then lightly sand with #360-grit stearated sandpaper. This sandpaper is treated with stearates that lubricate the grit and prevents sanded finish particles from "balling up" on the sandpaper. You'll recognize this paper in its most common form, gray colored aluminum oxide grit. A final wet coat of lacquer is all that should be needed for a smooth and durable finish.

Other clear finishes such as polyurethane, shellac or varnish can be used and brushed on following the same "sand between" step mentioned above. Ragged-on wiping varnishes will also work, just take care not to brush or wipe too much or too hard and redissolve the dried stain, creating a smear of color.

– Steve Shanesy

Our simple Arts & Crafts finish uses just one step in the coloring process, accomplished with an easy-to-apply gel stain. Apply the stain liberally, then wipe off most of the excess across the grain. This will drive the color into the open pores so it collects there.

With most of the stain wiped off after wiping across the grain, wipe a second time with the grain until all excess stain is removed. Use long wiping strokes the full length of the stained areas. The final wipes should use a light touch, render a uniform color and complete the staining process.

The stained wood should have an even tone and the quartersawn white oak's medullary rays should show as highlights against a somewhat darker background. Check edges and corners where excess stain may not have been wiped to an even color consistency.

Gustav Stickley Plant Stand

Does good work have to be flashy? Building a piece that focuses on existing skills can please both you and other woodworkers.

The clock read 3 a.m., but my body was still on East Coast time, so I was wide awake and shuffling around Gary Rogowski's house in Portland, Ore., like an unshaven ghost.

Rogowski is a long-time furniture maker and the owner of the Northwest Woodworking Studio school. And like most woodworkers, his house is filled with his own work. As I fumbled in the dark looking for the stairs, my hands came to rest on a dresser in the hallway.

The oak piece had simple Arts & Crafts lines and pleasing proportions, but it was not the sort of object that shouts for attention from the other side of a room. With time to kill and a curiosity about his work, I scrutinized the dresser the way only a woodworker can.

I pulled out each drawer. I poked around the interior of the carcase. I looked for filler in the dovetails. I examined the surfaces for defects in planing, sanding or finishing. It takes a lot to impress me before my first cup of coffee, but Rogowski's piece did just that.

Though simple in form, the piece was perfect in execution. For me, that dresser served as a reminder of something that I tend to lose sight of as I strive to become a better woodworker. Simply put: Refining your existing skills is as important as acquiring new ones.

So when I returned to Cincinnati, I vowed to build a piece that used basic joints, but that would require complete mastery of them to produce a finished project that could withstand the scrutiny of a fellow woodworker poking around my house in the wee hours.

The Gustav Stickley Plant Stand

For many years I've wanted to build a replica of this Gustav Stickley plant stand. The form doesn't

The goal was to get the details right. Though simple in form, this piece is a challenge to do well. Building it will improve your ability to execute precision joinery and crisp corners.

show up in the catalogs I have for Stickley's furniture company, but I have stumbled upon signed examples at auctions and have seen them in a number of books.

Composed of only 16 significant sticks of wood, this plant stand is not flashy like a Morris chair or sideboard. But it is a well-proportioned and thoughtfully engineered piece of furniture.

All of the joinery has to be spot-on for the piece to work.

The version shown here had to be redesigned a tad for a practical reason. The green tile top in the original was an odd size (10" x 10") that you are unlikely to find at a store. So if I'd slavishly followed Stickley, you would be stuck cutting down a larger tile or commissioning a ceramic artist to make you one.

With a little work on the computer, I resized the project to accept a common floor tile from a home center (price $1.46) and it changed the overall dimensions of the piece by only 1" .

So the first step in building this plant stand is to shop for a tile. The so-called 12" x 12" floor tiles at the home center were slightly smaller than $11^{3}/_{4}$" x $11^{3}/_{4}$". So I scaled all my parts around those dimensions. My tile doesn't match the beguiling green of the Grueby-made tile in the original, but I came close. As you shop for tile, check out the natural slate tiles, which vary in color. I found a few slate tiles that were a better historical match. When I returned to the bin the next day to buy them, they were gone.

Perfection Begins With Selection

When you build a simple and small piece of furniture, the importance of wood selection is magnified. Every stick carries more visual weight. Plus, this project doesn't have a front or back. It has to look good from all angles.

The trickiest part of stock selection is in the legs. Making legs with quartersawn white oak is a challenge because each board has two faces that exhibit quartersawn grain and two faces that exhibit flat-sawn grain. And they look so radically different that it is distracting.

To duck this problem, you can veneer quartersawn oak on the flat-sawn faces (a trick employed by Gustav Stickley on some pieces). You can

Here are my four legs for the plant stand. Except for the leg at top right, they are rift-sawn. I got lucky with the leg at top right. Even though it is quartersawn on two faces and flat-sawn on the other two, its grain pattern is consistent all around. Trees are weird that way sometimes.

With 22 tenons to cut, I opted to make these joints with a dado stack in a table saw. A fence with a stop ensures the accuracy you need for this operation. The tenons' face shoulders and edge shoulders are both $1/4$" so you can make all these joints with the dado stack protruding $1/4$" above the table.

make each leg out of four pieces of quartersawn material mitered at the corners (a trick employed by Gustav's brothers Leopold and John). Or you can do what I did: Don't use quartersawn oak for the legs.

I used rift-sawn (sometimes called bastard-sawn) white oak for my legs. Technically, a board has been rift-sawn when its annular rings intersect the face of the board at an angle that's somewhere between 30° and 60°. With quartersawn boards the angle is higher than 60°. With plainsawn boards, that angle is lower than 30°.

The beauty of rift-sawn boards is that their faces and edges look similar, especially if you select boards that have the annular rings at 45° to the face. As a result, a rift-sawn leg will usually look the same no matter where you are in the room.

A Tangle of Tenons

Another challenge with this project is making all the mortise-and-tenon joints come together. While all the stretchers and aprons join their legs with a simple mortise-and-tenon joint, the first complication is that the tenons intersect one another at the corners inside the legs. Plus, the four wide aprons aren't centered on the legs. Instead, they're pushed to the inside a bit to nestle closer to the tile top.

As a result, the tenons on the top stretchers are 1" long and are mitered to meet at the corners. The stretchers on the aprons can only be $3/4$" long and these are also mitered to meet at the corners. This means you have to lay out the loca-

I mark out the location of my mortises by using my tenons like a ruler. Note that you can see here how the top stretcher has a longer tenon than the apron does.

tions of your tenon shoulders with great care. All the stretchers and aprons need to measure exactly $11^{3}/_{4}$" from shoulder to shoulder. And then you add a third tricky part to the project's joinery: A through-tenon that pierces the lower stretcher and is secured with a tusk.

We'll tend to that through-tenon later. First cut the $1/4$" -thick tenons on all the aprons and stretchers – by hand or by power – then prepare to use those tenons to lay out the locations of your mortises in the legs.

With the tenons cut, you can use those joints to lay out the location of mortises on your legs as shown in the photo above. This method requires less measuring and therefore offers less opportunity for error.

Mismatched Mortises

The mortises for the top stretchers and the lower stretchers are centered on the legs. So set up your hollow-chisel mortiser (or your mortising gauge) to poke a $1/4$" -wide x $1^{1}/_{8}$" -deep mortise in the legs. Then make all those mortises.

Note that getting mortises that are dead-center on a leg is a challenge for many machines and

Here I'm making the mortises for the aprons, which are located ½" in from the inside edge of each leg. Each of the apron mortises measures ¼" wide, 3¾" long and ⅞" deep.

their operators. To side-step the problem, get the machine set as best you can. As you work, ensure that you always work with an inside face of the leg against the mortiser's fence. This ensures that even though the mortise might not be centered, all the mortises will match up on all four legs.

Then you'll need to adjust your machine (or layout tools) to cut the mortises for the four aprons. These aprons are set ¼" in from the inside corner of each leg, so the mortises for the aprons should be located ½" in from each inside corner. These mortises don't need to be as deep either – ⅞" deep will be enough to house the tenon and allow for a little gunk and glue at the bottom.

The mortises for the top stretchers and aprons intersect, which means you'll likely get some splintering on the inside corner where they meet. There's little you can do to prevent it (mortising is quite violent). If it's a minor split, you can pull the splinter out and ignore it. With oak, sometimes it splits badly and I'll glue the splinter back in and secure it with tape as the glue dries.

More Mortises Yet

The lower stretchers each get a highly visible through-mortise, which will house the through-tenons and tusks. I've experimented a lot with different methods to get clean through-mortises (see "Make Clean Through-mortises" on page 158). For mortises that are nearly square, the best technique I have found is to first make a plywood pattern and rout them out. Then you come back and use the same pattern to chisel the corners square.

Gustav Stickley Plant Stand

	NO.	PART	SIZES (INCHES)			MATERIAL	NOTES
			T	W	L		
☐	4	Legs	1⁵⁄₈	1⁵⁄₈	26	Oak	
☐	4	Top stretchers	¾	1¼	13¾	Oak	1" TBE
☐	4	Aprons	¾	4¼	13¼	Oak	¾" TBE
☐	2	Lower stretchers	¾	3½	13¾	Oak	1" TBE
☐	1	Cross stretcher	1¼	1⁵⁄₈	17⅛	Oak	
☐	2	Tusks	⅝	⅞	2½	Oak	Start with 7" long
☐	4	Top strips	¼	¾	11¾	Oak	
☐	1	Panel	¾	12¼	12¼	Oak	Notched at corners
☐	2	Bottom cleats	¾	¾	11¾	Oak	

TBE = Tenon both ends

Yes, it seems like a lot of trouble. But this is a visible joint and worth the effort. I make my plywood patterns by sawing up scraps of plywood and assembling them into a panel that has a hole shaped like the mortise I want.

With your pattern assembled, use it to lay out the location of the ¾" x 1⅛" mortise and trace its shape onto the lower stretcher. Waste away as much of the mortise as you can using a Forstner bit (Forstner bits allow you to overlap your holes).

Then clamp the plywood pattern to your work-piece and install a pattern-cutting bit into your router. Cut around the mortise (go clockwise) until you have wasted away everything the pattern-cutting bit can get. Don't remove the pattern from your work.

Here are the four pieces of ½"-thick plywood that I have sawn up and will glue back together into a panel. Note that I don't use biscuits or dowels to join these pieces, just glue. The edge grain of the plywood is strong enough for this light-duty application.

When you glue up the pattern, wrangle the pieces as best you can so that they line up at the seams. Mis-matched seams will end up as bumps that your router will have to travel over – spoiling your accuracy.

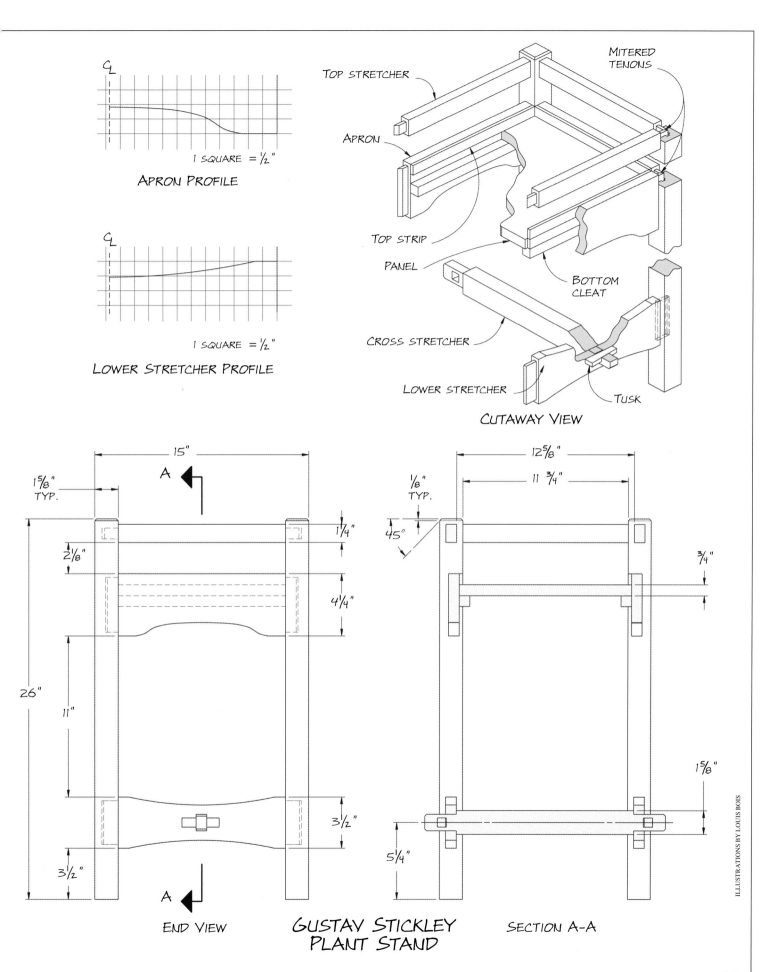

C_L

1 SQUARE = $\frac{1}{2}$"

APRON PROFILE

C_L

1 SQUARE = $\frac{1}{2}$"

LOWER STRETCHER PROFILE

TOP STRETCHER

MITERED TENONS

APRON

TOP STRIP

PANEL

BOTTOM CLEAT

CROSS STRETCHER

LOWER STRETCHER

TUSK

CUTAWAY VIEW

15"

A

$1\frac{5}{8}$" TYP.

$1\frac{1}{4}$"

$2\frac{1}{8}$"

$4\frac{1}{4}$"

26"

11"

$3\frac{1}{2}$"

$3\frac{1}{2}$"

A

END VIEW

$12\frac{5}{8}$"

$11\frac{3}{4}$"

$\frac{1}{8}$" TYP.

$45°$

$\frac{3}{4}$"

$1\frac{5}{8}$"

$5\frac{1}{4}$"

SECTION A-A

GUSTAV STICKLEY
PLANT STAND

ILLUSTRATIONS BY LOUIS BOIS

I used a ⅝" Forstner bit to waste away most of the mortise in the lower stretchers. You could use a smaller bit and a handheld drill as well. That just makes more work for the router.

Clamp the pattern on your work and cantilever things off your bench (you don't want to mortise your benchtop). Then use the pattern-cutting bit to hog out the waste that the Forstner bit couldn't get.

Use the plywood pattern as a chiseling guide to clean out the corners. Shown is a ⅜" corner chisel, though a garden-variety bench chisel will work just as well. It will just take twice the number of whacks.

When you band saw a curve, the temptation is to leave a lot of waste behind so you don't accidentally cross the line. I try to saw right next to the line. I get smoother curves and have less waste to remove with a rasp or router in the end.

I actually do the bulk of my routing with a laminate trimmer. This small tool has more than enough power for most work-a-day tasks, plus the smaller footprint makes clamping setups such as this a breeze. A full-size router would run into my bench's hold-downs.

Fetch a chisel or a corner-cutting chisel, and use the pattern to cut away the rounded corners left behind by the router bit. Don't try to remove all the waste in one whack. If you do, your chisel will try to push the pattern out of place. Take two or three small bites instead of one big one.

Precision Curves

An Arts & Crafts piece with eight curved edges is a bit unusual, but it is these curves that really set apart this design from similar plant-stand designs that competitors built and sold during this era. The curves on the lower stretcher are simply a segment of a 24"-radius circle. The ogee-shaped edge on the aprons is a somewhat more complex piece of work.

When confronted with a curve or two, I'll band saw out the bulk of the waste and shape the curve with a rasp. But because each of these patterns is repeated four times on the piece, I thought it best to produce a plywood routing pattern then clean up the edges by hand.

I made one plywood pattern for both shapes: One edge had the simple curve; the other edge had the ogee shape. I scribed the 24"-radius curve with a set of trammel points. To make the ogee edge, I first scaled up photographs of original plant stands to full size and created the pattern from those – I wanted this unusual curve to be just right. You can use the scale drawings to make your plywood patterns. Then I used these patterns to lay out the curves on the aprons and lower stretchers.

Saw out the bulk of the waste, then use your plywood pattern to clean up the edge with the help of a router and a pattern-cutting router bit. Then clean up your edges with a scraper and sandpaper – the surface left behind by a router bit isn't good enough to finish.

Cleanup and Test Assembly

At long last it was time to break out the handplanes – the fun part. After cleaning up all the flat surfaces with a jointer plane and a smoothing plane,

After routing, I scuff each edge with #120-grit sandpaper. This makes it easy to see my progress with a card scraper. When all the fuzzy grain from the sandpaper is gone, the edge is clean and ready to finish.

When you miter the ends of tenons, it's unlikely you'll get them to mate at the center of the joint. That would be asking a lot (but if it happens, great). Instead, miter them so that they barely miss one another. That ensures your tenons will seat completely in their mortises.

With the plant stand clamped up, mark on the top edge of the lower stretchers where the cross stretcher will be located. Then lay the cross stretcher on those marks. Use a ruler to then measure the distance between the two lower stretchers.

If you cut the tenons on your cross stretcher with a router, you'll need to set up a fence with a stop. Honestly, I did this setup to see how much of a pain it was. By the time I started adding the fence to the miter gauge, I would have been done if I'd just cut these by hand.

The hole for the tusk is offset a bit so that part of the mortise will be inside the lower stretcher. This is a critical point for a snug-fitting tusk.

Take small bites when cleaning out the rounded corners of the mortise for your tusk. Begin with the corners that will be buried in the lower stretcher – if you botch these they will never show.

I hand-fit all the joints then mitered the corners of the aprons and top stretchers.

Now you can assemble the project without glue to determine the size of the cross stretcher that is wedged between the two lower stretchers. Clamp up the entire plant stand and determine the exact distance between the two lower stretchers – that will be the distance between the shoulders of your cross stretcher.

Now you can mark out the ³⁄₄" x 1¹⁄₈" tenons on the ends of the cross stretcher. The tenons should be 2¹⁄₄" long, but you should confirm this with your dry-assembled piece. Now consider how you will cut these tenons. Using a dado stack will leave a surface that will require a lot of cleanup. I think you'll get cleaner results using a router or cutting them by hand.

That Touchy Tusk

If your tusks are designed properly, then installing them in the tenons is a simple operation. Most tusk troubles occur when the tenon is too short

to handle the tusk. Then it's tap, tap, crack – and the end of your tenon pops off. That's why the tenons are so long on this project's cross stretcher.

The first step is to bore a ⁵⁄₈" -diameter hole through the through-tenon. The location of this hole is critical. Knock together the cross stretcher and lower stretchers then trace a line around the through-tenon where it emerges from the lower stretcher.

Now lay out the location of the $5/8$" hole so $1/16$" of it crosses over this line. This space ensures the joint will tighten up when the tusk is knocked home. Drill the hole and square out the corners with a chisel.

Use a sliding bevel gauge set 4° off vertical to help guide your eye as you chisel out the mortise. The goal is to remove a wedge of material that is $1/16$" thick at the top that tapers to nothing at the bottom of the mortise.

One face of this through-mortise needs to be angled to match the angle on the tusk. I've found a 4° angle to work nicely. To lay out a 4° angle on your mortise, simply scribe a parallel line that is $1/16$" away from the edge of the mortise. That will give you the 4°. Then use a bench chisel to chop an angled ramp on this one face of the through-mortise. All the other faces of this mortise are left perpendicular.

Most people struggle with making the tusks. Here's the easy way: Start with a piece of oak that is $5/8$" x $7/8$" x 7" and cut a 4° taper on the width of the piece. Drive this overlong piece into the through-tenon until everything fits snugly and the tusk is roughly centered on the mortise. Then mark the final length of the tusk and cut it to size with a handsaw.

One Last Detail

One of the hallmarks of Arts & Crafts furniture is a small chamfer on the ends of legs, tenons and posts. I've always judged other people's work by these chamfers because they can be done quite poorly (got a belt sander?). Even when it looks like the maker wanted to take extra care, the grain can be easily torn out or splintered at the corners.

Once again, this is an area where I've experimented a lot with both hand and power techniques. And though I'll never give up my chamfer plane for long-grain chamfers, making them on end grain is a task best handled by a disc sander.

Assemble in the Right Order

I like to break all the long edges of my work right before assembly. It's easier to reach all the long edges with the sandpaper, and it prevents you from having sharp edges in tight corners where

your sandpaper wouldn't go. Plus, it's just as fast as doing it after assembly.

Glue up the two ends of the plant stand that have lower stretchers. Paint the inside of the mortises with glue and clamp things so the open mortises face the ceiling to prevent excess glue from running everywhere.

Once the glue is dry in the end assemblies, paint glue on all the blind mortises, slip the cross stretcher in place and clamp up the remaining top stretchers and aprons. Now you can turn your attention to getting the tile in its proper place.

"The perfection of a clock is not to go fast, but to be accurate."
— Luc de Clapiers, marquis de Vauvenargues (1715 - 1747), moralist and essayist

A Raised-panel Tile?

The tile rests on a panel of secondary wood that is sandwiched between strips of wood that are fastened to the inside of the aprons. The strips of wood create a groove that the panel floats in.

Four of these strips are visible. These $1/4$" x $3/4$" x $11^3/4$" strips rim the top of the aprons and fill in the space between the legs and aprons. Fit these strips between the legs and secure them with glue, pins and clamps.

When the glue dries, flip the plant stand on its head and fit the panel in place. You'll need to notch out its corners and allow a little expansion gap (unless you use plywood for this piece), but that is easily handled by a backsaw and block plane. When the panel fits, secure it against the

Plane down the over-long tusk until it fits snug in the through-mortise. The advantage to using a plane is that you remove a predictable amount of material with each pass – and the tusk is ready for finishing when you are done.

I wouldn't dream of cutting the tusk to length with power equipment. It's too dangerous. A backsaw and a bench hook make short work of the task.

top strips and nail in two ³⁄₄" x ³⁄₄" x 11³⁄₄" cleats below. The cleats should properly cross the width of the panel.

For the finish, I used the formula developed for the Spring 2007 issue ("Authentic Arts & Crafts Finish"). The recipe is as follows: Stain the bare wood with Olympic Interior "Special Walnut" oil-based stain. Let the wood soak for 15 minutes under the stain then wipe off the excess.

The next day, apply Watco's "Dark Walnut" Danish oil with a rag. Let it soak for 15 minutes then wipe off the excess. On the third day, apply one coat of Zinsser's Bulls Eye amber shellac. Shellac gets quite glossy, so you can add a coat of paste wax to reduce the sheen. Or you can apply a satin wiping varnish, which will give you extra protection (this project will see some water) and also reduce the sheen.

Attaching the tile is the easy part. I used a bead of tile adhesive. Draw the adhesive onto the wooden panel then press the tile into place. Take care not to use too much adhesive because it can easily squirt out from below the tile and make a mess of things on your finished project. Allow it to sit overnight. If you expect the plant stand to see lots of overflow, consider grouting around the edge of the tile as well.

This project will not end up in my home (we seem to kill all forms of foliage), but it will have my name on it. So if there are ever jetlagged woodworkers poring over this project, they'll know who got the details of this piece just right.

— *Christopher Schwarz*

Lay out your chamfers by lightly scoring the ends of your legs using a cutting gauge set to ¹⁄₈". Don't make this mark too deep or it could be visible on your completed work.

Set a miter gauge to 45° and use that to guide the leg gently to the spinning disc of the disc sander. (I have one of these sanding discs as an accessory for my table saw. It works great.) When your chamfer reaches your scribed line, back the leg away from the disc.

After you clamp up the ends of the plant stand, inspect the open mortises. It's possible that excess glue ran all over the open mortise. If it dries there, it could interfere with your final assembly. Tease it out (I use a coffee stirring stick).

Take care when installing the strips at the top of the aprons. You want the strips and the apron flush, and you don't want unnecessary glue squeeze-out. Cleaning up this seam is tough thanks to the top stretcher.

Nail, but don't glue, the cleats in below the panel. If the tile ever breaks it will be easier to repair if you can pry off the cleats, remove the panel and replace the tile.

Make Clean Through-mortises

Woodworkers expect this joint to be tidy and tight, not ragged and gappy. We explore the best ways to make this sometimes-vexing hole.

The history of the through-mortise begins with a joint that was necessary because of the tools and technology of the day, and it ends with a joint that flaunts the skills of the modern woodworker like a prize chicken at a county fair.

A through-mortise – which is where the joint passes entirely through a leg or stile – is rarely structurally necessary in modern furniture thanks to high-strength glues and machine-cut joinery surfaces that maximize the amount of wood-to-wood contact.

But they are sometimes necessary for other reasons: They are a hallmark of certain furniture styles, including some early American and European pieces, Arts & Crafts furniture and stick chairs, such as Windsors and Welsh chairs.

And in contemporary work, through-mortises are often used as the calling card for a handmade piece of furniture. Few furniture factories go to the trouble of making this joint, so individual makers use it to differentiate their work from the fiberboard garbage that clogs our stores, homes and landfills.

The reason the through-mortise is a poster child for handmade furniture is that it is a challenge to make well – much like the dovetail joint. People's eyes are drawn to expressed joints like this, and small gaps make big impressions.

I've spent years investigating various techniques for making this joint tidy and show-worthy. The following story is the result of my trials and occasional revelations.

Real-world Through-mortises

Through-mortises appear in the earliest extant furniture. Egyptian beds and stools typically used the through-mortise to join their legs and rails. Exactly why this joint was employed isn't

The torn grain, gaps and general loose fit around these through-mortises are unacceptable to the modern woodworker – though these defects were once common. This is an Arts & Crafts bookcase that once graced a church library in Lexington, Ky.

known, but we can guess. With a lack of reliable glues, a through-mortise joint allows lots of wood-to-wood contact – friction if you will – that will keep the joint together. Sometimes these joints were even lashed together, and the tenon passing through the mortise allowed this.

As furniture evolved through the 18th and 19th centuries, it became much more the norm to obscure joinery rather than show it off. Furniture craftsmen avoided the problem of unreliable glues by cutting a blind mortise (which is open only on one end) and then driving a peg through the finished mortise and tenon to mechanically lock the pieces.

"Only the mediocre are always at their best."

— Jean Giraudoux (1882 – 1944)
French diplomat, dramatist and novelist

However, in the world of the workers who fitted out houses with doors and window sash, the through-mortise remained a staple of the trade. When joining the rails and stiles of windows and doors, through-mortises are typical even in houses built at the dawn of the 20th century.

The reason for that is two-fold. Doors and windows are made up of heavier pieces that need to take more abuse than a piece of fine furniture. Plus, a through-mortise has other advantages. It can be cut using fewer jobsite tools (a chisel and a mallet is all that is needed) and you don't have to take the time to clean the bottom of the mortise. It can be assembled and wedged with fewer clamps – you can put one clamp on the joint, wedge it from the outside and immediately remove the clamp. And things can be more easily dismantled for repair – dig out the wedges and pull the joint apart.

And because the result was usually hidden by

paint or by its location on the edges of doors or in a window casing, the joint didn't have to look perfect. It just had to hold things together.

That's how things stood until the furniture factories came along. Some of the earliest factory machinery was designed to cut mortises and tenons. But in an effort to make less-expensive furniture for the masses, factories began using less-reliable joints – such as dowels – that could be made quickly and cheaply with precision machinery.

From the outside of the furniture, the results looked the same. A blind tenon and a doweled joint are indistinguishable from the exterior of a piece. And I've even seen doweled pieces that have a fake exterior peg, which implies there is a tenon in there instead of two skimpy bits of dowel.

Some furniture consumers were unhappy with this mass-produced flimsy furniture coming out of the factories. And from this discontent rose the Arts & Crafts movement. At its best, the Arts & Crafts movement celebrated stout joinery. High-quality pieces used through-mortises as a way to show the consumer how the joint was made. (Let's ignore, for a moment, the Arts & Crafts shysters that would nail on a fake through-tenon to fool the customer.)

These visible joints were put in visible places – on the tops of chair arms, on the fronts and ends of casework pieces, on legs. However, making these visible joints must have proved to be a challenge. They appear on only the best pieces. And they don't always look tidy (especially the ones that are close to the floor).

And then the through-mortise began to disappear again from furniture as the popular styles began to change to favor surface ornamentation to structural honesty.

Today the through-mortise joint is used when you are reproducing certain furniture styles or are attempting to display your craftsmanship. No matter why you make this joint, the standards for what is acceptable have changed. Gaps between a through-mortise and its tenon aren't acceptable in good work.

Two Kinds of Through-mortises

So the imperative is to make this joint look perfect, and the tolerances are tough to hit. Where do you begin? First, it's helpful to know there are two kinds of through-mortises, each of which requires a different strategy.

The first kind of through-mortise has an opening that is skinny and long – for example, $\frac{1}{4}$" wide x 3" long. This is the kind of through-mortise you would see when you join a side rail on a Morris chair with the chair's front leg. It also is common to see this mortise where a shelf intersects the side of the carcase.

The other kind of through-mortise is simply larger – it can be either rectangular or square. This is the kind of through-mortise you would see when you join a chair leg to an arm.

This through-mortise on the lower leg of a Gustav Stickley rocker would not pass modern muster. The ends of the mortise were left round and the tenon was square. On other joints in this chair you can see tearing left from the boring machine.

This through-tenon on an arm of a Charles Stickley side chair shows what good work looks like in a highly visible area. The joint isn't airtight, but it's quite good considering the 100 years that have passed since its making.

On the show side of a mortise, the edges must be crisp and not rounded over by the tool. Make lots of light cuts, then sweep the first bits of waste away using your chisel's edge flat on your work.

Let's walk through some of the techniques for cutting each of these.

Skinny and Long: Use Square Tooling

For any through-mortise, you can use a mortise chisel and a mallet. And if I have four or fewer to do, that is typically how I'll proceed. You lay out the mortise opening on both sides of the joint and then begin the banging. When I make my layout marks, I score them as deeply as possible on the face of the joint that will be visible. Deep score lines help you remove waste cleanly.

This is particularly important if the long axis of the mortise runs across the grain (like it does in the bookshelf in this issue). When you chisel out a mortise across the grain, it has a tendency to tear out around the joint, particularly in woods such as oak and ash.

Begin chopping out the side that will be obscured. Working from this side first allows you to get your chisel skills warmed up. If the chisel is cutting true, I'll drive down beyond the halfway point. Though removing waste is more

difficult in deep cavities, it's more important to get the two ends of the mortise to meet. So don't stop if things are going well.

Then flip the work and make a light cut on the face that will be visible. Some people will chop up the surface of the mortise with tight cuts then sweep the waste off the top of the mortise using the shaft of the chisel.

Once the initial opening is cut, you can drive more deeply. Just be certain not to lever the chisel against the ends of the mortise when prying out the waste. This pry-bar action rounds over the rim of the exit wound.

If you are not going to cut the through-mortise by hand, two other common options are to use a hollow-chisel mortiser or a plunge router with a straight bit and an edge guide.

I almost always choose the hollow-chisel mortiser. Here's why: The router method is slow. Through-mortises that are shaped this way (long and skinny) are typically in thick material – 3" thick is not uncommon. That can be a lot to ask of a $\frac{1}{4}$"-diameter router bit. In fact, I've snapped off quite a few in deep cuts. If you go the router route, take little bites. It slows you down, but it's easier on the tooling.

You also have to square up the ends of these router cuts (unless you want to make an authentic and gappy Gustav Stickley-style joint). This is a lot to ask of a hand-held chisel in thick material.

You have to take care and take smaller bites so your tool doesn't go astray.

The hollow-chisel mortiser is fast and can make a clean cut if you set up the machine with care. Let's begin there. You need sharp tooling. File the cutter of the auger-bit part of the tooling and stone the inside and outside of the hollow

chisel. For complete details on choosing the right bit and sharpening it, read our story on hollow-chisel tooling in the Spring 2007 issue.

You need to have your hollow chisel set dead parallel to the machine's fence. You can get there by trial-and-error. But here's how to make it there with less error. Lay out a sample mortise on some test scrap. Bring the hollow chisel close to your layout lines. Now press a 6"-long ruler against the hollow chisel and compare it to your layout line. The ruler will exaggerate any twist in the chisel and allow you to fine-tune it in the bushing of your hollow-chisel mortiser.

Now make a sample mortise to confirm that you are cutting where you want to cut and that the chisel is parallel to the fence. Now get ready to prepare your live stock. Normally, most instructions assume that your project parts are square. When making through-mortises, your parts have to be as square as possible. Double-check each part after you square it up and before you make your mortises. Small errors make joints that won't go together. I've found that it pays to have the part's jointed face against the mortiser's fence.

To bore the mortise, first work halfway through on one side. Then flip the work over and do the same thing on the other. If the machine is set up well, this work is extremely fast and clean.

In router-cut mortises like this, the corners are tough to square up without botching them. You can score your layout lines with deep knife cuts, which helps. Ultimately, if you take this path you are going to have to get good with a chisel.

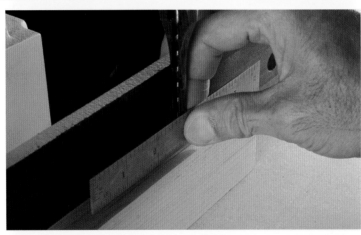

Press and hold a ruler to a flat face of your hollow chisel. Compare the ruler to your layout lines to see if the chisel is twisted. This trick is remarkably accurate.

I'm in the habit of using the leap-frog method of mortising. Skip a space with every hole, then clean up between the holes. Other craftsmen I respect say the holes should overlap slightly to improve chisel cutting. Try both and decide.

Here you can see the result of accurate machine setup and careful layout. The mortise goes clear through, and the rim of the mortise is crisp enough for close inspection.

Bigger Joints Require Different Tools

The rules change when the through-mortises get bigger. Once your joints are wider than $\frac{1}{2}$", then hollow-chisel mortisers become difficult to use. When your mortises are wider than $\frac{1}{2}$", you have to shift your work both left-to-right and back-to-front to clean out the mortise. That's not always a simple thing to do with accuracy. And you really need an X-and-Y sliding table. (Side note: I'm aware there are bigger bits available for hollow-chisel mortisers, but they don't work on the common benchtop machines.)

Here's the other thing that changes: Usually with larger through-mortises, you are working on thinner stock, typically $\frac{3}{4}$"- to $\frac{7}{8}$"-thick stuff.

So a new strategy is in order: router templates. Because your stock is thinner, the 1"-long straight bits have no problem cutting these joints with ease. Plus, as you'll soon see, the routing template can also be a chiseling template for squaring up the corners.

You can make these router templates to use either a pattern-guided straight bit or a bushing installed in your router's baseplate. The tem-plates for pattern-guided bits are simpler to make (no math), but it's tricky to get your bit's bearing and the thickness of your pattern all playing nice together.

On the other hand, the templates for bushing-guided bits require a little math (addition – plus its tricky friend, subtraction). But you're fooling around a lot less trying to match your bit and the thickness of the material out of which you are making your pattern. So really it's a wash as to which method is faster.

No matter which path you choose, you need to make a pattern out of plywood (or solid wood) that has an opening with perfectly sharp corners. Making that pattern is fairly simple: I saw up bits of plywood (typically $\frac{1}{2}$" in thickness) and reassemble them as a panel that has the right-sized hole for my routing pattern.

Remove as much of the waste as you can with a Forstner bit, then clamp the router template in place. Be sure to secure the template to the outside face of your work. Rout out the rest of the waste but don't remove the template because its job isn't over. You can use its sharp corners to guide your chisel to square up the rounded corners.

This technique yields nice crisp corners on the outside of your work and ragged, torn-out corners on the inside surface (because there was no template to guide your chisel). This isn't a problem as long as the tearing isn't too severe.

Once you get the mortise cut, the tenons are easy. I cut them close on my power equipment, then trim them to a snug fit with a shoulder plane, which also removes the marks left by the power tooling.

— *Christopher Schwarz*

The pattern-cutting bit (left) seems simpler (just make a pattern that is the correct size), but you have to set things so the bearing rides the pattern and there is enough cutter showing to do the job. Bushing-guided patterns simply require a slightly oversized pattern.

Here you can see how a pattern was assembled for a through-mortise. I use only glue on the edges to join the parts – no biscuits or dowels. With plywood, there's always enough long grain at the edges to make this panel plenty strong.

Take little bites with the chisel. If you try to remove the entire corner in one whack, bad things can happen. The template can shift. Or the chisel will steer itself outside the template – but below the surface of your work.

THIS-AND-THAT

White Water Shaker Bench

We build a reproduction of a rustic and sturdy walnut bench using hand tools and local walnut.

The Shakers in the White Water community built these walnut benches so that visitors would have a place to sit while they observed the Shakers' worship services.

While going to a church just to watch might seem a bit odd to us moderns, I probably would be in the front row if I could travel back in time to the 1830s. Their worship services were marked by choreographed, rhythmic and practiced dances, and original and moving hymns.

Though I've never gotten to observe Shaker dancing in person, I have had the privilege of hearing their hymns reenacted on a few occasions. Many of the hymns are devoted to the daily tasks of life (such as sweeping), and are simply beautiful.

The White Water community in Hamilton County, Ohio, has one of the closed village's original benches in its possession; it's a 13'-long behemoth made from six pieces of walnut nailed together. I was permitted to measure the original and pore over its details to build two reproductions that *Woodworking Magazine* is donating to the Friends of White Water Shaker Village (whitewatervillage.org).

The walnut for this bench was graciously donated by Dr. David Bryant, a local woodworker and turner with a band-saw mill. As a result, the bench shown in this article was built using wood that was cut about 10 miles from the original village.

We've scaled the 13'-long version down to a more home-friendly 6' long in the construction drawing. However, if you have a big family and would like a SketchUp drawing of the 13'-long version you can visit our web site and download it for free.

The original bench had tool marks that indicated it was built with hand tools using wood that had been processed (probably) by the Shakers' sawmill with a reciprocating blade (sort of like a giant jigsaw). In that spirit, I decided to use hand tools as much as possible for this project.

The joinery on this bench is simple, yet the original has held up remarkably well to regular use. And if you are a budding hand-tool user, you'll find this bench a great practice piece.

Processing the Stock

The original sitting bench was built using boards that were wide enough to be used without having to glue up several narrow boards into the necessary widths for the seat and the legs.

While finding walnut (or wood of any species) this wide can be a struggle these days, it's worth every effort. A seat made from a single wide board makes quite an impression on the viewer.

I roughly surfaced these boards (with some assistance) using a powered jointer and planer, then dressed them all by hand, first with a jack plane to get them flatter, and then with a jointer plane, which removed slight twists and cups. Then I ripped and crosscut the top and aprons to their final sizes.

White Water Shaker Bench

	NO.	PART	SIZES (INCHES) T	W	L	MATERIAL
❑	1	Seat	1	$12^{3}/_{4}$	72	Walnut
❑	2	Aprons	$^{5}/_{8}$	$2^{3}/_{4}$	68	Walnut
❑	2	Legs	$^{7}/_{8}$	$12^{3}/_{4}$	15	Walnut

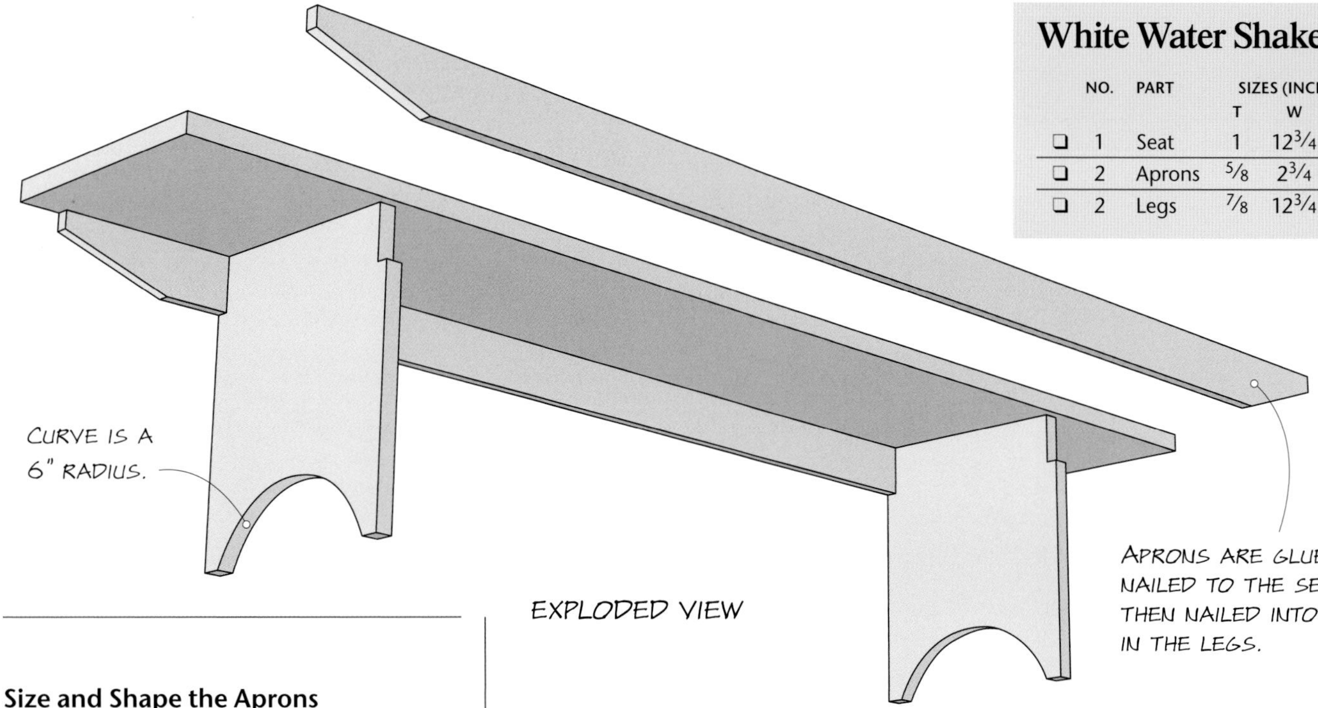
CURVE IS A 6" RADIUS.
EXPLODED VIEW
APRONS ARE GLUED AND NAILED TO THE SEAT – THEN NAILED INTO NOTCHES IN THE LEGS.

ILLUSTRATION BY CHRISTOPHER SCHWARZ

Size and Shape the Aprons

There are several ways you could build this bench, and I have no way of knowing how the Shakers went about it originally. Here's how I decided to proceed: First I shaped the aprons, then I nailed and glued them to the underside of the seat. Then I notched the legs so they fit between the aprons and nailed them in place. If you're going to do it my way, the first step is to deal with the aprons.

Plane the aprons so they are flat and true using a jointer plane. Then mark the taper at both ends using the drawings as a guide. To cut the taper, I put each apron on my sawbenches and cut the taper with a panel saw filed with rip teeth. Then I cleaned up the sawn edge with a block plane.

Attach the Aprons to the Seat

The most critical joint in this project is the way the aprons attach to the underside of the seat. A good joint ensures the seat will stay rigid and will keep the legs in place as well. I was impressed by how tight this joint was on the original, even after 150 years or so.

To ensure this joint was tight, I took extra pains to dress the top edge of the apron so it was perfectly flat and square. Then I made sure that the apron mated with the seat without having to pull out any warping with clamps. This, by the way, is a challenge when you have 13'-long boards and an 8'-long workbench.

First I use a jack plane set to take a thick shaving to dress the long edges of the seat. I follow that up with a jointer plane, which straightens the edge and leaves a nicer surface. Finally, a smoothing plane prepares the edge for finishing.

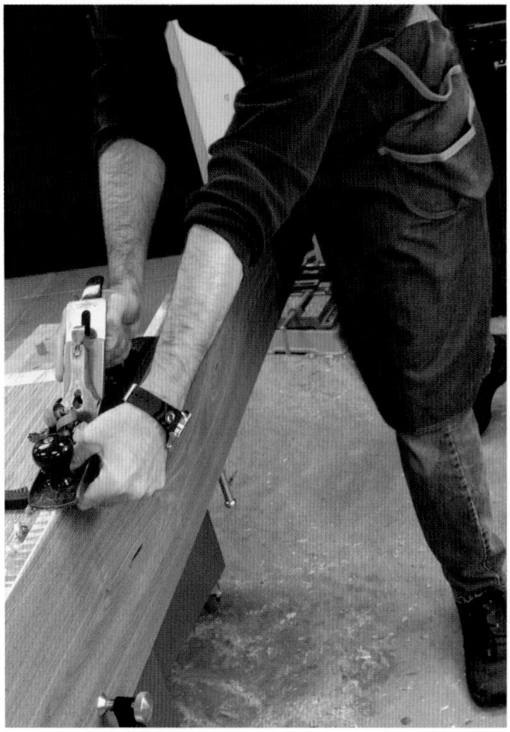

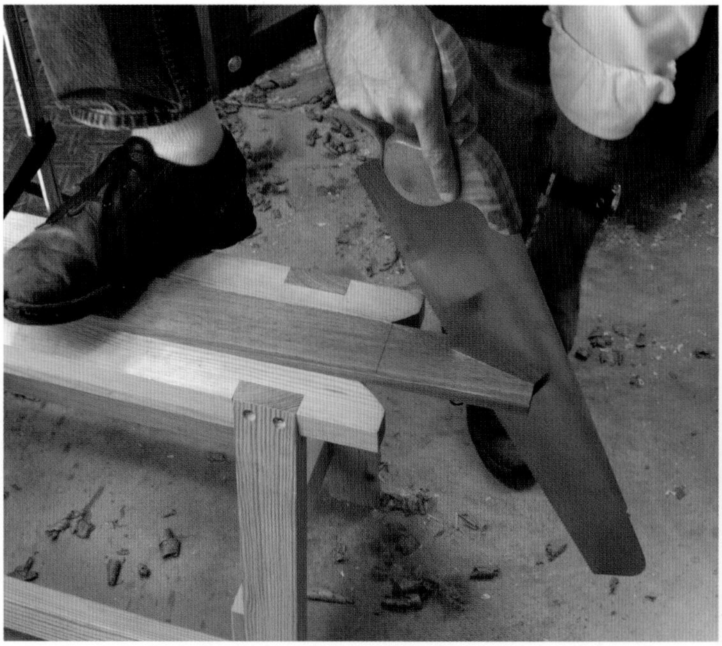

Sometimes it's easier to take the tool to the work. Here I'm using a panel saw to cut the tapered shape on the end of an apron. The apron is resting on one of my two sawbenches, which are a handy workshop appliance.

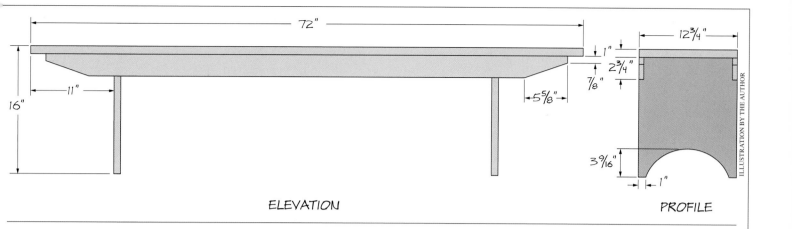

72"

1"
2¾"
⅞"

16"

11"

12¾"

5⅝"

3 9/16"

1"

ELEVATION

PROFILE

Then I glued the aprons to the seat. I used a modern yellow glue – our hide glue had gone missing that day. I let the glue cure overnight. Then I nailed the seat to the apron using *6d* cut nails spaced every 8½", just like the original.

Once you've driven the nails, set them below the surface with a nail set. For cut nails, I use a

It only takes a few strokes to clean up the sawn edge with a plane. Any sharp plane will do – planing downhill is always easy work.

homemade nail set made from an inexpensive punch. I filed its round tip to a rectangle, which is much more effective when setting rectangular-head cut nails.

Then plane the edge of the seat and apron flush and smooth.

Shape and Notch the Legs

The legs are simple but effective. The two feet are formed by cutting a curve on the bottom edge. Then you notch out the top and nail the leg in place. To begin, lay out the curve on the bottom of the legs using a compass.

Cut the curve using a bowsaw or some other frame saw, then fair the curve with rasps. The original craftsman stopped at this point. You can continue to refine the curve with sandpaper if you wish.

Now you can lay out the notches on the top of each leg. I think you should lay out and fit each leg individually. Don't just use the drawings to lay out your joints. Instead, place each leg where it will go on the underside of the seat/apron assembly and mark out the locations of the notches.

"Practical appeals to me because people will pay for it. I learned that people will buy 10 practical pieces for every room brooch."

— Hank Gilpin (1946 -)
furniture maker

Then use a combination square to gauge how deep each notch should be. Again, don't trust your cutting list or the drawing. Take the measurement from the actual apron where the leg will go. This is one of the keys to tight joints in handwork.

Now saw out the notches on the top of each leg. If you have a full nest of saws, use a tenon saw to rip the long section of the notch and a carcase saw to crosscut the waste free. If you have only one saw, a crosscut carcase saw can do the whole job.

One common error is to make the notches a little too long. The result is that the bottom of the notch won't fit tight to the apron. To fix this,

Some creative clamping ensures a tight joint. The clamp on the far right ensures that the apron will be flush to the edge of the seat at the ends. The F-style clamp keeps the tapered apron against the seat. Thank goodness for its swiveling clamping pad.

I laid out the nails using dividers (shown on the left). Then I drilled ³/₃₂" pilot holes and drove in the *6d* nails and set them with a homemade nail set.

A sharp bowsaw makes quick work of this curve. The biggest challenge is keeping the blade level during the cut – the tendency is to tip the far end of the saw up. To train yourself, I recommend marking the curve on both faces of the leg and stopping every few stokes to gauge your progress.

A couple rasps make quick work of cleaning up the curve to your pencil line. Rasps are two-handed tools. Beware of your left hand. Until you build up callouses, you can cut yourself this way.

Here's the leg in place and balancing on the aprons. I'm marking the location of the notches. This is a remarkably accurate way to work.

To make the workholding easy, I clamped a block on my bench and affixed the top to that block with some double-stick tape. Note that the face side of the tabletop is getting taped down to the block.

To make the workholding easy, I clamped a block on my bench and affixed the top to that block with some double-stick tape. Note that the face side of the tabletop is getting taped down to the block.

plane the top edge of the leg on a shooting board, which will tighten up the fit between the leg and the apron.

Now you can nail the legs in place. I clamped each leg tight to the apron and secured the leg to each apron with two 6d nails. Then I nailed the seat to the leg with five evenly spaced 6d nails. You can reinforce the legs with glue blocks.

Finishing Up

After setting all the nails, I finished up all the visible surfaces with a smoothing plane. However, the original craftsman didn't bother. The pencil lines from construction are still visible on the exterior surfaces.

It's unclear what sort of finish was on the original – if it had a finish at all. The bench doesn't exhibit any evidence of a film finish, and it is water stained in some places, so I opted for a boiled linseed oil finish. Boiled linseed oil is appropriate to the period and it would become stained if exposed to water. But I hope that won't happen with this reproduction.

I applied four coats of boiled linseed oil and followed that up with wax. Then it was time to take a seat and wait for the dance to begin.

— *Christopher Schwarz*

Arts & Crafts Mirror

The style is powered by the industrial revolution, and the joinery is some of the strongest in woodworking. This mirror is built for the long haul.

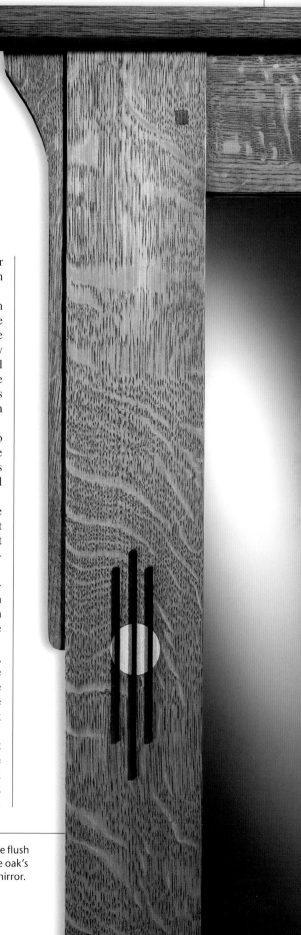

Arts & Crafts furniture, sometimes known as craftsman or mission, is simple in style and solidly built. This style first appeared in the United States about the turn of the 20th century. Although Gustav Stickley, a New York furnituremaker, had conceived this design in his shop and is credited as the American inventor of the style, it was not until the manufacturers of Grand Rapids, Mich., picked up the ball and made this furniture available to the masses that the design picked up steam. This design boasts clean lines, great wood grain and strong joinery.

In building furniture there is no joint stronger than the mortise and tenon, which is used in the construction of our mirror. While the joints on our project are not through-mortise and tenons (where the end of the tenon shows on the outside of the stiles), as they are on many pieces in this style, they are classic examples of the joint. The chamfering on the edges of the top, along with the corbels (another often-seen element of this period), provide you with a great introduction to the Arts & Craft-style of our furniture history.

We could not leave well enough alone when it came to the mirror's design. We decided to add inlay – a common feature on some mission-style furniture – to kick it up a notch.

If you have tackled inlay in other projects this will be a walk in the park. If this is your first foray into the world of inlay, rest assured that this is a simple introduction. You will have no trouble with this eye-popping addition. But, let's not get ahead of ourselves – the frame comes first!

Strength in Joints

Mirrors of the Arts & Craft style tend to have varying thicknesses of material that add an extra shadow line to the work. Be careful as you mill the pieces for this project – the stiles are thicker than the rails. This is important because we are going to cut the mortises in the stiles based on the thickness of the rails.

In order to have the back of the mirror fit flush to the wall, we need to keep the four parts of our frame flat at the back face, so we will position the mortises in those stiles off-center.

When I lay out the mortise measurements on the stiles, I begin by defining the width of the rails. Those lines are drawn across the entire edge of the stile. I then know not to extend my mortise cuts beyond that line or the mortise will show in the finished project. In the mirror, the top rail is aligned with the top edge of the stiles while the bottom rail is held 1" above the bottom end of each stile.

Next, I define the mortise length with two short lines (see picture on the top left of page 21). This measurement reflects the $\frac{5}{8}$" shoulders of the tenon. It is between these lines that I will cut the $1\frac{1}{4}$"-deep mortises.

Finally, I mark the location of the mortise in relationship to the front and back. It is offset toward the back edge of the stiles. I then repeat these exact layout steps for each and every mortise that I cut.

There are a number of ways to create the mortise. You can use a drill press to remove a portion of the material and finish cleaning things up with a chisel, make the cut with a plunge router or use a dedicated mortise machine.

The mortise machine is my choice. To begin, you need to place the $\frac{1}{4}$" tooling into the machine while setting the back edge $\frac{1}{4}$" away from the mortiser's fence. This measurement makes the math easy. A tenon of that thickness in $\frac{3}{4}$" stock will result in two $\frac{1}{4}$" shoulders as well.

Position the stile with the back face against the machine's fence and cut the mortise using the step method (center top photo, next page). As you cut the spaces you'll notice that there is always equal pressure on the opposing sides of the cut.

The inlay design of the raised ebony strips with the flush maple circle bounces off of the quartersawn white oak's mellow tones and adds to the overall look of the mirror.

Developing a routine to mark out mortise measurements keeps confusion at bay. Clamping two pieces together for layout saves time. The long lines indicate the inner edges of the rails; the short lines indicate the length of the mortises.

Plunge the first cut then skip an equal amount of waste material. Plunge again and repeat the steps until you move along the entire mortise. Next, return to remove the balance of the waste material. This extends the life of the chisel and bit set.

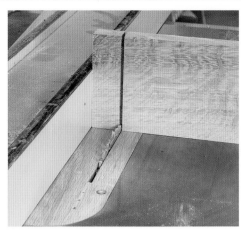

There is no need for a step-off block because we are not cutting completely through the rail. Adjusting for the edge cuts is simply a matter of raising the blade height from the previous step.

With the mortises complete we now need to make the matching tenons. I create the tenons at the table saw. First, set the blade height to ¼" then set the rip fence to cut the 1¼" length of the tenons (1¼" between the fence and the far side of the blade). Use the miter gauge to guide the cut on each face of the rails, while holding the piece tight to the saw's fence.

Next, raise the blade height to slightly above ⅝" in height without relocating the fence and make these cuts on the edges of the rails, forming the edge shoulders of the tenon.

The second phase is to cut the tenons' cheeks. I use a shop-made tenon jig. To begin, set the table saw's blade height to the top edge of the shoulder cut made in the previous step and adjust the fence to cut the cheeks of the tenon. This is where you need to be precise. The idea is to cut one face cheek, without trapping the waste between the blade and fence, then reverse each rail in the jig and make the second cheek cut with the balance of material resulting in a tenon of the correct thickness, as shown in the photo at right. This ensures that the tenon will be located in the center of each rail. Test the fit of the tenon to the mortise, making any adjustments as needed. You need a snug fit that does not require the use of a mallet to assemble.

The last step to create the tenons is at the band saw. Set the fence to remove ¹¹⁄₁₆" of material at each edge cheek. I recommend cutting a bit more than the lay out measurement of ⅝" so that you can adjust the rail in the mortise at assembly time to achieve the correct final positioning without significant loss of joint strength – remember, end grain does not have great holding power.

Inlay Makes it Pop
The inlay needs to be created prior to any assembly because it is easier to work with the individual pieces rather than an assembled frame. The inlay is fit and then removed prior to staining to achieve

Whether it is shop-made, as shown, or a commercially available jig, consistent thickness of your material is the secret to getting repeatable results in cutting the tenons.

Using hand pressure should be all that is necessary to fit a mortise-and-tenon joint. The primary gluing surface is the face grain of each piece, therefore it is not necessary to achieve a perfect fit over the width of the tenon.

the desired results. If it were stained like the mirror frame, the inlay would lose its impact.

I suggest running through these steps on a piece of scrap wood first, then once perfected you can work on the frame.

Beginning the inlay is as simple as drilling a hole. Chuck a 1⅜" Forstner bit into the drill press and drill a hole that is ¹³⁄₃₂" deep. Why so precise? The circle inlay for this project is actually a 35mm hinge hole repair kit (see Supplies box at the end of the story). Because of the tapered sides of the inlay piece, it is necessary that the inlay not only be tightly fitted to the circumference of the hole but that it seats tight to the bottom as well.

Next, install a ¼" drill bit in your drill press and bore through the frame at the center of the larger hole. This smaller hole provides access for the maple disk to be removed by pushing a small dowel in from the back of the mirror.

Position the round portion of the inlay into the hole and use a low-angle block plane to flush the circle to the stile. Pop the disk out and then lay out the lines for the string inlay on the stile

according to the plan and remember to establish start and stop limits for each string piece.

You need to secure the round inlay temporarily when routing the string inlay to keep it from spinning. I used a brad that I drove in from the backside of the stile. Find a non-routed area to install a brad (I used a 4d finish nail that I trimmed to ¾" in length), drill a pilot hole, put the disk in place and set the brad in from the back.

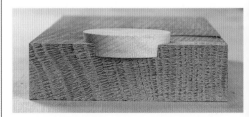

Setting up the hole for the circle inlay is precise work. The edge of the inlay must fit tight to the circumference of the hole drilled and be able to be affixed to the bottom.

A fence guide with your router is required for cutting the grooves for the inlay. If you overshoot the exact entry point for the bit, carefully climb-cut back to the beginning of the groove before completing the pass.

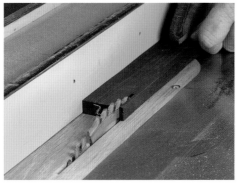

Cutting the ebony using the table saw wastes more material than the band saw, but the consistency of its cut makes it easier to fit the inlay.

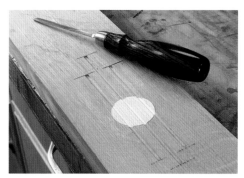

The router bit will leave a rounded end on the grooves. The choice is to square the ends with a ⅛" chisel or round the inlay with a file. Either method proved successful in the shop.

String Inlay, Rout On

Now you're ready to rout the recesses for the string inlay, which will sit proud of the stile when you are done. The 5¼"-long center string extends 1" below the 3¾"-long flanking pieces. Install a ⅛"-diameter upcut spiral bit into a plunge router with an edge guide attachment and position the bit to cut at the exact center of the stile. Set the depth of cut by zeroing out the bit against the face of the stile, then set the depth adjustment to the desired depth of cut on your plunge router. I set the depth of cut scientifically – with a good ol' American nickel (which is ⁵⁄₆₄" thick).

Start the router with the fence of the edge guide tight against one edge of the stile and plunge the bit into the cut at one end of your layout lines. Carefully move the router forward until you reach the opposite end, all the while holding the fence tight to the stile's edge. Repeat these steps for the second stile.

Now prepare to rout the second set of recesses. Adjust the edge guide to leave a ¼" of material between the center recess and an outer recess. Run the grooves as before, first with the edge guide's fence against one edge of the stile, then again with the edge guide's fence against the other edge of the stile. The hard work is done!

Ebony is my wood of choice for the stringing. To cut the strips safely I make a first pass at the table saw to rip the edges of my stock parallel. Then I adjust the fence to have the off fall of the next cut be the piece that is used as inlay.

To do this, set the fence closer to the blade by ¼" – one ⅛" for the blade thickness and one ⅛" for the inlay. Set the thickness a bit on the strong side. It is easy to pare the string down to fit the groove with sandpaper or a cabinet scraper. Once the fit is complete it's time to cut the individual pieces to length.

First things first: You have a decision to make. You can either square the rounded ends of the recess left from routing with an ⅛" chisel or you

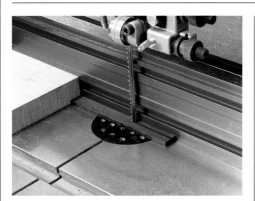

The band saw is the tool of choice when resawing the ebony to final size. The top edge of the string can be sanded and the pieces are small enough to rule out a table saw cut.

After fitting the inlay and stringing, remove the pieces and bundle them with blue painter's tape. This will ensure a proper fit after the finish is applied.

can round the ends of the inlay to fit the rounded recesses. Whichever path you choose, fit one end of the inlay to the groove then mark the opposite end. Cut the pieces with a handsaw, keeping them long enough to trim to a snug fit. A disk sander, file or sandpaper will do the trick.

The string inlay is held proud of the face of the mirror. If you set the depth of cut as explained in the text, you need to resaw the ebony to ³⁄₁₆"

thick. Step away from the table saw! The band saw is the correct tool for this cut. Set the fence appropriately and slice the pieces making sure to use a push stick or block for safety.

Fit all the stringing pieces into the recesses, then remove each assembled inlay set. Make sure to keep track of the orientation of each piece so that the sets will go back in the correct orientation at the end of the project.

Arts & Crafts Mirror

	NO.	PART	SIZES (INCHES) T	W	L	MATERIAL	NOTES
☐	1	Top	¾	2	26½	QSWO*	
☐	1	Top rail	¾	4	16	QSWO*	1¼ tenon on both ends
☐	1	Bottom rail	¾	3	16	QSWO*	1¼ tenon on both ends
☐	2	Stiles	1	4	60	QSWO*	
☐	2	Corbels	¾	1¾	16	QSWO*	
☐	2	String inlay	³⁄₁₆	⅛	15	Ebony	
☐	1	Circle inlay	½	1⅜		Maple	35mm hinge repair kit
☐	1	Mirror backing	¼	14⅜	53	Plywood	
☐	1	Mirror	¼	13⅞	52½		

*QSWO= Quartersawn White Oak

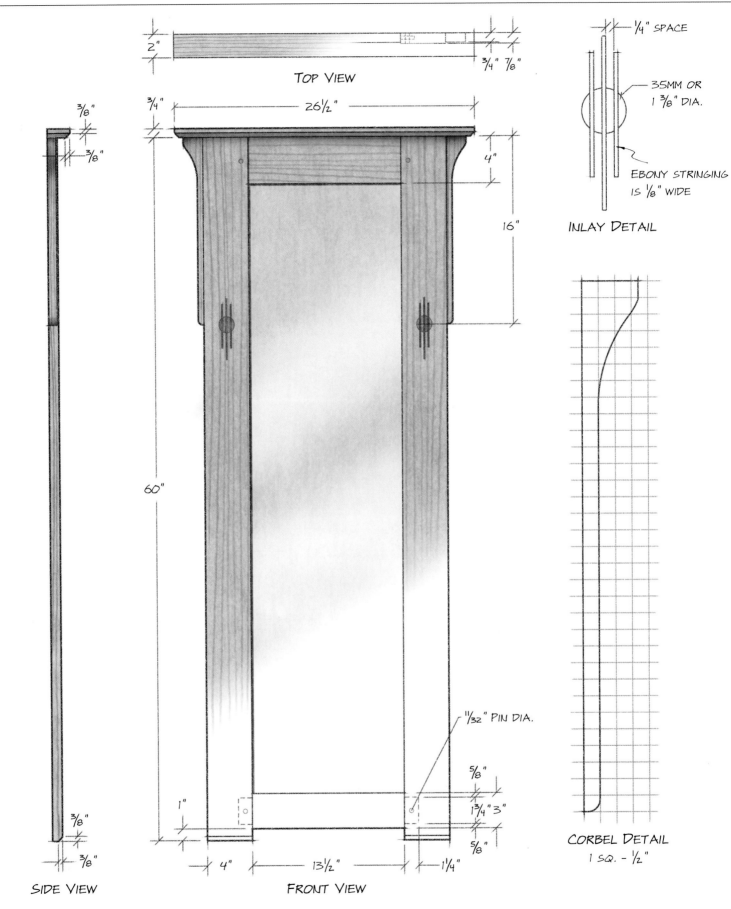

TOP VIEW

2"

3/4" 7/8"

3/8"

3/8"

3/4"

26 1/2"

4"

16"

60"

3/8"

3/8"

1"

11/32" PIN DIA.

5/8"

1 3/4" 3"

5/8"

4"

13 1/2"

1 1/4"

SIDE VIEW

FRONT VIEW

1/4" SPACE

35MM OR
1 3/8" DIA.

EBONY STRINGING
IS 1/8" WIDE

INLAY DETAIL

CORBEL DETAIL

1 SQ. - 1/2"

CRAFTSMAN MIRROR

Some Assembly Required

A few additional steps should be completed before gluing the frame's rails and stiles. The bottom end of each stile needs to have a $3/8$" x $3/8$" chamfer created, the interior edges of the frame need to be sanded and the sharp corners need to be knocked down with sandpaper.

I elected to cut the chamfer using the miter saw. It is simple and effective. You could also use a chamfer router bit. Adjust the saw to a 45° cut and remove the front $3/8$" of material. Make sure that you are cutting the front face of the stiles.

The different thicknesses of the pieces of the frame make it necessary to sand certain areas prior to assembly. The inside edge of each piece and the face of each rail need attention at this time. Also, because of the $1/8$" setback above the rails, the thicker stiles need to have their corners lightly sanded or knocked down at this time.

The pieces of the frame are now ready for assembly. It is especially important to not get glue onto the faces of the frame. Over-application of glue in the mortises or on the tenons will result in squeeze-out and considerable clean up. I apply glue into the mortises and move it around with an acid brush in order to coat all sides. Pull any excess out with the brush and paint it on the tenons.

Working with the rails is a bit more delicate. I add glue to the backside face cheeks of the tenons rather liberally because squeeze-out here is not a big issue. But, for the fronts, I add a very thin coating – just enough to smear a layer into the grain of the wood and not starve the joint.

Slip the joints together and slide the pieces up or down in order to align the top of the stiles with the top edge of the rail (remember the heavy cut on the tenon at the band saw allows positioning of this piece). The bottom rail needs to be placed according to the plan. Add clamps and allow the glue to dry.

When the assembly has cured it is time to add the pocket-screw holes that are used to attach the top to the frame. Follow the instructions for your particular jig to create the holes. Place one screw location in the center of each stile and then evenly space two additional holes along the top rail.

A New Tool for the Shop?

The mortise-and-tenon joints of the mirror are reinforced with $11/32$" x $11/32$" pegs. First drill an $11/32$" hole through the frame so that the hole is centered on each rail and is $5/8$" into the stile from where the two parts meet.

Again, why so precise with the size of the hole and the peg stock? This time it has to do with one of my favorite tools in the shop. I don't like to shave the corners off of my peg stock with a knife or chisel. I revert back to those early school days and the oversized, first-grade pencils. Remember the apparatus used to sharpen those bad boys? That style of pencil sharpener has for years created all the pegs I've used in my furniture. Dial in the largest hole on the sharpener, which happens to be $11/32$" in this case, and cut the tapered end on all your pegs.

Next, add a bit of glue to the peg, position it into the hole and tap the stock until the end of the peg is flush with the front of the frame. It is possible to be artistic with this process by choosing to use pegs of ebony to match the inlay, but I decided on a scrap of white oak.

To prepare the frame for the mirror and its backboard I elected to use a double rabbet cut: one rabbet for the glass and a second rabbet to house the plywood back. Creating this two-fisted cut on the back of the frame is a snap with an adjustable-bearing rabbet bit and router.

The first pass is set up to create a $1/4$"-deep cut that is $1/2$" wide. To prevent any tear-out of the wood I like to climb cut all around the frame to start, then follow up with a standard pass to clean the rabbet to size. Clamp the frame to the bench and work all the interior edges. Climb-cutting requires a firm grip on the tool, so be careful.

For the second rabbet, change the bearing to make a $1/4$"-wide cut with the rabbet bit and lower the cutter to take another $1/4$" of material. Hang the frame off the edge of the bench to complete this cut because the depth of cut causes the bearing's screw to extend beyond the thickness of the frame. It's important to keep the base plate of the tool flat to the frame.

Cap it Off

Creating the top is straightforward. Mill a wide piece of stock to thickness and cut it to the correct length. Do not rip it to final width, however, until after you have chamfered the piece.

To chamfer three edges – the two end-grain edges and one long edge – I turn to the router table with a chamfering bit. Set the bit so it is $3/8$" above the table. Always rout the end grain prior to cutting the long grain. This will minimize any chip out problems.

Cutting the bevel on the front edge of the bottom of each stile is best completed at the miter saw. Make sure that you are cutting the face of the stile and that the piece is set flat on the saw's table.

A backer piece of scrap material will keep the hole from blowing out of the frame back. Spring clamps will do the job. If you are feeling artsy, use different materials or turn the peg to a 45° angle in the hole so it appears diamond shaped.

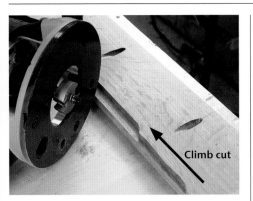

Start the rabbet by climb-cutting (cutting from right to left) will help to reduce tear-out from the router bit as you complete the cut in the standard left-to-right fashion. You should be able to make this cut with the project resting on the bench.

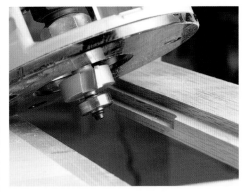

The second setup for the rabbeting is accomplished quickly after changing the bearing of the bit. Repeat the steps as before, making sure that the router's baseplate is resting on the work surface and that the tip of the bit is off of the bench.

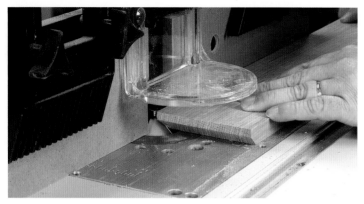

Moulding a wide piece that will then be cut to the final size needed for the top is much safer than working with narrow stock.

Cut the corbels from a larger piece of stock at the band saw. Cleaning the cut at a spindle sander makes short work of the task.

Once the edges are routed, rip the top from the wide stock at the table saw and sand the piece to #150 grit, making sure to sand the end grain.

To attach the top to the frame, position the top so it is centered on the frame and add a couple clamps to hold everything in place as you flip the mirror onto its front. Allow the top to extend past the edge of your bench and for the stiles to lay flat to the bench top. All that is left is to drive home the pocket-hole screws.

The corbels, present in a number of Arts & Crafts furniture designs, are the finishing touch. Transfer the pattern from the plan to your stock then cut the pieces at the band saw. A quick session at the spindle sander will have them ready in no time. Position the pieces against the frame for a quick check to ensure proper fit and make a light pencil mark at the bottom edge of each piece.

Now is the time to sand the edges of the stiles as well as the corbels and to knock off the sharp edges on each. Just as with the variations between the stiles and rails, the stepped thicknesses presented here mean that future sanding would be difficult at best.

Because the long grain of the corbels matches the long grain of the stiles, you can use glue to secure them in place. No additional fastening is required. Add a thin coating to both the corbel and the frame, right up to the pencil line, and then slide the pieces in place. No glue is needed on the end grain of the corbels. Clamps or small brads will work until the glue dries.

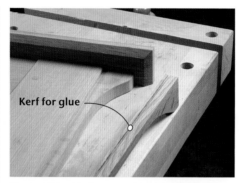

Kerf for glue

The last thing that you want to see is glue squeeze-out on the project. Before adding the glue for the corbels cut a kerf on the table saw to create a glue reservoir. Apply the glue to the wide area left after the cut.

Install the circle inlay in the correct orientation. Use a string inlay piece to fine-tune the setting. The grooves must be aligned.

Final-sand the mirror to #150 grit and fit painter's tape into the circle and string inlay areas to protect them from the finishing products. Keeping the oils off of the inlay is key to attaining a good glue bond when you are ready to install the pieces for the final time.

Now the mirror is ready for finish. Robert W. Lang, senior editor for *Woodworking Magazine* and author of "Shop Drawings for Greene & Greene Furniture" (Fox Chapel), has a finishing process that could not get any easier. He walks you through it on page 176.

Before adding a topcoat to the mirror, remove the painter's tape from the recesses and, if necessary, scrape away any stain or oil that crept into those areas and glue the inlay into the frame.

The maple disk will fit into the holes without a problem, but you want to make sure that the grooves line up and that the stringing will glide into place. Unless you achieved perfection in routing the grooves, the alignment will fit in only one direction. Find that fit and apply glue into the recessed hole and onto the back of the disk. Apply glue sparingly; you need only attach the disk into the frame. You do not want any squeeze-out.

The string is set into the grooves with a small amount of glue as well. I used the nose of the glue bottle in the groove to lightly spread the glue. Position the appropriate piece to the groove and tap in place with a mallet. If any glue escaped from the recess you need to clean it with a dry cloth. Depending on the tightness of your fit of the inlay, you may need to apply pressure to the pieces with a clamp. Once the glue has dried, apply a final topcoat of finish.

Finally, have a mirror cut to fit into the first step of the rabbeted frame and a piece of ¼"-thick plywood that will fit the second step. Slide the two in place and attach the back.

It is your choice on how to affix the plywood back to the frame. You can use small brads and a nail gun or, as I have elected, add a number of ⅝" screws spaced along the back's edge. It helps to add a bit of wax to the screws to drive them more easily without pre-drilling into the frame.

Now attach a heavy-duty mirror hanger (kits are available at any hardware store), find a well-suited wall for hanging, and this classic Arts & Crafts designed mirror will last forever and look exquisite.

— *Glen D. Huey*

Properly Pegged Joints

Pegging is an ancient furniture tradition – but does it result in a stronger joint? We investigate this method using a microscope powered by history and science.

If we are to discover the proper method for pegging joints, we make an assumption that, until now, may have never entered our thoughts. That assumption is that the joints actually should be pegged. Is this something that we need to do? It's been the practice throughout history, but why?

To choose to peg a joint is something with which I was not familiar. I always pegged the joints. Why? I was building reproduction furniture and the pieces that I copied were pegged. Bingo! Decision made.

When the time came to build furniture that was not a reproduction of anything in particular, I found myself pegging the joints anyway. I developed a penchant for pegging. I liked the way it looked. But was I doing it right? Is pegging a joint strengthening it or weakening it?

To answer those questions we need to first examine the history of woodworking for a moment. What types of materials were used in the past and what is being used today? How did the advancement of tools, including glue, change the way that we work wood? And are we properly fitting this joint? Only then can we decide if the joint should or should not be pegged and, if so, the proper method for doing so.

A Historical Perspective

In the mid-17th century, furniture was built to meet a need, not a want. Furniture was constructed using "green" lumber – lumber that was freshly cut from the tree lot and was not dried.

Because woodworkers used green wood they needed to compensate for movement as the wood dried over time. According to John Alexander, a long-time student of 17th-century woodworking techniques and author of "Make a Chair from a Tree: An Introduction to Working Green Wood" (Taunton), the stiles would become diamond shaped as they dried and would have a tendency to push the tenon out of the joint if it wasn't pegged. This is because wood dries twice as much in the direction of the growth rings (tangentially) as it does radially or across the growth rings, and drying wood exerts tremendous force.

The fact that glue could not stand up to that

Whether you use a round peg in a round hole or a square peg in a round hole, if the mortise-and-tenon joint is made correctly, the connection will stay coupled for years.

PHOTO BY AL PARRISH

force was only part of the problem. In addition, period glue was hide glue and its bonding strength is reversible when subjected to water, which the newly cut trees had in abundance. Therefore the hide glue would not work in this set of circumstances. Woodworkers of the 17th century had to peg the joints in order for the joint to stay together. They pegged out of necessity.

American Furniture Comes of Age

At the close of the 17th century, something changed. The adoption of the dovetail joint and the desire for wide boards to be used in the furniture of the period caused woodworkers to move away from riving their lumber from the logs – a process that produced only narrow boards.

To get those wide boards, one needed to saw the lumber and thus the pit saw was introduced. This process had a secondary effect on the lumber. The time lag from the cutting of the timber to delivery into the shop meant that the wood was arriving drier than in the past. Now the hide glue had a better ability to hold.

Did furniture builders of this period jump to using hide glue? Maybe, maybe not. There is no clear evidence to point either direction. But,

This high chest of drawers is representative of furniture from the mid-18th century. The advent of the dovetail, along with the use wide boards, changed how furniture was built. However, pegging was still used.

Hide glue has been found in the tombs of Pharaohs. These days, it's available as a liquid, or as crystals or pearls that need to be heated. PVA glues, such as yellow glue, have been used for more than 60 years.

The dedicated mortise machine, a relatively new tool for the woodshop, uses hollow chisels with an auger bit to remove waste material with relative ease, compared to hand-style mortising work of the past. The result is a straight, fairly smooth-sided mortise with squared ends. Machining the tenon ensures proper joint fit.

we know that they continued to peg joints for the next 200 plus years.

Today we have the ability to purchase our lumber so it is kiln dried to a 6 to 8 percent moisture content. Certainly this is dry enough to allow today's glues to hold our joints. Is glue the answer? Could these products now replace the need to add pegs to our furniture?

The Holding Power of Glue

Hide glue, the glue used for centuries, and polyvinyl acetate (PVA), developed in the mid-1940s (yellow woodworking glue is PVA), function much the same way – the water evaporates from the mixture and the glue solids are left to hold the connection. In fact, each type of glue is roughly half water and half solids at the outset. So, which is better to use?

According to Dale Zimmerman, a technical specialist with Franklin International, the makers of Titebond products, the glue with the higher solids would be a better choice. Titebond's hide glue is a 50 percent solids while the company's yellow glue is 45 percent solids. Thus, the hide glue should be the choice.

How about the holding power of these glues? Franklin tested shear strength (the amount of force needed to break the glue joint) of its glues using 1"-square blocks of hard maple with a long-grain to long-grain joint – the strongest type of glue joint for wood. The hide glue recorded a slightly higher figure than that of the yellow glue, which was 3,600 pounds per square inch (PSI).

Again, hide glue would be the choice.

The most interesting bit of information that Zimmerman stated was that the glue only adds strength to the joint, but it is the mechanical fit of the mortise-and-tenon joint that contributes the greater strength.

No amount of glue can compensate for a poorly fit joint. Any sloppy joints that are glued will result in a honeycomb effect in the glue where the solids pull to either surface of the joint and create air pockets at the middle of the glue. That weakens the overall bond and will result in joint failure. How the joint is fit is critical. A proper fit is the major factor in the longevity of the mortise-and-tenon joint.

If it Doesn't Fit, Don't Commit

There are a number of methods that can be used to properly fit a mortise-and-tenon joint. Bottom line: The fit should be snug without forcing the joint together.

If the mortise is not cut appropriately with straight sides and cut to a consistent depth, a matching, properly fit tenon cannot be made. In the past the woodworkers created this joint using hand tools. In order to get the fit that is required one would need to be somewhat skilled in using those hand tools, and that could take time to develop.

Today we have tools that make creating a mortise much easier than in the strictly hand-tool days. The router table and the dedicated mortise machine each make the cutting of this half of the

A properly fit mortise-and-tenon joint will slide together without the use of a mallet and will hold its position when released.

joint a snap for most any woodworker.

Creating the tenon in the past was also a matter of handwork. Handsaws and chisels did the necessary work with a generous amount of skill from the woodworker. Today we can use a stacked dado or a tenon jig at the table saw to accurately cut the tenon. We can produce both sections of this joint to the standard needed to ensure a proper, ideal fit.

That ideal fit is when you can push the tenon into the mortise with hand pressure and when lifted off of the bench, the joint stays together. That is the fit that we aim to accomplish. Just as using additional amounts of glue to try to reinforce an ill-fitting joint will not work, using a peg in a joint that is not properly fit will also not work. It may help to hold the joint together, but longevity will not follow. Eventually, the joint will fail and the amount of stress that would normally be placed on the joint as a whole will now be placed directly onto the peg – sometimes causing extreme damage on the mortised piece.

Making the Call

Once the joint is properly fit you can choose whether or not to use a peg. What is the proper technique?

The most important call is the placement of the peg. It should be placed within the heart of the tenon. Use a 1"- to 1¼"-tenon length at minimum and place the peg centered in the tenon from top to bottom and from side to side.

If it is placed too close to the end of the tenon, the chance of blowing out the end grain, even when housed in the mortise, is greater. This will weaken the joint. You would not see this defect until the joint is cut apart or it fails.

Conversely, if you place the peg too close to the shoulder of the tenon, or too near the edge of the mortise, the stress to the joint will cause the walls of the mortise to break and this would also cause joint failure.

The size of the peg should not be more than ⅜" for a mortise-and-tenon joint that is 1¼" in length (I use a ¼" peg for the majority of my work). Pegs bigger than ⅜" will weaken the connection by removing material that is too close to the edges of the joint.

The material that you select for the pegs is also a choice to consider. The practice most opted for is to use a wood that is equal to or harder than the lumber from which the project is constructed. This will allow you to match your project or to use a hardwood that will contrast with the piece for the added visual effect.

In addition, your pegs may be round, as in using a dowel, or square if you wish to create a more historical look. You've heard of the square peg in a round hole problem? It's not a problem. Whatever you decide, the hole can be round, and drilled the same size as the peg material.

Should the hole be drilled through the entire joint? If you are working a joint on a table, apron to leg, of course it is not necessary to push through the entire leg post, but on a door mortise and tenon I have not encountered an antique piece where the hole was not completely through the door thickness.

Once the hole is drilled it is up to you to leave the round hole, the result of the drill bit or, if you are using a square peg, you can use a chisel or other tool to match the hole to your peg. Traditionally, square pegs were driven into round holes so that the edges of the pegs would cut into the hole to add additional holding power.

To install the peg you will find it a huge help to start the peg, be it round or square, with a tapered

Blowout occurs when the peg is placed and driven to close to the end of the tenon. This will weaken the joint.

Driving the peg to close to the edge of the mortise or the intersection of the rail and stile can result in a split shoulder. This joint is scrap.

Drilled holes can accept either round or square pegs. As the square peg is driven into the hole the edges of the peg cut into the sides of the hole to increase the holding power. The squared hole is created after the drilling to help keep the edges of the peg crisp. This square hole was cut with a hollow chisel mortise bit.

It's your call on whether to use round or square pegs for the mortise-and-tenon joint, but whichever you choose, it is best to taper the leading end. I use a pencil sharpener for this task.

Add the glue to the peg and use your hammer or mallet to set the peg through the joint. Make sure that the peg extends past the back face of the joint. Trim where needed. If all the pieces are properly fit, you have just created a pegged joint that should last for years to come.

front end. This allows the peg to be driven into the hole with more ease.

Add glue to the tapered end and position the peg at the hole. Take the time to align the peg – square for a traditional look or as a diamond if you are looking to accent the piece. Neither alignment has a negative effect on the peg's strength.

A firm hit with your hammer will set the peg into the joint. Continue to drive the peg into the hole until the end is flush with the front face of your piece. All that is left is to trim the peg flush at the back face.

— *Glen D. Huey*

Authentic Arts & Crafts Finish

We discover a three-step process that looks great and is incredibly simple to apply.

Simplicity is a hallmark of Arts & Crafts furniture, but the proper finish has become a matter of mystery and complication. Gustav Stickley might be the cause of this. Writing in his magazine, *The Craftsman*, in the early 1900s he explained how to use ammonia to fume white oak, how to even out the color with dye dissolved in shellac, and how to top coat with shellac and dark wax. Then Gus throws a curve ball and states that in his factory they have greater facilities, so they use something different.

Stickley never details what methods he actually used. In the early years of production, his factory did use fuming and shellac, but as his furniture became more popular, these methods couldn't keep up with demand. And there is good evidence that circa 1906, Craftsman furniture began to be finished with aniline dye-based stains, and early versions of lacquer.

One of the common misconceptions about the original Craftsman finishes is the appearance of the flakes or rays of the quartersawn white oak. Today, people want to accentuate those rays to make them "pop." Most stains, followed by a clear finish, will give you that effect. An authentic finish, however, is more subtle; the flake of the grain is evident, but it doesn't smack you in the face.

The big advantage of fuming is that it changes the color chemically, resulting in an even color between the flakes and the rest of the grain. Exposing the wood to ammonia fumes, then top coating with amber shellac followed with a dark paste wax, will give you color and sheen that will closely match original Arts & Crafts pieces.

The disadvantage of fuming is that you're working with some dangerous chemicals. To get a good effect in a reasonable amount of time you need to work with 26 percent ammonia. The easiest place to find it is from a company that sells supplies for blueprinting. Janitorial ammonia, at about 10 percent solution, can be found in many hardware stores and will work, but

You don't need deadly gas or a complex process to get a good color – just products from a home center.

not as quickly. To make a fuming tent, I cobble together a frame from wood and cover it with plastic, securing the seams with spring clamps to make it airtight. I wear eye goggles, rubber gloves and an approved respirator while I pour the ammonia into a plastic container. When the fuming is completed in 24 to 48 hours, I put the protective gear back on, open a flap on the plastic and put the lid on the container. Then I vent the remaining fumes outside with a 20" box fan.

The next best finish I've found is alcohol-soluble aniline dye (W.D. Lockwood "Fumed Oak"), followed by shellac and wax. This produces nearly the same coloring and effect as fuming, but the risk is that the color will fade because dyes aren't entirely lightfast. In the Spring 2005 issue, we recommended General Finishes "Java" gel stain, a color that has since been discontinued. Some of our staff liked it, but I thought it a bit too dark and too red. I also don't like working with gel stains, so I went in search of a finish that would look right, resist fading and be easy to apply.

There are some recipes that involve several steps to get the color right and evenly applied. The general idea is to apply the color in stages to tone down the ray flakes. The results look good,

but the process is complicated. After several experiments I lighted on a simple method using products available from a home center. It uses a stain to get a good base color, a tinted Danish oil as a glaze, and amber shellac for warmth and a slight golden tone.

It's important not to sand the wood to too fine a grit. Sand to #120 grit with a random-orbit sander then hand sand with #150 grit. If you go finer, the oak becomes polished and the stain won't absorb well. After dusting the surface, apply Olympic Interior "Special Walnut" oil-based wood stain with a rag, saturating the surface. Let it sit for 15 minutes then wipe the surface dry. The next day, rag on one coat of Watco "Dark Walnut" Danish oil. Again, saturate the surface, let it sit for 15 minutes then wipe dry. The next day, rag on one coat of Zinsser's Bulls Eye amber shellac.

When the shellac has dried overnight, the surface is lightly rubbed with a nylon abrasive pad and given a coat of paste wax. The color is very close to the warm brown you see in antiques, and can be made darker by applying more coats of Danish oil or shellac. Achieving a good finish doesn't get much easier than this.

— *Robert W. Lang*

Circular Cutting Board

Bring your woodworking into the kitchen with this simple, circular project. It will make you look like a big wheel as you practice circles.

Solid maple makes an ideal surface for a cutting board, and feet in a wood of a contrasting color help it sit solidly, and make it easy to lift. A canola-oil finish contributes to an elegant look and is easy to maintain.

A well-equipped kitchen deserves to have a nice maple cutting board, especially if the kitchen is in a woodworking household. The cutting board may be an animal-shaped survivor from 8th grade shop class, or a more sophisticated design. For many woodworkers it is an introduction to working with shapes that aren't straight.

Maple has been used as a food preparation surface for hundreds of years and there are good reasons to follow tradition. While getting a perfectly smooth, tear-out free surface may be vexing, the finished product is both practical and attractive, despite unsuccessful attempts in recent years to label it as unsanitary.

This design began as a way to practice making circles. The three feet raise the cutting board above the counter, allowing it to be easily picked up and put down. The size and contrasting color of the feet add some visual interest, and if you have an adjustable trammel jig, like the one shown on page 139, it's easy to add them, bringing a simple project to a slightly higher level.

The cutting board shown here is about 18" in diameter. The basic design can be scaled down if you prefer. To obtain a piece wide enough, I glued together two pieces a little larger than 9"-wide. A simple butt joint is more than strong enough in this application. I selected the pieces, and when I had them arranged the way I wanted them, I marked the faces with a carpenter's triangle.

If you plan on surfacing the finished board with a handplane, arrange the boards so that the grain on the edges runs the same way. Maple is notorious for tearing out, and if one piece runs downhill while the other runs uphill, you may find it impossible to get a good surface after gluing.

I ran the edges to be glued over the jointer just before assembly, with the face of one board against the fence and the face of the other away from the fence. This cancels out any minute deviation of the jointer's fence from square. Even if the angles are slightly off from 90°, they will be complementary, ensuring a flat surface.

Straight matching edges and a level surface to lay the pieces on when gluing are important when gluing solid wood edge-to-edge. I ripped a few strips of scrap to a consistent width and placed them across my bench to support the pieces. After lining the triangle sides back up, I rotated one board up on edge and applied a bead of glue to one edge only.

Because this will be used in the kitchen and washed frequently, I used a waterproof poly-

> "... when you make something that says 'sleep,' by God you've made a bed."
> — Art Espenet Carpenter (1920 - 2006)
> cabinetmaker

urethane glue (Gorilla Glue). This glue tends to foam after assembly, so after laying on a bead from the glue bottle, I spread the bead with a palette knife to cover the edge with a thin, consistent film. I wiped the other, unglued edge with a damp rag because this glue cures only in the presence of moisture.

There are some other glues that also could be used; the key element is water resistance combined with some flexibility in the cured glue line. A waterproof PVA (such as Titebond III) would likely work as well as polyurethane. I have had epoxies fail after three or four years in cutting boards. I think this is due to the epoxy drying to a hard, brittle line. Wooden cutting boards are the objects of some inevitable abuse; soaked and dried repeatably as they are used, cleaned then put away.

Clamping Considerations

Despite the tendency of some of us to use as many clamps as is possible to fit for an "optimal" glue joint, practical experience demonstrates that two or three clamps across the joint will produce a good joint. The goal is a glue line that is barely visible, and this can be achieved with firm even pressure. I scraped off any wet glue that squeezed out to observe the glue line. This also allows the glue to cure in less time and with a better bond than letting it dry on the surface.

After letting the glue cure for 24 hours, I cut the circle on the band saw and trimmed it with the router and trammel jig as described on page 139. The particular piece of maple I used tore out a few times when trimming the edge. I think it would have preferred to serve humanity by staying in the woods and being tapped for syrup rather than being cut into lumber. For this project, it didn't make a difference that the circle was a fraction smaller than originally planned.

Best Foot Forward

After I had a good clean edge on the entire maple circle, I reset the trammel jig so that the outside edge of the cutter was lined up with the outer edge of the maple. This set the distance for the rabbets in the top of the feet. I screwed a scrap of the same material used for the feet (walnut) to my bench to serve as a center point.

I drew the outline of the board on the bench so that I could screw down the blanks for the feet securely, while avoiding the path of the router bit. I set the depth of cut to ¼" and routed an arc in the blank. I used a compass to scribe the inner and outer profiles of the foot on the top surface. At the band saw, I cut to the pencil lines, and cleaned up the saw marks.

I came close to a perfect surface with my smoothing plane and card scraper, but there were a couple torn spots that resisted my efforts. Following the dictum of, "If at first you don't succeed, try something else," I resorted to a random-orbit sander, and Abranet abrasives. Abranet is a new product from Mirka, with a mesh instead of a paper backing. It works very well, and stepping through the grits of #150, #240 and #320 left a very nice surface.

I use a 30°-60° drafting triangle to lay out the locations of the feet, one on the center line and the other two 120° apart. I again used Gorilla glue to attach the feet to the board, with a pair of small spring clamps to hold them in place. I left the clamps on overnight, and after rounding all the corners slightly with a piece of Abranet, the cutting board was ready for finishing.

For the finish, I saturated the wood with canola oil from the grocery store, let it sit for about 15 minutes then wiped it dry. Two coats a day apart are the initial finish, and I'll apply another coat of oil every month or so as the board is used. When it starts to look a bit dry, it's time to refresh the finish. To keep the board from warping, I will make sure to wash both flat surfaces with soap and water every time I use the board.

— *Robert W. Lang*

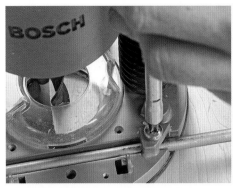

After the maple circle is trimmed, the bit is adjusted so that it is flush with the outer edge of the large circle.

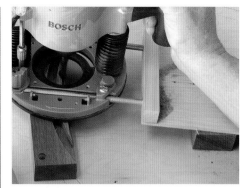

This setting is used to rout a ¼"-deep rabbet in the blanks for the feet.

A compass is used to scribe an offset line from the edge of the rabbet. The feet are then band sawn to shape.

Cooking oil makes a good finish for a cutting board. It's cheap, easy to apply and can be renewed on a regular basis.

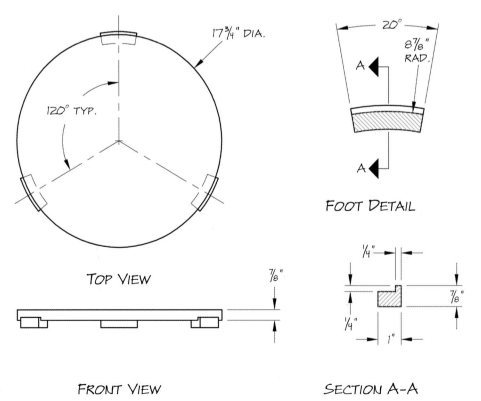

17¾" DIA.

120° TYP.

TOP VIEW

FRONT VIEW

20°

8⅞" RAD.

A

A

FOOT DETAIL

¼"

¼"

⅞"

⅞"

1"

SECTION A-A

ILLUSTRATION BY LOUIS BOIS

Tool Tote

A good bevel gauge makes the angles in this simple piece easy to make (and perfect dovetails be darned – sloppy will hold just fine).

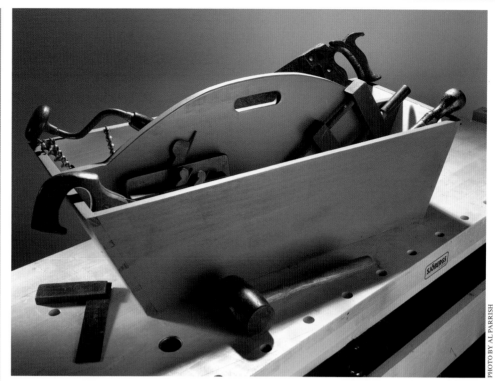

Don't let the angled ends put you off – this simple tool tote is a great beginner project. Even if your dovetails don't look perfect, they'll still impart the strength necessary to hold up under a heavy load.

Before the advent of plastic tool boxes, carpenters, joiners and the like would carry their tools from job to job in a wooden tote. (In fact, we have a family picture of my great grandfather carrying a similar tote, and he was a plumber). For this tote, we took the 24" interior bottom length (just long enough to hold a framing square) from an early 19th-century Canterbury, N.Y., Shaker example that sold for $400 at a recent Willis Henry auction. I decided on $12\frac{1}{2}$" x $6\frac{1}{2}$" for the interior width and height. The ends are about 22° off vertical.

This piece presents an excellent opportunity to practice your dovetails without having to worry about cutting them perfectly. Even if your pins and tails look like an illustration from an 18th-century dentistry tome, they'll still hold. And after all, this is a working piece, which means it's going to quickly get munged when you toss tools into it and lug it around the house or to a job site. (And paint is an excellent way to cover small gaps and wonky cuts.)

But first things first. I chose to use poplar not only because it's affordable and readily available, but because it's relatively lightweight. Once this sucker gets loaded down with hunks of metal, it's fairly heavy, so it's best to avoid adding to the tare weight, which can tear up your back.

Mill all your stock except the handle to $\frac{5}{8}$", then joint the edges. The sides are $7\frac{3}{4}$" wide x $30\frac{1}{4}$" long, and the ends begin at $8\frac{1}{2}$" wide x $13\frac{1}{4}$" long (however, the angle dictates the width, so rough-cut and tweak your final width later after the pieces are dry fit). Initially, I had milled the handle to $\frac{1}{2}$" to gain a smidge more interior room, but concluded afterward that $\frac{1}{2}$" cut into my palm too much. So, I milled another piece to $\frac{3}{4}$" and rough-cut it to 11" x 30".

Glue up a 14" x 25" panel for the bottom (a bit larger than finished size in width and length so you'll have enough extra stock to angle the ends and to fit it) then set it aside to dry.

Now, lay one of your side pieces flat on your workbench, and grab your sliding bevel gauge. Set it to an angle that pleases your eye and lock the blade in place. You're going to leave your bevel gauge at that setting until you're done with construction. Mark that angle on one end of a side piece.

Because you're going to gang cut the sides on the miter saw, you need only mark the angle on one end of one piece. Line up your two side pieces at the top and bottom, then secure them together by sinking a 1" nail into the waste portions at both ends.

With the saw off, pull the blade down on your work and adjust the cut angle by eye. When you're close, press the handle of your bevel gauge against the miter saw fence, and tweak the saw blade angle until the gauge's blade is flat against the saw blade along its entire length. Lock in the angle. (As with your bevel gauge, once you lock the angle on the miter saw, leave it set until the project is complete.)

Now align the angled mark on the side piece with the blade and make the cut. Flip the pieces over carefully (you've cut away one of the nails securing them together), measure $24\frac{3}{8}$" along the bottom edge, and make the second cut.

It's time to cut the angles on the top and bottom of the end pieces – maybe. You may prefer to cut your dovetails now using your preferred method, and plane the top and bottom edges to the correct angle once the box is assembled. These are not compound joints, but regular old dovetails, so if you haven't cut too many dovetails, it might be easier to leave the edges square while you do so – just be sure to leave enough overhang at the top and bottom so that you can plane the angles flush with the sides when you're done.

Or, you can set up your table saw for an angled cut (again using your bevel gauge to set the blade), and cut the proper angle at the bottom of each side, then line up the bottom edges of the side and

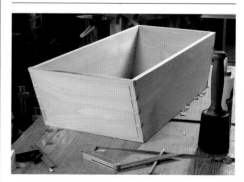

As you can see, all my tails are a bit proud, and the fit at the baseline is gappier than I'd like. But they'll do for a workaday project like this one.

ends before marking out and cutting the joints. I chose this option because I'm not a virtuoso with the plane; the table saw blade was far more likely to result in a matching profile to the sides, ensuring the tote would sit flat on a surface.

After I cut and dry-fit my dovetail joints, I pulled them apart, added yellow glue, then reassembled them. Check the bottom edges of the box for square (theoretically both the top and bottom edges should be square, but because you have to fit the tote bottom, if it's a choice between the two, go with the bottom).

Once the glue is dry, use a block plane to bring the top edges of the end pieces flush with the side pieces (and if you didn't cut the bottom angle before dovetailing, flush the bottom edges now as well).

Now align, glue and nail $\frac{1}{2}$" x $\frac{1}{2}$" cleats to the bottom edge of the side pieces. For added strength, you could also add angled cleats to the end pieces, then plane them to flush the angle with the ends. But that's fairly involved.

Measure $\frac{5}{8}$" up from the cleats, and calculate your measurements for the size of the bottom panel from that point. Cut the ends to the proper

angle at the table saw, or plane them to fit. The bottom panel should drop in and sit flat on the cleats. There's no need to secure it; the handle will keep it in place.

Now it's back to the miter saw to cut the angles on each end of the handle. As you did with the side pieces, simply mark one angle with the bevel gauge, make the cut, flip the board end for end then measure 24" at the bottom's length and make the second cut. (It's a good idea to confirm your length by measuring at the bottom of the tote, or make your initial cut a little long, and sneak up on the final dimension.)

What I found trickiest about this project was shaping the handle – or actually, deciding on what shape and handhold size looked and felt best. As I mentioned, I first milled wood to $\frac{1}{2}$" thick for the handle, and after cutting out the handhold, found that was too narrow a width to be comfortable. So I went with $\frac{3}{4}$" instead. To lay out the curve at the top, I first measured in 3" from where the handle ends would meet the box at the top edge, and sunk a nail just outside the line on the waste side on either end.

I then found the centerpoint at the top edge, grabbed a thin offcut from the trash can, and used the nails to hold it in place while I pushed up at the center to find the curve. Then I marked it with a pencil (see picture at right).

I cut to my line at the band saw, then measured $1\frac{1}{4}$" down from top center, and $1\frac{1}{4}$" to the right and left from that point. I chucked a $\frac{7}{8}$" Forstner bit in the drill press, lined up the center of the bit with my two outside marks, and drilled holes (you may wish to make a larger handhold, depending on your hand size). I cut away the rest of the handhold with a jigsaw, curving the top edge slightly to match the handle profile, and to provide a more comfortable grip.

With a rasp, I rounded over all the edges in the handhold, then used #120-grit sandpaper to break all the edges and clean up the rasp marks.

I decided to paint my tote a smoky gray-blue … my default color. But, to make it a little more interesting (and to avoid constantly chipping the paint with the movement of tools), I masked off the inside top edges with tape, and painted only the outside surfaces of the box (filling in my dovetail gaps in the process) and the handle.

After the paint dried, I marked the centerpoint on each end piece, dropped the handle in place, drilled three pilot holes through each end into the handle, and secured the handle in place with $1\frac{1}{4}$" cut nails.

— *Megan Fitzpatrick*

Two nails and a thin piece of offcut make a fine (and cheap) arc marker.

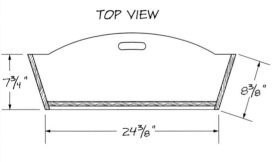

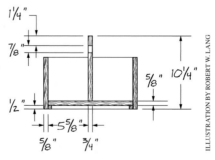

TOP VIEW

30$\frac{1}{4}$"

13$\frac{1}{4}$"

FRONT VIEW SECTION

7$\frac{3}{4}$"

8$\frac{3}{8}$"

24$\frac{3}{8}$"

SIDE VIEW SECTION

1$\frac{1}{4}$"

$\frac{7}{8}$"

10$\frac{1}{4}$"

$\frac{5}{8}$"

$\frac{1}{2}$"

5$\frac{5}{8}$"

$\frac{5}{8}$"

$\frac{3}{4}$"

ILLUSTRATION BY ROBERT W. LANG

Use a drill press to cut the outside ends of your handhold, and a jigsaw to remove the remaining waste. You'll do the final shaping with a rasp and sandpaper.

Tool Tote

	NO.	PART	SIZES (INCHES)			MATERIAL	NOTES
			T	W	L		
❏	2	Sides	$\frac{5}{8}$	7$\frac{3}{4}$	30$\frac{1}{4}$	Poplar	Dimension w/out angles
❏	2	Ends	$\frac{5}{8}$	8$\frac{1}{2}$	13$\frac{1}{4}$	Poplar	Dimension w/out angles
❏	1	Bottom	$\frac{5}{8}$	12	24	Poplar	Dimension w/out angles
❏	1	Handle	$\frac{3}{4}$	10$\frac{3}{4}$	29$\frac{1}{8}$	Poplar	Dimension w/out angles
❏	2	Cleats	$\frac{1}{2}$	$\frac{1}{2}$	23	Scrap	

Dining Room Tray

Not sure you can drive a nail? This project is a great confidence builder for the beginning basher.

Like the Enfield Shaker Cabinet, this project is adapted from Ejner Handberg's "Shop Drawings for Shaker Furniture & Woodenware Vol. 1" (Berkshire House). And like the Enfield Cabinet, we are left to connect some of the dots as to how it was assembled. I connected the dots with nails.

After building a few of these trays, here's the easiest way to make them with minimum fuss. Cut the sides and ends to size; plane them or sand them so they're ready for finishing. With glue and two bar clamps, glue the ends between the sides using yellow glue. Give the glue an hour to cure, then get set to reinforce each corner with $1\frac{1}{2}$"-long (4d) cut headless brads.

First, lightly scribe a line across the end of each side piece that's $\frac{1}{4}$" from the end. This is the line for your nails. Now drill a deep $\frac{1}{16}$" pilot hole that's $\frac{3}{8}$" in from each long edge. Drive a cut headless brad into each pilot hole. Angle the nails a bit to wedge the side piece against the ends. Countersink the nails below the surface of the wood with a nail set and a couple hammer raps.

Cut the handle to length to fit between the ends. You want this joint to be tight so I'd cut it close with your table saw and trim the end grain a bit to fit using a low-angle block plane. Lay out the curves and handle hole on the workpiece. Cut the curves on the handle using a band saw or bow saw. Clean up the saw marks first with a fine half-round rasp and then a file (or a spokeshave). If you have a spindle sander, that also will do the

Solid maple makes an ideal surface for a cutting board, and feet in a wood of a contrasting color help it sit solidly, and make it easy to lift. A canola-oil finish contributes to an elegant look and is easy to maintain.

PHOTO BY AL PARRISH

job. Then spokeshave a $\frac{1}{16}$" x $\frac{1}{16}$" chamfer on the long edges of the handle.

Bore out as much of the waste in the handle hole as you can with an auger bit or Forstner bit. (Tip: The curved ends of the hole are formed by a $\frac{3}{4}$"-diameter bit). After trying a couple different methods, I found the fastest way to remove most of the remaining waste was by light chopping with a chisel. Then a few strokes with a half-round rasp made the hole ready for sandpaper.

Glue and nail the handle centered between the ends. Two headless brads in each end of the handle will do the trick. Flush up all the bottom edges of the tray and get ready to install the bottom. Handberg's drawing shows the bottom as one piece that's glued or nailed to the sides and handle. I am not that brave when it comes to facing the possibility of future wood movement.

Make the bottom from three pieces that are either shiplapped (like in the back for the Enfield Cabinet) or use a tongue-and-groove joint. Make your bottom pieces just a bit too long ($\frac{1}{16}$" will do) and a bit too wide (even less than $\frac{1}{16}$"). This

will allow you to trim the bottom to a perfect finished size. To join the bottom boards, cut a $\frac{3}{16}$" x $\frac{3}{16}$" groove on the edges then cut a matching tongue on the mate. Prepare all the bottom pieces for finishing.

To attach the bottom, run a small bead of glue down the bottom edge of the handle and then center the middle bottom piece on it. Nail it to the handle – five brads down the handle will do. Ensure the other two bottom pieces will fit tight against the ends and the side pieces.

Run a bead of glue down the edge of the side pieces only and insert the bottom pieces. Position each so there's a $\frac{1}{16}$" gap between it and its neighbor. Nail each bottom piece to the sides only. Trim the bottom pieces flush with the outside of the tray. Break all the sharp edges with sandpaper.

This is a good project to also practice your finishing strategies for cherry. We ragged on a coat of linseed oil, let the project sit outside for an afternoon, then finished it up with some spray lacquer from an aerosol can a week later.

— Christopher Schwarz

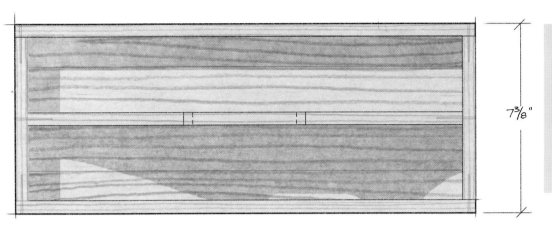

TOP VIEW

7³⁄₈"

Supplies

Tremont Nail Co.
800-842-0560 or tremont-nail.com

■ 4d (1½") cut headless brads, one-pound box, #CFB-4-1, $57.85

Price correct at publication deadline.

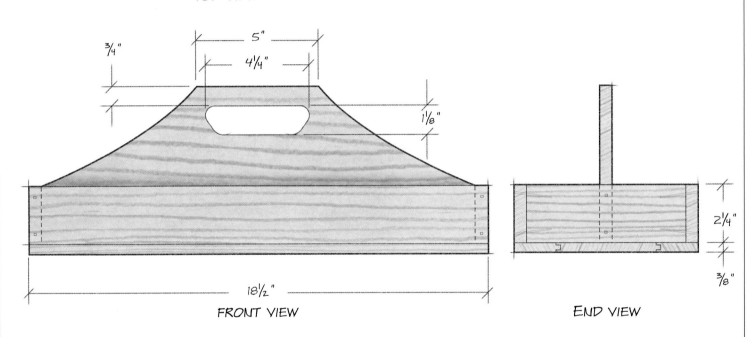

FRONT VIEW

5"

4¼"

¾"

1⅛"

18½"

END VIEW

2¼"

³⁄₈"

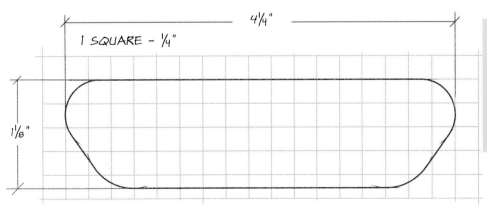

FULL-SIZE HANDLE PATTERN

4¼"

1 SQUARE – ¼"

1⅛"

Dining Room Tray

NO.	PART	SIZES (INCHES)			MATERIAL
		T	W	L	
❑ 2	Sides	½	2¼	18½	Cherry
❑ 2	Ends	½	2¼	6³⁄₈	Cherry
❑ 1	Handle	½	6⅛	17½	Cherry
❑ 1	Bottom	³⁄₈	7³⁄₈	18½	Cherry

DINING ROOM TRAY

Tile Trivet

Practice makes perfect sense; this small tabletop project will give you something practical to show for your effort as you build your skills.

A reproduction tile is the perfect complement for quartersawn white oak in this small accent piece.

PHOTO BY AL PARRISH

If I've been out of the shop for a while, I like to get some practice before tackling a large project. It gets my skills back in shape, and if I'm a little rusty my mistakes only generate a small amount of firewood. I'll make a few joints to be sure that my skills and tools are ready for the real thing.

Most people with hobbies do this. Golfers hit buckets of balls, softball players head to the batting cages and marathon runners jog through the neighborhood. But for some reason, many woodworkers are reluctant to practice without having something to show for it.

This trivet makes a great warm-up for any project that requires mortise-and-tenon joints, and if you're not sure which method you're most comfortable using, you can try a different technique at each corner. If things go wrong, you'll have material for kindling, not a bonfire; and if they go well, you'll have a nice accessory for your kitchen counter or dining room table.

We chose an attractive reproduction Arts & Crafts-style tile from Ford Craftsman Studios (www.fordcraftsman.com or 877-204-9961), but any 6" x 6" tile will work well. Purchase the tile before making its frame because tiles can vary in size from the stated dimension, and the sizes of all the wood parts depend on the size of the tile.

The tile sits in a $\frac{1}{2}$"-wide rabbet cut on the inside edge of the completed frame, so the length of the rail from shoulder to shoulder should be $\frac{15}{16}$" less than the width of the tile. When the frame is together, cutting the two $\frac{1}{2}$" rabbets will leave room for the tile to drop in place with a little room around the edge. The tenons are 1" long, so the overall length of these pieces will be 2" more than the shoulder-to-shoulder distance.

The length of the stiles is the shoulder-to-shoulder distance of the rails plus two times the width of the material. We used $2\frac{1}{4}$"-wide material and our tile was 6" square. Our rails are $7\frac{1}{16}$" long, and the stiles are $9\frac{9}{16}$" long. After figuring the lengths, lay out the location of the tenons and hold the parts against each other to make sure the assembled frame will be the same length on all four sides.

The tenons are $\frac{1}{4}$" thick and 1" wide, and are offset toward the outside of the frame to avoid interfering with the rabbet. After double-checking the layout, cut the joints and assemble the frame. Measure the exact thickness of the tile. It should be about $\frac{1}{4}$", and the depth of your rabbet should leave about $\frac{1}{16}$" of the tile proud of the surface of the wood.

If the trivet frame were mitered, it would be easier to make the rabbets before assembly, but with mortise-and-tenon joinery, the rabbets on the long stiles need to stop before they reach the end. I cut the rabbets with a router after assembly with a $\frac{1}{2}$"-wide rabbet bit, guided by a bearing below the cutter. This leaves the inside corners rounded, but these can be easily squared off with a sharp chisel.

To do this, set the back of the chisel against the vertical edge of the rabbet, and rock the end of the chisel toward the corner. This will make a scoring cut that will maintain a straight line into the corner from each direction. When the scoring cuts meet at the corner, place the sharp edge of the chisel in the cut and remove the end-grain material first. Then chop the long grain, and pare the bottom smooth, using the surface of the rabbet made by the router as a guide for the back of the chisel.

The square foot blocks on each corner give the trivet some character, and make it easy to place

your hand under the edge to pick it up. A cove cut in the bottom edge improves the appearance of the feet. I made the cove cuts on the router table, routing one edge and both ends of a piece about 12" long (see photo below). Using the long piece lets me safely make the cuts using a square piece of scrap to back up the work piece. I wouldn't attempt to rout the edges of parts as small as the feet at their finished size.

After the edges are done, cut the feet to size and glue them to the bottom of the stiles. Make sure the grain on the feet is oriented in the same direction as the grain in the stile. After the glue is dry, sand the top faces and edges; lightly chamfer the edges and finish. I used the finish formula described on page 176, followed by two coats of water-based polyurethane for extra protection.

— *Robert W. Lang*

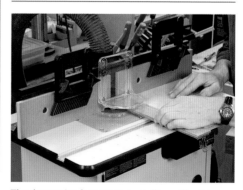

The decorative feet are too small to mill safely when cut to their finished size. Rout the profile in a piece about 1' long, using a square piece of scrap as a push block to move the narrow end of the stock across the router bit.

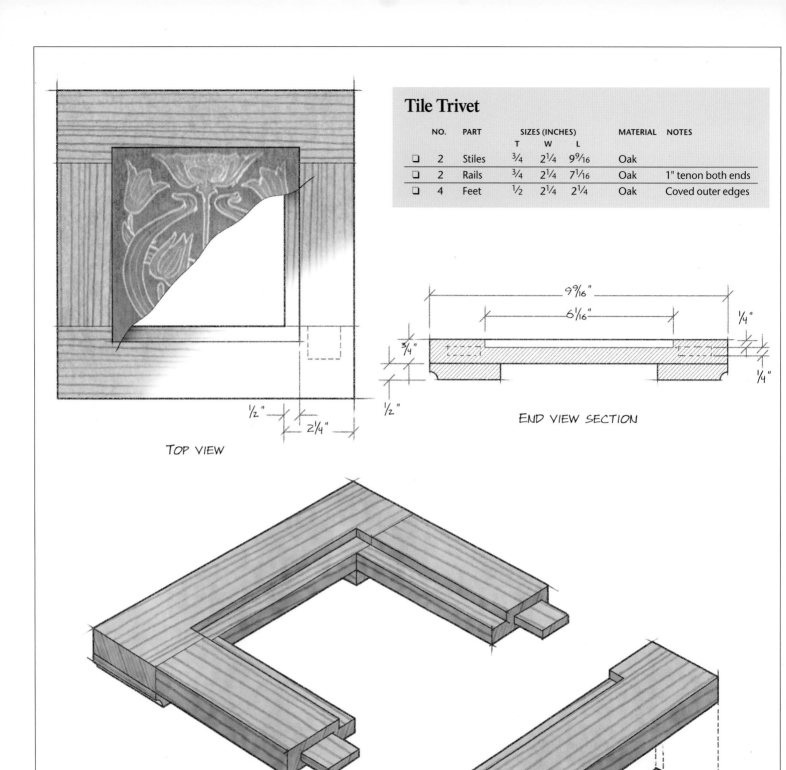

Tile Trivet

NO.	PART	SIZES (INCHES)			MATERIAL	NOTES
		T	W	L		
☐ 2	Stiles	¾	2¼	9⁹⁄₁₆	Oak	
☐ 2	Rails	¾	2¼	7¹⁄₁₆	Oak	1" tenon both ends
☐ 4	Feet	½	2¼	2¼	Oak	Coved outer edges

TOP VIEW

END VIEW SECTION

EXPLODED VIEW

TILE TRIVET

Hanging Shelves

This simple project with authentic details provides practice with little risk, and a handsome and useful display.

Hanging shelves are one of the most adaptable projects in woodworking. A small shelf can fill a need in the kitchen or bath, while a larger one can hold books in the den, or a collection of tools in the shop. The method of making them provides an opportunity to develop skills and use leftover material. It's all a matter of scale.

The illustration on the next page shows some variations in size and shape, and the techniques for making the shelves (and attaching them to the wall) are a good way to practice your joinery. If the project turns out well, put it in the living room. If the end result contains flaws, find a dark corner in the guest bathroom or a dusty place in the shop.

Size the components based on the overall size and the intended purpose. I wanted a small set of shelves for spices in the kitchen or small cosmetic items in the bath. These shelves are 4" deep and the overall height is 20". While sketching, I settled on an overall width of 13¾". I milled the ash boards I had to a thickness of ⅝" to maintain an overall sense of proportion.

I milled all of the stock to 4" wide and cut the parts to the lengths given in the list. All of the shelves finish ⅛" narrower than the sides, but I waited until after making the through mortise-and-tenon joints to reduce them in width. This left a little leeway for fitting the joints.

With both side pieces next to each other on the bench, I oriented them with their most attractive surfaces facing out, and I laid out the locations for the through-mortises. I used a wheel marking gauge to incise the edges of the mortise locations. This gives a more precise location than a pencil line, and when it comes time to clean up the edges

A simple set of hanging shelves is enhanced with decorative joinery, hidden shelf supports and a hanging method that shows no fasteners.

of the mortises, it's easy to see where to stop.

Method to Make Square Holes

I decided to forego using a hollow-chisel mortiser or a router with a jig to make the through-mortises. The small size and location across the width complicated the setup for either of these options. Instead, I removed most of the waste with a ⁵⁄₁₆"-diameter Forstner bit in the drill press. I set a fence on the drill press table to center the bit in the mortise at the top of the sides vertically,

---

"In theory, there is no difference between theory and practice. In practice there is."

— Yogi Berra (1925 -)
former Major League Baseball player and manager

---

and drilled a series of overlapping holes.

After resetting the fence, I drilled another series of holes to locate the bottom mortises. Making the mortises this way involves some risk of tearing out the wood on the back of the joint. This can be minimized by knifing in the layout lines on both sides of the joint, and using a piece of scrap wood below the work when drilling and paring.

Using a ¾"-wide chisel, I pared away the scallops that remained where the holes overlapped. As the scallops disappear, and the paring cuts get closer to the edge of the mortise, it takes more effort to make these cuts. I positioned my shoulder directly over the chisel so I had extra leverage as I pushed down. It's also easy to sight along the back of the chisel to be sure it is vertical from this position.

After working the wide top and bottom edges, I used a ¼"-wide chisel to pare the ends of the

Hanging Shelves

NO.	PART	SIZES (INCHES)			MATERIAL
		T	W	L	
❑ 2	Sides	⁵⁄₈	4	20	Ash
❑ 2	Fixed shelves	⁵⁄₈	3⁷⁄₈	13³⁄₄	Ash
❑ 2	Adjustable shelves	⁵⁄₈	3⁷⁄₈	12¹⁄₄	Ash
❑ 1	Cleat	⁵⁄₁₆	1¹⁄₄	12¹⁄₄	Ash
❑ 2	Cleat	⁵⁄₁₆	⁵⁄₈	12¹⁄₄	Ash*

* 45° bevel on edge, one piece attaches to wall, the other to the top shelf

Simple hanging shelves can be made in a number of sizes and shapes. You can hone your skills and fill a need at the same time.

mortises down to the lines. A cut in this direction is trickier to control, even though the effort to make the cut is easier. These cuts go with the grain, so taking too big a bite can cause the wood to split along the grain.

I stopped paring when the cuts got close to the layout lines and switched from a chisel to a rasp for the wide parts of the joint, and a small flat file for working the ends. This gave me more control and a better surface for the last few cuts that define the mortise.

With one hand above and the other hand below the work, hold the rasp vertically and watch the flat side of the rasp and the layout line as cuts are made on the down stroke. Use the same technique with the file to create a crisp line and corner on the end of the mortise. Use a small adjustable square frequently to check the joint.

In addition to the lines on the finished face being straight and square to each other, I also checked that the walls of the mortise were square to the face of the board. If there is some variation,

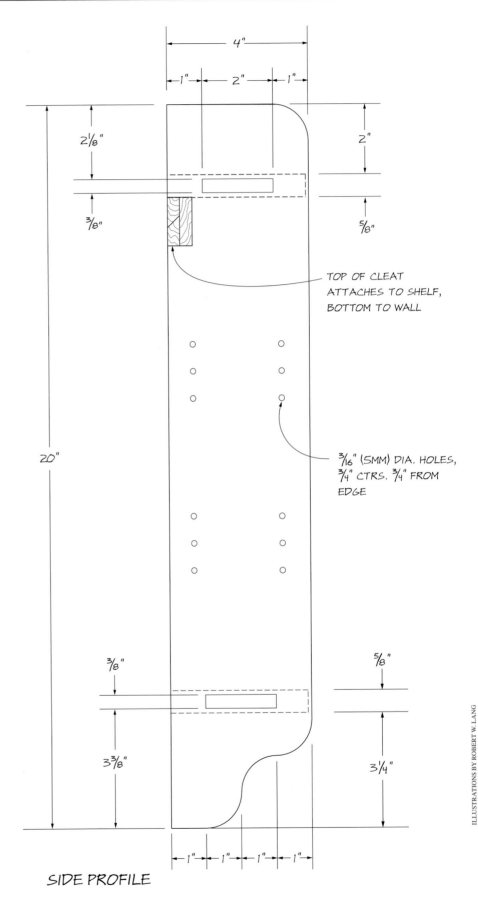

TOP OF CLEAT ATTACHES TO SHELF, BOTTOM TO WALL

³⁄₁₆" (5MM) DIA. HOLES, ³⁄₄" CTRS. ³⁄₄" FROM EDGE

SIDE PROFILE

HANGING SHELVES

After paring close to the layout lines, a hand-cut rasp is used to remove the last bit of material, leaving a straight and crisp line.

A small flat file is ideal for perfecting the ends of through-mortises.

it should be held to the inside face of the board. The joint will still function if the mortise isn't perfect, but to look good it must be a tight fit on the show side.

Tenons to Fit

On a good day, all the mortises will be the same size. I used a pair of fractional dial calipers to check before cutting the tenons. Just as there are many ways to make the mortises, there are a number of methods to make the tenons. I set up a 1"-diameter straight bit in the router table, with the edge of the bit $^{13}/_{16}$" from the edge of the fence. I set the height of the bit lower than I needed to keep from overcutting the tenon cheeks.

Using a square scrap of wood as a push block, I ran the end of a shelf along the fence and over the bit. I then flipped the board over to cut the other side. Using the calipers, I measured the resulting tenon to compare it to the mortise size. This method of trial and error ensures that the errors land in scrap wood and don't result in a skinny tenon. I made slight adjustments to the bit height to make the tenons a few thousandths of an inch bigger than the mortises.

I fit the tenons for height first, placing a corner into the mortise and removing small amounts of material with the rasp held flat across the tenon cheek. When I could force each corner into the mortise, I placed the shelf vertically on the side, lined up the edges of the shelf and side, and marked the ends of the tenon directly from the mortise.

I used a dovetail saw to remove the excess material from the tenon, cutting close to, but just outside the pencil line. Again, this keeps any error manageable without ruining the part. After sawing, I used a chisel, then a rasp, to work the tenon down to the finished size. Before giving the tenon a test fit in the mortise, I put a small chamfer on the ends of the tenon with a rasp. I also put a very light chamfer

around the inside edge of the mortise. These chamfers help get the joint assembly started, and they keep damage to a minimum as the tenon comes through the show side of the mortise.

In theory, the joint should come together with hand pressure. I aim for that, but it almost always takes a few tries to get the fit just right. I push until the tenon gets stuck, then take the joint apart by tapping on the inside of the mortised piece with a dead-blow hammer. Tight spots will show as shiny areas where the two pieces rubbed each other. If you have trouble seeing them, rub the tenon with a soft pencil and push it into the mortise as far as you can. When you take the joint back apart, you can see where the graphite has rubbed off.

If the wood is hard, you can get away with lightly tapping around the mortise to get the joint

together. The wood will make a different tone in tight areas than it will in loose ones. It takes some experience to know where to hit and how hard to hit. The risk is splitting the wood, and it doesn't really work to beat on it until something breaks, then beat it a little less.

I make most of the adjustments to the tenon, unless I discover a high spot within the mortise. This is a process of testing the fit, taking the joint apart, making a few strokes with the rasp then testing the fit again. I switch to a card scraper at the very end, aiming for a finished surface on the exposed part of the tenon as the final fit is reached.

Turning the Corner

When the joint finally goes together, I find something – either a metal straightedge or a scrap of

Holding the rasp at a 45° angle quickly brings the chamfered ends down to the layout line.

wood that is as thick as half the exposed portion of the tenon. In this piece, the end of the tenon protrudes $^3/_{16}$" beyond the face of the side, so I laid a $^3/_{32}$"-thick straightedge against the side, and marked around the tenon with a pencil. This established the limit of the chamfers on the tenon ends, which I cut with a rasp.

Before disassembling the sides and shelves, I marked the edges of the shelves so that I could trim them to be flush at the back, and $^1/_8$" in from the front edge of the sides. I made the rip cuts on the table saw, then I used a block plane to remove the saw marks and chamfer the shelf edges.

With the joints fit, I used double-sided tape to temporarily hold the two sides together, oriented with the outside faces out and both front edges together. I then laid out the curved profiles at the top and bottom. I used my adjustable square to draw a grid on one side, and a compass set to a 1" radius to mark the curves.

I cut the curves at the band saw, and removed the saw marks with an oscillating-spindle sander. The sander is nice to have, but these edges can also be cleaned up with the curved side of the rasp, followed by a card scraper.

Room for Adjustment

After taking the sides apart, I laid out the holes for the adjustable shelf pins. I marked the holes on $^3/_4$" centers, $^3/_4$" in from the front and back edges. I spaced the sets of holes so that the shelves would divide the space in thirds when the shelf pins were in the center holes of each group of three. After marking, I drilled the $^3/_{16}$"-diameter holes at the drill press. I used small brass shelf pins, with a 5mm shank. This was a tight fit in the $^3/_{16}$" holes, but it worked.

I didn't want the shelf pins to be visible, so I used a $^3/_8$"-diameter core box bit to cut two stopped grooves in the underside of each end of each shelf. I set up the bit in the router table, with a square block extending from the fence to guide the edge of the shelf as I pushed the shelf into the bit and against the fence.

After sanding all the parts with #120 grit with a vibrating sander, then with #180 grit by hand, my shelf was ready to assemble. Before assembly, I brushed yellow glue on the end-grain surfaces of the mortise and the shelf. After letting this dry for 10 minutes, I started the tenons in the mortises, and brushed glue on the cheeks of the tenons. I was frugal with the glue so that there wouldn't be any squeeze-out to clean up.

With all the tenons in place and the glue applied, four bar clamps brought the assembly together. I removed the small amounts of glue squeeze-out with the back of a sharp chisel and a damp rag, and then I let the work sit in the clamps overnight. After removing the clamps, I lightly chamfered the edges of the sides and shelves with a fine rasp and a piece of #120-grit sandpaper.

To hang the shelf from the wall, I milled some scrap stock to $^5/_{16}$" thick. After establishing the length to fit within the sides of the shelves, I ripped one piece of this thin stuff to $1^1/_4$". I set the blade of the table saw to cut a 45° bevel and

Supplies

Rockler
800-279-4441 or rockler.com
1 ■ brass shelf pins
#22252, $4.29 pkg. of 16
Price correct at time of publication.

the fence to rip two pieces $^5/_8$" wide. I glued one of these angled pieces to the flat piece, as seen in the photo below right.

When the glue dried, I planed the edge where the two pieces met flush, and glued this assembly to the bottom back edge of the top shelf. I set the other angled piece aside to screw to the wall. The angled edge attached to the shelves drops over the angled edge of the piece attached to the wall. This provides a secure connection, and the only thing visible from the front of the shelves is the face of the piece below the top shelf.

I hand-sanded all the pieces with #180-grit Abranet (an abrasive mesh) before staining. I applied a heavy coat of Olympic "Special Walnut" oil-based stain with a rag, let it sit for 10 minutes then wiped off the excess. For a topcoat, I sprayed semi-gloss lacquer from a can, sanding between coats.

A small simple project such as this is a good way to spend some time in the shop, and have something useful and attractive to show for it.

— *Robert W. Lang*

Stopped grooves made at the router table with a core box bit hold the shelves securely and conceal the shelf pins.

The completed through mortise-and-tenon joint is incredibly strong, and it adds a decorative accent to a simple project.

A hidden French cleat slips over a matching angled cleat to hold the shelf to the wall.